W9-BMY-241

TS-257

Overleaf: This is either a young caterpillar mascarading as a Mouseketeer or a fabulous Skye Terrier puppy. OWNERS, ROBIN STILES AND SUSAN PARSONS.

Title page: The Australian Shepherd makes friends wherever he goes: he's an all-around family friend and an athletic working dog. OWNER, KATHY HAUER.

Acknowledgments

A moment to thank some special people, whose encouragement and enthusiasm have made this a better book: Rick Tomita and Bill Scolnik, BJ and Bill Andrews, Nona Kilgore Bauer, and Dr. Samuel Draper, super dog people and super friends!

To Sherise Buhagiar, for outstanding design and typography.

To Fred Mayo, Carole and John Hessels and Chris Farley, for performing Shiba duty.

To Jaime Gardner, Linda Lindner, Joseph Janish, Marcy Myerovich, Candida Moreira, Tom Roberts, Pat Marotta, Mike Secord and the whole TFH staff for hard work and dedication on this book.

© 1996 by T.F.H. Publications, Inc.

Distributed in the UNITED STATES to the Pet Trade by T.F.H. Publications, Inc., One T.F.H. Plaza, Neptune City, NJ 07753; distributed in the UNITED STATES to the Bookstore and Library Trade by National Book Network, Inc. 4720 Boston Way, Lanham MD 20706; in CANADA to the Pet Trade by H & L Pet Supplies Inc., 27 Kingston Crescent, Kitchener, Ontario N2B 2T6; Rolf C. Hagen Ltd., 3225 Sartelon Street, Montreal 382 Quebec; in CANADA to the Book Trade by Vanwell Publishing Ltd., 1 Northrup Crescent, St. Catharines, Ontario L2M 6P5 ; in ENGLAND by T.F.H. Publications, PO Box 15, Waterlooville PO7 6BQ; in AUSTRALIA AND THE SOUTH PACIFIC by T.F.H. (Australia), Pty. Ltd., Box 149, Brookvale 2100 N.S.W., Australia; in NEW ZEALAND by Brooklands Aquarium Ltd. 5 McGiven Drive, New Plymouth, RD1 New Zealand; in Japan by T.F.H. Publications, Japan—Jiro Tsuda, 10-12-3 Ohjidai, Sakura, Chiba 285, Japan; in SOUTH AFRICA by Lopis (Pty) Ltd., P.O. Box 39127, Booysens, 2016, Johannesburg, South Africa. Published by T.F.H. Publications, Inc.

BY T.F.H. PUBLICATIONS, INC.

Choosing
A Dog
for Life

Andrew De Prisco and James B. Johnson
Featuring the photography of Isabelle Français

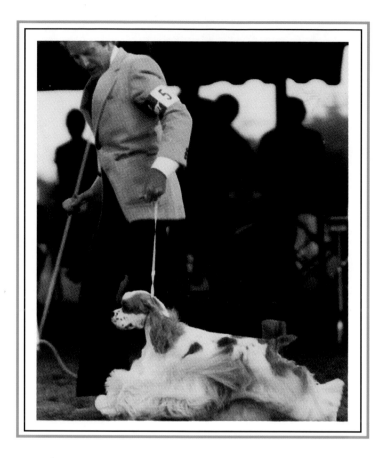

Ted Young, Jr., put the capital "P" on Professional Handler, one of the dog world's most beloved sportmen. Ted here is gaiting Cocker Spaniel Champion Kamp's Kaptain Kool. Teddy is greatly missed by the fancy and the dogs that he made great. Teddy represents just one of the thousands in the fancy who have died from AIDS.

To Paul Monette and "Puck"
and all other dog lovers and fanciers that
AIDS has taken from us and their dogs
before their time.

Andrew

Contents

Call on the Belgian connection.
OWNERS, P. KOLLER, K. ADAMS AND C. ARGENTO.

Champion Schipperke and his young pro owner-handler Chandler Hahn.

Eenie-meenie-miny-mo....catch a Frenchie by the toe.

Vote PONs and turn to page 274!
OWNERS, L. SHIELDS AND D. ZALIS.

Treasures from the Garden of Eden: Go, go, go Xolo! OWNER, SUSAN CORRONE.

Surrender to a Shiba! OWNER, ANDREW DE PRISCO.

Jacquet's Tengu and Maikohime of Akatani ("Kabuki") are author Andrew De Prisco's housemates. Although these two Shiba darlings have more energy and innovation than most owners would know what to do with, the author finds their love-life attitude as rewarding as it is challenging.

Preface

If you read *Time Magazine* or watch *20/20* you might think there's nothing "pure" about purebred dogs. According to such high-profile media, purebred dogs suffer from bad temperaments and unsolvable genetic diseases, and therefore cannot make happy, health pets. We are not here to defend purebred dogs, instead we're here to defend you, the potential owner of a purebred dog, with the facts you need to know about each of the 166 breeds presented in this book. The authors have surveyed hundreds of breeders and owners about their breeds. We trust that our contributors have been both candid and realistic.

You are not the ideal owner for every dog in this book. The purpose of this book is to lead you to the right breed or breeds, to make you aware of a dog's needs, virtues and drawbacks (including temperament, health, and training), and to prepare you to make the best decision. You also must be honest with yourself about your means, lifestyle, and living accommodations: do not be seduced by every pair of twinkling puppy eyes that adorn the next 300+ pages. No matter how important the decision to buy a dog is to you, it's infinitely more important to the dog whose life you are choosing to look after.

A Dog For
Life

A best friend is one who knows all your faults and loves you just the same. The slogan "Man's best friend" referring to the dog has made the title of books, movies, bumperstickers, tattoos, and other likely things. Despite its overuse, much truth and poignancy still remain in it. Today man has as many faults as ever, and our dogs love us just the same.

Perhaps man's greatest vices are his greed and selfishness, vices which have taken their toll on his friend the dog. We live in a fast-paced society, one that is obsessed with speed and instant gratification. People value spontaneity and efficiency.

People buy dogs with their Visa cards.

Too often these same people cannot pronounce the name of the breed they've just purchased, but know that it is the in-vogue dog of the month.

Author Andrew De Prisco with his Shiba friend for life, Kabuki. OWNER, ANDREW DE PRISCO.

Education and forethought, along with knowledge and craft, have been cast aside like the aging village sage.

If you intend to own a dog, you require a certain education. You need to know that dogs are a lot of work: they need to be fed and watered, sort of like the cripple Wandering Jew houseplant on your back porch; they need attention, time and training, like the children who are nagging you to buy a puppy; they get sick, rowdy, disobedient, depressed, also like your kids; they bark, hopefully not like your kids; they mess, dig, fight, fart, whine and howl.

And remember, puppies are *for keeps*....or so we'd like to think.

Dogs, like it or not, are much like adopted children, your own children. They love and need love, responding honestly and without conditions or catches. They are dependent. Selfish people shouldn't have children, and they shouldn't have dogs either. Usually the children and dogs of such people are unhappy and unpleasant to be around; though it's more likely the dog who gets cast into the street, usually. Homeless dogs are a problem, as are homeless people. About ten or twelve million dogs are destroyed annually in the United States alone. The figures on homeless people, frighteningly more daunting, are not as accurate, as they evade both censuses and dog catchers.

Owning a dog has never been more fashionable than it is today. Hollywood stars, athletes, princes, presidents and serial killers each have favorite dogs. The public needs to know this information and

Two fashionable beauties from Jacquet Kennels. The Shiba Inu became the author's first dog: Jacquet's Tengu. BREEDER, RICHARD TOMITA.

consumes it regularly. Seeing elegant greyhounds, clever corgis, and mauling mastiffs on the big screen heightens a breed's mass appeal, making the demand for certain breeds higher than ever before. Was that an *American Bulldog* in that Disney flick?! Breed booms aren't a recent phenomenon, though they are bigger today than ever. If a breed is super popular, avoiding it is your best and most painless option. Too many entrepreneurs enter the market, with

The ever-popular German Shepherd and his smaller herding dog buddy, the Pembroke Welsh Corgi, need ample exercise time and space. AGENT, JAMES MOSES; OWNER, JANE FIRESTONE.

Standing on his hinds, the Lakeland Terrier still doesn't reach the heights of popularity—even when he's owned by superstar Bill Cosby!
OWNER, WILLIAM COSBY.

skulled, large-brained" Dobermans of the '80s to the rotten and wilder Rottweiler (who can't run) of the '90s, breed booms have taken horrible tolls on the favored "dogs of the week." Fortunately, dedicated breeders (those breeders who have been in the breed for a couple decades) come to the rescue. These breeders have maintained good representatives of the breed with sound bodies and even temperaments. They were breeding before the dog's name was a household word, and will continue breeding after the breed boom has become a mushroom cloud and a memory.

Yet there are ways to acquire a worthy example of a popular dog breed. The authors reemphasize the value of a dog owner's education. You really have to know about the breed, its requirements, temperament and suitability before running to the pet shop with your Visa card! While you're still paying interest on the dog you bought, you may be enduring some ugly surprises as your darling bundle of

no understanding of dogs, and attempt to make quick profit on the breed in demand. Such breeds in the limelight are mass-produced and resultingly have the overall worst temperaments, bad conformation (poor hips, weak hindlegs, bad bites) and genetic and medical problems to match.

Almost without exception, the hyperpopular breeds over the past three decades have been ruined by profiteering amateur "breeders" who understand nothing about dogs and less about their reproduction. From the near-schizoid Irish Setters of the '70s to the "small-

Beardies are bouncing, lovable purebreds that enjoy moderate but steady popularity.
OWNER, PENNY HANIGAN.

puppyfur grows taller than your Volkswagon or starts eating one of its tires....and your veterinary bills will likely exceed comprehensive on your car.

This book is written for the people who are interested in finding a dog that suits their lifestyle, commitment, and personality—a dog that won't end up as a statistic in an animal shelter or on the returns-line at the pet shop. Dogs are for keeps, so we intend that the dog you choose indeed becomes *a dog for life.*

Fortunately, the dog world is populated by many caring folk who believe that all dogs deserve a fair shake. In recent years, rescue societies have been established. These organizations, sometimes operating directly out of a breeder's home, are designed to locate abandoned dogs of a particular breed and to find them a loving, permanent home. Too often dogs are bought on a whim. Fads in dogs are bad mostly for the dogs. No matter how miserably bred a dog is, even if his hips don't work like they should, the dog is still a dog, and dogs by nature are trusting, loving creatures who thrive on their loving relationships with man.

The stories of animal shelters and rescued dogs will nick even the coldest of hearts. Those of us who are innately soft toward the canine species have our hearts shattered regularly. We understand that dogs are social creatures. They derive from pack animals and don't do well as the "lone wolf." Socialization is the key to a good pet. Only caring breeders are able to socialize a puppy properly. Socializing means giving the puppy real-life experiences, letting him hear the noises of the world, letting him feel human hands and lick human faces. Well-bred dogs aren't necessarily show-dog per-

The 1990s are marked in black and tan: the Rottweiler swiftly has become the most talked-about purebred on the block—but even the well-bred ones are not for everyone.
OWNER, SUZANNE E. BURRIS.

fect, they are just reliable, socialized, temperamentally stable, people-loving companion animals.

It's not easy being a dog. Being a dog—a good dog that is—takes training. Breeders of show dogs may breed for the perfect pretty dog, but every breeder, regardless of the breed, must first breed for steady temperament and freedom from genetic and medical problems. Breeders breed *dogs* first, show dogs second. About 80 percent of all the dogs a breeder produces become "just pets." Every dog bred must be functional!— functional pets who are able to walk and run and play, pets who can enjoy good health for more than five or six years. While the life expectancy of each breed varies, we must expect our dogs to reach ten years of age, and more

Puppies need hands-on love and attention. Never select a puppy that is hand shy.
BREEDERS, LARRY AND ANGELA STEIN.

likely into their teens. When buying a puppy, find out how old his grandparents lived to, and his great-grandparents if possible. Some statistics on larger and popular dogs should frighten away most potential buyers. The man–dog bond is a strong one, and who wants to lose a friend before his time?

The work of the Delta Society, an American organization dedicated to strengthening the bond between humans and animals, has brought forward much information about the relevance of animals in our lives. Their studies have revealed how communicating with a dog can lower a person's blood pressure, add smiles and years to a lonely elderly person's life; how pets can positively affect the development of children and reach autistic children and abused adolescents. The Delta Society also serves the handicapped, blind and deaf through fostering and promoting

A Bulldog possesses a face that only a mother could love—but sometimes that face is its best feature.

Dogs and cats have a natural calming effect on people. Teach children while young to handle pets with respect and kindness.

the owner's absence. So much can be said about the strength of the man–dog bond and its relevance in our modern world.

In theory, the man–dog relationship should be the easiest relationship for a human to uphold. Dogs have few expectations, not to say they don't have needs. Since in human relationships, expectations most commonly do us in, choosing a dog to share your life with should be relatively painless and hopefully rewarding. Understanding the dog's mind and his instinctual patterns will greatly benefit an owner. The dog's intelligence has been estimated to be equivalent to a five-year-old child. Consider that these days five year olds are doing homework at their computers and playing complicated video games requiring mental and physical dexterity. Children, of

therapy dogs, hearing dogs, Seeing Eye dogs, and other assistance dogs. Therapy dogs bring light to the dark halls of nursing homes, hospitals, mental institutions, and even prisons and penitentiaries.

One offshoot of Delta known as the POWARS program provides a very timely service for Pet Owners With AIDS. This service helps AIDS patients to keep their pets by providing volunteer dog walkers and feeders, etc. POWARS is also prepared to care for the pet in

Dachshund escaping from the stresses of daily life. A dog's life ain't always easy.
OWNER, DIANA BARTLETT.

course, are human; dogs, of course, are not. When our dogs talk, or try to tell us something, we don't always understand; this doesn't make the dog dumb, but rather it tells us how important it is to understand basic canine language.

Some experts purport that, next to the higher primates and the ever-cleverer pig, the dog is by far the most intelligent land animal. If we consider the kinds of tasks and tricks that dogs are capable

buried under 20 feet of snow and ice. Dogs can learn the difference between the smell of cocaine, heroin, marijuana, and other illegal substances for the sake of drug-detection work. Similar feats have been accomplished by dogs in the arson-detection business. As assistants to the disabled, dogs have been taught to push the snooze button on alarm clocks; use light switches, toilets, elevators; hold doors and pull wheelchairs. Dogs have also been trained to act in movies, doing stunts which faithless non-doggie apostles assume are camera tricks instead of dog tricks.

The family of dogs is the most diversified of any species on earth, thus making the choosing of

The Golden Retriever ranks among the most people-oriented and responsive of all dogs. Goldens can be trained to do everything from difficult land and water retrieves to searching out substances and jumping from helicopters.
OWNER, DEBRA M. WALES.

of, we may quickly understand just how intelligent the dog is. And very likely, we've just begun to comb the surface of this animal's abilities. Society has given the dog many jobs and the dog has performed in these various capacities with skill and ingenuity. Dogs have been trained to locate a man lost in the Swiss Alps, even if that man is

a breed of dog a most mind-boggling venture. Dogs have been developed for various work tasks; others have evolved to fill an ecological niche; others have been developed for appearance, uniqueness or for no apparent reason at all. Owners will be interested in examining the different kinds of dogs before delving into the different breeds of dog.

The earliest type of dogs to develop, still maintaining its wolf-like appearance and a good amount of its forebear's primitive style, is the Nordic dogs. These are the breeds of the nomadic Arctic, sometimes called spitz breeds. In appearance they are very natural, with wild color patterns, erect ears, thick coats, broad and long snouts, curled tails, banded guard hairs like the wolf's, and much elasticity. Gregarious and yet aloof, they are good-natured, independent canines who bond closely to man. Among the dogs in this group are the sled pullers like the Siberian Husky, Samoyed, and Alaskan Malamute, the Nordic herders like the Elkhound, and Chow Chow, and other companion dogs such as the American Eskimo, Keeshond, and Pomeranian.

The spitz breeds thrive as pack dogs: they are most intelligent and bond closely with humans. Siberian Huskies remain one of the favorites of the Nordic breeds.
OWNER, MAUREEN KENT.

Another ancient group of dogs is the pariahs, survivor dogs that likely descend from the earliest of domesticated dogs. The Basenji of Africa, the Pharaoh Hound of Malta, and the Canaan Dog of Israel are examples of these dogs. These breeds typically are less people-oriented than the Nordic dogs, who were not outcast from man's camps as were the pariahs.

Close to the pariahs are the

Quicker than a rabbit, the Whippet is a graceful yet playful sighthound breed.
OWNER, SHARON SAKSON.

No small wonder, the Saint Bernard has served man in many capacities, from protection dog to a search and rescue lifesaver.
OWNER, MICHAEL PARKER.

tions, with distinctive elongated noses, deep chests, long powerful legs, flexible spines, and a swift rabbit-like gait when in full throttle (some attaining speeds over 40 miles per hour).

The breeds we know as mastiffs developed as guardians from hereditary giants. Man's fascination with such oversized wonders, nearly to the point of worship, resulted in the creation of life-size monsters with the biddability of other domesticated dogs, and incredible strength and supernatural protective instincts. These dogs were employed as beasts of war, watchdogs, and flock guards. Among the breeds which survive from these dogs are the Mastiff, Tibetan Mastiff, Great Pyrenees, Great Dane and Saint Bernard.

Mastiffs crossed with other breeds to create quite different offspring. The sighthound–mastiff match brought forth dogs like the

sighthounds or gazehounds. These dogs were developed in southern Asia and northern Africa to hunt on open grasslands by using their eyes, as opposed to their noses. These breeds are ancient too and are represented in today's family of dogs by such breeds as the Greyhound, Saluki, Afghan Hound, and Whippet. These animals all have like conforma-

The Kuvasz, originally bred to protect a flock, today excels as a family guard dog par excellence, though his popularity is far less than it deserves to be!

Scottish Deerhound and the Irish Wolfhound. Crosses to terrier types brought forth the Bull Terrier and Staffordshire Terriers.

Other offshoots of the mastiffs or acromegalic strains were scenthounds, large heavy dogs like the Bloodhound, Basset Hound and other European hound dogs. These dogs have deep jowls, excess skin on the head and long floppy ears. Following these hounds are the more familiar and lighter Beagle, other foxhounds and the coonhounds.

The sporting breeds, as they are called, derive from similar stock and in this group we have such dogs as the Dalmatian, pointers, setters, spaniels and retrievers. The pointing dogs are the most ancient of this group and

The Bloodhound epitomizes man's quest for perfection: his nose is thousands of times more sensitive than man's own nose.
OWNER, MRS. DORIS McCULLOUGH.

were employed for their ability to point concealed game. Spaniels for water and land include dogs for finding woodcock (called cockers) and dogs for springing birds from cover (called springers). Setters developed later, from pointer-springer crosses, with the coming of the shotgun. These dogs locate prey and then flush it on command. Retrievers, of all these dogs, are the most mastiff-like, as they are heavier in body and broader in

The Weimaraner represents the best of all sporting dogs—a pointer, springer, flusher, cocker and retriever in one beautiful dog!
OWNER, AUDREY R. SOLTIS.

Miniature sporting dogs: Cavalier King Charles Spaniels in four lustrous colors awaiting the royal treatment.
OWNER, CINDY BEEBE.

group of dwarfs absolutely excel as good friends for elderly people, homebodies, apartment and/or city dwellers, as well as the disabled.

Likewise the terriers are small, compact dogs with strong musculature and hard, wiry coats. These dogs were developed for the extermination of rodents and other pests, mostly on the British Isles. Nearly all the known terrier breeds today come to us from the English, Irish, Scotch and Welsh people. Terriers vary in size from the tallest (the Airedale) to the tiniest (the Yorkshire). In character these dogs are bold and fearless and noisy, often stubborn but very inventive.

face. Among the breeds developed to retrieve from water or land are the Labrador, Golden, Flat Coat, and Curly Coat, plus the Poodles, who were developed expressly for water.

Miniaturized versions of all these different groups have afforded us a veritable menagerie of companion dogs as well as vermin hunters. The breeds typically called toy dogs derive from dwarf mutations that occurred and later were bred for. Some of the toy breeds are very ancient, such as the Italian Greyhound and Chihuahua, while others are more recent concoctions, like the Toy Poodle, Chinese Crested, and Cavalier King Charles Spaniel. Unfortunately toy dogs receive bad press for their alleged lack of utility. Since most dogs today function primarily as companions, the small breeds included in this

The temperaments and utility of the different groups become a common denominator for the breeds included therein. Owners rather instinctively know what kind of dog is for them, and what dogs are not. Choosing a dog by his appear-

Tiny terrier puppies from Ireland: the Glen of Imaal is a less common Irish terrier breed with uncommonly good taste.
OWNERS, ARA LYNN AND PAUL BUSH.

ance can lead to disaster, as the temperament of the animal is equally, if not more, important. And let us not overlook the health of our pets. Given the vast number of breeds in the world, admirers of the dog have a tail-wagging rainbow of dogs from which to choose, coming from dozens of different nations around the globe. Of the 400+ existing breeds of dog in the world today, about 150 are accessible to American readers, probably a few more are accessible to British readers, given their closer proximity to the European continent (barring importation and quarantine). As the international dog scene continues to advance, more and more breeds will come to the delight of our eyes and hearts.

Once shunned as mismarked Cairn Terriers, the West Highland White Terrier enlightens thousands with its kind nature and happy disposition.
OWNER, CHRISTINE FORBES.

Potential dog owners need good information about the "abouts" and whereabouts of the different breeds of dogs. Subscribing to a dog magazine, attending an occasional local dog show, calling the kennel club for breeder references, contacting animal shelters, and going to the library are all ways that new owners can keep abreast of the dog scene. Selecting a dog can be a fun adventure, one that leads to finding the perfect new friend—a dog for life.

A Polish treasure finally arriving on our shores, the Polish Lowland Sheepdog cannot be beat as a hardy companion dog with lots of heart.

Finding
Your Best Friend

There are dog people, and then there's everybody else. Dog people are those people whose lives are not complete without a dog, or two or three. Not all dog people are good dog owners but are people who have always owned dogs, so they continue to do so. Often you hear, "My mother used to breed Pomeranians, so now I have a Cocker and a Shar-Pei." Then there are dog people who understand the commitment necessary in owning a dog: not just walking and feeding, but spending quality time

What child can resist a lapful of Boxer babies?
BREEDER, RICHARD TOMITA.

with the animal and making him feel a real part of the family. Active families choose active dogs like Golden Retrievers or Labradors, and challenging these talented dogs is a full-time job.

Having decided that you actually want to own a dog, or be owned by a dog, it is now necessary to evaluate what you want from a dog. Dogs are versatile and talented, huge and tiny, fat and thin, quiet and rowdy. Do you have a job for the dog?: a watchdog, herding dog, indoor companion, babysitter, hunting mate, etc. Choosing a dog may be compared to choosing a mate. Usually the young debutante thinks that she knows what she wants in a mate, though very often she falls in love with the mutt down the road instead of the dual champion from three generations of best in show winners.

Mutts are easy to love too, and offer dog people a hearty cornucopia of great attributes. Mixed breeds or mongrels, many say, are closer to the "natural" dog, not having their gene pool tampered with or isolated by humans. The argument for hybrid vigor remains a strong one and mutts outlive purebred dogs two or three to one, and are generally much healthier.

Back to the debutante who instead pays no mind to the mutt down the street but holds out for the purebred of her dreams: "Some day he'll come along, the dog she loves." She must decide what he will look like, big and strong, or lithe and tall; must he be protective, a guardian; or must he be sensitive and domestic?

The lady's choice! Doberman Pinschers serve as excellent guard dogs as well as biddable, affectionate companions.
OWNER, ELIZABETH KAMAU.

There are at least as many dogs to choose from as spouses in the world, and puppies are easier to train than spouses. And puppies listen to you when you talk.

The potential dog owner also must evaluate the time he has for

The English Setter is a sporting dog that requires moderate exercise and does well in most living environments.
OWNER, MARY OLDHAM.

23

Concern yourself with temperament, even of a docile breed like the Labrador Retriever. The litter should demonstrate an outgoing people-oriented character.
OWNERS, JUXI BURR AND SONYA NINNEMAN.

lated and wormed, and ready for you to continue with the schedule they provide. Ask to see the parents of the litter, if possible. Generally the dam is available. Keep in mind that she has been tending a busy litter for six to eight weeks and may look a little ragged. Even though she may have lost a lot of coat after whelping, she should not appear ghastly and be nervous about people touching her puppies. While some mothers are more protective than others, the kind temperament of the mother will indicate the likely personality of her get.

Owners are not encouraged to pursue any of the "purebred" crossbreeds you may find, though many are cute as buttons. Among the cute buttons we have seen are

Chow Chow puppies should be affectionate and confident. A well-socialized Chow puppy is the only Chow puppy to own, love and show.
OWNERS, FRANK AND SANDRA HOLLOWAY.

the dog, the accommodations he has (e.g., size of his apartment or house, fenced yard, neighborhood, puppy kindergarten and obedience schools in the area, etc.), and the family or other people who will share the home with the dog.

The puppy you choose should be socialized, temperament tested, and well adjusted to the world of humans. Puppies must be outgoing and not shy, showing all the expected signs of vitality and health that such an animated little creature should have. Breeders should be ready for all your questions and be responsive to any of your concerns. The puppies will be inocu-

A dog for life—
Choose your lifetime
companion with
care.
OWNER, DAVID
MELVARD.

Cockapoos, Peekapoos, Terripoos, and Pugapoos. These dogs come in all the colors of all the breeds incriminated, and Cockers, Poodles, and Pekingese come in dozens of colors! However, all of the inherent problems of all the breeds may be kicking up their cha-cha heels in any of these mixed-up little tykes.

When you are buying a dog, the seller should put no pressure on you. Breeders usually interview potential buyers in person to find out the kind of living accommodations available for their puppy. For breeds larger than toys and terriers, the breeder may require that you have a fenced-in yard. Others may wish to meet the entire family and find out what the family's schedule will be. Some dogs do not do well staying at home alone all day. Very often breeders mandate that the puppy be crate-trained, and will not sell to you unless you sign an agreement to that effect. The best breeders insist that the

Breeders of American Staffordshire Terriers are very selective about placing their puppies. These dogs require experienced and responsible owners.

puppy be returned directly to them should you decide not to keep it.

Rescue societies are a viable outlet for obtaining a purebred dog at a reasonable cost. It is less likely that a puppy can be found at these places since the stock from rescues is mostly abandoned animals. This book attempts to apprise the potential buyer of the individual breeds discussed by listing potential problems known to occur within the breeds. Your seller should be able to present valid information about their stock's health. For instance, in the United States, the parents might be OFA-certified for hip dysplasia. The OFA is

Although most breeds of purebred dogs require screening to check for inherited problems, the Bichon Frise is happily clear of most defects.
OWNER, LORI KORNFELD.

the Orthopedic Foundation for Animals and offers dog owners an opportunity to check their animals for inherited bone disorders. In addition to HD, the radiologists render an opinion on the occurrence of craniomandibular osteopathy (CMO), osteochondritis dessicans (OCD), ununited anchoneal process, Legg-Perthes disease and fragmented chronoid process PennHIP is another such registry. It's necessary that your puppy's parents be cleared through an organization like these. We can only pray that OFA and other such registries remain above-board and honest with their records—money and politics can only blur our vision, and our dogs suffer most in the long run.

This eye-catching dog can even see through his heavy corded coat. The Komondor thrives on a large estate—he is a choice sentinel with a high exercise requirement.
OWNER, RUBEN COLLADO.

Perhaps the most beautiful eyes in the dog world belong to the Weimaraner: no colored contacts here. Screening serves to bring about problem-free eyes in the breed.
OWNER, LAUREL LOCKHART.

Be aware that screening is not a mere show dog qualification. In more severe cases, hip dysplasia is a crippling condition leaving your dog hardly able to run, and very often in much pain just to move about. It is only reasonable to require that such affected dogs be altered so that they do not continue to pass this dread disease to their offspring.

Another American organization is CERF, the Canine Eye Registration Foundation, which provides a similar service for eyes. Eye problems are prominent in a number of popular breeds and owners must be aware of the occurrence of entropion, ectropion, pannus, retinal dysplasia, luxated lens, progressive retinal atrophy (PRA), Collie eye anomaly and others. Some of these disorders are apparent in puppyhood and should be checked by CERF.

There are other organizations designed to help breeders and owners become aware of the hereditary problems of dogs. Unfortunately, only the ethical breeders are realistic about the problems affecting their breed. Many are continuing to breed affected, unstable animals, which may be profitable in the short run but ultimately damning to the breed they supposedly love in the long run.

This book also gives detailed descriptions of what the dog should look like as an adult, and how the puppy grows up to look like that. If you want to

Puppies need to chew. Gumabones® are the only safe and tasty option.
OWNER, NANCY A. PITAS.

Pet shops sell the best nylon bones and toys from Nylabone® and every dog needs them for good teeth and health.
OWNER, LINDA S. BRENNAN.

buy a certain breed of dog, you must know what it should look like. Is it really that obvious? For instance, if you are buying an eight-week-old Pomeranian and the seller hands you a 23-pound fluffy porker and say's "Here's your new Pom," RUN! If your Labrador seller has a very rare brindle puppy with a feather tail and says "Here's your new Lab," RUN! If your Boxer puppy is mostly white; if your Rottweiler puppy can't run smoothly and at eight weeks is the size of a full-grown Boxer; if your Pit Bull puppy growls at your three year old, RUN, RUN, RUN!!

Get a copy of your breed's standard of perfection and read it. A breed standard is a written description of what the breed should look like for conformational perfection in the show ring. Even if you are not interested in showing the dog, the standard will tell you what to avoid. A breed's disqualifications aren't just esthetic drawbacks but more likely are structural problems which make the dog incorrect for the breed. The word "type" is an important word in evaluating a purebred puppy. This word is often found in breed standards as well. The American Kennel Club (AKC) defines type as: "The characteristic qualities that distinguish a breed; the embodiment of a standard's essentials." In plainer words, type is what sets one breed apart from the next. Type distinguishes your Golden Retriever from your Labrador; your Shih Tzu from your Maltese. It's elements of size, color, temperament, facial features and

The lovely Shih Tzu comes in all colors and markings. Each one is more beautiful than the next....hence Shih Tzu owners tend to keep two or three at least.
OWNER, LYNNE BENNET.

Type for the Keeshond includes his dramatically marked gray coat, spectacles around the eyes, his ruff and trousers. This pup is still growing into his trousers.
OWNER, PAULA WEIMAN.

expression, and much that is ineffable. May we say that if you love the Shih Tzu but wish you could find a white one, you probably don't love the Shih Tzu....you love the Maltese. White is "type" for Maltese. Likewise, if you love the Labrador Retriever but are infatuated with the brindle color pattern, you probably want a Boxer, Tennessee Treeing Brindle or Mountain Cur, not a Labrador. All of the wonderful qualities of the individual breeds can only be expected from well-bred, *typey* examples of the breed. But, nonetheless, we see lesser breeders producing oversized Rotties, unathletic blonde Goldens, short, piggy Labradors, and manic Toy Poodles....and lots of other purebreds who are mere caricatures of their breed.

Your emphasis on temperament must be high. Pets must act like pets in the home and with the family. Breeders conduct some kind of temperament testing as they are socializing and training their young brood. There are social

29

tests to see how outgoing a puppy is. Generally speaking, a shy puppy is one to be avoided. Never buy a shy puppy because you feel sorry for him. Dominance tests try a puppy's spirit. The pup should be confident and motivated, not wild and wired. Alertness tests and obedience tests are designed to check an animal's personality. Ideally the puppy will come when called and be biddable, no matter how excited he is with your company. Some breeds are less inclined to come when called, so if the entire litter is too busy to come to you, it's probably the breed.

Although these Sheltie puppies are much too young to go home, they are just beginning to develop their personalities and fondness for the human touch.
OWNER, LINDA ZIMMERMAN.

When dealing with a breeder, it is more likely that he will choose the puppy from the litter for you. This has become common practice. The old-school idea about following your heart and the puppy's choosing you is mostly bunk—romantic bunk, but still bunk. You must make the breeder aware of what you intend for the dog. If you intend for the puppy to be solely a companion, the breeder is not likely going to sell you a top-of-the-line show-quality puppy (even if that puppy likes you best). It only behooves the breeder and his program to sell his best puppy to someone who will show the dog so to further establish that breeder's reputation. Show wins count for breeders. If you need a watchdog or an obedience competitor, the breeder will know the temperament and subtle personality differences and be better prepared to recommend which puppy is your best choice. Unfortunately, in some breeds, color is an important factor for the owner. Many people only want a black Lab or a fawn Whippet or a red Corgi. Such prejudices do not benefit dogs. Many of these prejudices are not just up-

Likely your breeder will choose the puppy for you. His experience with the breed and the litter serves him well to make the wiser decision.
OWNER, MATTHEW L. DOWNING.

held by color-conscious pet people but by blind judges who only acknowledge certain colors in a breed. The breeder therefore must compromise and choose the best dog from a fraction of the litter, since you won't take a yellow Lab or a blue Whippet. Our hats are off to all those open-minded colorblind pet folk and to any judges out there putting up blue Whippets and roan Field Spaniels... or chocolate Labradors at field trials.

Locating a breeder of a rare breed, or even a popular breed, should not be a difficult matter and phone calls to the AKC (New York City) or Kennel Club (London) can be most resourceful to locate a breeder or breed club in your area. Often the individual breed clubs or even an all-breed club can help by recommending a quality source for a particular breed. With the less common breeds, you may be placed on a waiting list, sometimes for as long as two years. Anything worthwhile is worth waiting....and why rush the selection of your next best friend?

Once mom has shown her young charge the ropes, it's time to meet the new family. These water-bounding hounds are Otter Hounds, among the least seen of all breeds though one of ancient and endless charms. OWNER, ROBIN ANDERSON.

Affenpinscher

A monkey-like expression and mustache introduce *le Diabletin Moustache,* the little devil with a mustache—the Affenpinscher.
OWNER, MRS. PATRICIA PATCHEN.

DESCRIPTION

The adult Affenpinscher distinguishes himself by a jaunty monkey-like expression with a grand little mustache, bushy eyebrows and hair tufts. He must be balanced and compact, standing ideally at ten inches at the withers, essentially a square dog (females are slightly longer than males). The head should not be too large, but proportional to the body; the eyes, full and round, also should be in proportion to the head, not bulging. The bite should be undershot, with teeth and tongue not visible when mouth is closed. In color the Affen varies greatly and commonly comes in black, gray, silver, black and tan, and red. Furnishings are often lighter than coat and black masks are common too. The coat should be dense and rough, about an inch in length.

OWNER SUITABILITY

Affens are fun little dogs. Monkey-like in more than just appearance, the Affenpinscher would rather monkey around with older children, but with proper supervision can coexist with toddlers. They are too delicate to take rough handling. Be wary that this monkey business doesn't include much jumping since Affens have delicate legs. Affens are game and fearless little tykes who are never afraid to protect themselves or the family with whom they bond closely. Perhaps rightly called yappy, Affens make great alarm dogs and thrive on indoor life. If taught to shush from a young age, adults may be desirably more quiet.

A sturdy toy dog, the Affen is balanced and compact, most commonly seen in black.
OWNERS, DR. AND MRS. BRIAN J. SHACK.

32

Growth

Affen pups average 3 to 5 ounces at birth, maturing with good rate to a fully developed 7 to 8 pounds. Tails are docked by five days, creating a tail of about one-third inch. Optional ear cropping is usually done around 16 weeks. When selecting an Affen, avoid frail and undersized pups. Breeders mark the start of adolescence at about 12 weeks, and the end around 12 months. Adolescent Affens eat well and can easily overeat if not monitored. Permanent teeth usually begin to emerge around five to six months. Uncropped ears tend to rise and fall during the teething period. If the coat is not stripped, the changeover to the adult coat usually starts around six to eight months, with the true adult coat in place some time around 18

Consider the texture of the mother's coat (very stiff and wiry) when choosing a pup from the litter.
OWNER, NANCY E. HOLMES.

months. An adolescent coat may have gray shading to it. Testicles should be fully in place by four months, though Affens sometimes retain one testicle longer. Females typically experience their first heat between eight and 14 months.

Health

Possibly the greatest problem is broken bones, due to the Affenpinscher's petite size and bold nature. Patellar (knee) luxation is a recognized problem, and breeders must screen for this. Gentle eye care will help to avoid cornea lacerations, which can be problematic. There is a breeder concern about Legg-Perthes disease (degeneration of the femoral head in the absence of bacteria or other disease-causing agents). As with other toy breeds, instances of hydrocephalic

At a few weeks of age, Affen pups are gangly but irresistible.
OWNER, NANCY E. HOLMES.

puppies and cardiac problems in young puppies are well documented. Incidences of open fontanels (soft spots in the center of the head) are noteworthy. These are active dogs who, owing to their small size, require supervised exercise. Grooming entails some stripping, or plucking, which must begin at a young age. It is usually best that a professional groomer or breeder walk you through the grooming process a few times until you can do it yourself. Aside from their occasional finickiness, Affens have no special dietary concerns and live ten to 11 years.

Red adolescent coming into his coat.
OWNER, HIGHLAND KENNELS.

Affenpinscher

Afghan Hound

DESCRIPTION

The aristocratic appeal and supreme dignity of the Afghan Hound make him the flashiest of dogs and a top show-dog contender. He is exotic with his long silky coat and unusual pattern, Eastern expression, and commanding stature. The head is long and refined, with a silky topknot; the eyes are almond shaped, nearly triangular, and are never full or bulgy. The neck is of good length and not too thick. The hipbones are most prominent; the backline appears level and the shoulders and loin exhibit impressive power. The stifle often looks more exaggerated than it truly is, due to the profuseness of his leg furnishings or trousers. The coat is not clipped and the tail has a curve or ring at the end, not set on too high and always carried up. In height, the adult Afghan dog stands 27 inches and bitches 25 inches. Weight: 50 to 60 pounds.

With unreserved drama, the Afghan Hound defines regality in its expression and aristocratic bearing.
OWNERS, GREGG, SCOTT AND TODD RECHLER.

OWNER SUITABILITY

Afghan Hounds, despite their aloofness and noble sensibility, are clowning and people-oriented dogs. Many are especially wonderful with children. Stubborn and headstrong, the Afghan is a confident, very intelligent and often high-strung dog like most other sighthound breeds. The appearance of the Afghan for many is a super plus, quite unusual and nearly human. They love to be outdoors, but can also cuddle around the fire with their much admired human keepers. Consistency is key to training the Afghan: due to his stubborn nature, he can become irritable, spooky or shy. Do not rush him and be patient but strong; he is a steady-dispositioned fellow.

Afghans need plenty of room to stretch.
OWNER, HUTCHINGS.

Growth

The weight of the newborn Afghan varies considerably, most commonly 10 to 18 ounces but some several ounces less. The breed matures very slowly, and owners must not rush this process. The true color of the Afghan may be masked by the black guard hairs of the young puppy coat. Actual coat color should be apparent by four weeks of age. Spotting and incomplete pigmentation should disappear by no later than three months. Proper socialization is imperative, as Afghans are sensitive animals. Breeders state that between the ages of seven and 16 months is a critical time for personality development. Respect and consistency are the keys. Physical development is slow as well, and adolescent Afghans often appear awkward (exercise must be monitored to avoid injury) and go through the "uglies" as they lose their puppy coat. Extra grooming is necessary to avoid the new coat matting with the old. Breeders recommend at least three weekly sessions. Adolescent Afghans can easily become finicky, spoiled eaters. Avoid treats at this time and ensure a balanced diet. Pups are generally difficult to housetrain.

Afghan pups mature slowly and are surprisingly delicate despite their size. By four weeks, pups need plenty of human interaction. OWNER, LUCIA BROWN.

Saying the Afghan is just a "coat" breed is like saying Zinman's is just a "coat" store! These three glamour hounds would impress any Fifth Avenue shopper. OWNER, RENEE WOLCOTT.

Health

The Afghan's unique hip structure allows for excellent moving and turning at high speeds, yet the ever common hip dysplasia affects the breed; elbow joint malformation is also known to occur. Necrotic myelopathy, which culminates in death from respiratory paralysis, is restricted to Afghans (usually starting at three to six months of age). Milk allergies are common in young pups, and the breed has a known sensitivity to chemical preparations (e.g., flea powders). Afghans have a known sensitivity to anesthesia, tranquilizers and cortisone, which can cause coat drop. Ear mites and yeast infections commonly affect the breed and should be checked for regularly. Ask the breeder about cataracts and hypothyroidism in the breeding stock. In addition to plenty of running time, Afghans need plenty of social time, or otherwise they may become aloof, introverted, and potentially degenerate in health. Grooming the luxuriant coat is demanding, up to two hours a week, plus monthly bath time. Afghans live 14 years or more.

Adolescence is marked by uneven growth, gawkiness, and loose limbs. OWNER, RENEE WOLCOTT.

Afghan Hound

Airedale Terrier

The tallest of terriers, the Airedale possesses a wiry outer coat over its distinctive outline.
OWNER, LINDA HOBBET.

DESCRIPTION

The Airedale Terrier stands apart from the other terriers for its great size and unequaled versatility as a sportsman. The adult stands about 23 inches tall, more inches than an earth dog truly needs for his bred-for tasks. The Airedale is beautifully balanced with its head long and not too broad between the ears, which are V-shaped and dropped towards the sides of the head. The nose is black and rather sizable; the eyes are dark and not prominent. Despite his bigger size, he is all-terrier and his expression must say so. The back is strong and short; shoulders long and sloping. The coat should be hard, dense and wiry, close lying and straight. The breed is a classic tan and black pattern, sometimes with a red mixture. Whether dog or bitch, the animal is well boned and muscular.

OWNER SUITABILITY

The Airedale offers an owner the best of every possible world. This is a sweet-dispositioned sports dog, with remarkable agility, intelligence, and keen senses. He is able to swim tirelessly, hunt on land, go to ground as an exterminator, and work as a police professional. Overall he is a confident, well-put-together dog who must be reminded that he should be a gentleman, since he is naturally quite dominant. He is sometimes rowdy, always protective; his love of fun and people and high activity level embolden this animal's spirit. He loves to please and can be most obedient.

Puppies given the opportunity to spend at least eight weeks with mom learn good manners and better understand their limits.
OWNERS, SCOTT AND DOTTIE BOEVING.

Growth

Airedale puppies begin life weighing around 12 to 15 ounces. They GROW at a consistent rate to attain their mature 50 or so pounds. When puppies commonly leave for their new homes, at about eight weeks, they usually weigh about 12 pounds. Rear dewclaws, when they appear, are removed as early as possible, and the tail is docked to about two-thirds its length. The ears often rise and fall during the teething process, and many breeders recommend setting them. Your breeder, veterinarian, or groomer should be consulted on this process. The Airedale's temperament and willingness to please make adolescence not a terribly difficult time. Owners should use this time to initiate training and properly channel their dog's protective instinct.

Some puppies are blessed with naturally good standing ears, others have heavy overly houndy ears and need to be "set." OWNER, SANDRA HAMER.

The young Airedale grows evenly, giving the impression of an adult in miniature. OWNER, LINDA BAAKE.

Health

Highly intelligent and trainable dogs, Airedales need plenty of active time with their owners and are happiest when challenged with physical tasks. Hip dysplasia, unfortunately, has a relatively high incidence and screening is a must. Airedales can be expected to live from 10 to 15 years. Older dogs have been known to develop cancer, especially pancreatic cancer, nasal sinus tumors, lymphoma, and bladder cancer. Otherwise, the Airedale suffers from few breed-specific problems. Undershot bite, umbilical hernias, hot spots, and dry skin are the primary medical concerns. Since certain eye problems have been reported, screening is a big plus. Skin irritations, related either to flea allergies or possible thyroid problems, are known. Growth-hormone deficiency (dwarfism) is noted. Grooming is very important to lessening the incidence of skin irritations and other problems. Stripping is needed about every 12 weeks, and owing to the Airedale's size, fulfilling this obligation may prove time consuming, though the amount of grooming depends greatly on the quality of coat—better coats require less grooming. An important note: Airedales are known for their high tolerance to pain and thus may be hurting more than they show.

Airedale Terrier

Akita

DESCRIPTION

A dog of substance, power and dignity, the Akita has a broad, triangular head that is massive but always in balance, characteristically small triangular eyes, erect ears and a Nordic tail curled and large enough to balance the dog's head. A beautiful, balanced picture is true to the breed. The muzzle must be broad and full and the skull flat; dewlap is undesirable. The neck is thick and muscular, short and widening towards shoulders. The body is slightly longer than high and the chest is wide and deep. The back is level with a well-muscled loin and moderate tuck up. The Akita is not light-boned or rangy in body type. The skin is pliant but not loose. Dewclaws on front not removed. The coat is double with a thick, dense, soft undercoat and outer hairs that are straight and offstanding. The standard describes the Akita's color as "any color including white; brindle; or pinto." The pinto pattern features white with patches of other colors evenly placed. Males stand 26 to 28 inches; females 2 inches less.

The Akita is a bear dog (not a bird dog): he should be substantial and powerful, whether male or female, as is this extraordinary dog: Champion The Widow-Maker O'BJ, the number two Akita sire of all time.
OWNERS, BJ AND BILL ANDREWS.

OWNER SUITABILITY

The Akita is truly the perfect house dog, although his great size may make you wish he were only a house guest. Females are better with children than males, who tend to be testy. Choose the Akita carefully as he is a one-family dog. Training from an early age is a must, because once the Akita puppy gets ahead of you, you'll spend both your lifetimes catching up. If any dog can reason, it's the Akita! A devoted guardian, he requires a family that is self-assured and strong-willed, like himself. He will not get along with other dominant dogs, but is quite amenable to cats. As with all large guarding breeds, the Akita should be closely supervised with unknown children. Akitas are challenging and fascinating: this is a powerful but gentle animal, who is both elegant and utilitarian, non-destructive, and above all the cleanest of all breeds (even burying his own feces like a cat).

GROWTH

Akitas weigh 12 to 20 pounds by eight weeks. Females attain full physical maturity around three years of age, males about four years. (Some Akitas develop more quickly.) The characteristic tail curls over the back by around four weeks. Ears become erect as early as six weeks or as late as six months. Vitamin and calcium supplementation is often recommended until the ears are fully erect. Correct bite may not be established until one year of age. Adolescence is marked by the emergence of dominance and possibly stubbornness. Proper training is vital. This breed does not respond well to aggressive training. Consistency and positive reinforcement are the keys. As the Akita matures, angulation decreases, buttocks tend to narrow, backs appear longer, and long narrow muzzles appear more snipy. Coat color changes are common for the first two years of life.

HEALTH

Akitas in general are long-lived and hardy dogs. A life span of 15 years is not uncommon, though certain lines may never see ten. The breed suffers from few breed-specific abnormalities. Nervous disorders have been diagnosed in the breed, including epilepsy. Hip dysplasia is a known problem and screening a must. PRA, vWD and achondroplasia also affect the Akita. Also, entropion is reported, but owing to the Akita's relatively small eye size, the condition may not really be entropion and the pup will grow out of (or into) the inward eyelids. Auto-immune diseases and hypothyroidism are common and must be inquired about. During shedding time, plenty of brushing is required to upkeep the Akita's plush coat, and, of course, generous outdoor activity is needed. As with all curled tailed dogs, hot spots should be guarded against.

The five-week-old Akita needs much human interaction. The mama dog should have a people-friendly, stable disposition. OWNERS,WALTER AND VICTORIA DONACH.

Akitas grow at various rates; maturity is achieved between three and four years. The adolescent requires a sturdy but kind hand. Never punish or hit an Akita. OWNER, RUTH ZIMMERMAN.

Akita

Alaskan Malamute

DESCRIPTION

Distinguished for his full and thick coat in shades of gray and white, his strong appearance, his powerful head and intelligent expression, prick ears, and of course his full plume tail carried over the back in a typical Nordic fashion, the Alaskan Malamute stands 25 inches and moves with proud carriage. The coat pattern features a cap over the head and/or a black mask. The eyes are brown, not blue, and almond shaped and positioned in a wolflike way, although the breed's expression remains soft and friendly. The body is compactly but substantially built; the back is straight and slopes to the hips; the loins are powerful and of good length to facilitate an easy stride. The coat is double and the outer coat or guard coat stands out; the neck is heavily furred, as are the shoulders and legs. Weight: 75 to 85 pounds.

A strong and powerful hauling dog, the Alaskan Malamute must be compact and substantially built.
OWNERS, MIKE AND JACKIE COSENTINO.

OWNER SUITABILITY

Although the Alaskan Malamute will grow out of his puppy fur, he never grows out of his puppy fun. This is a good-natured and high-spirited dog who needs dedication and firm training. Like all of the other northern breeds of dog, the Malamute is a dog-oriented dog who is not a one-man dog. This pack mentality also makes it necessary for the owner to assume the role of pack leader or number-one dog. This is a good outdoor dog that loves the snow and cold.

The cap is a distinguishing breed feature. The Malamute never has blue eyes.
OWNERS, MIKE AND JACKIE COSENTINO.

GROWTH

Litter size varies considerably, and whelp size can be 12 to 22 ounces. Growth rate is great during the first few weeks, and by eight weeks breeders report a weight of 24 pounds. It should be understood that there is considerable size variance in the breed, and owners should take note of the individual line from which their prospective puppies derive. Full maturity may take as many as four years to complete, and this too may vary with different lines. Breeders stress the importance of temperament in selection. Checking the temperament of the parents is ideal when possible. Puppies and their parents must be friendly towards people. Adolescent Malamutes are known to rebel, to challenge the pack authority of their owners. Owners must be firm and

The eight-week-old puppy can weigh up the 24 pounds; although the breed grows quickly, maturity may not be achieved until four years of age.
OWNERS, SANDEE REEVES AND CHERYL PATERSON.

consistent, and this phase will pass without complication.

HEALTH

A very strong and naturally hardy animal, the Malamute's most significant problem is hip dysplasia. Dwarfism, known as achondroplasia, has also struck the breed; it is apparent at birth. Hemeralopia or day blindness (the inability to see in bright light) and renal cortical hypoplasia (a congenital kidney condition that usually culminates in kidney failure by six months to two years of age) and hypothyroidism are conditions reported in the breed. Malamutes may be genetically predisposed to copper and zinc deficiencies. Firm, consistent (not harsh) training must begin at an early age to cap the Malamute's high-energy propensity towards mischief. Shedding can be a real nuisance, and owners must guard against excessive heat exposure as well as hot spots. Malamutes are happiest when working and playing hard in the cool (or cold) outdoors.

Puppies should exhibit a people-friendly attitude. Ears may drop during the teething phase but usually stand up with little fuss.

Alaskan Malamute

American Bulldog

DESCRIPTION

A light-footed heavyweight of a dog, the American Bulldog is a powerful medium-large-sized dog whose first impression is that of a very large, athletic Bulldog (and not a terrier). The head is described as box-shaped and the skull is large and square, not narrow or tapering. The eyes are round and wide set; the ears, rose or drop. The body is robust and powerful, not exaggeratedly wide, with a deep chest and a fairly short back. Neck is fairly short and shoulders broad and heavily muscled. Rear legs moderately angulated; front legs straight and well muscled. Tail should be long enough to reach point of hocks and is moderately thick and not straight or docked. The coat is short, hard and shiny. The ideal dog stands 25 inches and weighs 120 pounds. Males stand 22 to 28 inches at the shoulder, bitches 17 to 26 inches; males weigh 90 to 135 pounds, bitches 25 pounds less. In color the dog is at least 50 percent white with patches of brindle or shades of brown; all-white dogs are acceptable. Solid black, black/tan, black/liver, merle and fawn with black mask are not acceptable.

American Bulldogs vary greatly in size and type. Breeders disagree about what is the ideal specimen. Whether stocky and small or taller and heavy, these dogs are healthy, reliable guard dogs.
OWNER, LOUIS MALDARELLI.

OWNER SUITABILITY

Tough as nails and high-spirited, the American Bulldog has become a popular choice as a guard dog. He is ridiculously athletic and sweet tempered, with an exceptional silly fondness for children (and yet he is still a fierce protector). He craves attention and needs an owner who is firm, since he tends to be a little muscle-headed at first. His main purpose in life is to please his master. Adults are sensible, happy dogs who are fond of good clean fun.

GROWTH

At seven weeks, males weigh a solid 10 to 15 pounds, bitches slightly less. Size variance is due in part to the differences between individual lines. Prospective owners should avoid excessively large dogs. The breed is naturally large and big-boned. Taking this to excess only encourages HD, joint malformation, bloat, and other related problems. American Bulldogs mature slowly, especially physically. Mature development may not be attained until after two years of age. Generally, full height is attained in the first year or so, and the dog will broaden out during subsequent months. Adolescence is marked by the emergence of dominance and guarding instincts. These must be properly channeled. Dominance especially must be curbed from a young age, and aggression never tolerated.

HEALTH

Because of its relative rarity, the American Bulldog lacks much veterinary analysis. However, prospective owners must be wary of hip dysplasia and joint and bone malformation, excessively undershot bites, narrow rears, and many other conditions affecting all bulldog breeds. Additionally, partial or total deafness and/or blindness must be suspected in all-white dogs and lines containing such dogs. Firm, consistent discipline must be initiated early on, as this is an immensely strong, dominant dog. Abundant non-aggressive exercise and rigorous training help keep the Bulldog happy and content. Grooming is minimal at most. Appetite abounds!

The brawny American Bulldog can be dog-aggressive, despite its sweet disposition.
OWNER, LOUIS MALDARELLI.

Puppies grow at a slow but steady rate. Owners must establish themselves as "top dog" early on to avoid boisterous puppies taking over the house.
OWNER, LOUIS MALDARELLI.

American Bulldog

American Eskimo

DESCRIPTION

The American Eskimo is an elegant, solid-white dog who boasts classic northern type: prick ears, a curled tail, thick double coat and wedge-shaped skull. The breed occurs in three sizes: standard, miniature and toy. The toy variety is less common than the larger two. The body is strong and compactly built, with a strong, somewhat broad chest and a straight level back. The front legs should be parallel and straight and the hind well developed with good angulation. The eyes are slightly oval, not slanted, and the ears are slightly rounded at the tips. The muzzle is medium in length, as is the neck, which must blend into the shoulders gracefully and carry the head proudly. The tail should be carried over the back, but is not tightly curled or double hooked. The coat should be full, though quality is more important than quantity, and has a noticeably thicker ruff around the neck. Standards stand 15 to 19 inches; miniatures stand 12 to 15 inches; toys less than 12 inches (females always an inch less).

The American Eskimo has a pure white coat of excellent quality. The tail is carried curled over the back in typical Nordic fashion.
OWNER, MARGARET A. CANNON.

OWNER SUITABILITY

Sweet-natured and mild-mannered, the American Eskimo is a great family dog of medium size, not fragile but not so large he'll plow over the kids. Do not choose a shy puppy as this can be a difficult dog to work with. Although he is almost intuitive, the Eskie needs patient and firm training. When an Eskie wants to learn, he can do so in minutes—the trainer's job most of the time is convincing him that obedience is fun and worthwhile. These are high-activity dogs, inside and out. Like other spitz breeds, they are boundless in snow and cold. Commit much time and love to your American Eskimo: although the breed tends to be high-strung and independent, only if ignored and bored will the dog become barky and hyper.

GROWTH

The American Eskimo comes in three varieties by size. Birth weight, of course, varies accordingly. By eight weeks, toys weigh under 3 pounds, miniatures weigh 3 to 5 pounds, standards 6 to 8 pounds. The average for physical maturity is one year, though typically toys mature the quickest, standards the slowest. Prospective owners should check for good pigmentation and proper bite (undershot bites are common); the nose and eye rims should be black by six weeks. The puppy coat is shed at five to six months; seasonal shedding thereafter. Bitches are known to experience a severe coat blowing (to the point where they may appear to be balding) during their third summer. Testing of authority is common in adolescent males. Early obedience is recommended.

American Eskimos are more ideal for experienced dog owners. They can become difficult and aloof if not handled and trained appropriately.
OWNER, CYNDI RICHARDS

HEALTH

Make certain your Eskimo comes from stock having excellent bone and joint construction—OFA and obedience titles are big pluses in the pedigree. The Eskimos are prone to some of the same defects affecting their German Spitzen ancestors, including cryptorchidism and monorchidism, weak joints, hypoglycemia (in toys), and improper skull development (open skulls at birth). Also, patent ductus arteriosus affects the breed, a condition in which the tear ducts do not close. The Eskimo can be a delight to train and loves to run and play—take advantage of these traits in your training and exercise routines. Grooming entails plenty of brushing, and shedding is excessive during the seasonal changes. Avoid excessive bathing—it's not necessary despite the white coat, which breeders refer to as almost self-cleaning. Dry your Eskimo well to avoid hot spots.

The Toy American Eskimo develops faster than the other two varieties. The black pigment can be complete as early as two weeks of age.
OWNER, MARILYN A. PIKE.

American Eskimo

American Foxhound

DESCRIPTION

The Foxhound in America can vary in appearance as different types have been developed by hunters and keepers throughout the country. Despite these variations, the American Foxhound is a clean, muscular animal built for the chase. The forelegs are straight; the hips and thighs are strong and muscled; stifles strong and well let down. The tail is not long and carried gaily, set moderately high. The coat is close and hard, typical of the hound breeds. The skull is fairly long and slightly domed, never flat. The muzzle should be neither too long nor snipy. The ears must be long (able to reach the tip of the nose) and set on low and soft to the touch. The eyes are large, set well apart, and the expression is convincingly

The leaner of the two recognized Foxhound breeds, the American Foxhound is designed for the chase. He is a robust athlete.
OWNERS, JAMES M. AND JUDY G. REA..

pleading and gentle. Color is never a consideration in the Foxhound breeds but, of course, the classic tri-color pattern is most common.

OWNER SUITABILITY

The American Foxhound is first a social family dog, and second a working dog who hunts in packs. These dogs are dogs through and through. They love people and children, and usually take to strangers like they do to the scent of a fox. Of course as pack dogs they are good with other dogs and are big-voiced watchdogs.

An expression that convinces one of the Foxhound's gentle spirit.
OWNER, JUANITA TROYER.

GROWTH

American Foxhounds weigh in around one pound at birth and gain an additional 5 to 6 pounds on average by six weeks. By six months, weight averages about 50 pounds and height around 22 inches. Physical maturity is commonly attained by 18 months of age, with a weight of around 65 pounds and a height of 24 to 25 inches. Typically all dewclaws on front and rear legs are removed as early as possible, as dewclaws on a hunting dog can easily lead to unnecessary injuries. Ears must be houndy (long, set low, and fairly broad) at birth and most notably by eight weeks of age. Coat quality and color changes are minimal; however, by one year the dog should possess its medium-length, hard, all-weather hound jacket.

American Foxhounds thrive as companion animals: they are naturally friendly and love to please their folks. OWNER, JUANITA TROYER.

HEALTH

Relatively free from hereditary problems and resistant to disease, perhaps the greatest danger to these dogs is their abundance of energy and rather fearless nature, which can lead to lacerations and broken bones. Avoid all dogs coming from lines containing merle to merle crosses, as such breedings are known to create complications in all dogs. Some back (spinal) problems have been reported, including osteochondrosis. Inquire about thrombocytopathy, a blood (bleeding) disorder unique to the breed. Foxhounds do best in the company of other hounds and should receive plenty of daily running and romping. This dog is a tireless worker, not an inactive house pet—any Foxhound should be kennelled outdoors. Grooming is minimal, but the ears and eyes should be checked at least weekly for signs of infection and foreign objects.

The Foxhound is a "survivor" in the classic sense of the word. Excepting the rigorous exercise requirement, he is an easy keeper and commonly lives to about 13 years of age. OWNER, LISA SCHINKER.

American Foxhound

American Pit Bull Terrier

DESCRIPTION

The true canine gladiator, the American Pit Bull Terrier is a medium-sized dog who weighs 35 to 60 pounds; females 30 to 50 pounds. The head is medium length and wedgelike; it is flat and widest at the ears and the cheeks are prominent. The muzzle is square, wide and deep with well-pronounced jaws. Ears are cropped or uncropped and set high on head; eyes round; neck slightly arched and muscular. The shoulders are strong with wide sloping blades; back is short and strong, slightly arched at loins. The chest is deep but not too broad; tail shortish and tapering to a point. The legs are large and round boned and hocks down and straight. All colors are possible and the coat is short and stiff to the touch.

The athletic Pit Bull Terrier is a natural "doer," requiring suitable outlets for his energy and a responsible owner to provide them.
OWNERS, VICKI CLENSY AND GARY CLEARY.

OWNER SUITABILITY

The Pit Bull Terrier is a good family dog and if raised with children literally thrives on the "mauling" toddlers give him, exhibiting far more tolerance than most breeds. The dog must be kept on leash when in public since he loves to spar with other dogs, consistent with his terrier/fighting-dog background. If you are brash and irresponsible, this is not the breed for you, as the Pit Bull requires an educated, sensible person as his owner. About 40 percent of the dogs are aggressive towards cats (and other animals), also consistent with their baiting ancestors. These dogs exhibit rock-steady dispositions, love people more than anything, and are athletes par excellence. They are a little soft to correction and can be a trifle stubborn; they love to be indoors and enjoy relaxing as much as a good physical workout.

Pit Bull puppies need a loving hand to train them, despite their potential stubbornness.
OWNER, BETH JONES

GROWTH

Because there is considerable size variance between the lines of this breed, so too are there differences in the size of pups. However, on average, seven- to eight-week-olds weigh 10 to 15 pounds. Physical maturity is not reached until around two years of age, though maximum height is usually attained around one year. Breeders report no unusual points in development. It seems that these dogs simply require a good-quality puppy food, plenty of socialization and exercise, and consistent training. Breeders note that possible aggression toward other dogs usually emerges around 18 months, and that owners must thereafter keep their dogs on lead to avoid confrontations.

HEALTH

Breeders claim relative freedom from the major hereditary and congenital problems of to-

The gladiator of the dog world! The American Pit Bull Terrier is unmistakably a tough, confident dog.

day—including hip dysplasia. However, potential owners must guard against undershot bites, loose joints, and excessive bone and muscle (especially in the shoulder). Kidney stones (cystine uroliths) are reported. Perhaps the greatest detriment is the Pit Bull's own strength, coupled with its very high tolerance to pain. Torn muscles, broken teeth, and ruptured ligaments are common injuries. Grooming minimal. Exercise requirements high. Avoid dominant training tactics, and *never* teach aggression.

Observe the dam's disposition. With proper training and socialization, the pup will develop its mother's good nature and temperament. OWNERS, MARY MARTIN AND MARY HAPPEL.

American Pit Bull Terrier

American Staffordshire Terrier

DESCRIPTION

Muscular and agile, the American Staffordshire Terrier may be viewed as the show-ring version of the American Pit Bull Terrier, as these two breeds are nearly indistinguishable by sight. The American Staffordshire Terrier, the accepted breed name for AKC dogs since 1972, is a stocky, sturdy animal standing about 18 to 19 inches; he exudes strength for his size. The head is of medium length, the skull is broad and the cheek muscles are duly pronounced. The ears are set high and are either cropped or natural. The back is fairly short, slightly sloping from withers to rump with the loins slightly tucked. The ribs are deep in rear and well sprung. Legs set rather wide apart to make room for the dog's deep chest. The coat is short, close and stiff. The tail is low set and not docked. While color is never an important consideration in the breed, dogs must not be all-white, over 80 percent white, black and tan nor solid liver.

The American Staffordshire Terrier is a strong, sturdy terrier breed with a steady, outgoing temperament. OWNERS, YUNHEE AND KIHONG KIM.

Choose a confident and enthusiastic puppy (with a scissors bite). OWNER, KAREN HINES.

OWNER SUITABILITY

The American Staffordshire comes from the same lines as the American Pit Bull Terrier, though the AmStaff is generally perceived as the more sophisticated breed, the show-ring dog. Regardless, these dogs are dominant, very bold dogs who are perfect family dogs and gentlemen with familiar people. AmStaffs from good breeders are great with children and are of the most stable dispositions. These are high-activity dogs who love to exercise and to be outside. They do not get along with other dominant dogs, and are less friendly with cats than most breeds.

AmStaffs possess colorful personalities and coats! OWNER, J.D. WAYMIRE.

Growth

The newborn AmStaff weighs around 11 to 13 ounces at birth. These dogs grow steadily throughout the first year, usually attaining their full height by 12 to 14 months. Both dogs and bitches will continue to broaden and develop through the second year, and dogs possibly into the third. The full-grown male can easily attain a weight of 65 pounds. Because of their development and their activity level, AmStaffs require highly nutritious meals, especially through their first year. Despite the dog's excellent appetite, owners must guard against overfeeding to prevent joint problems and obesity. Unlike in other breeds, an improper bite usually does not improve with the emergence of the permanent teeth.

Health

The AmStaff has a known history of hip dysplasia, making OFA a must. Also elbow dysplasia, loose joints, and excessive bone and muscle (especially in the shoulders) must be checked. The breed's tremendous strength and high pain threshold can easily lead to injuries such as torn muscles and ligaments and broken teeth. A ruptured anterior cruciate (the ligament supporting the rear leg) is not uncommon and can be debilitating if not treated immediately—suspect all lameness. False pregnancies are known to affect females, and bilateral

The soundest, most consistent puppies will be delivered by a fully mature bitch (two years of age). A trusting nature is indispensable for this breed.
OWNER, J.D. WAYMIRE.

AmStaff puppies are gentle and people-loving, if a little rowdy at play.
OWNER, JUDY HAIGHT.

As early as four weeks of age, AmStaff pups should be handled by humans to promote their inborn sense of trust.
OWNERS, MARY JEAN MARTIN AND RUTH TEETER.

cataracts are reported in the breed. Allergies are also noted. Brush the coat daily and look for dry patches of skin and any redness or irritation. Train consistently from a young age, and *never* teach aggression or encourage dominance.

American Staffordshire Terrier

American Water Spaniel

DESCRIPTION

The American Water Spaniel stands 15 to 18 inches in height: the proper size is very important as is the symmetry of the dog's parts. The breed should be slightly longer than tall, appearing neither square nor compact. The coat texture and color must also be considered. The proper coat can range from uniform waves to close curls and need not be consistent throughout. The dog's dense undercoat is vital to its ability to work in water or difficult terrain. In color the dog should be either solid liver, brown, or dark chocolate (white on toes and chest is permissible). The dog's head is moderate in length and the ears are long and wide; the eyes can range from a light yellowish brown to brown (bright yellow eyes are a disqualification). Overall, this is a sturdily constructed, agile animal of great athletic ability.

A delightful, but uncommon sporting breed, the American Water Spaniel has a unique curly coat colored in liver, brown or chocolate. OWNER, SHARON DOUGHERTY.

OWNER SUITABILITY

This is an eager-to-please hunting dog with very strong pack instincts who is rarely kept as a pet. Yet, despite his dearth of opportunity, he makes a terrific pet if he knows who is boss! He is of a good size and a very hardy keeper. Though larger than the Cocker, he is not a Cocker in temperament: he is a thinker and needs firm fair direction. He gets bored easily and needs a job to do. Patient trainers excel with this breed. Choose a homebred puppy that is not timid or fearful, for an outgoing dog promises peaceful, productive coexistence. Not necessarily good with children, the breed bonds strongly with his owners. Rather possessive, he

A fantastic little hunting dog with a lot of brains. Despite his pleading expression, he is less easygoing than the Cocker, though sufficiently merry. OWNER, L.A. ALEXANDER-SUESENS.

knows what is his own and will not hunt for strangers. Females bark more readily than males. Do not choose this breed on a whim: older dogs do not transfer well with a second owner.

GROWTH

At seven to eight weeks of age, American Water Spaniel puppies weigh 7 to 9 pounds. Physical maturity can be rather slow, sometimes taking up to 24 months, though 12 months in some lines is reported. The mature dog weighs from 28 to 45 pounds, females 25 to 40 pounds. Prospective owners should select for a compact dog with a thick curly or wavy coat. The head should be square with a medium-length muzzle and a good bite. Avoid pups with yellow eyes, straight coats and pups which are shy or hyperactive. Adolescent dogs change little physically; there will be a darkening of the eye color, an increase in body substance, and a thickening of the coat. Adolescent males are known to test their owners, and females may become aloof; both are known to become possessive. With proper socialization and training, this phase will pass easily.

HEALTH

Little veterinary research is available on the breed. Breeders report incidences of hypothyroid, hip displasia and PRA, as well as dwarfism. All breeders must test for HD and PRA.

A puppy should possess an outgoing personality, a curly coat and other than yellow eyes. The dam's coat will of course be fuller and denser than the puppy's.

Conditions to inquire about of the breeder include hypothyroidism, juvenile cataracts, diabetes and the incidence of rat tails and yellow eyes. Breeders also report possibility of bad temperaments. Be sure your AWS is well socialized and brought up in a home, not a kennel. Plenty outdoor exercise is required, and swimming is an excellent activity. Owners can work (play) with their dogs either in actual hunting, with Frisbee™, fetch or other retrieving games to satisfy this dog's strong instincts. Grooming is easy but necessary, as the coat is thick and may become oily. Owners are encouraged to check the dog's ears, skin and anal glands regularly.

Breeding stock should be checked for potential eye problems. OWNERS, PAUL AND LYNN MORRISON.

Well-socialized breed members can make excellent, reliable home companions and watchdogs. OWNER, SANDRA W. BRACKEN.

American Water Spaniel

Anatolian Shepherd Dog

DESCRIPTION

A muscular, well-proportioned dog who stands from 29 inches, bitches from 27, and weighs in excess of 100 pounds, bitches more than 80. A large dog who must be hard and lean, with a proportioned head with a strong muzzle, triangular ears, medium-sized eyes set apart for good sight; slightly arched neck, powerful and muscular. The forequarters are relatively long and well boned; hinds are muscular and angled proportionally. The coat varies substantially in length (from short and straight to longer and slightly wavy), but always has a thick undercoat. Curly or corded coats are bad. A variety of colors is acceptable, including fawns, black-masked fawns, brindles and white. The tail is set rather high and reaches to the hock; when relaxed it is carried low and curves upward; carried high and wheel-like when alert.

An impressive, upstanding guardian breed, the Anatolian Shepherd is a large-boned, powerful dog seen in dozens of colors and patterns.
OWNER, VERNON AND DI MILES.

OWNER SUITABILITY

A highly territorial, natural guard dog who requires a lot of attention growing up to rear him properly into a calm, biddable guardian dog. He is gentle with children, though children under five are not recommended as he is too large and strong. Dogs cannot be trained by force and need patience and respect to train effectively. Traditional training techniques may not work with this breed, and owners should keep in contact with their breeder. Adults of the same sex may not tolerate one another. Generally not given to roaming, he is still strongly territorial. He does not do well in cities as he needs a large confined area for off-lead exercise. He is courageous and fearless and a rewarding animal to own.

Potentially dog-aggressive, Anatolians should not be kept in same-sex pairs. Their attitudes develop faster than their bodies: firm training is vital.
OWNERS, WANDA STUTZER AND EDITHA COLLINS.

54

GROWTH

Anatolians are big dogs, bigger than they appear in pictures. Weight at eight weeks is approximately 35 pounds. The breed is slow to mature, not reaching full maturity until four years for males, about three years for females. Owners should select for dark eyes and a broad deep head and muzzle. Coloration should be fawn with a black mask. Temperament should be bold, and parents should display a natural guarding instinct but never be aggressive. The developing Anatolian will eat tremendous amounts of food, but this will drop drastically after full size is reached. Generally, there is no need to overfeed as the adult's appetite is small for his size. Adolescent males may become disobedient and overly "macho." Socialization is vital in making the Anatolian a viable companion animal.

HEALTH

The Anatolian has long been bred strictly for function according to the most harsh selection process by Turkish shepherds. This has resulted in a dog virtually free from hereditary health problems. Today there is some incidence of HD, entropion, hyperthyroidism, unilateral and bilateral cryptorchidism as well as wry mouths, overshot jaws, and bad temperaments. Prospective owners must insist on proper screening, both for physical and temperamental traits. Responsible breeders encourage owners to shop around and learn as much as possible about the breed before making their selection. Exercise requirements are considerable, though can be easily satisfied by long walks. Grooming needs are also simple though considerable, owing to the breed's dense coat. Anatolians live 12 to 13 years, some as long as their late teens—most amazing for such a big dog!

At just eight weeks, Anatolians can weigh as much as 35 pounds. The dam should be bold and confident.
OWNERS, LOUISE AND ELIZABETH EMANUEL.

Young pups will have much energy and massive appetites.
OWNERS, LOUISE AND ELIZABETH EMANUEL.

The breed is naturally protective and gentle with its charges.
OWNER, GAYLE BOUDER.

Anatolian Shepherd Dog

Argentine Dogo

DESCRIPTION

A moderately large, very muscular dog with a completely white coat that consists of short hair and no undercoat. In profile, the breed must exhibit a clear, clean line flowing smoothly from nose to tail. Dogos weigh 80 to 100 pounds and stand 24 ½ to 27 inches for males, females 23 ½ inches minimally. The skull is massive; the muzzle the same length as skull; bite must be scissors, never undershot or overshot; eyes dark brown or dark hazel; nose black; ears well set and cropped close. The neck is thick and softly arches (the skin must not be too tight). Chest is wide and deep; withers high and strong, sloping to rump; rear legs muscular with straight pasterns. The tail is long and thick, falling naturally, never curling over. Eyes should never be blue or China (with uneven melanin distribution); lips must never be loose and hanging; nose never pink or split; small black spots on head are permissible, but never more than one black patch on the head.

A solid white dog with a clean, muscular build: the Dogo is a no-nonsense guard dog that adores its people and thrives on affection.
OWNER, JOSEPH KRAER.

OWNER SUITABILITY

This native Argentinian may be more "dogo" than the average person can handle. Developed as a hunter and defender, the Argentine Dogo makes a top-notch candidate for guard work. Although they have been described as "overgrown Pit Bulls," the breed is closer to the Boxer in temperament. With children they are absolutely wonderful and thrive on their affections and petting. Dogos possess superior canine intelligence and often pose a challenge to train. Described as a "primitive thinking breed," owners must begin training as early as 12 weeks in order to properly channel their natural enthusiasm and high-energy personalities. Dogo males are no more aggressive with other dogs than other working breeds are. Females tend to be easier to train. Most Dogos adjust well to life indoors and make pleasant housemates.

The Dogo toddler soon develops its dark pigment on its nose and eye rims.
OWNER, JOSEPH KRAER.

56

GROWTH

Puppies should weigh about 15 pounds at seven to eight weeks of age. They do not reach physical maturity until two to three years of age. Puppies should appear well proportioned and moderate; puppies that are overly heavy or overdone will likely grow to become improperly proportioned adults. Males develop more slowly and remain mentally immature for some time. Ear cropping is typically done at eight or nine weeks. Dogos are highly regarded for their extremely stable temperaments and their versatility as companions and protectors. Adolescent males tend to bond closely with their owners, more so than females, who are less demanding. Some zestful young dogs exhibit "lap dog" tendencies and are unabashed in showing their joy upon their owners' return—dancing on their hinds in a two-step tango quite unique to this hot-blooded South American purebred.

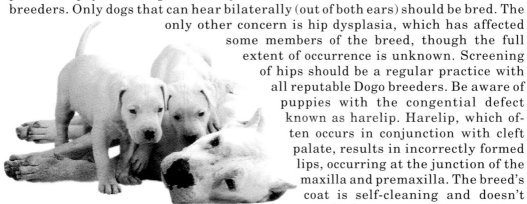

Choose an even-tempered, well-balanced puppy. By seven or eight weeks of age, the Dogo will reveal its symmetry (or lack thereof).
OWNER, JOSEPH KRAER.

HEALTH

Like most other white dogs, deafness is the breed's most notable health problem. By six weeks of age, a puppy's hearing can be evaluated. Unilaterally deaf puppies (deaf in one ear) are sold strictly as pets on a spay/neuter agreement by most breeders. Only dogs that can hear bilaterally (out of both ears) should be bred. The only other concern is hip dysplasia, which has affected some members of the breed, though the full extent of occurrence is unknown. Screening of hips should be a regular practice with all reputable Dogo breeders. Be aware of puppies with the congential defect known as harelip. Harelip, which often occurs in conjunction with cleft palate, results in incorrectly formed lips, occurring at the junction of the maxilla and premaxilla. The breed's coat is self-cleaning and doesn't smell doggy—grooming requirements are minimal. Although some breeders report Dogos that have lived 15 to 17 years, a modest life-expectancy estimate is 10 to 12 years.

By six weeks of age, a pup can be checked for hearing imperfections. A well-bred, properly trained Dogo can become an affectionate, long-lived *amigo*.
OWNER, JOSEPH KRAER.

Argentine Dogo

Australian Cattle Dog

The Australian Cattle Dog abounds in symmetry, musculature and soundness. He is a working dog that may be suspicious of strangers yet amenable to handling. OWNERS, LINDA BERNARD AND THE RUBEN HORTAS.

DESCRIPTION

A true working dog, the Australian Cattle Dog suggests strength, agility and endurance in a compact and well-constructed package. The head is broad of skull, slightly curving between the ears; the cheeks are muscular but not overdone; foreface is developed and filled in under the eyes. The eyes are oval in shape and not prominent or sunken in. Ears are moderately sized; small ears are preferable to large ears. The neck is exceptionally muscular with no appearance of throatiness. The topline is level, back strong, rump long and sloping, chest deep with well-sprung ribs. Tail is set on low and medium in size. Coat is straight and medium in texture with a short dense undercoat. The Cattle Dog is either blue or red speckle in color; black, tan, red or blue markings on the head are desirable but never on the body. In blues, tan undercoat permissible. Height: 17 to 20 inches.

OWNER SUITABILITY

A good protector of family and property, the Australian Cattle Dog is a real outdoorsman, who is not ideal for indoor living. Owners need to be strong and decisive as the AuCaDo is a strong-willed, "smarter-than-your-average-cowherder" cowherder. Training from a young age is necessary. Despite rumors of being wild and savage, the breed is sound and protective. These are super-adaptive and versatile dogs who give lots of satisfaction to their family members: they enjoy time with the family working, playing and resting. They generally prefer to be the family's one dog.

Puppies will grow into their ears, sometimes taking as long as nine months. Show puppies should not have spoon or bat ears. OWNERS, BILL AND SUSAN STREAKER.

58

GROWTH

Australian Cattle Dog pups weigh on average 9 to 11 pounds at seven to eight weeks of age. Full physical maturity is usually not attained until two years of age, or even later for some males. The breed experiences a rapid growth period between nine and 12 months, during which time dogs may appear leggy and gangly. Exercise may have to be adjusted accordingly, and nutrition requirements must be met. Fortunately the breed is known for its good appetite. AuCaDo pups are born white. Black marks are undesirable. The desirable blue or red coloration usually begins to emerge around two weeks. AuCaDo adolescents can experience two or three coat changes, which breeders note as possibly dramatic, with the dog dropping all its top coat and undercoat. Temperament changes through adolescence are also common, especially periods of failing self-confidence. Breeders state that owners must be consistent and reassuring, especially through these "fear" periods. Dewclaws on the hind legs are definitely undesirable, as are

At eight weeks of age, the AuCaDo is a sturdy dog with a tremendous desire to please and do. Puppies need activities to occupy their paws, jaws and imagination. OWNER, RHUE JEFFERSON.

a stumpy tail, curled tail, tail carried high, sway and roach back.

HEALTH

Likely because of its broad genetic base and stringent early selections for working ability, the AuCaDo is largely free from genetic conditions and has a low susceptibility to disease, even cancer. PRA and deafness are possible concerns in the breed. Proper selection for good breed type is the owner's greatest responsibility, as cobbiness and weediness, straight shoulders and stifles (knees), cow and bow hocks are all common physical traits that could cause complications as the dog ages. Kidney stones (cystine uroliths) are reported.

These two youngsters were actually born solid white: their blue speckled coloration emerged only a few short weeks ago. OWNER, JAMIE HANSEN.

Proper grooming of the thick undercoat is essential to avoid skin problems such as eczema. Life expectancy is nine to 12 years.

Australian Cattle Dog

Australian Kelpie

DESCRIPTION

Lithe and active, the Kelpie appears to have great stamina and suppleness, with no sign of cloddiness or coarseness. Dogs stand 18 to 20 inches; bitches 17 to 19 inches. Larger, longer examples of the breed are preferable—the Kelpie should never appear square. The head is broad between the ears with a flat skull that tapers to the muzzle. The ears are of moderate length and of good size (neither bat nor spoon ears). The eyes are widely spaced, almond-shaped and dark in color (light-colored eyes lend a mean appearance). Neck is strong and full; shoulders clean and sloping with close-set withers (shoulders should not be set too far forward or too straight). The chest is deep rather than wide; barrel ribs are undesirable. Hindquarters should show breadth and strength with a longer than short haunch bone; no dewclaws on hinds. The tail bends in a slight curve, raised when excited, and reaching the hock. Coat is moderately short, flat with a good undercoat. Colors include black, black and tan, red, red and tan, fawn, chocolate, and smoke blue.

The Kelpie's expression should never be mean or coarse. As a working dog, he has few equals. OWNER, PHILIP DELATHIERE.

OWNER SUITABILITY

One of the toughest of herding dogs, the Kelpie is a quiet worker capable of moving any livestock, though chiefly suited toward sheep and cattle. They are athletic and mostly independent. Likely the Kelpie has too much energy to be kept solely as a pet, though they are markedly affectionate, especially with children. You must keep a Kelpie busy. Potential owners must take into account this dog's strong herding instinct and realize he will not be happy if you and your family are all he has to herd. He is not suited as a guard dog.

Athletic and energetic, the breed possesses super-canine stamina. Keep a Kelpie busy or else he'll find his own busy work. OWNER, PHILIP DELATHIERE.

Kelpie training should begin as early as possible: these dogs are tough in mind and body. Firm instruction and a kind hand go far to teach the Kelpie his place.
OWNER, PHILIP DELATHIERE.

ROWTH

Kelpies were initially bred and culled according to natural selection, which has created a very natural and problem-free breed. Kelpie pups grow at a normal, uncomplicated rate, reaching physical maturity some time around two years of age, weighing in around 30 pounds. Initial sheepdog training is usually begun around four months of age, though herdsmen note that Kelpies peak around three years of age as true working dogs. Because of their metabolic rates and outstanding athleticism, all Kelpies require nutritious feedings, and actual working dogs will require excellence in their nutritional plan.

HEALTH

An exceptionally athletic and adaptable dog, the Kelpie suffers little from genetic or hereditary conditions and possesses a strong defense against disease. Inactivity is highly stressful to these dogs, and plenty of exercise and mental stimulation are vital. Otherwise this very active dog can literally self destruct—stress is a leading factor contributing to disease. Hip dysplasia should be considered, and arthritis is common in older dogs, likely attributable to their usually rigorous lifestyle and zesty approach to every task. Deafness is known in some lines. Kelpies typically live to ten years of age, though some have lived to 17.

Australian Kelpie

Australian Shepherd

Description

Longer than he is tall, the Australian Shepherd has a coat of moderate length, variously colored, with a natural bobtail. He must be the picture of symmetry and stamina, with apparent agility. The head is clean-cut and strong, with a flat to slightly rounded skull; muzzle tapers slightly and stop is moderate. Neck is firm and medium length; body is firm and topline appears level. The chest is deep and loin is strong and broad. Tail does not exceed 4 inches. The quarter assemblies are balanced and give the dog complete support, moderately angulated with sufficient shoulder slope. The coat is of medium texture to provide protection from the elements and its quantity should not be exaggerated. Colors include blue merle, red (liver) merle, solid black, solid red (liver, with or without white and/or tan points). Body should not exhibit white splashes. Patterns vary from roan, flecked, mottled to marbling, splotches and bold patches. Males stand 20 to 23 inches, females 18 to 21 inches.

The picture of symmetry and stamina: the Australian Shepherd combines a flashy appearance with an unbeatable work ethic and a peach of a personality. OWNER, J. FRANK BAYLIS.

Owner Suitability

The Aussie is a thinking herder. He is instinctive and protective of his charges, necessarily aloof with strangers. As family dogs they are loyal and devoted, as well as courageous. Aussies will take the initiative and are industrious workers and highly adaptable. Many dogs work in Texas heat while others herd in below-zero Canadian winters. They need much exercise and an outlet for their talents, and in the home they are well behaved and mellow.

Adult Aussies are level-headed, independent companion dogs who are enjoying growing popularity as their many virtues are revealed. OWNERS, MARY-LOU E. TRONE AND JOAN DELLA ROCCO.

GROWTH

There is considerable variance between the different strains of this breed, both in terms of size and rate of growth. Newborns weigh between one-half and one pound, with a full-grown weight of up to 70 pounds attained at physical maturity by three years of age. Larger strains experience more dramatic growth periods, during which times skeletal development often exceeds muscular development, leaving the dog rangy or leggy in appearance. Proper nutrition at this time is vital to curb potential joint problems. Exercise may have to be adjusted accordingly. Color changes are common in the breed. Pups are born with flesh-colored noses, which darken with age, as does the merle coloration. Any copper coloration tends to intensify starting a few weeks after birth. Bite is usually determinable by six months, though bite may improve as late as two years. Dewclaws in most cases should be removed at an early age.

To ensure your puppy's good temperament, observe the dam. She should be well adjusted, trusting and calm. OWNER, SANDRA K. NOELL.

HEALTH

The Australian Shepherd is a hardy breed, tolerant of its environment and resistant to disease. The most common problem suffered by this hardy herder is injury due to accidents—the breed has a propensity to chase bicycles, cars, and other moving objects, in an attempt to satisfy its insatiable love to herd. And working dogs, of course, are subject to kicks from livestock. OFA and CERF screening should be requirements, as hip dysplasia, PRA, and retinal detachment are known to occur. Other eye problems also reported in the breed include microphthalmia (small eyes), Collie eye, and cataracts. Potential owners must watch for homozygous merles, the possible products of merle to merle crosses, as such dogs are highly predisposed to health problems. Some animals can be affected by deafness, blindness and other disorders, such as kidney stones. Grooming needs are considerable, though not demanding or excessive. Hot spots can be guarded against by feeding a top-quality food. Nasal solar dermatitis has a known high incidence. Aussies live 12 to 15 years.

Merle-colored dogs have blue eyes and their coats tend to darken with age.

Australian Shepherd

Australian Terrier

DESCRIPTION

Small but sturdy, the Australian Terrier is a diminutive working terrier who stands 10 to 11 inches at the withers. The coat is distinctive for its rough ruff and apron—soft topknot—and overall harsh texture ($2\frac{1}{2}$ inches in length, except tail). The body is considerably longer than it is tall. A dog in good working condition exhibits fine balance and weight; the dog is medium in bone. The ears are pricked with no tendency to flare off the skull and the tail is docked. In color the Australian Terrier is blue and tan, solid sandy or red; smutty marks in colored portions are a fault, as is an all-black body coat and white marks on feet and/or chest. The head must be long and strong with a smart expression. Notice an inverted V-shaped area with less hair extending from nose to muzzle. The neck is long and slightly arched. The ribs are well sprung but never round in appearance; loin is fairly short with slight tuck-up; never cobby. Forelegs are straight; hind strong and well angulated at stifles and hocks.

The Australian Terrier's expression is keen and intelligent; his head is graced with a soft top knot.
OWNER, AMY R. MARDER, DVM.

OWNER SUITABILITY

The Australian Terrier always has something to do: this is a very busy little dog who can be constructive and obedient. Instruction is necessary or else the Australian Terrier will devise his own itinerary. Quick problem solvers and natural workmen, they provide owners with hours of assistance and amusement. Good watchdogs, they are not yappy but spirited; easygoing but purposeful; plucky but obedient.

Always shown in hard working condition, the breed possesses a harsh-textured coat complete with ruff and apron.
OWNER, AMY R. MARDER, DVM.

64

GROWTH

Newborns generally weigh about 6 ounces, and rear dewclaws if present should be removed at the earliest possible time. The tail is docked to about two-fifths length between three days and one week of age. Ears are never cropped and should stand in proper position by four months. Teething and other demands on the body may cause the ears to rise and fall. If not in proper position by four months, taping may be in order. Australian Terriers generally are physically mature by one year to one-and-a-half years, though they often reach their full height by seven months. Adult weight is 12 to 14 pounds. Incorrect bites are not common. No unusual development patterns in

At a few weeks of age, the Aussie is black with small tan highlights. These areas expand as the pup grows. OWNER, DEBRA L. AUSTIN.

the breed, though experience indicates that human handling has a positive influence on both physical and mental growth. Owners are encouraged to be consistent and loving with their dogs.

HEALTH

Owing both to its utilitarian development and rugged conformation, this Aussie is one very hardy breed, nearly free from such common problems as hip dysplasia, entropion, and congenital heart problems. There is a minor incidence of Legg-Perthes disease and PRA. Diabetes mellitus and cryptorchidism are the two major concerns, and even these problems are not common. Aussies do best as house dogs, not subjected excessively to the elements, and should live a happy 14 years. A high-energy dog, the Aussie both requires and enjoys plenty of exercise. These dogs love to please and do well at obedience work—don't be misled by their small size. Also, while this little guy exudes the typical terrier air of superiority, he actually needs plenty of human response and praise to keep his ego intact. Grooming needs include stripping the hard terrier coat, a job which is not excessive but does requires some specialized skill. They must *never* be clipped.

Throughout its life, Aussies thrive on reinforcement. Their confidence may wane during adolescence, so be encouraging and supportive. OWNERS, DANIEL L. AND PAT A. TURNER.

Australian Terrier

Basenji

DESCRIPTION

The beautiful and smart Basenji is short-backed and lightly built, distinct for his wrinkled brow and tightly curled tail...not to mention his barklessness (he is not mute but rather yodels!). The head is elegant, intelligent in expression and carried proudly on a well-arched, well-crested neck. The eyes are almond-shaped and set obliquely with dark rims. The ears are small and erect and slightly hooded. The skull is flat and the foreface tapers from eye to muzzle with a visible stop. The short back is balanced by a short-coupled body which appears to end in a waist. Chest of medium width and tail is set high and curls over the side. The coat is short and fine, and skin is pliant. The Basenji has white feet, chest and tail tip, and the body is either chestnut red, pure black, black and chestnut red (tricolor), or brindle.

An African yodeler who is always on his toes, the Basenji attracts more than his share of attention. OWNERS, DIANNE T. BLEECKER AND GUSTAVO DE LA GARZA.

A tricolor Basenji. OWNER, ARTHUR R. GILBERT.

OWNER SUITABILITY

The Basenji is quick of mind and foot. Keeping up with this little dog turns into a full-time job, but worth every moment. The Basenji offers high intelligence and much affection, though he is aloof with strangers as a rule. Training is tricky and patience has never been a truer virtue. They are anxious and spirited, easily bored, and cleaner than most cats, grooming themselves regularly. Many even climb like cats, including on fences and trees. Approach the Basenji slowly and treat him with respect, for he is a sensitive soul. Due to their barklessness, Basenjis do not make good watchdogs.

The brindle (left) and the chestnut red (right) are two possible Basenji colors. OWNER, SUSAN CAMPEAU.

ROWTH

The average weight of the newborn Basenji is between 6 to 8 ounces. Both front and rear dewclaws should be removed as soon as possible. Noses are pink at birth, but turn black with age. Paw pads also darken with age. Basenjis that will be red when mature are dark brown as juveniles. Selecting a puppy with a good bite is important, as undershot bites tend to worsen with age.

HEALTH

Be not dismayed, but the Basenji has shown some rather

Training the Basenji may compare to "keeping a wave upon the sand." These are highly intelligent, aloof canines whose trainability is likened to that of cats. OWNER, ARTHUR R. GILBERT.

unique problems. Persistent pupillary membrane (the persistence of pigmented strands across the pupil) is passed hereditarily. Pyruvate kinase deficiency, characterized by severe congenital anemia, also transmitted genetically, culminates in early death. Hemolytic anemia, Fanconi's syndrome and calculi (affecting the kidneys), retinal deterioration, lymphangiectasia, hereditary red-blood-cell disease, and malabsorption disease are being worked on by breeders. Basenjis seem more prone to enteritis (bacterial infection of the intestines) than other breeds. Umbilical hernias are common in pups. Many Basenjis are prone to allergic reactions to chemicals, such as flea dips. However, the healthy Basenji is one very active and long-lived dog, averaging ten to 13 years of life. Plenty of play and training are required to keep this dog interested and happy. Unique to the Basenji bitch, estrus is once annually.

The Basenji dam is a natural whelper and good mother. Unlike other dogs, however, she only cycles once per year (instead of twice).
OWNER, AMY RIDDLE.

Basenji

Basset Hound

DESCRIPTION

A dog of great bone and characteristically short legs, the Basset Hound is a deliberate and tireless working dog, who is also tireless in his affection. The Basset's head has a well-domed skull with a pronounced occipital protuberance (never flat). The skin around the head is loose and falls in wrinkles over the brow when lowered. The muzzle is heavy and deep; the lips pendulous; dewlap is very pronounced. Slightly sunken, the eyes are proverbially sad, revealing his soft heart. Prominent haw is preferred.

One of the great scenthounds of England, the Basset Hound stands low on its massive short legs. He can weigh 60 pounds or more despite his mere 14 inches.
OWNERS, GABRIO DEL TORRE AND PAT AND ROGER TURPEN.

The ears are excessively long and velvety. The chest is deep with a prominent sternum. The shoulders are well laid back and strong, not steep, turned in or bending out at the elbow. Front legs are never knuckled over, but are short and powerful. The dog stands firmly on its hinds, showing a well-let-down stifle and straight hind feet. The Basset stands no taller than 14 inches. The coat is hard and smooth and sufficiently dense, never long. Colors vary, as in all hounds.

OWNER SUITABILITY

A walking proverb, the Basset Hound goes placidly amid the noise and haste, a little bit stubborn but with utter determination. He is beyond a doubt a gentleman who must be treated as such. Harsh or even overly vocal reprimands are completely inappropriate for the Basset. He must be treated kindly and gently. Strong-minded and loyal, he commits himself to a single person if given that opportu-

Basset puppies aren't the most active puppies you'll ever meet, but they rival any for sweetness and philosophy.
OWNER, PAMELA T. ROBBINS.

nity. For a fine family dog, the training should be assumed by a few patient members. The Basset's sonorous bark works wonders for him as a watchdog.

GROWTH

Bassets in general throw large litters, with 15 or more puppies not too uncommon. Thus, while one-half to one pound is average for a whelp, considerably under that weight is not necessarily an indication of a problem. What prospective owners must check for, especially with very large litters, is that all pups receive proper nutrition. Breeder-supplemented feedings are the norm. With

Basset pups should not be overfed, overstressed, or over-exercised. Like their mom, they will take everything in stride.
OWNER, LAURA BAILEY.

proper nutrition, Bassets will weigh between 10 and 15 pounds by eight weeks of age. Owners and breeders must guard against overfeeding and obesity, and calcium and other bone-development nutrients should be given only on the advice of a veterinarian, as skeletal abnormalities may be the result. Exercise must be limited, especially during rapid growth periods, as joint complications may occur. Proper dentition should be apparent at a young age. The Basset is a sweet breed, and temperament problems are rare.

HEALTH

The Basset's conformation predisposes it to many bone and joint disorders, most commonly shoulder and foreleg lameness. Irregular growth of limb bones (producing bow-leggedness, among others) and joint deformities are noted problems. Additionally, the Basset has demonstrated a predisposition to achondroplasia, interdigital cysts, subaortic stenosis, calculi, and some cancers. Wobbler syndrome may affect the Basset's spinal column before six months of age. Entropion, ectropion, and glaucoma are noted. A blood platelet disorder and vWD are passed hereditarily in the breed; in American dogs the platelet disorder is quite widespread. Good-quality Bassets are easycare animals, with little grooming needs and hardy appetite. Life span is eight to 12 years. Guard against the breed's proclivity to overeat and underexercise, which can be linked to bloat and back problems in later life, and check the ears regularly for irritation as ear infections are common.

Ideally your Basset will never quite grow into his ears, and even on his merriest day, his eyes exude profound sadness.
OWNER, DAWN TOUNE.

Basset Hound

Beagle

DESCRIPTION

A beautifully balanced dog with a gentle, sweet expression, the Beagle has a broad, full and fairly long skull, which is slightly domed at the occiput and never flat. The ears are long and nearly reach the tip of the nose; they are entirely flat-lying and broad. The eyes are large and set well apart; their expression is gentle and pleading. The nose must not be Roman or upturned to present a dish face and the muzzle must never be long, snipy or very short. The neck rises easily from the shoulders and is neither short nor cloddy. The throat is clean and never shows dewlap. The shoulders are sloping and never straight; the chest is deep and broad and never overly wide or deep. The forelegs are straight and the pasterns short and straight; the stifles strong and well let down; hocks moderately bent and firm, never straight. The tail is set moderately high and carried gaily, never long. The coat is close and hard and of medium length, not short, thin or soft. Beagles come in all true hound colors. Beagles are categorized in two varieties: not over 13 inches and 13 to 15 inches, not over.

Why not a Beagle? The all-around Beagle has much to offer most people: compact size, a great personality, good looks and easy care. OWNERS, MARK LISTER, BRUCE TAGUE AND J OHN AND GRETA HAAG.

OWNER SUITABILITY

Clever and classic, the Beagle is an affectionate, biddable family dog who is ever gay and hardy. The Beagle is a professional debater: he can convince his owners of many things. Begin training early or else you will have an overweight, barky Beagle who soils in every room. They are gregarious with other dogs and

A pile of pre-school Beagles. BREEDER, RICHARD PRESTON.

have an insatiable desire to please their masters. All in all, the Beagle is a wonderful dog.

Growth

Size and growth rate of course vary with the variety. Pups of the larger variety tend to grow more rapidly, though not excessively so. Pups of the smaller variety vary more in size, with some being larger. Caesarian sections are more common in the smaller variety because of this. Dewclaws should be removed from both front and rear limbs, where present. Beagles are a natural breed, with no unusual growth or development patterns. Beagles do well on a balanced diet and mature at a consistent pace. Most Beagles are black and white at birth, with the true coloration emerging around three weeks. Lemon and whites are usually all white at birth, and blues are a grayish color. Improper bites are somewhat common and can be determined at an early age. Bad bites should be avoided and dogs having them never bred, though for the pet person a slightly off bite should present no problems with responsible dental care.

By three weeks of age, the Beagle's true coloration begins to emerge. OWNER, RICHARD PRESTON.

Health

Eye disorders, including cataracts, glaucoma, retinal dysplasia and PRA, are found in the breed, making screening a requirement. The Beagle's conformation seems to predispose it to intervertebral disc disease, and multiple epiphyseal dysplasia (a condition in which the hind leg joints sag causing a swaying gait) has been passed hereditarily. Hip dysplasia, however, is very uncommon. Hemophilia A is a sex-linked hereditary recessive trait which must be inquired of the breeder. Kidney disease, glandular enlargement, amyloidosis, IgA deficiency, meningitis, pulmonic stenosis and congenital anemia (pyruvate kinase deficiency) are also reported. A well-bred Beagle, however, is a hardy and happy animal who enjoys a long 12-to-15-year life expectancy, requires little grooming, and eats well.

Only acquire your Beagle from stock that has been tested for potential eye, kidney and blood problems. Let nothing interfere with the potential long life of your dog. OWNER, CHRISTINE L. VORONOVITCH.

Beagle

Bearded Collie

A natural herding dog, the Bearded Collie comes "as is," whether for the show ring, the living room, or the sheep farm. His coat naturally parts in the middle and is never trimmed or sculptured.
OWNERS, VIRGINIA AND MICHEL HANIGAN.

DESCRIPTION

The Bearded Collie is an unspoiled, active dog, enjoying the hardiness and agility of a true working dog. The dog possesses a medium-length coat that is harsh and shaggy, though never woolly or curly, naturally parting to either side and accentuating the lines of the body, instead of hiding them. The body is long and lean and not heavy: approximate ratio of 5 to 4, length to height. Ideally the height at the withers is 20 to 22 inches. The head is well proportioned and the skull is broad and flat. The eyes are large and well set apart but not round nor protruding. The nose is large and squaring; the muzzle is never snipy. The shoulders are well laid back; the legs straight but not too heavy. The chest is deep and reaches at least the elbows; the loins are strong and a flat or steep croup is a serious flaw. The thighs are well bent and the hocks are low; the abundantly furnished tail is low set and reaches at least the point of hock. The coat epitomizes naturalness and is not trimmed or sculptured, nor is it ever long and silky. In color the adult Bearded Collie can be any shade of gray from black to slate to silver, or any shade of brown from chocolate to sandy; or light to dark shades in blues or fawns. White only occurs as a foreface blaze, on the skull, tail tip, chest, legs, feet and around the neck. Eye color adheres to coat color and lighter color eyes on a blue or fawn are correct.

No airs about the Beardie, he is a fun-loving, by-your-side companion. Keep him busy, give him time outdoors, and make him feel involved, and you'll have a priceless, well-behaved pet.
OWNER, CAROL THURSTON.

OWNER SUITABILITY

A great indoor dog, the Beardie loves children and his people. He does not like to be left alone and mourns your absence. Quality time for playing and exercise is vital and the Beardie is a curious little man (like a two-year-old human). Outside time makes the Beardie a more balanced and relaxed indoor pet. These are soft souls who don't cope with rough correction or handling. Be gentle yet firm. If you're inclined towards a winsome shaggy dog who will lick you on your saddest days, vote Beardie!

Growth

Weight at birth varies considerably, correlating to litter size, which also varies. Average whelp weight is 8 to 10 ounces. Beardie pups grow quickly and in general are rambunctious. Early weaning is often initiated for the sake of the dam. Owners should select for outgoing personalities that demonstrate good confidence, and of course for good health. A condition called adolescent trauma occurs in the breed, especially affect-

Select puppies on their bouncy temperaments and sparkling health. Show puppies should be balanced with dark pigmentation and sound build.

ing males. Owners must avoid stressing the dog during this time. Breeders advise just to continue good socialization and training. Attention is a big must to avoid frustration and potential destructiveness. Beardies grow fast. They grow like a weed and can be as unsightly as one. Adolescents can grow unevenly, especially skeletally/muscularly, and coat changes can definitely lead to a case of the uglies. Color often fades to appearing almost white for about one year. Feed plentifully between two and six months to encourage proper development. If testicle(s) are undescended by five months, they will likely remain so. An incidence of smooth coats, in which the long guard hairs are absent, is reported—this is visible by eight weeks of age. Beardies attain full physical maturity around two years of age.

Beardies grow fast but mature slowly. Adolescence, otherwise known as the "uglies," is characterized by gangly limbs and uneven coat growth.
OWNER, JUNE E. HARTZOG.

Health

The Beardie enjoys relative freedom from congenital and hereditary problems, and breeders deserve handsome applause. However, HD, PRA, and persistent pupillary membrane (persistent pigmented strands across the pupil) do occur with heretofore low incidence. Perhaps the most significant problem (and this too is not common) is a fading of skin pigment around the eyes, lips, and nose. This condition may be hereditary or an allergic reaction. As a note, Beardies often have a low resting heart rate (60 beats per minute) and a body temperature of 102–102.5°F. Grooming, especially brushing, is a considerable must. Beardies have sensitive skin and may be prone to hot spots. Flea control is vital to a healthy Beardie. Owners should plan for at least a weekly grooming of one-half to one hour for the adult coat. Daily brushing for the adolescent changing coat can be of great benefit. Feeding habits may be a problem, so ensure a healthy diet of quality foods and do not spoil the breed with table treats. Life expectancy is 12 to 14 years.

Bearded Collie

Bedlington Terrier

DESCRIPTION

An unusually distinct terrier breed, the Bedlington is a hard, athletic dog of much grace and style. The head is described as narrow but deep and rounded; long in jaw and short in skull. There is no stop and the line from nose to crown is unbroken. The head is neither cheeky nor snipy. The eyes are almond shaped, small and well sunken; set is oblique and fairly high on the head. The ears hang flat and are set on low, triangular with rounded tips. The jaw is long and tapering; muzzle is strong and well filled up with bone under eye. The neck is long and tapering, never throaty. The head is carried high. The body, longer than high, is muscular and lithe; the hindlegs are longer than the straight forelegs; pasterns long and sloping are slightly bent; hocks strong and well let down, never turning in or out. The coat is a hallmark of the breed, a mixture of hard and soft hair which stands out from the skin; not wiry to the touch, the coat is crisp and tends to curl. The tail is low-set, and shaped like a scimitar (tapering). The Bedlington can be blue, sandy, liver, blue and tan, liver and tan. Dark patches on all colors are encouraged. Preferably, the dog measures $16\frac{1}{2}$ inches at the withers; the bitch $15\frac{1}{2}$. Weight ranges from 17 to 23 pounds.

These dark eyes are the windows to a very sophisticated terrier soul. The head piece on the Bedlington is most unique, giving the breed a look unlike any other dog.
OWNER, DAVID P. RAMSEY.

OWNER SUITABILITY

Blessed with a clear sense of the absurd, the Bedlington ranks among the clowns of the canine world. The dogs need appropriate attention from the family. Raised in the home, the breed is very tolerant of children, extremely loyal and loving to its humans. They are not ill-tempered or hard, though dogs raised strictly for ratting work can be ungodly fearless. Their affection for people, however, has been understated. It is not difficult to raise more than two Bedlingtons together and they are not ill-tempered, as some would have it.

Crisp with a tendency to curl, the Bedlington's coat stands out from the skin, a combination a soft and hard hair.
OWNERS, DOUG LEHR AND DESIREE WILLIAMS.

GROWTH

There is much difference between the Bedlington adult and puppy. Breeders note that only the most discerning eye can really judge the potential of a pup. For starters, Bedlingtons are born black, chocolate brown, or dark coffee, and mature to blue, liver and sandy respectively. This change can take the better part of the first year to be completed. Prospective owners should avoid dogs with long backs, narrow chests, gay tails, and dogs that are markedly oversize or lacking in substance, as these faults will likely not correct with age. Proper bite should be a reverse scissors, with close-fitting lips. Owners should check for missing teeth. Bedlingtons usually consume their meals without protest, thus ensuring a properly balanced diet should not be a problem.

HEALTH

Bedlingtons in general are healthy, long-lived dogs. They are true terriers, and exhibit that distinctive terrier spunk. Grooming demands are great, as the breed's hallmark clip

Bedlington puppies are dark through most of their first year, gradually lightening to their adult colors. Selecting a puppy for show requires an experienced eye as Bedlingtons can grow unpredictably in coat, color and conformation. OWNER, JEAN L. MATHIEU.

likely will require some professional assistance. Breeders note that these dogs fare better when not kept at consistently warm temperatures, especially when the coat is kept longer. The most significant problem is a condition in which copper is retained in excessive amounts in the liver. It is estimated that at present up to 50% of the breed may be affected; however, many of these dogs may live normal lives. Prospective owners must insist on a "biopsied normal" certificate from both parents of any litter. Another known problem is retinal dysplasia, which is also hereditary and makes screening a necessity of the parent stock. It is a lively terrier breed that does best with plenty of constructive exercise and obedience training.

The Bedlington variety of spunk differs from that of other terriers. Potentially aloof and stubborn, the breed needs a strong but patient handler. OWNER, K. DONOVAN.

Bedlington Terrier

Belgian Sheepdog, Groenendael

DESCRIPTION

The black Belgian Sheepdog is a square dog with an impressively proud carriage, agile, strong, and very alert. Well proportioned and elegant, the male stands 24 to 26 inches, the female 22 to 24 inches. The head is strong and well proportioned to body. The eyes are medium in size and almond shaped, never protruding. The ears are triangular and erect, never hanging. The neck is round and long enough to allow for proud carriage of the head. The withers are slightly higher and slope into the back; the topline is level and straight; the chest is deep but not broad. The abdomen is neither tucked up nor paunchy. The croup is medium long and sloping. The forelegs are strong and parallel; hindlegs are also parallel and of good substance, with oval bone rather than round. Feet slightly elongated. The tail is strong, never cropped or stump. Coat is straight and abundant, not silky or wiry; texture is medium harsh. Undercoat is extremely dense, varying with climate. The color is always black (or with limited white markings).

A well-built, solid black herding dog of medium size, the Belgian Sheepdog, Groenendael is commonly referred to simply as Belgian Sheepdog.
OWNER, JULIA E. FIECHTER.

OWNER SUITABILITY

The Belgian Shepherd has achieved a moderate popularity as a pet animal, and is commonly confused with a solid black German Shepherd. All the Belgian herding breeds excel at any number of pursuits, including obedience, herding, sledding, agility, search and rescue, police work, and arson and fire detection. A remarkable breed that is a great companion for children and loves to play outdoors. Inside he is well behaved and most consistent, though too active for apartment living.

The ideal Belgian Sheepdog puppy is outgoing and people friendly, if a little reserved. The well-socialized litter shines with personality and good health.

GROWTH

The Belgian Sheepdog weighs 12 to 14 pounds at eight weeks. Full maturity takes up to four years, and females typically mature quicker than males. Belgian Shepherd breeders on the whole are an ethical and responsible herd, and physical soundness in the breed is the norm. Still, owners should have a clear understanding of the standard and select for physical soundness. Temperament is also important. Belgians are known for their loyalty

The puppy's coat is soft and downy though usually solid black. Some puppies may have white markings on the chest which may darken with maturity.

and intelligence. Pups may be naturally suspicious but never shy or aggressive. Adolescence is marked by the change of the soft downy puppy coat to the dense, black adult coat. Adolescent dogs need plenty of exercise and lots of time with the owner and human family. Training should be initiated at a young age. Chewing needs are strong and outlets must be provided.

HEALTH

Hip dysplasia affects the breed, though not as commonly as it does other sizable working dogs. Epilepsy, which can be confirmed by an EEG at an early age, is also reported, though infrequently. An unusual reaction to immunizations and a sensitivity to anesthetics have been noted in the breed and should be checked with both the breeder and veterinarian. Shedding is considerable, and the breed has shown a tendency to develop dermatitis during its shedding season. Plenty of training and exercise are vital. Belgian Sheepdogs typically live into their teens.

The long coat of the Belgian Sheepdog adult distinguishes it from a solid black German Shepherd, with which the breed might be confused.
OWNERS, WILLIAM G. AND CATHY H. DAUGHERTY.

A balanced puppy with a good gait promises the best adult dog.
OWNERS, JAN MANUEL AND CAROLYN KELSO.

Belgian Sheepdog, Groenendael

Belgian Sheepdog, Laekenois

DESCRIPTION

The Belgian Sheepdog is a square dog with an impressively proud carriage, agile, strong, and very much alert. Well proportioned and elegant, the male stands 24 to 26 inches, the female 22 to 24 inches. The head is strong and well proportioned to body. The eyes are medium in size and almond shaped, never protruding. The ears are triangular and erect, never hanging. The neck is round and long enough to allow for proud carriage of the head. The withers are slightly higher and slope into the back; the topline is level, straight; the chest is deep but not broad. The abdomen is neither tucked up nor paunchy. The croup is medium long and sloping. The forelegs are strong and parallel; hindlegs are also parallel and of good substance and oval bone rather than round. Feet slightly

The Laekenois breed is distinguished by its reddish fawn coloration and its harsh, wiry coat. Otherwise this breed is identical to its Belgian Sheepdog brethren.
OWNER, MONA B. MOORE.

elongated. The tail is strong, never cropped or stump. Coat is harsh, wiry dry with no curly or fluffy areas. Length is about $2\frac{1}{2}$ inches; eyes are not obscured by hair; muzzle hair does not make head appear square; tail is not plumed. In color, the dog is reddish fawn with black shading, mostly on muzzle and tail.

OWNER SUITABILITY

The Laekenois breed is little known in the United States, though there are a small fraternity of breeders in England. He is a strong-minded, tough dog and can rightly be called the "black" sheep of his herding family. His wiry coat is quite unique for a shepherd dog, and he is the only Belgian Shepherd that couldn't be mistaken for a GSD. Like his Belgian brothers, he is a good babysitter and can stare the most unwilling child to his room at bedtime. (The breed employs a "hard-eye" staring method to herd its sheep into their pens.)

GROWTH

Newborns at about one pound grow steadily and reach 9 to 12 pounds by the eighth week. Puppies are born with soft, fuzzy coats which gradually is replaced by the correct wire coat, which develops slowly and begins to show its full bloom by around 18 months (slower with some dogs, up to three years). Dogs will lighten with age. Ears are erect by the third month. Expect the maturing adolescent to challenge authority. Treat him with respect but be firm and consistent in training.

HEALTH

The four Belgian Sheepdogs are all closely related and share very uniform physical conformations (excepting coat and color). Hip dysplasia needs to be considered, and epilepsy, too, should be kept in mind. Evidence of adverse reactions to immunizations or anesthetics exists, and such possibility should be checked with the breeder and veterinarian. The Laekenois's crisp coat requires little in the way of special care, despite its unique appearance. As with the other three Belgian Sheepdogs, exercise requirements are high.

The eyes are clear and the expression alert. Although as a puppy the Laekenois's coat is soft and fuzzy, the adult coat should show no signs of curl or fluff.
OWNER, MONA B. MOORE.

While an independent and resourceful worker, the Laekenois counts among the most trainable of dogs. He is not stubborn and thrives on pleasing his owner. This is the least common of the Belgian Sheepdogs in the States, though England has a moderate number of breeders.
OWNER, MONA B. MOORE.

Belgian Sheepdog, Laekenois

Belgian Sheepdog, Malinois

DESCRIPTION

The Belgian Sheepdog is a square dog with an impressively proud carriage, agile, strong, and very alert. Well proportioned and elegant, the male stands 24 to 26 inches, the female 22 to 24 inches. The head is strong and well proportioned to body. The eyes are medium in size and almond shaped, never protruding. The ears are triangular and erect, never semi-prick or hanging. The neck is round and long enough to allow for proud carriage of the head. The withers are slightly higher and slope into the back; the topline is level and straight; the chest is deep but not broad. The abdomen is neither tucked up nor paunchy. The croup is medium long and sloping. The forelegs are strong and parallel; hindlegs are also parallel and of good substance, with oval bone rather than round. Feet

The Malinois is a strong, proud breed of herding dog with a dense, short coat, black mask, and collarette around its neck.
OWNER, REBECCA J. WASNIEWSKI.

slightly elongated. The tail is strong, never cropped or stump. Coat is characteristically short, straight, hard, and weather-proof, with a dense undercoat; somewhat longer around neck to form a collarette, as well as on the tail and back of thighs. The color is rich fawn to mahogany with black hair tips to create an overlay.

OWNER SUITABILITY

A versatile and attractive herding dog, the Malinois appears a great deal like the German Shepherd, which has been its blessing and its curse, since it will never escape being in the shadow of the infinitely popular GSD. Its lesser popularity makes it a viable choice for people who are not inclined to find a top-notch German Shepherd or who want a hard-as-nails guard dog. Nonetheless, the Malinois has many wonderful virtues to offer an owner: he is protective, strong, affectionate and trustworthy with children, obedient and overall quite undemanding.

Black hairs create an overlay or ticking effect over the Malinois's fawn to mahogany coat.
OWNERS, SHARON AND JAMES BURKE.

GROWTH

Newborn Belgian Sheepdogs on average weigh about one pound. Weight at eight weeks is about 9 pounds. Rate of development may vary from individual to individual; 18 months is average for physical maturity. When selecting their dogs, owners should avoid oversize (Belgians are medium-sized dogs) and seek a square, solid construction. Coat should be short. The coat coloration can vary from light to dark, but the characteristic black mask and ears should be apparent. While some white may occur on the newborn, an excess of white, usually on the chest and extending down inside the front legs, is definitely a fault. A whitening on the muzzle, commonly called a "frost," is not uncommon and is acceptable. Prospective owners should check for undershot or overshot bites. The black coat overlay will become more apparent with age. The adolescent dog will lose its soft puppy coat and gain its dense protective jacket. Young males may act rebellious and dominant (so may females) but this is a passing phase. Lots of socialization and early training should result in a loyal, obedient, and naturally protective canine.

The puppy's black mask and black overlay darken with age. Puppy buyers shouldn't be concerned about small white marks or frost on the muzzle but should avoid oversized puppies. OWNERS, FRANK AND CAROL KNOCK.

HEALTH

While the Malinois is among the more healthy and hardy breeds of the canine family, HD does affect the breed. The incidence of this problem has been largely controlled by responsible breeding. According to some sources, the incidence today is only about five percent. Epilepsy is also known to affect the Belgians. Reports tell of adverse reactions to immunizations or anesthetics—be aware and discuss this with your breeder or veterinarian. Dermatitis may occur during the shedding period of both the Groenendael and Malinois. Eye screening should be performed by all breeders. The Malinois's shorter coat demands less grooming but his exercise and training requirements are just as high. Many Malinois go gray very young (as early as two years). Life span is approximately ten to 14 years.

The Malinois puppy possesses a softer coat than the adult. Accustom the puppy to grooming early on so that it learns to welcome the attention. OWNERS, FRANK AND CAROL KNOCK.

Belgian Sheepdog, Malinois

Belgian Sheepdog, Tervuren

DESCRIPTION

The Belgian Sheepdog is a square dog with an impressively proud carriage, agile, strong, and very alert. Well proportioned and elegant, the male stands 24 to 26 inches, the female 22 to 24 inches. The head is strong and well proportioned to body. The eyes are medium in size and almond shaped, never protruding. The ears are triangular and erect, never hanging. The neck is round and long enough to allow for proud carriage of the head. The withers are slightly higher and slope into the back; the topline is level and straight; the chest is deep but not broad. The abdomen is neither tucked up nor paunchy. The croup is medium long and sloping. The forelegs are strong and parallel; hind legs are also parallel and of good substance, with oval bone rather than round. Feet slightly elongated. The tail is strong, never cropped or stumpy. Coat is straight and abundant; neither silky or wiry, nor wavy or curly; texture is medium harsh. The ears are well tufted; collarette around the neck; fringe on back of forearms; abundant breeches and well covered tail. The female is never as fully ornamented as the male. Undercoat is extremely dense, varying with climate. The body color is a rich fawn to a russet mahogany with black overlay. No solid black or liver dogs.

The Tervuren coat is straight and abundant with well-tufted ears and furnishings on neck, legs and tail. Show dogs possess these features to glorious perfection. OWNERS, JUDY BAUMEISTER AND STEVE SORENSON.

OWNER SUITABILITY

Tervuren folk are thoroughly convinced that the Terv is the most versatile of the Belgian Sheepdogs, and at least as talented as the more popular German Shepherd. The Terv needs encouragement but not a lot of forceful reinforcement. He learns and remembers. His endeavors are extensive and he naturally excels at obedience, as his strongest desire is to please his owners. These are active outdoor dogs that are not recommended for apartment living. They are excellent with children and prove consistent babysitters able to round up the kids for bedtime.

Welcome to a trouble-free, multi-talented loving companion: the Terv has it all. OWNER, JOELLE G. WHITE.

GROWTH

The Tervuren weighs 8 to 13 pounds at eight weeks. Development is characteristically steady, though some individuals experience growth spurts where their legs outgrow their bodies. Breeders allow three years for physical maturity, though some dogs and particularly bitches mature sooner. Owners should carefully select for temperament, insisting on pups which have been well socialized through the first eight weeks. Tervuren pups should be adaptable and confident, and of course friendly. Ears should be erect by four months, though they may drop momentarily during teething. Adolescent Tervs often are poor eaters, and proper nutrition must be ensured. Adults are typically good eaters. The Tervuren coat becomes redder and blacker with each shedding.

HEALTH

Hip dysplasia is uncommon in the Tervuren, though it does occur and screening is still a must. Epilepsy is known in the breed; it can be determined by an EEG at an early age. Thyroid secretion and pancreatic problems have also been reported and breeders should be questioned as to their likelihood. Some breeders advise a diet with less fats to avoid pancreatic

The puppy's ears should stand naturally by four months. These are perceptive, quick-thinking puppies that require an owner on his toes.
OWNER, ROBIN M. WEST.

problems. Hypothyroidism, which can be marked by seizure-like occurrences, has been identified in the Tervuren. Inquire also about reactions to immunizations and anesthetics. The Tervuren's abundant coat can shed plenty and daily brushing is recommended. Exercise and training requirements are significant, as for all the other Belgian Sheepdogs. Life expectancy is 12 to 16 years.

Growth is usually steady, though sometimes the legs can get a little ahead (or behind) of the adolescent.
OWNER, ROBIN M. WEST.

Belgian Sheepdog, Tervuren

Bernese Mountain Dog

DESCRIPTION

Strikingly aristocratic, boasting his illustrious tricolor pattern, this Swiss working dog stands up to $27\frac{1}{2}$ inches tall (dogs range from 25 to $27\frac{1}{2}$ while bitches range from 23 to 26 inches). The coat is thick, moderately long, slightly wavy or straight; it is not trimmed but shown natural; overly curly or dull coats are discouraged. The head is flat-skulled on top and broad with a defined but unexaggerated stop. The ears are medium size, set high and triangularly shaped with rounded tips. The eyes are somewhat oval in shape. The Bernese is a dry-mouthed breed, with little development of the flews. The topline is level; the chest is deep with well sprung, not barrel-shaped, ribs; the back is broad and firm. The bushy tail may swirl upward when the dog is alert, but never curl in spitz fashion. The shoulders are moderately laid back and never loose;

The classic Swiss tricolor pattern on an abundantly coated $27^1/_2$ -inch dog distinguishes the Bernese Mountain Dog. He possesses a notable air of the aristocratic combined with intelligence and agility.
OWNER, HEATHER BREMMER.

the forelegs are straight, well under the shoulder. The hocks are well let down and straight. The tricolor pattern consists of a jet-black ground color (without exception) with symmetrical markings in rich rust and clear white.

OWNER SUITABILITY

The Berner is a good-natured dog who is not as outgoing as some believe. (Many liken him to the Golden Retriever in temperament though he was not bred to be quite so people-happy.) He is independent yet affectionate with his people, generally aloof to strangers. He is an outdoorsman and prefers to spend time outside. The Berner seems to not be able to resist the attention of children. His faithfulness is most noteworthy and he has a healthy enjoy-life attitude.

The puppy is clearly marked in rust over the eyes, on the cheeks, chest and legs by three weeks of age.

GROWTH

Newborn Berners are a large 1 to $1\frac{1}{2}$ pounds, with an apparent correlation of pup size to litter size. Smaller pups most commonly attain a size similar to larger ones by maturity. Responsible breeders will not let pups leave the litter until at least eight weeks of age, which has been determined to affect the dog's character positively. High metabolisms and rapid growth rate necessitate a prescribed diet for the Berner puppy and adolescent. While these diets vary from breeder

Unlike most other puppies, the Berner puppy will need to be fed no less than three or four times per day for the first year. Low-protein diets help ward off possible joint problems.

to breeder, essentially they all are of low-protein content with vitamin and mineral supplementation. This diet is important to preventing skeletal problems. Generally young pups are fed four times a day, later reduced to three when growth rate becomes even and steady. Most joint problems become noticeable between the ages of four to eight months. Markings can generally be noted by three weeks of age. Proper adult bite is difficult to determine with certainty in pups, because bites have been known to change as these dogs mature. Rear dewclaws should be removed at an early age.

No sooner than eight weeks of age should Berner puppies be released to their new homes.

HEALTH

The Berner is a big, gentle, determined dog. Exercise demands are not great, though these dogs greatly benefit from long walks and delight in cart (or child's wagon) pulling should they get the chance. Grooming needs too are not excessive, though plenty of brushing keeps the coat clean and mat free, and also reduces the inevitable shedding. Hip dysplasia, osteochondrosis and osteochondritis (two similar cartilage conditions) are among breeder concerns, as is PRA. The Berner has the dubious distinction of being the first breed to exhibit elbow dysplasia, a hereditary condition that affects many breeds. Osteochondrosis (and chondritis) usually occurs during the maximum period of growth, typically four to eight months. Fragmented coronoid process, which exhibits signs similar to elbow dysplasia, is also well documented in the breed. Breeders report umbilical hernias, though state that they are rarely severe. Cerebellar degeneration has a genetic basis in the Berner. Although meningitis is not common in the breed, veterinarians link vasculitis as the likely cause. Aside from screening and sound selection, the single most important factor to the Berner's health is his diet.

Large-breed puppies should not be over-exercised. It seems Berner puppies grow in their sleep!

Guard against over-feeding, especially protein, and smaller daily meals twice a day will help guard against bloat. Avoid high-impact exercise until the Berner is fully developed—he is a cart-puller, not a jumper.

Bernese Mountain Dog

Bichon Frise

DESCRIPTION

The most balanced and sound powderpuff in dogdom, the Bichon Frise is a small, solid white dog with a gaily carried plume of a tail that befits his merry temperament. Contrasting with his snow-white coat are his dark eyes, whose expression is soft but alert. This white angel has "halos" around its eyes, which are the black skin surrounding the eyes, enhancing expression. The ears are drop and of medium length, covered with long, flowing hair. The skull is slightly rounded. There is a slight chiseling under the eyes, but not too much to give an impression of a weak or snipy foreface. The nose is prominent and always black. The neck is long and arched; topline is level except for a slight arch over the loin; chest is suffi-ciently wide to allow free movement of forequarters; the forechest is well pronounced, protruding slightly; underline has moderate tuck-up. The tail is set on level with topline, well plumed, and gracefully curved over the back. Tail cannot be docked, corkscrew, droopy, low set or carried even to the back. The texture of the outercoat is coarser and curlier than the soft and dense undercoat; to the touch the coat feels silky and fine. The coat is trimmed to show natural contours of body; overtrimming is discouraged; in England the breed is shown untrimmed but "tidied up" at the feet and muzzle. The Bichon color is white, but markings of cream, buff or apricot are acceptable (more than ten percent is discouraged). Height ranges from 9 to $11\frac{1}{2}$ inches at the withers.

From the Island of Tenerife hails this handsome snow-white beauty: beneath his flowing cotton should be a solid little frame.
OWNERS, ANITA CAROLLS, BARBARA B. STUBBS AND LOIS K. MORROW.

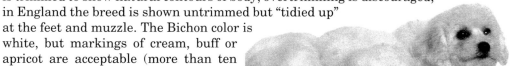

By two weeks of age the pup shows his true white color; some pups have shades of tan or cream on their ears.
OWNER, JOYAN NOLAN.

OWNER SUITABILITY

Adaptable and family-loving, the Bichon makes a delightful children's dog. He is easygoing and gives from his heart without conditions. Bichons excel as show dogs, as their coats are extraordinary. They also do well as obedience dogs since they are that rare combination of smart and obedient. You can find a sweet dog who can fit into any lifestyle. He does not like the heat and prefers to be indoors most of the time.

86

GROWTH

Newborn Bichons weigh about 4 ounces at birth. The average Bichon weighs 4 to 6 pounds by eight weeks of age. The Bichon puppy coat is darker than the adult coat and this color fades by maturity. The juvenile nose is pink, but should achieve its black pigmentation by three months. Eyes should be dark brown or black with fully pigmented lids. Full physical maturity is not attained until one to one-and-a-half years of age. Bichons may not reach mental maturity until three or four years—hence a really long puppyhood. Breeders note that adolescence is not marked by complications as it is in other breeds. Bichons are typically good eaters with few temperament problems. The coat change is generally without the ugly stage so common in other plushly coated breeds. The coat starts out full but single, becoming a full double coat by maturity. One possible complication is teething, as Bichons are known to be slow in cutting their permanent teeth. Owners should monitor this process and be sure to provide plenty of safe and effective chewstuffs to assist the new teeth along.

A Bichon puppy outcuddles the best of them. Never experiencing an awkward stage, the Bichon's coat develops plushly and naturally.
OWNER, JEROME PODELL.

HEALTH

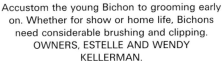

Accustom the young Bichon to grooming early on. Whether for show or home life, Bichons need considerable brushing and clipping.
OWNERS, ESTELLE AND WENDY KELLERMAN.

The Bichon is a lively and very healthy breed, resistant to disease and relatively free from hereditary and congenital problems. Exercise requirements are minimal owing to the breed's small size, though owners must not neglect regular outings and plenty of play. The dog's desire to please lends itself well to obedience training, and owners should capitalize on this. Socialization problems are rare in the breed. In America show grooming demands are great, with professional assistance necessary. Grooming is important too, to prevent matting and subsequent skin problems. Patellar (kneecap) luxation and epilepsy have been documented in the breed. Bladder stones occur more frequently in female Bichons. Most important to Bichon owners is proper care of the eyes, teeth, and coat. Owners must learn to care for and/or prevent tearing and subsequent staining. Additionally, the Bichon has shown a tendency to develop dental problems such as pyorrhea and pemphigus, and regular dental prophylaxis must be maintained. Otherwise the Bichon is a hardy long-lived dog, averaging 17 years of age.

Bichon Frise

Black and Tan Coonhound

DESCRIPTION

The specialist's dog, a trail and tree worker, the Black and Tan Coonhound has become America's most recognizable coonhound breed: he is a large, powerful dog colored in coal black with rich tan markings above eyes, sides of muzzle, chest, legs, breachings, and toes. The head is quite sizable and cleanly modeled, with well developed flews but skin devoid of folds. The ears hang in graceful folds outlining the head majestically. The neck is sloping and muscular, but devoid of excess dewlap. Back is level; chest reaches elbows; tail is long and carried high and freely. The coat is short and dense. The Black and Tan Coonhound stands 25 to 27 inches for a male; 23 to 25 inches for a female; height is in proportion to the animal which

An American original in black and tan, the Coonhound is a powerful, substantially built hunting dog.
OWNERS, JAMES S. AND KATHLEEN M. CORBETT AND MARGO SENSENBRENNER.

never appears leggy nor close to the ground. White marks on chest or other parts are undesirable; a white mark an inch in diameter will disqualify the dog from the show ring.

OWNER SUITABILITY

A consummate hunter and a gentle people-dog, the Black and Tan is a most capable animal whose adaptability is nearly uncanny. These dogs cope with harsh winter temperatures as well as the near-tropics. While they are easygoing and genuinely like human folk, they are happiest when doing their bred-for work. They are bold and crafty and need patient training. Leash training is a must for pet dogs since he will be off and treeing at the blink of a coon's eye!

Soulful eyes and a gentle spirit.

Bred to hunt in packs, Coonhounds are gregarious work and play mates.
OWNERS, KATHERINE SETTLE AND ARILLA E. TURNER.

Growth

A fast-growing bundle of loose skin, the Black and Tan puppy appears to be tripping on his Dumbo-like ears for the first few months—he slowly grows into these and his velvety coat. He reaches adolescence without his breed's full-bodied robustness. Dogs mature fully by their second year. Puppies require a fair amount of encouragement to boost their confidence. For a large dog, the Black and Tan is remarkably long-lived, averaging to 15 years. He doesn't become a senior citizen until about 10, spending his first decade of life as an active, fun-to-be-around canine buddy.

A Coonhound pup is trusting and sweet natured, requiring his owner's encouragement to become a confident, capable hunter and watchdog.
OWNERS, JAN BRUNGARD AND LINDA D. PINCHECK.

Health

Hip dysplasia is the major concern, with OFA an absolute requirement. Ectropion (outward turning eyelids) occurs with perhaps too much frequency but can be avoided with proper selection. Hemophilia B, characterized by prolonged bleeding, is a prospective owner concern. It is a sex-linked recessive hereditary trait. Hunters and field trialers should be aware of polyneuritis (a.k.a., coonhound paralysis), which maybe acquired seven to ten days after a raccoon encounter; it is an immune-mediated syndrome that will improve in three to six weeks. Check the long pendant ears regularly as they are subject to external-ear infections (otitis externa).

Although primarily an outdoor dog, the Coonhound is mellow and well mannered in the home.
OWNERS, JAN BRUNGARD AND LINDA D. PINCHECK.

Black and Tan Coonhound

Bloodhound

DESCRIPTION

The solemn Bloodhound is among the heaviest of the hounds, with males attaining a weight of 110 pounds and bitches 100 (though the average is about 20 pounds less). Most notable is the noble head of the breed, which is narrow in proportion to its length and long for the body. The occipital peak of the skull is very pronounced. The eyes are deeply sunken. The ears are soft to the touch and thin, extremely long with folds

The king of canine noses: the Bloodhound. OWNERS, DR. JOHN AND SUSAN HAMIL AND DR. MARLENE ZAHNER.

and very low-set. Wrinkles abundantly adorn the head; skin falls especially over the forehead and sides of the face. The neck is long and the chest well let down to form a deep keel; the forelegs are straight and heavily boned, with squarely set elbows; the hocks are well bent and let down. The loin is slightly arched and deep and the back strong. In color the Bloodhound can be black and tan, red and tan, and tawny; small amounts of white are permissible. The average height of dogs is 26 inches; bitches, 24 inches. The larger animal is preferred provided that quality and balance are maintained.

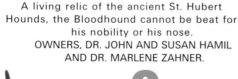

A living relic of the ancient St. Hubert Hounds, the Bloodhound cannot be beat for his nobility or his nose. OWNERS, DR. JOHN AND SUSAN HAMIL AND DR. MARLENE ZAHNER.

Wrinkles reign from the beginning. OWNER, GRETCHEN SCHUECKING.

OWNER SUITABILITY

Renowned for his nose, the Bloodhound is the best tracker and probably the calmest dog of all. He is determined and tireless. Like most of the other hound breeds, the Bloodhound likes people, especially people with fun smells. He is quiet in the house, though often operatically vocal out of doors, making use of his cavernous howl. Owners need a lot of property as Bloodhounds can wear down your land quickly. Fences are a must, too, as Bloodhounds can be on a scent like the wind! His nose is said to be two million times as sensitive as a human's. Despite his size, he is no guard dog and never attacks. Among the kindest and most patient souls in dogdom, this dog is more profound than he is quick-minded, much like the architects of Western thought.

The classic black and tan pattern. OWNER, ROBERT SHARPS.

90

GROWTH

Litter size varies greatly in the Bloodhound, from very few to as many as 15 pups. Naturally, whelp size varies as well, with larger litters containing smaller pups. If provided with a good diet and supplemental feedings for larger litters, smaller whelps attain the same size as larger ones. Bloodhound pups are almost entirely black or red at birth, changing to black and tan or deeper red, respectively, as they mature. Bloodhounds grow rapidly and should be fed a breeder-prescribed diet. Finicky eating may be a problem with the adolescent, and this proclivity must especially be curbed during the high-growth periods, when proper nutrition is vital to avoid developmental problems. The Bloodhound does not attain full physical maturity until around two years of age, and males may continue to fill out past this time. Females may not experience their first estrus cycle until one year, or even later. Undershot bites may develop between three months and one year of age.

The Bloodhound pup grows quickly though does not become fully mature until two or three years of age.
OWNERS, GRETCHEN SCHUECKING AND JIMMIE AND DELORES JACKSON.

HEALTH

In many ways, the Bloodhound is an easycare companion. He has a sweet and even temperament, and exercise requirements can be largely fulfilled by long leisurely strolls. The breed is also relatively free from serious hereditary and congenital conditions—though HD and elbow dysplasia are reported. The most common problems involve the eyes (ectropion and kerato conjunctivitis sicca); the former usually as a result of the lower eyelid drooping and thereby collecting debris—which can lead to complications. Owing to the long, pendant ears, infections are also common. Always check between the skin folds for signs of irritation. Bloodhounds are known to suffer from bloat (gastric torsion) and are best fed two smaller meals a day, exercised regularly and moderately, and allowed plenty of water. Finally, complications in bone growth are known in the breed and should be discussed with your veterinarian at checkups throughout the growth period.

The Bloodhound's ears and eyes require an owner's regular attention to keep clean and trouble-free.
OWNER, MRS. DIANA DIXON.

Bloodhound

Border Collie

DESCRIPTION

The Border Collie possesses a durable and athletic frame, with a smooth outline to reveal a dog of grace, quality and balance. The skull is fairly broad with full cheeks; a tapering, moderately short muzzle; distinct stop; well-set-apart oval eyes; erect or semi-erect ears. The neck is slightly arched and of good length. The body is longer than tall; hindquarters broad, sloping to tail set on; thighs long and deep, stifles well turned and well-let-down hocks. Tail is moderately long, raised in excitement (but never over back). Borders come in two coat varieties: the more common is the moderately long, in which the coat furnishes a mane, breeching and brush; and the smooth. All colors are possible and permissible, provided that white does not predominate. Borders stand about 21 inches, bitches less.

A working dog in every sense: appearance is completely secondary to the dog's ability to do his bred-for job—herd sheep. OWNER, SHARON HOLM.

OWNER SUITABILITY

An action dog with much energy and intelligence, the Border Collie is the original workaholic sheepdog, born to please and move sheep. If the owner is not a shepherd or doesn't have sheep, he must find other tasks to keep the Border happy. These dogs excel in obedience and agility and, of course, herding trials. They are quick to learn and obedient by nature, bred to follow the signals of a shepherd. The Border Collie may be the most intelligent of all dogs, with the possible exception of the Poodle.

"All work" has not made the Border Collie a dull dog: many of the smartest trainers consider the Border the most intelligent of all breeds. OWNERS, PETER AND ANN STACEY.

GROWTH

Border Collies begin life at about one pound, which is somewhat sizable for a breed that matures at 30 to 45 pounds. The Border Collie is a natural breed and experiences few growth or developmental problems. Of course, these active and athletic dogs will be very rambunctious pups and require plenty of patience. Exercise and obedience training can

Border puppies are active in mind and body, needing an owner's patient and constant attention. OWNER, JERRI A. CARTER.

begin at an early age. Many dogs destined for the ranch or for herding trials begin sheepdog training at around four months of age. While the breed is generally physically mature at one year, or slightly later, it will take at least another year or two for the dogs really to peak as performance animals.

HEALTH

The Border Collie is considered a very hardy, healthy animal, generally free from hereditary and congenital problems and highly tolerant of his environment, making him largely resistant to disease. Hip dysplasia and PRA both exist but are rare, as are Collie eye and epilepsy, owing to careful breeding. Posing more of a problem, especially for males, is osteochondritis dessicans, a cartilage condition that develops most commonly during the rapid growth period of four to eight months. Proper feeding (a breeder-prescribed diet),

Responsible breeding and screening have made the Border Collie virtually health-problem-free. OWNER, JERRI A. CARTER.

without oversupplementation, is vital during this time. Bad bites, allergies, primary ciliary dyskinesia (a respiratory problem), deafness and cryptorchidism are all reported, though not serious concerns. The Border Collie requires a goodly amount of brushing, exercise and mental stimulation. This dog averages ten to 14 years of age, though some have lived to 18.

The ears can be erect or semi-erect and the coat can be moderately long or smooth. OWNER, LINDA HUSSON.

Border Collie

Border Terrier

DESCRIPTION

A medium-sized working terrier who is "hard as nails" in the field and whose otter-like head sets him apart from the other terriers. The working Border Terrier male weighs 13 to $15\frac{1}{2}$ pounds, female $11\frac{1}{2}$ to 14 pounds. He is of medium bone, well put together, though rather narrow in shoulder, body and quarters. Characteristic is his broken, very wiry jacket that lies closely to his body (never wavy or curly); Borders are exhibited in their natural state, only slightly tidied up. The eyes are described as "full of fire and intelligence." The ears are small and V-shaped; not set on high but dropping forward close to the cheeks. The muzzle is short and well filled; a moderately broad curve at the stop is desired. The neck is clean and muscular, gradually widening to the shoulders. Back is strong and does not dip behind the shoulder. Ribs carried well back and not oversprung; underline fairly straight. Tail is moderately short, thick at base and tapering. Hindquarters strong and racy; thighs long. Borders can be red, grizzle and tan, blue and tan or wheaten; dark muzzle is desirable; white on chest tolerable but not on feet.

A terrier's terrier: the Border Terrier possesses the head of an otter and the spirit of a cobra, fearless and quick.
OWNERS, BETSY KIRKPATRICK, CINDY PEEBLES, AND W. HENRY ODUM III.

OWNER SUITABILITY

This plain little brown dog is one of the best hidden secrets of the fancy! The Border Terrier is an unusually wonderful family dog, full of charm and life. Being a 110% terrier, he is critter-oriented and will chase mice, rabbits, squirrels, etc. Although the family cat is safe, other small mammal pets are not. Owners must have a fenced-in yard (high enough that he doesn't jump over and deeply imbedded that he doesn't dig under). Reliably easygoing, sensitive, friendly and affectionate, the Border is an independent spirit and likes to make his own decisions. Begin training early. His independent hunting nature also makes him believe he needs to find his own dinner, which makes walks interesting. Not given to bad habits or pestering, the Border gains his admirers from the sensible dog folk, not moved by a fluffy coat or a passing fad. Many owners opt for a second to keep the first company.

In doors or out, Borders like being around people and protecting them from harmful vermin. Though critter-minded, Borders make sensitive company.
OWNERS, WAYNE AND JOYCE KIRN.

Growth

Newborn Border Terriers weigh on average 10 ounces. Borders are slow to mature for a small dog, not reaching full adult conformation until about one-and-a-half years, though some lines mature earlier. Uneven growth rates could signal a puppy that may not mature into a show-quality dog. Prospective owners should select for good balance. Borders weigh $3\frac{1}{2}$ to 5 pounds at eight weeks. The characteristic harsh coat should be apparent starting at three months, though it becomes more coarse as the dog matures and the puppy coat is stripped. Temperament changes are usually not a problem, though consistent socialization (human and dog) is vital to avoid introversion. A shy period is common, and owners must simply be patient and encouraging while continuing with socialization. Nonetheless, owners should avoid overstimulation to prevent an unmanageable adolescent, which could carry over to adulthood. Testicles may descend as late as six months.

Choose a puppy who has a balanced outline at eight weeks of age. Commonly by ten or twelve weeks the puppy's legs may appear shorter, but the puppy will usually grow past this phase.
OWNERS, ROBIN JONES AND TERESA TIPTON.

Health

The Border Terrier provides years of exhilarating canine companionship, with a long life expectancy up to 15 years. Provided with good socialization and plenty of constructive exercise, including chewing exercise, Borders prove good-natured, fun canines. Besides the necessary terrier stripping, which does require a certain amount of skill, the Border Terrier is an easycare dog owing both to its small size and hardy nature. Congenital heart problems, hip dysplasia,

Borders mature slowly, and white spots on chests usually shrink with age. Avoid white marks on the toes for a show puppy.
OWNERS, WAYNE AND JOYCE KIRN.

Young puppies are seal brown and eventually the tan undercoat comes through.
OWNER, HAZEL WICHMAN.

and PRA have all been documented in the breed; and, though their incidence is low, screening should be required of all breeding stock. Pups should be checked at a young age and then annually for heart murmurs and other possible problems.

Border Terrier

95

Borzoi

DESCRIPTION

Unmistakably elegant, the Borzoi is a vision of grace and aristocracy. Standing 28 inches at the withers (bitches 2 inches less), the Borzoi ranks as one of the tallest sighthounds and is identified by his long, silky coat, his long, narrow skull and deep powerful jaws, capable of pinning a wolf. The ears are small and fine, lying back in repose or raised when alert. The eyes are set somewhat obliquely, never round, full nor staring. The neck is clean and never throaty; with coat frill profuse and curly. The shoulders are sloping and never coarse or lumbering. The chest is rather narrow with deep brisket; ribs very deep, only slightly sprung; back rises at the loin and curves gracefully. The hinds are long and powerful with well-bent stifles. Tail is long and set on low, carried low in motion. The coat can be either flat, wavy or curly, never woolly. The Borzoi can be any color. Weight ranges from 75 to 105 pounds, bitches about 15 pounds less.

The Borzoi or Russian Wolfhound, as he is sometimes called, has the jaws to grasp and hold a wolf! This is a powerful yet undeniably elegant sighthound.
OWNER, AMY L. SORBIE.

OWNER SUITABILITY

This ex-wolf hunter has become a gentle and well-mannered member of society. Most owners are fascinated by the Borzoi's great size and sophistication. For all his size, he is generally undemanding on his owners, though he needs adequate space to exercise and is very active when outdoors. Indoors he is less active. With his sophistication comes his stubborn nature, so good habits should be ingrained at a young age. He is stable with children and somewhat sociable, though the romper room isn't his favorite place.

Although a vigorous outdoor dog, indoors the Borzoi is reserved and well behaved.
OWNER, DEBBIE TAPLEY.

GROWTH

The Borzoi is a rapid-growing though slow to mature breed. This fact makes selecting from genetically sound breeding programs all the more important, as physical defects including metabolic bone disease can especially affect this breed. Borzois essentially complete their rapid growth phase by nine months to one year of age. During this time proper nutrition is of utmost importance. Owners must not spoil the breed with treats or table scraps to avoid a finicky eater. A breeder-prescribed diet should be followed especially for the first year. During the rapid growth phase, enlargement of the long bones and joints is common. Owners should still check for pain and any signs of limping, as this could signal a problem. Full physical maturity is not attained until around three years of age. A breeder-prescribed socialization program is also a good idea, as roaming, irritability, and shyness are reported behavior problems in improperly socialized dogs.

HEALTH

The Borzoi's size may deter an owner at first sight. However, Borzois prove easycare animals because of their mellow disposition and minimal grooming re-

Although the breed is not outgoing, your Borzoi pup's mom should be neither unfriendly nor hand shy. Temperament of the dam is an ample reflection of the breeder's socialization program. A calm, approachable puppy is your best bet. OWNER, LENA S. TAMBOER.

quirements. Grooming primarily involves brushing, though some trimming around the areas of the anus, eyes and ears may help prevent infection. The two most detrimental conditions facing the breed are metabolic bone disease and bloat (gastric torsion). Of course, bloat can be guarded against by feeding smaller meals at least twice a day, regular moderate exercise (never after meals), and allowing the dog plenty of water. Bloat claims most of its victims between the ages of two and six years. Metabolic bone disease, however, needs to be checked in the breeding lines. Borzois are known to be sensitive to barbiturates, anesthetics, and flea dips—be sure your vet is aware. Provide soft bedding for the Borzoi, as bedsores may tend to develop. Hip dysplasia is not a documented problem. Borzois live ten to 12 years.

Male puppies tend to experience a more awkward stage than do females, though awkwardness is detectable in both as their bones and joints grow. OWNER, LENA S. TAMBOER.

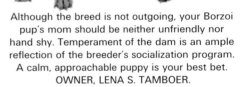

Even a full-grown Borzoi doesn't eat a czar's portion: despite their great size, Borzois have moderate peasant appetites. OWNER, HARDY.

Borzoi

Boston Terrier

DESCRIPTION

The Boston Terrier presents the body of a terrier topped by a distinctive short head. This is not a toy-size dog but rather medium sized, in any of the three weight classes: under 15 pounds; 15 to 20 pounds; and 20 to 25 pounds. Dogs are not to exceed the 25-pound upper limit. The Boston's coat is smooth and colored in brindle, black or seal (black with a red cast) with evenly marked snow white on muzzle band, foreface blaze, and forechest (and preferably on the legs too). This is a sturdy dog who is compactly built and balanced; he must never appear spindly or coarse, blocky or chunky. The head, a hallmark of the breed, has a square skull which is flat on top, with flat cheeks, no wrinkles, abrupt brow and a well-defined stop. The eyes are wide apart and dark in color (never blue). The muzzle is short and square, deep and wide. The nose must be black, and not speckled (dudley). The jaw is square and the bite should be even or slightly undershot. Avoid wry mouths. The body appears short-backed and the tail is set on low and straight or screw, and is never docked. To allow for terrier style movement, the shoulders must be sloping and well laid back and the legs should be strong.

Direct from Bean Town, the Boston Terrier slices a hearty hunk of Americana on any owner's plate. The Boston's coat is smooth and bright: with a bowtie, its formal wear is complete! OWNERS, ELISABETH McNEIL AND JODI GHASTER.

OWNER SUITABILITY

Exceptional with children and as a house dog, the Boston Terrier is a relaxed and responsive New England gentleman. Bostons are fastidiously tidy and bear no doggy odor, making them easycare companions. Although a little large for a lap dog, most owners don't seem to mind the extra weight! In the home he is quiet and good mannered, and makes a marvelous watchdog. Bostons are generally non-combative souls, but true to their heritage, they can take good care of themselves. Their prominent and somewhat bulging eyes are prone to injury if the game gets too rough.

The key feature to a Boston is its head: it must have a clear white blaze; the muzzle short and square; and the eyes wide apart. OWNERS, ELISABETH McNEIL AND JODI GHASTER.

GROWTH

Because of the variance of size within the breed, there is also a variance in size of the pups. Also, Boston puppies grow at various rates, and while most develop at an even pace some may experience spurts of rapid growth. Pups that experience these spurts may become uneven and awkward, and exercise should be adjusted accordingly to prevent injuries, and more importantly, frustration to the pup. Full size is generally attained by one year of age, though males will continue to add substance. Ear cropping and tail docking are both optional in the breed and are not encouraged. Ear cropping should be performed only if the ears are large, rounded, or will not stand erect. Breeders generally do not crop ears until after the dog is six months of age. Socialize diligently, especially males, to prevent excessive combativeness and other anti-social behaviors. Early obedience training is advisable.

The pup's eyes are vulnerable and prone to possible injury by scratching or rough playing. Breeders and owners must guard against this and other eye problems that occur in the breed, such as glaucoma, distichiasis, and cocked eyes. OWNER, ANNA M. BENEDETTO.

An all-around good companion, the Boston is an easycare dog that bonds closely to his owner. He's an excellent watchdog. OWNER, ANNA M. BENEDETTO.

HEALTH

While the Boston Terrier's potential problems may seem daunting to a new owner, the breed on the whole is hardy and long lived. The Boston Terrier suffers from many congenital and hereditary problems, including heart defects, deafness, and juvenile cataracts. Additionally, hydrocephalus (fluid in the brain cavity), walrus puppies (severely bloated, deformed pups), and swimmer puppy syndrome (a condition in which the pups can't lift themselves to stand) are all documented. Bite problems, straight stifles, luxated kneecaps, cherry eye, hyperadrenocorticism, and improper vertebra development may also occur. Malignant and non-malignant tumors and cysts are common in older dogs. Some Bostons have exhibited bad reactions to anesthesia. Because of its brachycephalic muzzle, the Boston is prone to sinus problems and heat stroke. This information underlines the importance of good breeding and careful selection. Grooming demands are very minimal, and exercise demands can be met with regular training sessions and daily walks. Bostons live 12 to 15 years.

Boston Terrier

Bouvier des Flandres

DESCRIPTION

Rough, strong, and compact, the Bouvier des Flandres is distinctive for his rugged appearance, accessorized by his beard, mustache and bushy upstanding eyebrows. The skull is well developed and flat; ears are highly placed, cropped triangular or not cropped; muzzle is broad and well filled out. The Bouvier's desired proportions are essentially square, and long-bodied dogs are undesirable. The curve of the rump is markedly wide and never sunken or slanted. The tail is docked to two or three vertebrae; tailless dogs occur and are perfectly acceptable. The shoulders are quite long and not loaded; elbows close to body; pasterns quite short, slightly sloping forward. The hindquarters present large powerful hams and are parallel to the fore. The coat is double and tousled in appearance: outer coat is harsh and dry, approximately $2\frac{1}{2}$ inches long; undercoat is fine and dense. Colorwise the Bouvier passes from fawn to black, including salt and pepper, gray and brindle (white chest stars are allowed); chocolate brown, white and particolors are to be avoided. Height for dogs is $24\frac{1}{2}$ to $27\frac{1}{2}$ inches, an inch less for bitches. Height deviations are severely penalized.

The psalm comes alive: the fierceness of a wolf and the gentleness of a lamb in one creature. For protection, companionship and crowd appeal—consider the Bouvier, the last werewolf in Flanders.
OWNERS, JEFFREY BENNETT AND NAN EISLEY-BENNETT.

OWNER SUITABILITY

The Bouvier, once a cow-mover, today herds new admirers for his guard dog ability and his excellence as a family dog. For all his burly ruggedness and flick-of-the-switch aggressiveness, Bouviers are thankfully delicate with kids. Famous for their work as police dogs, cart pullers, ambulance and messenger dogs during the wars, they understand their designated tasks rapidly and perform them with devotion.

The Bouvier's obedience and intelligence have earned him many service roles over the years.
OWNER, DEBBIE ARBUCCI.

Growth

Litter size and whelp size vary greatly in the breed, without a direct correlation between the two. Newborn Bouviers can weigh 8 to 24 ounces. Owners are encouraged to avoid excessively over or undersize pups, as these may not mature correctly. Oversized dogs particularly are prone to developmental problems affecting the bones and joints, as well as bloat. Dewclaws should be removed as early as possible, and the customary tail docking should be performed around three days of age. Ear cropping is also customary and is usually performed at about seven weeks. Most pups are ready to venture forth to their new homes around nine weeks, and will show their preliminary guarding instincts as early as three months. Dark-coated Bouviers tend to darken with age, becoming almost solid black by their senior years, while fawn dogs tend to lighten as they age. Proper socialization is important throughout the developmental period, as these large dogs could present real problems if neglected or overstimulated.

Select a solidly constructed, well-balanced puppy, not oversized nor too small. The young Bouvier should be active and playful. OWNER, EMMY WALTERS.

Health

World War II nearly destroyed the breed, and it has since been rebuilt on a narrow breed base. This close breeding has given rise to reproductive complications, including endometritis (inflammation of the lining of the uterus) and ovarian cysts. Stomach problems, noted by some owners, most often are easily treatable, though bloat should be guarded against by feeding two smaller meals. Overall the Bouvier is a remarkably strong and hardy breed, relatively free of HD and other debilitating conditions. Lymphosarcoma and hypothyroidism are reported, though in relatively small numbers. Most importantly, select from healthy bloodlines. Bouviers enjoy life and love to work even past the age of ten years. In general the life expectancy is 12 years. Grooming can be very considerable, with some stripping of the harsh outer coat necessary. Skin conditions are rare in well-maintained dogs.

Puppies with dark pigmentation will get even darker with age (lighter colored or fawn pups will get lighter). OWNER, DEBBIE GOLDSTEIN.

Bouvier des Flandres

Boxer

DESCRIPTION

The stamp of the Boxer is his beautifully chiseled head, always perfectly proportioned to the body, which is medium sized and square. The muzzle must be broad and blunt, but harmonious with the form and balance of the skull. The style of the Boxer defines the breed, and this dog is both elegant and of good substance. He is square with a short back, powerful limbs and a shiny coat clinging to his muscular curves. Intelligent in expression and strikingly elegant, the Boxer possesses a chest which is of fair width, and an obviously well-defined forechest; his

Elegance and good substance combine to make the Boxer a stylish, harmoniously put-together working dog.
OWNER, RICHARD TOMITA.

back is short, straight and connecting the withers firmly to the hindquarters; loins short and muscular; slight tuck up but always curving with grace; pasterns slightly slanting; the shoulders must be neither loose nor loaded. The hindquarters balance the fore in angulation, never steep or overangulated; the thighs are hard and developed, not overdone or light; hocks well let down and not overangulated (sickle). This construction is essential for a dog who must move with a powerful and efficient drive. In color the Boxer is fawn or brindle, black-masked, with white to enhance his appearance (never more than one-third of the body and never solid white). Males stand not less than $22\frac{1}{2}$ to 25 inches; females 21 to $23\frac{1}{2}$ not more; proportion and balance are key.

The English Boxer has natural or drop ears, not cropped in the style that has become famous in the States.
OWNERS, FREDERICK AND SOPHIE MILLER.

OWNER SUITABILITY

The Boxer is a strong-bonding dog whose devotion and affection for his people compose his being. These are playful, energetic family dogs that make great watchdogs. Despite his size, brawn and spine-chilling bark, the Boxer does not function well as a guard dog, since most Boxers will lick their intruders or invite them in with a Frisbee™ in their mouths. Although his name doesn't agree, the Boxer is a lover, not a fighter. Dogs in the States are regarded highly for their steady dispositions and absence of drooling. They are so human-childlike that they make a delightful addition to a home without children, or great playmates for a home with children!

GROWTH

There is considerable variance among the Boxer lines. Whelps range from 10 ounces to 1 pound. Some develop evenly and consistently while others may experience growth spurts, which are not a concern provided that proper nutrition is maintained. Eight-week-old pups weigh 8 to 12 pounds. Tail docking is done between three and seven days of age. Optional ear cropping is most commonly performed at eight weeks. Considerable post-surgery care is required, and owners must be informed of this by the breeder. Physical maturity can be as early as one year or as late as 18 months or more. Males especially will continue to add substance after full height is achieved. The adolescent Boxer is full of energy and typically consumes its meals with zest. Picky eaters should be coaxed with extra meats (fresh or canned) added to

White markings on a show puppy are considered flashy, especially if from an international winner from America's premier breeder at Jacquet Boxers. OWNER, RICHARD TOMITA.

their meals. Extra exercise and play are required during this time, and Boxers benefit greatly from obedience training. The well-socialized and properly maintained Boxer will emerge as a superior companion and watchdog par excellence. They are known for high intelligence and the ability to think before acting. Contrary to popular opinion, properly socialized Boxers do well in multi-dog households.

HEALTH

Boxers are easycare companions. Grooming demands are minimal, with regular brushing the primary requirement. Much has been said about the Boxer's health, and research has shown that, while many problems are reported, the breed in general is a hardy and healthy one. Owners are encouraged to research lines and discuss health concerns with breeders. The Boxer has shown a high incidence of tumors, both malignant and benign. Lymphoma, heart and lung tumors, heart murmur, subaortic stenosis, hyperadrenocorticism, inherited epithelial dysplasia, thyroid and testicular cancer, and osteosarcoma are all

If properly socialized from a young age, Boxers can be among the steadiest of all dogs, affectionate and protective to their family. OWNER, RICHARD TOMITA.

documented, with some lines showing a greater predisposition than others. Monorchidism is a concern, as is bloat. Bloat has claimed the lives of otherwise top-quality dogs and so owners must be on guard. Hypothyroidism and intervertebral disc degeneration have been reported, and an unusual condition called ulcerative keratitis (characterized by an erosion of the cornea) is considered peculiar to Boxers, though not common. Muzzle pyoderma (pustules on the muzzle) is treatable with antibiotics. Boxers live zestfully, but decline rapidly in old age. Life expectancy is commonly eight to nine years, but many dogs live to 13 and some even more. A condition called Boxer cardiomyopathy affects some older Boxers; it is marked by the degeneration of the heart muscle. The nutritional supplement L-carnitine three times daily is reportedly beneficial.

Boxer

Briard

DESCRIPTION

A sizable, handsome dog with an attractive, distinctive long coat, the Briard stands not less than 23 to 27 inches, bitches 22 to $25\frac{1}{2}$ inches. Like any other strongly built herder, the Briard has power without coarseness. The Briard is not cobby, but nearly square, slightly longer than tall. The head appears long, and is of sufficient width without being cumbersome. The standard describes the head as two equal-length rectangles merging; the wider one is the skull, the other the muzzle. The coat adorns and nearly conceals the head with its long, natural falling hair. The eyes, partially visible through the coat, must be dark. The ears are well apart and open, attached high; cropped ears are carried high and parallel, natural ears must not lie flat but are lifted slightly when alert. The muzzle with its moustache and beard is somewhat wide; and the nose is always black. The body is constructed with a slight incline, down from prominent withers to the straight back, to broad loin and slightly inclined croup. Tail is uncut, well feathered with a crook at the end, carried low. Rear legs are equipped with two dewclaws and are never removed. The coat feels dry to the touch and is slightly wavy; undercoat is fine and tight. Color of the coat must be uniform, deeper shades preferred and never white; coat should not be spotted and a white chest spot is acceptable unless exceeding one inch in diameter.

Unlike the fabulous gooey cheese from the same region of France, there is nothing soft or processed about the Briard: this is a natural, tough working dog. OWNERS, KENNETH AND VALERIE FOX.

OWNER SUITABILITY

Being protective by nature, the Briard makes a good family dog, with strong instincts to guard his flock. Briards do tend to bond more closely with one family member and have been known to protect the children from parental correction (a great dog for kids!). The Briard adolescent can be bossy so a firm but loving approach to training is necessary. As is the case with other smart dogs, Briards revel in testing their owners; smarter owners are top dogs who continue socializing the dog and making their Briards pliable and obedient. Adolescent Briards have been described as typical teenagers, always testing authority. The breed has a high requirement for human contact and companionship throughout its lifetime.

To ensure that the Briard will grow up people friendly, socialization should begin as early as three weeks.

GROWTH

By eight weeks, Briard puppies average 6 to 10 pounds. Briards grow rapidly, and by three months they may weigh as much as 25 pounds. Proper nutrition is vital to ensure proper growth. Full physical maturity, however, is not attained until about three years, though full height is usually achieved by one year. Ear cropping, when performed, is done during the fifth week. Socialization is paramount to achieving and maintaining the full potential of this breed. The Briard's color changes as it matures. Dark puppies will lighten to one year of age, at which time the tawny coloration is achieved. This color generally darkens again and the coat becomes coarser with maturity. Black pups may have gray hairs interspersed in the coat by the time they mature.

Briard mothers are protective of the small young ones. Puppies' ears are never cropped too early so as not to misjudge the growth of the ear.

HEALTH

In general, the Briard enjoys good health. Exercise requirements are high to satisfy the plentiful energy of this working dog. Grooming demands, too, are considerable, though no specialized grooming is required. Plenty of brushing, including linebrushing (the technique of brushing upward layer by layer) down to the skin, is necessary to keep the coat clean and tangle-free, and also to help limit shedding and dermatitis and other possible skin problems. Hip dysplasia at one time was common in the breed, but has been greatly reduced through careful breeding. Always insist on screening for HD. PRA also occurs with relative infrequency but is still an important concern. By far the most serious problem is bloat, and owners must follow a careful feeding and exercise program. Hypothyroidism is also known in the breed, as is night blindness and certain heart and blood defects. Briards enjoy an active ten to 12 years of life.

As with other large breeds, Briard pups grow rapidly and may experience awkward periods of uneven growth.

Darker puppies will lighten until one year of age.

Briard

Brittany

DESCRIPTION

A closely knit working gun dog, the Brittany should appear leggy for he is able to cover much ground, as well as rugged for he is vigorous and lively. Further, the dog is square with a tail docked to four inches or naturally short. He stands $17\frac{1}{2}$ to $20\frac{1}{2}$ inches and weighs 30 to 40 pounds. Proportion should never be lost and a long dog is not desirable, nor is one who lacks bone or is too heavily boned and cumbersome. The head is medium in length and rounded, very slightly wedge shaped, stop well defined but not too deep. The eyes are well set in with a protective eyebrow. Ears are set high and drop, well covered, tips rounded slightly, sometimes called vine-leaf shaped. The neck is medium and not overdone; topline slightly sloping; deep chest; back short and straight, flanks rounded and fairly full; shoulders are sloping, not too wide apart, never straight. Forelegs perpendicular and pasterns slightly sloping, never down. Stifles well bent, thighs powerful. The coat is dense, flat or wavy, but never curly; texture fairly fine, not wiry or silky. Feathering should not be too profuse. Brittanys can be orange and white or liver and white, in clear or roan patterns; ticking is desirable; tricolors also occur but are not preferred by Americans. Black on the coat or nose is a disqualification.

Brighter than your average spaniel, the Brittany has talent beyond expectation. He shares his gifts with his master on the field and in the home.
OWNERS, DR. DENNIS AND ANDREA JORDAN AND G.K. NASH.

OWNER SUITABILITY

Spaniels as a whole are possibly the brightest dog group, and the Brittany is brighter than the average spaniel. The Brittany proves to be one of the most gifted of the gun dog breeds and is as responsive a family dog as any. As a hunter he is vigorous and tireless, not to mention versatile beyond mere words; a true outdoorsman who needs an owner who will give him lots of daily time outdoors. Brittanys in fact love children and are happy to share their exercise time with them. He is also more independent than most and therefore needs more focused training.

Brittanys are intelligent but sensitive students. Praise them and they respond with enthusiasm.
OWNER, THERESA MANN.

GROWTH

Brittanys mature by two years of age. Adolescents are active and need extra exercise. Puppy tails which are long should be docked to $\frac{3}{4}$ inch at two days. Front dewclaws are to be removed. Brittany bitches experience their first heat cycle usually between 9 and 12 months. When selecting a puppy, look for balance and compactness, though allow for legginess.

HEALTH

The Brittany is a high-spirited, highly intelligent dog who places few health-related demands on his owners. Grooming requirements are small, though regular brushing and possibly some trimming of the fringe are required. As a drop-eared

Puppies of this breed define alertness. Perceptive beyond their days and more curious than a cat, Brittany pups will continually delight and challenge. OWNERS, WENDY ARCHINAL AND SHARON BUEHLER.

breed, the Brittany benefits greatly from regular ear cleaning, which prevents infection. While the Brittany enjoys relative freedom from serious diseases and conditions, hip dysplasia remains in the breed. Screening for HD is a must and ideally extends back several generations in the breeding program. Monorchidism, hypothyroidism, and hemophilia A also occur. Otherwise, the Brittany's natural and unexaggerated conformation seems to fare well, allowing it a life expectancy of 12 to 13 years.

Brittanys place few demands on their owners. They adapt to most any lifestyle but do require sufficient exercise to keep fit. OWNERS, BETSY WALLACE AND CLAIRE STIDSEN.

Brittany

Brussels Griffon

DESCRIPTION

To call the Brussels Griffon not a dog of beauty undermines our understanding of beauty, as beauty only exists in the eye of the beholder, and the tiny Griffon offers much to his beholder. Two varieties exist: smooth and rough, which are identical except for coat. The Griffon's most outstanding feature is his head, whose expression is described as "almost human," though it is truly most unusual. A large, round head with a domed forehead; small, high-set ears, cropped or dropped; long black eyelashes; a fringe on the rough-coated variety creates a brow around the eyes, a moustache under the nose, beard on the chin and whiskers on the cheeks. The dog's

Griffon means "wire coated" as this handsome breed member portrays. The snappy show dogs of today would make their Belgian "street urchin" ancestors proud.
OWNER, CLEOLA MOORHEAD.

body is short and thickset; the back is level; ribs well sprung; short coupled; tail set high and docked to one-third. The rough coat is desirably hard and wiry, never woolly or silky, nor shaggy in appearance. The smooth coat is straight, glossy, short and not at all wiry. There are four color possibilities: red, beige, black and tan, and solid black; no white anywhere on any color. Adult Griffons generally weigh 8 to 10 pounds, and should not exceed 12 pounds.

OWNER SUITABILITY

A dog with true Hollywood appeal, the Brussels Griffon is an unusual little star of a dog with a natural ability to manipulate, flatter and mug. If not properly trained, he may also "chew the scenery," as Brussels can develop bad habits if not properly instructed. These are bold and demanding tykes who make a living convincing their much-enamored owners to spoil them. He is very sensitive, delightful around the house, and perceptive enough to be human (at least in a past life).

In Belgium and the rest of Europe, the smooth variety is known as the Petit Brabacon.
OWNER, HOWARD OGDEN.

Growth

Brussels pups are born weighing 5 to 7 ounces. Dewclaws should be removed and tails docked to one third at about day five. Ear cropping is optional and should be delayed till about three months. Little post-op care is usually required, as there is sufficient cartilage to support the ears upright. Coloration at birth varies. Chocolates, marked by a complete lack of black pigment, and rarely blues, occur. These pups have pink paw pads, stomachs, and pink or liver noses. These colors, of course, are unacceptable faults. The adult coat of the rough Brussels emerges by six months of age. Consistent feeding practices, limiting treats, as well as providing lots of exercise and early training make for a healthy, mannerly Brussels.

Health

The young Brussels tot is fairly delicate and small, requiring a gentle hand. Adults however are hardy and resilient.
OWNER, CHERYL STEVENS.

Among the hardiest of the toys, the Brussels basks in relative freedom from breed-specific diseases. Hydrocephalus is known but not common. Shoulder problems and short skulls have also been reported, so insist on good conformation and well-boned parents. Puppies called "leakers" sometimes occur. These pups constantly release urine and are best euthanized as problems in later life are inevitable. Cleft palates and hare lips may occur in otherwise normal litters. Careful eye care is necessary as they are prone to injury. Feeding and exercise demands are easily met by feeding a good-quality commercial dog food and daily walks. Grooming demands depend on coat type, with the rough coat requiring stripping, a simple though specialized procedure. Because of the breed's characteristic undershot bite, regular dental care is a must to prevent gum disease and early decay. Puppies ofttimes lose their milk teeth slowly, and may even require extraction if they interfere with the primary teeth. Brussels live to 15 years, sometimes to 18.

The soft puppy coat will be replaced by a harsher coat by six months of age. Colors vary a great deal and generally will lighten with age.
OWNERS, DOUG MATNEY AND TERRY PAGE.

Many breeders wait until a puppy is at least three months before cropping the ears. Often puppies with good ears are left unaltered.
OWNERS, DOUG MATNEY AND TERRY PAGE.

Brussels Griffon

Bull Terrier

DESCRIPTION

Key to the Bull Terrier is his head, which should not be coarse, and whose expression is intelligent. The head is long, strong and deep all the way to the end of the muzzle; he has a full face that must be oval in outline, without any hollows or indentations. The head should be symmetrical with the body of the dog and not exaggeratedly large. The neck is long, arched and clean; chest broad and of great depth; body is well rounded with good spring of rib, back short and strong. The legs are big boned but never coarse; tail is short and set on low, tapering to a point. The breed is divided into two classes: White and Colored. On the White, patches of color on the head are permissible, but not elsewhere, and skin pigment is not to be faulted; the Colored can be brindle or any color other than white, or any color with white provided the white does not predominate; brindles preferred. The coat is short, flat and harsh to the touch, appearing glossy. Traditionally the breed standards do not indicate size requirements for the Bull Terrier, as the "maximum size for substance of dog consistent with quality and sex" should be one's guideline. Nonetheless, for the sake of reference (and comparison to the smaller Miniature Bull Terrier), the breed generally stands about 22 inches at the withers and weighs 57 pounds on the average. The Miniature stands less than 14 inches.

Classically known as the gladiator of the dog world, the White Bull Terrier proudly reveals his impressive musculature. OWNERS, JAY AND MARY REMER AND W. E. MACKAY-SMITH.

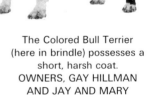

The Colored Bull Terrier (here in brindle) possesses a short, harsh coat. OWNERS, GAY HILLMAN AND JAY AND MARY REMER.

OWNER SUITABILITY

A sweet-natured gladiator, the fiery Bull Terrier is all heart. Owners find this dog a vigorous guard dog inspired more by love of his family and natural territorial instincts than any innate desire to fight. Bull Terriers are a popular choice of apartment dwellers who seek a protection dog, since he is as economy-sized as a guard dog comes. Not the brightest dog and a bit stubborn at times, the breed is considerably stable and fond of children. Firm training from day one is required for a well-behaved dog, especially if the dog is expected to live with other animals. They are naturally aggressive with other dominant dogs.

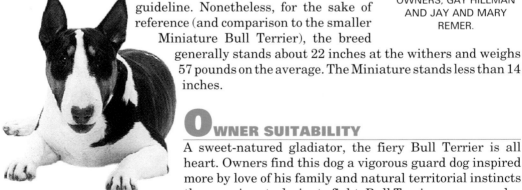

An economy-size guard dog, the Bull Terrier epitomizes compact power and ability. OWNERS, KAREN D. COOKE AND MARION DUSSAULT.

110

GROWTH

The average Bull Terrier whelp weighs between 10 and 14 ounces. Dewclaw removal is optional, tails are never docked, and ears are never cropped. The ears should stand erect of their own accord, though teething and other physical demands may hinder this. It is possible to assist the ears with various supports, the details of which can be provided by a breeder. Bull Terriers develop without difficulty, reaching full height by one year but continuing to add substance over the next year or so. Appetite is rarely a problem, and owners must guard against overfeeding and obesity. Proper socialization and training must begin at an early age. Dominance will emerge during adolescence and must be curbed and channeled to appropriate behavior. Because temperament is at least partly inherited, owners are advised to check for as much temperament testing as possible in the breeding program, and start their own dog in puppy kindergarten, etc.

The Bull Terrier's head is unique in dogdom: full faced, oval in outline, strong and deep to the end of the muzzle. OWNERS, JAY AND MARY REMER AND W.E. MACKAY-SMITH.

HEALTH

Having never attained overwhelming popularity and fairly escaping the hands of irresponsible breeders, the Bull Terrier suffers from few health problems. Deafness is the most serious condition facing the breed, particularly the White variety. Owners should insist on veterinary documentation regarding hearing. Hernias, particularly umbilical, and a condition called stud tail (marked by a bald patch near the base of the tail) are known to affect the breed, as are acne and acrodermatitis (a fatal hereditary skin disorder that lightens the color of affected puppy who may have infections on face and feet—death occurs by 18 months). Owners note that Bull Terriers are chewers and swallowers; caution is advised. Only proven safe and effective chewstuffs should be provided, and plentifully. Exercise demands are not great, though daily exertion is necessary and helpful in keeping the Bull Terrier content and well behaved. Grooming is a cinch, with little more than regular brushing and combing and inspection of the eyes and ears required.

A healthy Bull Terrier puppy grows at a normal pace, has glossy, clean skin, obviously can hear with both ears and is alert and playful. OWNER, DREWES.

Bull Terrier

Bulldog

DESCRIPTION

The Bulldog is a medium-sized dog, whose low-swung, thickset body and uncanny, massive, short-faced head bespeak proud generations of breeding for appearance and not function. While the Bulldog's original function has long passed, he must still be a sound animal of sensible proportions. Mature dogs weigh about 50 pounds, bitches about ten pounds less. The muzzle is extremely short, broad and turned upward; the jaws are massive and undershot; the nose must be black. The eyes are round, situated in front of the head, dark in color and neither sunken nor bulging; lids show no haw. Ears are set high and wide apart, termed rose ears, which are small and thin and folding inward at their back lower edge and upper front edge curving over, out and back, showing the burr (ears are never erect, prick button, or cropped). Neck is short, very thick and well arched. The topline should fall slightly behind the shoulders, rise to the loins and then curve suddenly to the tail to form an arch; this is very distinctive and correctly called wheel back.

The Bulldog possesses a stiff upper lip and an equally proud undershot jaw. His very being exudes all things British: gracious, polite and perhaps a wee bit stubborn.
OWNERS, ROBERT AND JEAN HETHERINGTON, JR. AND MARGARET K. CURTIS.

Begin the young dog's training straightaway. Avoid spoiling or chastising him—be fair and consistent. OWNER, EMMANUEL.

The chest is broad, deep and full; belly should be tucked up; tail carried straight or screw (not curved or curly). The forelegs are short, very stout and straight, presenting a bowed outline (the bones are neither curved or bandy); elbows are low and stand well out from the body. Hindlegs are longer than fore to elevate the loin above shoulder; hocks slightly bent and well let down. The dog moves in a characteristic loose-jointed sidewise motion, referred to as rolling gait. The coat is fine and smooth in texture and flat; head and face covered in heavy wrinkles, including dewlap; body is covered in soft and loose skin. Colors (in order of preference) are red brindle; all other brindles; solid white; solid red, fawn or fallow; piebald; combinations of any of these. Any clear color is desirable to a muddy, defective pattern. Solid black is highly undesirable.

OWNER SUITABILITY

For all his snoring, waddling and grunting, this breed is a most popular choice as a family dog. A peaceable, good-natured soul with soulful eyes and only love to share, the Bulldog enjoys rolling around with children, and adults can scarcely not find his ways charming and endearing. Correct the Bulldog gently but firmly—harsh reprimand can break the Bully's spirit. Since he is not very agile and happiest as a homebody, the Bulldog needs an owner who will do things with him, not for him. Bulldogs do not excel as guard dogs. He thrives as a companion for the elderly, with whom he shares a number of old-fashioned values.

GROWTH

The Bulldog at eight weeks weighs 7 to 8 pounds. Rate of development varies with lines, but in general full height is achieved around ten months, with full maturity some time between 18 months and three years. Prospective owners must carefully select for soundness. The young Bully should not be fat or heavy; its breathing should be free; the eyes should be clear, with well-fitting eyelids. A loose, straight tail is perfectly acceptable for a pet dog. A veterinarian should check the dog's palate and breathing ease. The bite too should be checked to see if it is viable; undershot is correct in this breed. Breeders remark that the adolescent Bull-

Select your Bulldog puppy for soundness, fitness, and general good health. Avoid a puppy who has visible breathing problems, runny, affected eyes, or irritated skin and wrinkles.

dog of good breeding presents little problem to its keepers. They are good eaters and delight in family activities. Feeding must be monitored to avoid obesity. Young Bulldogs may prove over-enthusiastic at times and perhaps willful too, but good training and socialization easily control such tendencies.

HEALTH

The Bulldog suffers from many hereditary and congenital conditions. Among these, cleft palates and walrus puppy syndrome are the more common and serious ones affecting newborns. Swimmer puppy syndrome also occurs in this breed. Hip dysplasia is a problem, and foreleg lameness is both common and very serious. Owners must have the shoulders of the selected animal carefully checked for looseness and insist on screening of the breeding stock. Entropion and ectropion, dermatitis, stenotic nares (which cause obstruction of the nasal passages), and elongated soft palates (with their associated conditions) all occur but can be treated. Muzzle pyoderma (pustules on the muzzle) can be treated with antibiotics. Veterinarians report cases of kidney stones, cherry eye, deafness, distichiasis, hypothyroidism, inherited metabolic liver defect, kerato conjunctivitis sicca, pulmonic

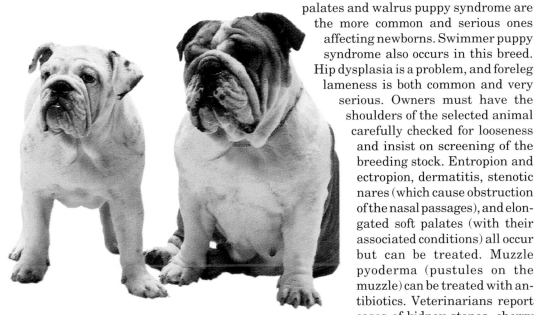

Bulldog puppies, like their parents, are less active than puppies of other breeds. They move slowly, if a little awkwardly, and can easily overexert themselves in too much excitement or play. OWNER, CONNIE GIBSON.

stenosis and ventricular septal defect. Prospective owners must select their dog carefully from a breeder whom they trust and make frequent veterinary visits through the first year, as early detection and responsible prevention can ensure a healthy life. Life span is eight to ten years.

Bulldog

Bullmastiff

DESCRIPTION

An adult Bullmastiff weighs in at 110 to 130 pounds, bitches about ten pounds less; the adult male can stand 25 to 27 inches, bitches an inch less. A powerfully built, sizable yet compact animal, the Bullmastiff possesses a large and broad head, with some wrinkles, a keen expression, strong foreface and a broad, deep muzzle; stop moderate; forehead flat. The neck is thick, nearly equal in circumference to the skull.

Topline must be level; wide and deep chest; short back. The tail is set on high and is straight or curved, but not carried like a hound. The quarters assembly is made for driving, free action: shoulders not loaded, never cow-hocked, forelegs straight, elbows not in or out; good angulation. The coat is short and dense and colored in red, fawn, or brindle; white mark permitted on chest only.

Bred for protection work, the Bullmastiff outsizes most other functional guard dogs, though he should not be overdone or cloddy to interfere with his smooth movement. OWNERS, MALINDA RABY AND PETER KOZEL.

OWNER SUITABILITY

Bred as a guard dog, the Bullmastiff, for his 130 pounds of sheer muscle, should daunt any intruder's intentions. They love their families and despite their size adore being indoors, where they are at home and relaxed with the family. The Bullmastiff will bond closely with the whole family and guard each member with his life, including the family cat and pot-bellied pig. He is fearless yet docile, and well-bred representatives are both alert and agile, enjoying exercise time with family members. Most dogs are dominant to unknown dogs and not sociable to strangers unless introduced by a familiar person.

Even puppies demonstrate a protective air about them, naturally suspicious of strangers. OWNERS, STEVEN AND LINDA ALLEN.

ROWTH

Birth weight varies from 12 to 24 ounces, and there seems no correlation between birth size and adult size. By seven weeks, most pups weigh 13 to 14 pounds, and by 16 weeks, 45 to 50 pounds. Avoiding oversized dogs is important in preventing bone- and joint-related health problems. The breed is naturally big, and excess is absurd. Prospective owners should take careful note of the puppy's construction: it should be solid, well-knit, and balanced. Check for short tails, screw tails, and cleft palates. Temperament too is a big concern, and a breeder's temperament screening in his line is a great bonus. Bullmastiff puppies should be eager to please and delight in human company. A natural suspicion of strangers is characteristic and desirable. With proper training, the Bullmastiff can become a superb guardian and protector. Feeding will be a big concern: Bullmastiffs are known to have individual requirements, and it is best to have a breeder or veterinarian assist in determining the nutritional program. Calcium supplementation is often harmful.

Puppies should be soundly constructed, move without difficulty, and be eager to please and approachable. OWNER, DEBBIE JONES.

HEALTH

Cancer and bloat claim more Bullmastiff lives than any other condition affecting the breed. While neither can be prevented totally, their incidence can be limited by providing a healthy lifestyle for your dog, including a prescribed diet and exercise routine. Hip dysplasia is a major concern for breeders and screening is a must. Skin and eye problems occur (including eczema, dermatitis, muzzle pyoderma and alopecia; entropion, glaucoma, and PRA). A reportedly hereditary back condition (cervical malformation) occurs to varying degrees, ranging from mild lameness to partial paralysis. Tumors and kidney stones may affect older dogs. Bullmastiffs typically live to ten years of age.

Be sure your breeder's stock has been screened for hip dysplasia and ask about the occurrence of cancer in his line.

Bullmastiff

Cairn Terrier

DESCRIPTION

A short-legged, strongly built terrier that stands well forward on its forelegs, with a foxy expression, hard coat and small pointy ears. The Cairn Terrier is not heavily built but is well muscled and in hard working condition. The head needs to be broad in proportion to length of skull, not too narrow, with a decided stop. Head is furnished with hair on top that is a bit softer than body coat. The muzzle is strong but never too long and heavy. Eyes should be rather sunken and medium, not too large or prominent. The ears should not be oversized nor rounded at points; they should be set wide apart on the head and not heavily covered with hair. Legs should be of good bone, not too light or heavy; forelegs not out at elbow, but straight (fore-feet can be slightly turned out and are larger than the hind). Body with well sprung deep ribs with level, medium-length back; body should not be too short backed or long and weedy. Tail set on at back level. The coat must be double with a profuse outer coat and a soft, close undercoat, never open, blousy, or too short; waviness permitted but not silkiness or curliness. Cairns can be any color except white (and no white markings); ears, muzzle and tail should be darker. Dogs weigh 14 pounds, bitches 13; dogs stand 10 inches, bitches one-half inch less; dogs measure $14\frac{1}{2}$ to 15 inches from front of chest to back of hindquarters, appearing neither leggy nor low to ground.

Named for the "cairns" (or crevices) from which the dogs would extract their vermin, Cairn Terriers represent the modern-day version of the original working dogs of Scotland. OWNER, BETTY HYSLOP.

OWNER SUITABILITY

Cairns are great with kids but do not tolerate too much grabbing—they will let the kids know when the game's over. Cairns are smarter than you think. As family dogs, they sometimes pick one special human, though everyone gets his share of love. Cairns are not lap dogs, usually not cuddly, nor will they hang on your every word: this is an independent-thinking, smart and active dog who can be willful and stubborn. Training must be gentle and firm and discipline need not include anything more than a well-chosen word or two. The breed is small enough to get exercise bouncing on and off the furniture, yet he is hard enough to go camping in the rough. Owners should understand the terrier manifesto: earth dogs dig; they like to find growing carrots from your garden and they instinctively seek vermin. Pretend to be charmed by the dead mouse with which your Cairn proudly gifts you—screaming will only confuse him. Likewise the Cairn is territorial, particularly males, and his property includes you!

Cairns delight in pleasing you. Patience and fairness in training go far to teach the Cairn how to best please you. Some even like leashes. MR. AND MRS. WALLACE.

GROWTH

Most important in the eight-week-old Cairn is balance. Cairns often experience uneven periods of growth during the first year. As one breeder puts it, the dog "will probably go through a stage when he looks like he is all ears, legs, and tail." So long as he was balanced at eight weeks, he should be balanced at maturity, which is usually about one year. Cairns will continue to add

The baby Cairn grows quickly the first few weeks.

substance until as late as three years. Tails are never docked. Rear dewclaws should be removed as early as possible; removal of front dewclaws optional. Males in particular are known to reach sexual maturity at an early age. Stripping the puppy coat begins when the fluffy baby coat looks loose. Coat should be somewhat hard to the touch as early as three months. The coat will generally darken as the adult coat takes its place, and in some creams and wheatens the coat will continue to darken with every coat change. Owners must monitor the teething process. Cairns have been known to retain puppy teeth, and these possibly may have to be extracted by a veterinarian. Overeating can be a problem, so feeding must be governed, and treats given limited to two or three per day. Adult dogs generally maintain their

Tails are never docked but left natural.
OWNER, SUSAN W. DE WITT.

weight on one-half to two-thirds cup of a quality dog food per day. Barking from young dogs is normal—curtail this from the start.

By eight weeks of age, the Cairn puppy should appear *balanced*—he will lose this during his adolescence but regain it by maturity.
OWNER, JON LAWRENCE.

HEALTH

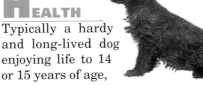

Typically a hardy and long-lived dog enjoying life to 14 or 15 years of age,

Screening for possible problems minimizes possible health risks in puppies.
OWNER, JON LAWRENCE.

the Cairn requires plenty of outdoor activity. Grooming is not demanding, though stripping the hard outer coat is required. Like all other breeds, there are some hereditary conditions affecting the breed today, though perhaps fewer than usual in the Cairn. An unusual condition known as craniomandibular osteopathy (CMO), or lion jaw, is reported; it affects pups and is marked by an acute swelling of jaws. It is treatable, possibly self-correcting, and rarely fatal. Krabbe's disease (globoid cell leukodystrophy) affects pups from a few weeks to a few months of age—it is a blood disorder that results in death. An unusual canine condition (believed to be passed hereditarily as a recessive) known as cerebellar hypoplasia has been reported in Cairns and a few other terriers; it is rare and its signs are varied, sometimes progressive and sometimes apparently self-correcting. Cairns have been known to develop secondary glaucoma and aberrant cilia. Hemophilia A and B and inguinal hernias are also known, as are PRA, vWD and Legg-Perthes. Breeders warn of a flea bite dermatitis that is somewhat common but can be controlled when caught in an early stage.

Cairn Terrier

Canaan Dog

DESCRIPTION

The Canaan Dog comes from the spitz family of dogs and is a medium-sized, square dog standing 19 to 24 inches in height. His head is spitz in type, blunt and wedge shaped, with a rounded skull and slight stop. The ears are prick with broad base and rounded tips. The neck is clean, well-arched and of medium length. The forelegs are straight and medium boned; topline straight; hindquarters broad with well-muscled thighs. The feet are round and catlike with hard pads. The tail is set high and bushy, carried over the back. Colors range from sandy to red brown, white or black with dark and white masks. White markings on the body are common, though gray and black/tan are incorrect. The coat is straight, harsh and of medium length. The legs should be well feathered and males have a mane.

A modern-day phenomenon: a Canaan Dog seeking an owner! The original survivor, the Canaan Dog spent its first 4000 years of feral existence without ever wearing a collar.

OWNER SUITABILITY

The national dog of Israel has yet to take a stronghold on an American or British fancy despite the immediacy and uniqueness of the breed's personality. In Israel the Canaan Dog is prized for its versatility, intelligence and convenient size. His abilities as a herding dog, guard dog, guide for the blind, search and rescue tracker, mine detector, and companion qualify him to compete with any dog. His "detective" abilities deserve recognition, and he can identify an individual's approach from far away. His protective instincts and his strong bark make him a superior candidate for watchdog duty. Training requires patience and time as the Canaan bores easily and doesn't subscribe to repetition. He is a thinking dog that needs to keep his active mind and paws busy. Set a good example for your Canaan: he learns by watching. Many Canaans are dog-aggressive and will fight if unsupervised.

Kelef K'naani, the "Dingo" of the Promised Land, boasts a pedigree longer than the Dead Sea Scrolls and can be counted among the most ancient of all dogs. Despite the Canaan Dog's somewhat ordinary appearance, he is as smart and talented as any dog and, like the perfect wedding guest, makes few demands.
OWNER, MYRNA SHIBOLETH.

GROWTH

Canaan Dog puppies begin life at 13 to 16 ounces and grow at a normal, healthy rate. Puppy weights vary considerably, as adults can weigh from 35 to 50 pounds at maturity. Few breeds compare to the Canaan Dog in terms of naturalness. Puppies' ears begin to stand by a few months. The soft puppy coat becomes thicker around six months of age. Adolescence may be marked by increased suspiciousness though most dogs pass through the stage with little trouble. Characteristically Canaans mistrust unfamiliar persons. Puppies are uncommonly vocal, born with an innate sense of language: some speak Yiddish and Hebrew; others speak in tongues; others simply chant in typical Middle Eastern fashion. Curtail barking from a young age or it may become problematic. Early socialization is recommended by breeders.

Given the Canaan's history as a feral dog, the breed is naturally mistrustful of strangers. Canaan puppies are not as outgoing as most other puppies. The breed bonds closely with its family but requires much socialization in order to accept outsiders. OWNER, ISABELLA ZIRRI.

HEALTH

The fittest canine on the face of the earth, the Canaan Dog would leave most of America's veterinarians starving. The breed's reputation as the only breed in existence to evolve without man's intervention leads one to believe that the Canaan Dog presents few health concerns to his owners. Such a natural dog as the Canaan Dog demands very little of his owner. The dog's appetite is moderate; grooming and bathing requirements are minimal to non-existent; exercise needs are easily met. Like most other double-coated dogs, the breed sheds twice annually. The parent club reports that HD and PRA have very minor incidence, among the lowest in any breed. Epilepsy may affect some dogs. Life expectancy is 14 to 15 years of age, and some dogs have reached 20. Many owners profess that older breed members remain sprightly and active into the golden years.

A clean bill of health is par for the Canaan's course. Canaans outlive most breeds, often remaining active and spry into their late teens.

Canaan Dog

Cardigan Welsh Corgi

Well dressed in his flashy brindle and white coat, the Cardigan has passed up long work days at the hoofs of pushy cows for a life as a stylish companion at the feet of his master.
OWNER, JACQUE SCHATZ.

DESCRIPTION

The Cardigan is a small, low-to-the-ground dog with moderately heavy bone and a deep chest. His trademark tail is described as a foxlike brush. This is a well-balanced, sturdy dog that stands $10\frac{1}{2}$ to $12\frac{1}{2}$ inches at the withers; adult males weigh from 30 to 38 pounds; bitches from 25 to 34 pounds. The dog appears much longer than tall—from nose to tail tip, the Cardi measures between 36 and 43 inches. Lack of balance as well as over- or undersize are considered serious faults. The head appears refined, with a gentle expression. The ears are prominent on the head, large and slightly rounded, always erect and sloping forward. The eyes are medium to large and not bulging, set widely apart; blue eyes are only permitted in merle-colored dogs. The cheeks should be flat; the muzzle is tapering but not blunt or pointed. Butterfly noses tolerated in blue merles. Neck is moderately long and strong. Tail set fairly low on and reaches well below the hock, never set on high or carried high. Forefeet, rather large and rounded, point slightly out; the front assembly should not be straight or so crooked as to appear unsound and the bone should not be so heavy as to interfere with agility or to appear coarse. The coat is medium in length and double, not wiry, curly or silky; while the Cardi is well furnished on the ruff, pants and tail, the coat should never be fluffy or distinctly long. In color the Cardi can be red, sable, brindle, black or black/tan, blue merle; white flashings are usual but should never predominate on the head or surround the eyes; predominantly white dogs are disqualified from showing.

Despite his low-to-the-ground station, the Cardigan is a medium-sized (not a small) dog.
OWNER, DOREEN PARGO.

OWNER SUITABILITY

A thinking people dog, the Cardigan excels as an intelligent and trainable dog who enjoys learning and wants to learn. As a matter of fact, if you don't train him, he will train you. Challenge is the spice of a Cardi's life, and agility, obedience and tracking are likely grounds for Cardi excellence. As companions the Cardigans are superb, and not just because they are handy-sized. They love swimming, hiking, and any sport and television too (especially during football season). Being low to the ground, some tend to have a fetish for a certain family member's feet.

GROWTH

Cardies on the average weigh about 8 pounds at eight weeks, and typically gain about a pound a week until some time around six months of age. By six months, the majority of growth is complete, though Cardies will continue to mature until about three years of age, at which point, development should be complete. The Cardi's ears should become erect by eight to 12 weeks. Teething may cause the ears to fall and rise (this is common in dogs) and temporary taping of the ears may be in order. The puppy coat should change over to the adult coat between the ages of six and ten months. Some Cardies will subsequently shed the adult coat once a year, while others will shed gradually year 'round. The Cardigan puppy must be kept from going downstairs until it is at least six months of age to protect his developing forequarters from serious injury.

Cardigan puppies grow at a steady rate and do not experience an awkward stage; they gain about a pound per week until six months of age. OWNER, CINDI BOSSI.

HEALTH

Eye problems, including PRA and secondary glaucoma, affect the breed, making screening a necessity. Bone and joint problems occur, especially at the shoulder and wrist, owing to the breed's conformation. Owners should limit (or eliminate) jumping and stair climbing in pups and young dogs, and avoid overfeeding. The Corgi's elongated back predisposes it to spinal problems, and owners must guard against obesity and laziness, particularly in older dogs. Breeders note that, despite the dog's long back, slipped and ruptured discs are not common problems. Not too uncommon, urinary calculi, especially in males, is signaled by straining during urination. Overall these are easycare, healthy dogs living around 12 to 14 years.

Socialization can begin when the Cardigan is a few weeks old. Ideally the puppy is friendly and good natured, happy to be in the company of humans. OWNER, CINDI BOSSI.

Cardigan Welsh Corgi

Cavalier King Charles Spaniel

DESCRIPTION

A miniature spaniel, active and graceful and in perfect balance, the Cavalier King Charles Spaniel stands 12 to 13 inches and weighs 12 to 18 pounds. The skull between the ears is almost flat and the stop shallow. The eyes are large and dark, set well apart, but not prominent; the ears are long, set high and well feathered. Neck is moderately long with a slight arch; chest moderate; shoulders well laid back; legs straight and moderately boned. The tail balances with body length and is carried happily, but not above the back. The coat is long and silky, generously feathered, never curly—slightly wavy is permissible. Traditionally the Cav comes in four colors: black and tan, solid red (ruby), red and white (Blenheim); and tricolor.

The Cavalier can take up to 18 to 24 months to mature fully. The coat furnishings, intensity of coloration and full body development come in time to fill out the potential show dog.
OWNER, CINDY BEEBE.

OWNER SUITABILITY

Most Cavalier owners are addicted to these beautiful dogs and want to own two or three at a time. Why not! They are small, clean and gracious. Cavs also enjoy being spoiled and enjoy the "fat life" with royal elegance. Sleeping on the master's bed and drinking from the mistress's glass are commonplace in Cavalier homes. They are both active and affectionate, among the "waggiest" wags to come from Britain (where they are hailed as a top breed in popularity). Perfect apartment dogs, they are well behaved indoors and can be paper-trained with ease.

Don't overfeed the Cavalier puppy. The breed has a hearty appetite and is happy to overindulge at every opportunity. Obesity, the plague of toy dogs, takes its toll on many spoiled Cavs.
OWNER, CINDY BEEBE.

GROWTH

The weight of newborn Cavs varies with litter size, with pups from small litters weighing more and generally maturing to larger size than puppies of large (six or more) litters. Nevertheless, the eight to ten week old weighs around 3 to 4 pounds.

Young Cavs are notoriously good eaters, and owners are encouraged to feed a strict diet with a minimum of treats and table scraps. Additionally young Cavs should receive a good amount of exercise and outdoor experience. Cavs should be maintained as small sporting dogs, not as delicate toys. Both testicles should be fully descended by eight weeks—but may be as late as six months. Undershot bites are common, but can be self-correcting as late as 18 months–when selecting, however, avoid extreme bite conditions.

Cavalier puppies can weigh as little as 3 pounds when you take them home. They are delicate and affectionate and depend on your loving, gentle care. OWNERS, JAMES AND CHRISTINE MEAGER.

The Cavalier puppy you select should have a glossy, clean coat. Be aware that mite infestation can affect the pup's coat and ears once he is four or more months of age. OWNER, LINDA STEBBINS.

HEALTH

The Cav is blessed with relative freedom from debilitating conditions. Most important is proper care of the eyes, ears, and skin—ear infections and mites are particularly common, owing in part to the long drop ears. A dandruff-like condition is common in adolescents. Feeding should be in accordance with a breeder/vet prescribed diet. Some heart problems occur, including a murmur by six years as well as a serious hereditary condition that results in premature death. A unique and uncommon hallucinating condition, commonly called fly-catching (in the absence of flies), has been reported. It is not fully understood. The Cav is a long-lived (average nine years, many 13 to 15 years, exceptional 19 years) and healthy animal with minimal grooming and moderate exercise requirements. Trimming of the Cav is forbidden, and only the hair between the paw pads should be clipped. Otherwise, brushing several times a week is the only grooming needed.

Cavalier King Charles Spaniel

Chesapeake Bay Retriever

DESCRIPTION

A well-put-together, unexaggerated working retriever, the Chesapeake is distinctive for his deadgrass-colored coat, in varying shades from dark brown to a dull straw color. He should have a broad and round skull with a medium stop, small ears, well up on head, medium-large eyes that are yellowish or amber in color. The body is medium in length with well-tucked-up flanks and a short back, well coupled, and a deep wide chest. The quarters assembly is essentially powerful with the hinds slightly higher than the shoulders, which are sloping and uninhibited for free action. The feet are well-webbed and harelike, and the legs are very straight; rear dewclaws removed. Tail extends to hock and is straight or slightly curved; feathering not too excessive. Of great import is the quality and texture of the coat: the outer coat is thick and short and not over $1\frac{1}{2}$ inch anywhere on body; undercoat is dense and woolly; curly coats are not acceptable. White marks on the coat (except breast, belly or spots on feet) are extremely undesirable on any dog, as is a solid black dog. In size the Chessie weighs 65 to 80 pounds for males, 55 to 70 pounds for females; males stand 23 to 26 inches, females, 21 to 24 inches.

A sports dog through and through, the Chesapeake Bay Retriever excels in countless arenas: the field or stream, the show or obedience ring, as well as the home. OWNERS, STEPHEN AND MARGEE S. WEBB.

OWNER SUITABILITY

Chessies are athletic, hardy dogs that enjoy the companionship of dogs and people alike. They tend to play rougher than most retriever breeds and work equally as hard as any. The dog does not thrive indoors, although he thoroughly enjoys family time. Outdoors he is vigorous and outgoing. Chessies are

Chessies take their time filling out, often not reaching full maturity until three years of age. OWNER, PAMELA WOODES.

more dominant than you might expect and therefore make reasonably good protection dogs. Training for general obedience as well as field work can begin in small doses from a young age.

Newborns weigh 10 ounces to 1 pound. Rear dewclaws removed, front optional. Young pups vary in size, largely depending on lines. An eight-week-old may weigh 9 to 15 pounds. The breed matures slowly, reaching full height by nine to 12 months, but not attaining full maturity until two-and-a-half to three years. Pups are born darker and lighten to their adult color, which tends to lighten with each shedding period. Pups are born with waves to their coats, but these waves soon disappear and then reappear with age. (At eight weeks, waves may be visible on tails, ears, and possibly forelegs, and generally the more apparent at this time, the wavier the coat at maturity.) The adolescent dog may appear uneven—all legs, high in rear, etc. Generally they are good eaters and meet the demands of their growth spurts. Males may test authority at this time, and early training is very, very important. Chessies mature to very calm dogs. They are protective by nature but typically do not show this characteristic until nine to 18 months of age.

Choose a Chessie puppy with a wavy coat and a good-natured disposition. The dam should be well balanced and even tempered. OWNER, PAMELA WOODES.

Puppies lighten with age, gradually reaching their adult color after a few shedding periods. OWNER, HELEN T. SIEGEL

HEALTH

While much veterinary research on the breed is lacking, PRA is a known occurrence. Also, entropion has been reported in young dogs. Hip and elbow dysplasia should be concerns, as they affect most of the other gundogs of similar size. Ear infections plague most drop-eared breeds. Veterinarians report cases of vWD and cataracts in the breed. The Chessie, created and maintained for its superb athletic ability, possesses a strong resistance to disease, and provided it is conformationally strong should enjoy a healthy life of 12 years or more. Owners should avoid pups with tails curling over the back and check for umbilical hernias. The all-weather coat requires very little care, but owners should employ regular grooming to limit the potential doggie odor. Of course, exercise and training requirements are high.

It's never too early to begin a Chessie's training. OWNER, JANICE BYKOWSKY.

Chesapeake Bay Retriever

Chihuahua

DESCRIPTION

The tiny Chihuahua is a well-balanced toy dog with a characteristic saucy expression and a desired apple-domed skull (with or without molera, which is the small gap in skull formation). Chihuahuas must not exceed 6 pounds in weight. The body is slightly longer than tall; shorter bodies in males are desirable. The eyes are full and not protruding and set well apart; ears are large and held upright when alert, flaring to sides when in repose; broken or cropped ears are a disqualification. Neck is slightly arched; ribs well sprung but avoiding barrel shape; tail moderately long, carried sickle up or out, or curled; tail should never be tucked between legs, or bobbed or docked. The two coat varieties are Long and Smooth. The Long coat is soft in texture, flat or slightly curly with an undercoat and fringe on ears, tail, legs and neck; never appearing bare from excessive thinness. The Smooth coat is soft, close and glossy, undercoat permissible; furry tail preferred. Colors vary tremendously, solid, marked and splashed; no color or combination frowned upon.

The Long coat Chihuahua is adorned with a plumed tail, culottes on the rear, a full ruff on the chest, and fringes on the ears and legs.
OWNER, MRS. KEITH THOMAS.

OWNER SUITABILITY

Considered the tiniest of all dog breeds, the Chihuahua necessarily is a gentle but swift-moving housedog. Dogs are not conscious of their size and the Chihuahua's big-dog bark clearly indicates that he is a confident, bold canine. Nonetheless, he is described as clannish and more comfortable with members of his own breed. He is territorial and will protect his master or mistress with his whole heart. Chihuahuas enjoy the good life and don't mind extra attention and coddling. To avoid the aggressive, yappy adult, socializing the Chihuahua with friends and other dogs is advisable.

The Smooth coat Chihuahua has a close-lying, easycare coat without the fringe of its Long coat brother.
OWNERS, BONNIE THOMPSON AND KATHERINE GLAMONA.

GROWTH

The eight-week-old Chihuahua weighs about one-half pound. Growth rate for this tiny breed varies with the lines. In general, full maturity occurs at about one year. A rule-of-thumb indicator for mature weight is to double the weight at three months. When selecting their dogs, owners are encouraged to avoid excessive smallness, as these dogs are more prone to health problems. Owners should check for proper head shape and beware of incompletely formed skulls (not to be mistaken for the molera in the skull, which is allowed for in the standard). Select for overall compactness and an outgoing confident personality. Shyness and nervousness can lead to serious problems in later life. The adolescent dog proves a real delight to its owners. Temperament remains even, and a persistently playful attitude prevails. There is little coat or color change.

HEALTH

A remarkably long-lived breed, Chihuahuas have been known to live 20 years. There are some health problems affecting the breed, however, including cleft palates, secondary glaucoma, hemophilia A, and several heart valve problems, all of which are limited in occurrence. Cystine uroliths (kidney

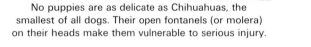

No puppies are as delicate as Chihuahuas, the smallest of all dogs. Their open fontanels (or molera) on their heads make them vulnerable to serious injury.

stones), cryptorchidism, hydrocephalus and pulmonic stenosis are reported but not alarmingly common. Shoulder dislocations can also be a problem. Owners must take note that the molera, an open fontanel, is acceptable in the breed and requires extra gentle handling. Of course, the Long variety requires more grooming time than the Smooth, but both are essentially easycare, easily fed and exercised dogs. Hypoglycemia is also reported to occur in the breed.

Outliving all other breeds, the Chihuahua, mighty but not meek, surely shall inherit the earth. OWNERS, JUNE AND JENNIFER FERRANTE.

A clan of Chihuahua babies. OWNER, BARBARA SPORER.

Chihuahua

Chinese Crested

DESCRIPTION

Hardly one's idea of a powderpuff of a breed, the Chinese Crested can be hairless or coated (called Powderpuff). The Hairless variety only has hair on the head, tail and feet; the Powerpuff is completely covered with a double soft and silky coat. This little toy dog stands from 11 to 13 inches, with some variation tolerated. The head is wedge-shaped viewed from above, with almond-shaped eyes, set wide apart, large uncropped ears held erect, clean cheeks, slight stop, and solid pigmented nose. The Hairless should not be faulted for the absence of full dentition; the Powderpuff is faulted for missing teeth. Neck is lean and slightly arched; topline level; flanks moderately tucked up; loin light, breastbone not prominent. The slender tail tapers to a curve, reaching the hock, and carried gaily in motion. Forequarters allow for good reach; moderate stifle angulation. In the Hairless, the skin is smooth and soft. All colors are permissible and the Crested enjoys some unusual doggie colors, including pink, blue, lavender and copper!

What the Chinese Crested lacks in hair it makes up in virtues: he's hypoallergenic, he doesn't shed and is odorless, he makes few demands, and he's *lavender* to boot.
OWNER, ORVILLE VAUGHN.

OWNER, ARLENE BUTTERKLEE.

The coated variety (Powerpuff) is identical to her naked sisters except for her fabulous coat, strands of long, flowing silk!

OWNERS, A. BUTTERKLEE, V. HELU, AND J. WENDELKIN.

OWNER SUITABILITY

A dog without hair! Chinese Cresteds—believe it or not—are more normal than many breeds of dog. Despite their unusual look, these dogs tend to be playful, affectionate and hardy. Owners must be aware that their near-naked charges must be handled properly and sometimes dressed properly too. During the fashionable winter, sweaters and vests are a must for the well-dressed Crested. The breed belongs indoors and loves family and tolerates good children. They are independent and intelligent.

GROWTH

Weight and growth rate varies between lines. At seven to eight weeks, weight can be 1 to 3 pounds. Owners must select puppies carefully. Make contacts and research the breed before buying such a genetically unique dog. Avoid any pup showing signs of over-refinement or frailty, as these dogs are health and injury risks. Also, check the teeth and skin. Any pup showing signs of unhealthy skin must certainly be avoided. The adolescent will require some extra care and patience. Temporary behavior changes are common, particularly during the teething period, and adolescent acne may develop. Conformation and color typically changes little during this time. Owners will be required to work with a breeder or other experienced owner to best ensure the proper care of their special canine friend.

HEALTH

The Chinese Crested is of course genetically unique in some ways. As far as health is concerned, the major consequence of the hairlessness is in dentition and skin care. Missing teeth, particularly molars and premolars, are common, as are various skin conditions. Otherwise, the breed is subject to those same common ailments affecting the other toy breeds, including Legg-Perthes, luxated patellas, glaucoma, lens

A Crested puppy should show the same signs of good health as a normal-coated puppy, plus clear, unaffected skin. The adult's skin feels soft but is thicker than that of other dogs and heals faster when injured. Cresteds sweat (like humans) instead of pant (like other dogs).
OWNER, JACKIE WENDELKIN.

luxation, cataracts, PRA, and aortic stenosis. This underlines the importance of careful breeder and puppy selection. Grooming needs are of course unique to coatless dogs (Powderpuffs require similar care to other dogs), and owners must follow the breeder's recommended plan of skin care, feeding, and other requirements. Sunburn is a common problem. Some Cresteds have allergies to wool and lanolin.

Powerpuff puppies, just like Hairless puppies, should be friendly and people-oriented, if a little more independent than other toy dogs.
OWNER, JACKIE WENDELKIN.

Chinese Crested

Chow Chow

DESCRIPTION

The Chow Chow enjoys many unique traits: his scowling expression, large head with his broad flat skull and broad deep muzzle, accentuated by his dramatic profuse ruff, his blue-black tongue, and his stilted gait. Correctly the Chow Chow is squarely built, not longer than tall, and has hind legs that show little angulation, with the hock joint and metatarsals directly beneath the hip joint, which thereby produce the breed's characteristic short, stilted gait. Two varieties of the Chow are recognized, the Rough and Smooth, both of which are double coated; quality and texture should outweigh length. The rough coat is abundant, straight and off-standing, rather coarse to the touch; the smooth is hard, and dense, without ruff or feathering. The Chow's head is large in proportion to the dog and carried proudly, but never makes the dog look top-heavy; skin not too loose. The ears are necessarily small and moderately thick triangles which round at the tips, erect and tilting forward. (Drop ears disqualify.) Nose must be large and black in color; tongue must be solid blue-black; spotted noses or other than black (excluding blue Chows) noses as well as pink or spotted tongues disqualify. In color the Chow can be red (light gold to deep mahogany), black, blue, cinnamon (light fawn to cinnamon), and cream. The average adult Chow stands 17 to 20 inches at the withers. The Chow is well proportioned, medium in size with muscular heavy bone development; cloddy, overdone dogs and snipy, fine-boned dogs are not desirable.

The Chow Chow is a square breed. The Rough is abundantly coated in a straight, coarse coat.
OWNERS, ROBERT BANGHART, FRANK HOLLOWAY AND EILEEN BALDI.

OWNER SUITABILITY

The scowling Chow Chow of yesteryear may not be the easygoing, affectionate Chow of today. Many breeders have successfully convinced the Chow that people are trustworthy and goodwilled. We believe that ill-tempered Chows are, for the most part, *not* a product of heredity but a victim of lack of training and socialization. They have had reputations of willful disobedience and impenetrable aloofness. Many Chows today are biddable and huggable, all the while maintaining their fuzzy nobility. Nonetheless, he is not the most demonstrative of lion-clad companions, remains dominant and somewhat stubborn. For all his lion-like big-headedness, training the Chow does not require a whip and a chair, just a convincing tone of voice and a lion's share of patience. Chows have many splendid characteristics and are handsome animals, though they are not for everyone. The Chow puppy must be socialized; that is, brought into contact with as many strangers and new environments as possible. Socialization should begin with early puppyhood. The adolescent Chow, if not properly socialized, may become quite willful and unmanageable. By nature independent, the young Chow wants to do things his way. Perhaps the most time-consuming chore for a Chow puppy owner is grooming, particularly when the adult coat first comes in. At this stage, the puppy must be groomed and bathed regularly in order that the new coat may grow in.

Litters from four to six, with birth weight between 10 and 20 ounces. Adult size variance accounts for varied size and growth rate of pups. The tongue, pink at birth, is usually completely blue-black by six weeks; if tongue has not changed by eight weeks, then chances for show may be diminished even though the Chow tongue has been known to turn as late as nine months. The coat darkens with age; in red or cinnamon coats, the more dark hairs at birth, the darker the mature coat. Chows are difficult to distinguish between blue and cinnamon at birth.

Chow puppies are born with the iron wills of an independent, thinking creature. Select a Chow puppy that is approachable and trusting of humankind (i.e., a properly socialized puppy). OWNER, SANDRA HOLLOWAY.

HEALTH

Hip dysplasia is unfortunately too common in the Chow. Only screened parents should be bred. Elbow dysplasia is also reported, but more important are loose and subluxated kneecaps, to which the Chow is predisposed owing to its straight (or only slightly angulated) stifles. Owners must monitor the development of the hind legs and exercise cautiously during the developmental stage. Some lines are prone to dwarfism. Congenital entropion, Collie eye, glaucoma, hypothyroidism and ectropion occur. Elongated soft palates and unusually short tails appear and should be checked for. Grooming the Rough Chow can be quite demanding, and shedding tends to be heavy at times. Flea infestation, allergies, and soap left in coats from baths cause skin problems for Chows. Since Chows are sensitive to heat, owners must guard against heat stroke, and this includes keeping excess weight off and avoiding overexposure to sunlight. Bloat must also be guarded against. Some dogs are badly affected by anesthetics. Chows live ten to 12 years of age.

The young Chow's coat will get harsher with age and is considerably softer, though never cottony. OWNER, LINDA ALBERT.

The Smooth Chow Chow is identical to the Rough except for coat. All Chows should have the characteristic blue-black tongue.

Chow Chow

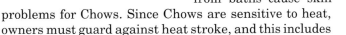

Clumber Spaniel

DESCRIPTION

Long, low and heavy, the Clumber Spaniel has a markedly heavy brow, a deep chest, and massive bone. His color is primarily white with lemon or orange markings; freckles are not uncommon but the fewer marks the better. Males stand 19 to 20 inches, females 17 to 19 inches; males weigh between 70 and 85 pounds, females between 55 and 70. The Clumber's head is massive with broad ears, set low, flat top skull and a pronounced occiput, marked stop, broad and deep muzzle; brown-colored nose (including shades of beige and cherry). The neck is long with some dewlap; back straight and firm; loin only slightly arched. The forelegs are straight and short, with elbows in close; pasterns only slightly sloped; feet large with thick pads; stifles well angulated. Essentially the body is rectangular in shape. The coat is straight and dense, soft in texture; feathers on neck, legs, belly, tail and ears.

A favorite of English royalty and one of America's first registered purebreds, the Clumber Spaniel modestly reveals its dignity, charm and work ethic. This modest show dog is Champion Clussexx Country Sunrise, the first Clumber to win The Westminster Kennel Club Dog Show (1996). OWNERS, RICHARD AND JUDITH ZALESKI.

OWNER SUITABILITY

A steady, easygoing spaniel graced with patience and understanding, the Clumber Spaniel is not a popular choice as a companion dog to spite the virtues here described. Perhaps the Clumber is suspiciously too nice: he is not mischievous, not prone to bad habits, nor is he hyper and reckless indoors. The Clumber loves kids and is a natural governess. Some say he is lazy and prefers not to move. Owners can encourage his activity as he is a natural hunter and loves to be on the field.

The Clumber's virtues well stock a good-news buffet. The Clumber lacks little except popularity: he is a kind, patient do-gooder who enjoys attention but expects little praise. OWNERS, DR. GERALD NASH AND JANICE FRIIS.

Growth

Newborn Clumbers weigh between 12 ounces and one pound, on average, with litter size most commonly between four and six pups. Clumber pups grow rapidly during early life, making the quality of their diet of importance. Fortunately they are notoriously good eaters, and getting a Clumber to consume a nutritious meal is rarely a problem. Yet while they grow rapidly, Clumbers actually mature slowly, not reaching true adulthood until three years of age. Because of this fact, vitamin and mineral supplementation are not recommended, as it could lead to developmental abnormalities. Clumbers are active and inquisitive young dogs, and should be engaged in a regular exercise and training program from a young age.

For a heavy dog like the Clumber, a life span of 12 to 14 years is promising and impressive. OWNERS, GEORGE AND DOROTHY O'NEIL.

Health

Limited and careful breeding can be credited with the Clumber's lack of hereditary problems. Entropion, and to a lesser extent ectropion, do occur and must be checked. Hip dysplasia is known in the breed, and screening should be a requirement. Also, undershot bites and missing

Since there is only moderate demand for Clumber Spaniels, only the very best dogs are bred. Resultingly there are very few hereditary and/or genetic problems in the breed. OWNER, MRS. G. BIRD.

Clumber puppies may be less active than some breeds, though breeders have little trouble keeping their puppies busy. Like all puppies, they are inquisitive and playful.

teeth must be checked for. Most importantly, owners must avoid overfeeding and provide moderate daily exercise (ideally field work and/or walking) throughout the dog's life. Otherwise this long, low, heavyset canine is prone to develop all sorts of joint and disc problems and undue stress may be placed on vital organs. The haw of the eyes is rather pronounced and perfectly natural for Clumbers. Grooming needs are minimal for this sportsman, though the Clumber should be thoroughly brushed out several times weekly, especially after any field work. Clumbers may live to 14 years.

Clumber Spaniel

Cocker Spaniel (American)

DESCRIPTION

The Cocker Spaniel is a small-bodied, compact spaniel noted for his refined, chiseled head and his full coat. The Cocker's skull must be rounded but not to exaggeration and with no tendency towards flatness; eyebrows and stop are defined; cheeks flat; muzzle broad and deep with square even jaws; foreface strong. Eyeballs are round and full, rims slightly almond shaped. The ears are long with fine leather, and well feathered. Neck is long; shoulder well laid back. Back is strong and sloping; tail is docked; chest deep and wide; forelegs parallel and straight, close to body; good hindleg angulation; feet compact and large with horny pads. The coat is silky, flat or slightly wavy, with feathering on ears, chest, abdomen, and legs. The three varieties of the Cocker by color include the Black (solid or with tan, never with any white); Any Solid Color Other than Black (called ASCOB); and Parti-color, including roans (primary color cannot exceed 90 percent). Ideal height for males is 15 inches, an inch less for females.

America's number-one spaniel, the Cocker Spaniel comes in three varieties: Black, ASCOB and Parti-color. This Black (with tan) exhibits the show Cocker's elegant style and well-groomed coat.
OWNERS, SAMUEL B. AND MARION W. LAWRENCE.

OWNER SUITABILITY

The Cocker Spaniel has remained a popular choice of companion dog for many reasons. He is small, easy to get along with, and most of all, loving and merry. Cockers will do anything to please their owners. They make happy house dogs but are demanding on an owner's time and patience. Even a Cocker in a pet-clip (shaved down) requires a great deal of coat-care time. Time and energy are also required to minimize the doggy odor. Cockers are less inclined to hunt than many other spaniel breeds whose members are less removed from the activity. His attractive appearance, stylish head and gentle, sweet disposition will win him admirers for as long as there are dogs.

Growing by leaps and bounds in the popularity department are the Parti-color Cockers, of which this black and white is an extraordinarily fine example.
OWNER, BRIGITTE BERG.

The buff Cocker Spaniel is called an ASCOB (Any Solid Color Other than Black); buffs are the most popular color of this most popular breed.
OWNERS, MARY MALONEY AND LEE BERGSTROM.

GROWTH

Newborn Cockers weigh about 6 ounces. They grow with a good rate and by eight weeks old should weigh 4 to 6 pounds. Tails are docked (leaving about one-third) and dewclaws removed between three and six days of age. Cockers generally achieve their full weight by nine months of age, though bitches reach maturity at 11 to 13 months, and dogs at 12 to 16 months. Puppies should be outgoing and not show any signs of fear. Insist on health information because many health problems are possible in so popular a breed. Cockers experience their coat change usually around 11 months, with a tendency to mat a lot at this time. The amount and intensity of coat will also affect this matting tendency. *Daily* grooming should keep the coat neat and tangle-free. Feeding should be twice a day till seven months, once a day thereafter, depending on the dog and his activity level, metabolism, etc.

If you have fond memories of the Cocker Spaniel of your childhood, be even more careful about choosing a well-bred one. Read carefully and ask the right questions before you bring home this ever-loving, merry little dog.

HEALTH

For all the Cocker's charms and merriment, an owner must be willing to care for the breed's abundant coat as well as care for its beautiful eyes and long ears.
OWNER, MICHAEL JONES.

Possibly owing to its overwhelming popularity, the Cocker has quite a few health problems, many of which are not serious and can be treated with proper care and early diagnosis. Eye problems include PRA, cataracts, primary glaucoma, and keratitis—inquire about them and insist on eye screening. Entropion, ectropion, and cherry eye are reported problems. Skin problems are rather common, particularly allergic rashes, seborrhea, epidermal cysts (cysts of the outer skin), and lip fold pyodermas (pustules on the lip). Cockers show vitamin-A responsiveness to skin problems.

Blacks are more prone to malignant oral cancers. Hip dysplasia and luxated kneecaps occur and no puppy coming from affected stock should be selected. Breeders should also be aware of Factor X, immune-mediated blood disease and IVD. Cockers suffering from cardiomyopathy respond well to taurine supplementation. Some lines are prone to pulmonic stenosis, hypothyroidism, distichiasis, calculi, and metabolic liver defects. Cockers can provide up to 15 years of quality companionship.

Many breeders color crossbreed in Cockers: the results are exciting though the main goal must always be health and soundness.
OWNERS, MICHAEL JONES AND JUDITH BEAUCHAMP.

Cocker Spaniel (American)

Cocker Spaniel (English)

DESCRIPTION

A sporting dog of much bone and substance, the English Cocker Spaniel is an active dog with a compact build. Males stand 16 to 17 inches; females 15 to 16 inches; males weigh 28 to 34 pounds, females, 26 to 32 pounds. Above all, the English Cocker is a dog of balance whose expression is soft and yet alert and merry. The head is strong and never coarse, with soft angles. The skull is arched and slightly flattened. Eyes are medium in size and full, set wide apart with tight eyelids. Ears are low-set, close to head and covered with long silky hair. Muzzle is well cushioned and equal in length to the skull. The neck is graceful and muscular, not throaty; chest is deep and medium wide; loin short and broad. The tail is docked. Forequarters and hind angle moderately; forelegs are straight; upper thighs are broad. Coat is flat or slightly wavy and feels silky. The breed is well feathered, less so than the American breed, and never so profuse as to interfere with the dog's work in the field. Solid colors include red, black, and liver; particolors are clearly marked, ticked or roan; tan may occur on solid black and liver as well as partis; markings on parti-colored dogs' bodies should be broken and even.

England's top dog, the Cocker Spaniel is merry, sturdy and sporting; of great intelligence and superior field ability, the English Cocker trains easily and lives to please. OWNERS, SUSAN FIORE-McCHANE AND JOAN DAVIS.

OWNER SUITABILITY

Sweet and biddable, the Cocker Spaniel of England is a lovely family-oriented dog. Children must be properly instructed not to rough-handle the pup and to allow him his sleep time. The English breed is less coated than the American Cocker but still needs daily attention. Cockers tend to be politely manipulative, turning on their soft, pleading eyes to get their way. Their alleged sad eyes are a bit of a misconception: the Cocker is a merry breed above all.

The Cocker's coat, though not as profuse and abundant as his American cousin's, is well feathered and requires a fair amount of upkeep. OWNERS, SUE AND ANNIE KETTLE.

GROWTH

Average litter size is five, though larger and smaller litters are common. Birth weight is a mere 2 to 4 ounces. Puppies grow rapidly for the first six months, then develop slowly thereafter. English Cockers will continue to add substance and some height at the withers until 18 to 24 months of age, at which time maturity is reached. English Cockers require increased exercise during the slow development period to stimulate growth and keep it at an even pace. Adolescents require firm but kind training, perhaps a little more firm for males, who may demonstrate more independence at this time. Temperament should be sweet and biddable at all times. The coat change occurs between six and eight months, during

The sweet temperament of the Cocker is as vital as the dog's ability to walk on lead, flush game or sit on command. Consider the parents of your puppy: is the dam friendly, happy and approachable?
OWNER, HELYNE COPPER.

which time the coat loses its fluffiness and takes on longer feathering on the legs, body, and ears. Increased grooming is necessary during this time to prevent mats and keep the coat and skin healthy.

Cockers grow quickly until six months of age; the following months the coat will begin to change, though the dog's overall growth will slow down, not reaching maturity until two years of age.
OWNERS, JOHN POUCHER AND TRACEY DEYETTE.

HEALTH

The English Cockers can easily live 12 to 15 years, but unfortunately often suffer blindness after age ten. Eye problems are the most prevalent condition affecting the breed. PRA, cataracts, and glaucoma are all well documented and occur with unfortunate frequency. Eye screening must be an absolute requirement. Swimmer puppies (pups who do not develop proper limb musculature and are therefore unable to stand) reportedly occur in the English Cocker. Cryptorchidism occurs, and, quite unusually, there is an incidence of hermaphroditism. Distichiasis and MAP uroliths are reported by veterinarians. The long drop ears predispose the breed to ear infections, which regular checking, cleaning, and ear powdering can minimalize. Proper feeding and daily exercise are vital to ensure proper bone and muscle development in this slowly maturing breed. There are some cases of vWD, a blood disorder, and familial nephropathy, a kidney disease.

Healthy Cocker puppies should have clear eyes; screening the parents and the puppy ensures the long life and good vision of your Cocker.
OWNER, CORKY MECK.

Cocker Spaniel (English)

Collie

DESCRIPTION

The familiar Collie, sweet, expressive and intelligent, comes in two very different coats, the Rough and the Smooth. Both dogs are perfectly balanced, harmoniously proportioned animals that carry no exaggeration or useless timber. The head appears as a blunt and lean wedge, of smooth and clean outline; never cheeky or snipy. The correct jaw is essential to the Collie's expression and must meet in a scissors bite. The muzzle and width of backskull must complement one another to create the correct Collie look. The ears can scarcely be too small, and must be carried correctly and tip or "break" naturally forward, about three-quarters erect. The foreface is chiseled for the eye set; eyes are almond shaped and medium in size, placed obliquely; never full and round. The neck, firm and sinewy, is heavily frilled in the Rough. The body is somewhat longer than tall and should be firm, not fat or weak. The forelegs are straight with a fair amount of bone; stifles and hocks are well bent. Tail is moderately long with end swirling upward. The outer coat of the Rough must be straight and harsh, never softer, open or curly; outer coat of Smooth must be short, hard and dense; undercoat of both is soft and abundant. Four colors are recognized: sable and white, tricolor, blue merle and solid white; only merle-colored dogs can have odd eyes. Dogs stand 24 to 26 inches and weigh 60 to 75 pounds; bitches stand 2 inches less and weigh 10 pounds less.

The smiling Collie expression says it all: a dog of beauty, personality and intelligence. OWNERS, NANCY McDONALD AND JOYCE DOWLING.

Less commonly seen is the Smooth Collie, possessing all the virtues of his well-clad brother except the abundant coat and grooming needs. OWNERS, DUNCAN C. AND LIBBY BEILER.

OWNER SUITABILITY

No mystery that the Collie is the proverbial children's dog! The Collie is a dynamic, sweet dog who is always tuned in to his owner's moods. Essentially he is a most obedient dog, easy to train and interested in pleasing his owner. While Collies thrive as family dogs, they do very well in a kennel environment, being outdoors most of the day and night. Most important is for the new owner to correct the barky Collie pup from the very beginning. Many Collies become incurable barkers and owners opt to have the dog debarked, which is a shame as it renders them useless as watchdogs. Collies need to be entertained and occupied lest they become wired and stir-crazy.

GROWTH

Collies are predisposed to large litters, and litter size can affect birth weight, which ranges from 6 to 12 ounces. Collies grow rapidly, and males even more so. Weight at eight weeks can be as much as 25 pounds. Breeders stress the importance of high-quality meals which keep the pups solid but neither obese nor thin. Obesity leads to many problems, and overly thin young Collies may never attain their potential adult substance. New puppies should eat two or three meals a day; adolescents, two meals; and adults, one meal broken into two feedings—always of high quality. Owners should select for a sweet, outgoing, affectionate personality, and train with kindness, using positive reinforcement, never physical abuse or harsh verbal treatment. Coat change begins around eight to nine months, and is complete around one to one-and-a-half years, depending on line and coat type. Coat color may darken with change. Ears may need extra attention to keep them erect during the teething period.

The Collie puppy should be well fed and show substance, though not appear fat. Most pups grow fast, though there is much variation from litter to litter.
OWNER, JOE KOEHLER.

The Collie has a known adverse reaction to Ivermectin (heartworm preventative drug). Discuss this with your veterinarian and breeder.
OWNER, THERESA THOMAS.

HEALTH

Having mostly recovered from the overbreeding of the Lassie era, the Collie enjoys relative good health. Dwarfing still occurs in litters: apparently normal at birth, affected dogs grow slowly and never reach full size. Health problems in later life are common in affected dogs. Merle Collies may be susceptible to deafness. Skin problems are the most prevalent conditions, including demodicosis, nasal pyoderma and nasal solar dermatitis (a.k.a. Collie nose). Proper nutrition and good grooming practices, especially for the Rough Collie, help to limit such conditions. Despite the Rough Collie's long coat, grooming need not be undertaken more often than once a week. Eye problems (Collie eye and PRA) are concerns for some Collies. Roughs before one year of age may suffer from rod-cone dysplasia—screening is necessary. Some lines have incidence of hemophilia A, inguinal hernias, and epilepsy. Make sure that your vet is aware that some Collies have experienced adverse reactions to Ivermectin, commonly used for heartworm prevention. Be sure to avoid ticks which can lead to pemphigus in Collies. Your veterinarian should check for ectasis syndrome (Collie eye) at your first visit. Collies can lose their teeth early without proper care and chewing stimulation. The breed has a greater susceptibility to gingival hyperplasia than others—brush the teeth often and use Nylabones®. Collies typically live to around ten to 12 years. Veterinarians report cases of amyloidosis, osteosarcoma, base narrow, and patent duct arteriosus of the lungs.

By eight weeks of age, the Collie pup, whether Smooth or Rough, can weigh up to 25 pounds.
OWNER, THERESA THOMAS.

Collie

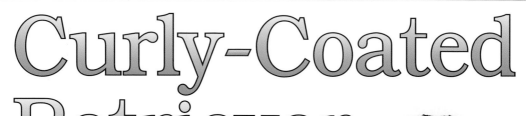

Curly-Coated Retriever

DESCRIPTION

An upstanding, enduring retriever breed distinctive for his coat of crisp curls, the Curly-Coated Retriever has a long and well-proportioned head, the skull is not too flat; the jaws are long and strong, never snipy. Eyes are rather large, not too prominent, and colored in black or brown, never yellow. The shoulders are very deep; chest not too wide, but deep; the body is short and muscular with deep powerful loins. The legs are of moderate length; quarters strong; hocks low and moderately bending as with stifles. The tail is moderately short and carried fairly straight, tapering. The coat must be curly all over, though slightly open coats are not uncommon or severely penalized. Saddle or patch of uncurled hair is undesirable as are any white patches (i.e., on chest). In color the Curly-Coated Retriever is solid liver or black.

The Curly-Coat is a snap-curl to train! He thrives on doing good and right by his master. OWNERS, GARY E. AND MARY MEEKS.

OWNER SUITABILITY

The Curly-Coat excels as a swimmer and retriever and is a natural huntsman. Calm and reserved, the breed is temperamentally easy to train. Good with children and family, the Curly-Coat does not do well with strangers and doesn't enjoy extensive handling. Breeders do strive to produce pliable pups that will accept any kind of handling. Never use harsh correction on the Curly-Coat. Since he is such a sportsaholic, owners should live near a lake or pond so that the dog can have the opportunity to swim—once he's in the water, it's hard to get him out.

This retriever's curly coat names him and stamps him with a distinguishing feature. He is a hardworking sporting dog with an adaptable even temperament and commendable watchdog abilities. OWNERS, GARY E. AND MARY MEEKS.

There is considerable size variance in the breed, both in pups and adults. Litters range from one to 15, and the whelp weighs 8 to 14 ounces. Rear dewclaws should be removed, front optional. At eight weeks, pups average between 12 and 15 pounds. A mature bitch may weigh 40 to 70 pounds, dogs 10 to 15 more. Owners are encouraged to check lines if size is important. Curly-Coats are slow to mature, reaching full height between one year and 18 months, though they may add an inch or two after that. Breeders mark full maturity at two to three years. Curly puppies (and adults too) are generally more discretionary than, say, Labradors. A litter of pups may be more inclined to observe a visitor at first rather than jump all over him. At eight weeks, the coat is fluffy, comparable to a young Poodle's. Adult coloration will be apparent. Livers will have liver-pigmented noses, eye rims, and lips. The eyes may range from yellow to brown, the darker the better. Blacks have dark (black) pigment and brown eyes. By four months, the adult coat is indicated. Prior to this time, it appears wavy and has a flatter feel, lacking the adult thickness and fringing. The breed grows in spurts (typically around ten weeks, seven to eight months, and possibly gawky at one year). By 18 months to two years, they're starting to look good.

For an owner needing a hypoallergenic dog—who just isn't a "Poodle person"—this may be the dog of your sneezeless dreams! OWNERS, MR. AND MRS. ROBINSON.

HEALTH

Breeders report some incidence of HD and PRA, nonetheless they emphasize the importance of screening. Owners should inquire about a condition known as patterning, which is a pattern of baldness that is inherited. It is partially hormonal but not fully understood. A responsible breeder should provide some form of written guarantee against it. Some cases of cancer and epilepsy are also reported, but at this time it is not clear if these are merely individual cases or if they point to a breed-specific tendency. This breed sheds all at once, typically in late spring to early summer, when the coat will fall out in handfuls. Use a slicker brush and comb daily. Otherwise shedding is minimal and grooming needs are virtually nonexistent. Breeders call the Curly a "wash and wear" dog. Toweling is to be avoided as it can stretch the hair and negatively affect the curl. Curly-Coats on average live ten to 15 years.

Curly-Coated Retriever

Dachshund

A product of Germany, the Dachshund derived as a "badger dog," named after its quarry. Today Dachshunds don't work for their daily biscuit, though they still boast their digging talents...and beg a lot too.
OWNERS, KAYE LADD AND ELIZABETH A. PATTERSON.

The Wirehaired Dachshund, the last of the three varieties to develop, possesses characteristic facial furnishings and a coat that requires special care.
OWNERS, KELLIE WILLIAMS AND DUAN AND EVELYN PETTYJOHN.

No matter the coat type, the silhouette of the Dachshund is unmistakable. The Longhaired variety has the coat of a setter: long, silky with a flag tail.
OWNERS, DR. ROGER AND DEBORAH BRUM AND SHERRY SNYDER.

DESCRIPTION

The Dachshund stands highest on the low-to-the-ground dog totem pole: he is utterly distinctive for his long back, short, thick legs and solid muscular frame. He carries his head with the bold spirit of a hunter who can boast a keen nose and full houndlike voice. Two sizes of Dachshunds are bred and shown: the Standard, weighing 16 to 32 pounds, and the Miniature, 11 pounds and under (at one year of age and over). The head tapers to the nose; eyes are medium in size, almond in shape; bony eye ridges are prominent; skull slightly arched, but not overly broad or narrow. Teeth fit in scissors bite, preferably not even. Neck is long, muscular, and without dewlap. The trunk is characteristically long and the abdomen is slightly drawn up. The chest is very prominent; forearm short with hard, pliable musculature; joints between forearm and wrist are closer together than shoulder joints (so that the front does not appear completely straight). Knuckling over must be avoided as it is a severe construction flaw (disqualification). Hinds are strong and muscular; legs turn neither in nor out; tail without kinks or curvature, tapering. The Dachshund occurs in three distinct coat types: Smooth, a short shiny coat; Wirehaired, short, thick, rough outercoat with a softer undercoat and facial furnishings, no soft hair anywhere on the body; and the Longhaired, a sleek, slightly wavy hair with a setterlike flag tail. Smooth and Longs can be colored in reds and cream; bicolors of black, chocolate, wild boar, gray (blue) and fawn (Isabella); dappled or brindle patterns. The Wirehair more commonly occurs in reds, wild boar and black and tan.

OWNER SUITABILITY

Dachsies are even in temperament and eager to please. Firm, consistent training is required early on to make a Dachsie understand that you are in charge. Many breed members are stubborn, or tenacious. They are relatively independent and able to entertain themselves for hours on end...and yet they love to be by your side if possible. They are good with children and elderly folk as well. Most Dachshunds are sweet and thrive on praise and affection—avoid rough handling as some dogs can become aggressive. With other dogs they are quite tolerant, even inviting. Choose a housebreaking method and stick to it!

GROWTH

Birth weight and growth rate of course differ between the two varieties. The Standard usually weighs 6 to 8 pounds at eight weeks, and reaches physical maturity around 18 months. The Miniature weighs proportionately less, around 2 to 3 pounds. Owners should select a strong, well-constructed pup who actively explores his surroundings. Snappy or shy pups should be avoided. The chest should be long, extending well be-

In Dachshunds, colors are a wondrous thing, as these dappled darlings and their dear mom illustrate.
OWNERS, MARY JEAN MARTIN AND RUTH K. TEETER.

hind the front legs to support the long back. Temperament becomes set during adolescence, and the nine-to-12-month period is especially critical. Avoid overstressing the adolescent dog, and the young bitch before her first two seasons. Dachshunds will welcome spoiling and quickly perceive themselves as top dog. Owners must remain consistent and authoritative, yet always loving.

Tan points on these Smooth pups are clearly evident at a few weeks of age.
OWNERS, MARY JEAN MARTIN AND RUTH K. TEETER.

HEALTH

Back problems, particularly intervertebral disk disease, can easily affect the Dachshund, owing to its short-legged, long-backed conformation. Select from quality breeding stock, and limit stair climbing, jumping, and other high-impact activities throughout the Dachsie's lifetime—also, keep off all excess weight. Eye problems, including walleye, PRA, microphthalmia, karoto conjunctivitis and ectasia syndrome are all reported—eye screening should be a must. Excessive ossification of the long bones, and osteopetrosis, which causes a condition similar to swimmer puppy syndrome, are documented congenital problems. Diabetes mellitus (an insulin problem), renal hypoplasia (a kidney problem), and cystinuria (a urinary tract problem) affect both varieties. Vitamin C supplementation is strongly discouraged. Grooming depends on coat types, none too exhaustive. Hypothyroidism should be watched for. Dachsies live 14 to 16 years. Veterinarians report cases of achondroplasia, deafness in dappled dogs, hyperadrenocorticism, and vWD.

Wire puppies showing off the first signs of furnishings— soon their beards and mustaches will be as pronounced as mom's!
OWNER, PAT LEONE.

Dachshunds do not react well to harsh discipline: be equitable and stern for best results.
OWNER, SHIRLEY J. STUMMER.

Dachshund

Dalmatian

DESCRIPTION

The Dalmatian stands out for his unique spotted coat, black or liver spots on a pure white background. The spots should be round and well defined, varying from the size of a dime to a half-dollar (in England, at a good rate of exchange, from one pence to 50 pence). Height ranges from 19 to 23 inches at withers; size deviation faulted, particularly oversized females. The breed's outline is approximately square. The head is of fair length and free of loose skin. Eyes are medium in size and set well apart, roundish, brown or blue in color, darker preferred. Ears are moderate in size and set rather high; lips clean and close-fitting; scissors bite required; nose fully pigmented. Neck nicely arched and fairly long; smooth topline; chest deep and capacious; back level; loin short and slightly arched; tail carried at slight upward curve; elbows close to body; stifle well bent. Cowhocks are a major fault. Feet are round, compact and well padded. Coat is short, dense, and glossy, never woolly or silky. Markings may not be other than black or liver; tricolors are very rare and disqualified; patches (not overlapping spots) will disqualify the dog from shows.

Formerly a carriage dog, circus performer, guard dog and hunter, the Dalmatian comes to us with a rich history of fascinating abilities: above all he is as unique as his spots.
OWNER, MRS. WALTER A. SMITH.

OWNER SUITABILITY

There are 101 Dalmatians on every block these days! Growing in popularity, this very recognizable breed is more familiar in pictures (and movies) than in real life. Real-life Dalmatians are good-sized dogs who are most energetic, even hyper, yet adaptable enough for city or country life, if properly reared and disciplined. A solely outdoor existence is not acceptable as these dogs crave attention. Be

Dalmatians are born solid white with visible pigment spots in the skin. By two weeks of age the spots emerge through the skin as pigmented hairs.

firm in training as the young pup easily grows into a tough adolescent, and bad habits are easy to scheme up and hard to break. Ideally these are mild-mannered, easily trained dogs. They are terribly affectionate and delightfully clownlike. Be aware that Dals have hunting instincts and love to run, jump and climb. While crate-training is recommended, never leave your Dal for more than a few hours as bladder/kidney complications may ensue.

GROWTH

Most newborn Dalmatians weigh between 11 and 15 ounces, and generally come from large litters. By eight weeks, a weight of 6 to 10 pounds is expected. Physical maturity is attained some time between 18 to 24 months. Owners should select for a dog that is properly socialized and of good temperament.

Select a Dalmatian who is calm and confident; observe the dam to see that she is neither hyperactive nor suspicious when approached.

Dalmatians should be outgoing and friendly (and certified for hearing!). Hyperactivity and aggression can be problems in poorly raised/poorly bred dogs. Adolescents need firm discipline and plenty of exercise. Dals are known to test their owners and males are particularly prone to seek dominance. Breeders encourage neutering to help curb this tendency. Provide ample chewing stimulation as Dals seem to teethe for a couple years.

HEALTH

Deafness, particularly bilateral, presents a major concern to breeders. Responsible breeding, including careful screening of breeding stock, has limited the problem, though it is by no means eliminated. Lack of pigment on eye rims and nose also occurs, and ofttimes is related to deafness. Incomplete pigmentation commonly worsens with age due to pigment migration. Color patches, rather than spots, are common. Blue eyes are acceptable, though not most desirable, in the U.S.—they are not

As incurably cute as the Dalmatian toddler is, remember this will grow up to be more dog than he appears. Not ideal for first-time owners, Dals begin to test their owners through adolescence (and may continue through adulthood if not corrected promptly).
OWNER, STEPHANIE PODEJKO.

Pet owners do not select for spots or eye color: sound temperament and the puppy's ability to hear outweigh all other considerations. *Never* accept a deaf puppy.
OWNER, BEN RILEY.

acceptable in the U.K. A unique condition known as urolithiasis/dermatitis syndrome causes serious health complications in the Dalmatian but can be partially relieved through diet. Kidney stones are common in the breed so never crate your dog for long hours (his need to urinate can aggravate the problem). Vitamin C supplements should be avoided. Epilepsy is not uncommon in the breed, and though the condition can be controlled by preventative drugs, affected dogs should be spayed as the condition is hormone-related. Breeding Dalmatians is difficult and genetically complicated—don't try it. Life expectancy is about ten to 12 years.

Dalmatian

Dandie Dinmont Terrier

DESCRIPTION

A sturdily built, low-stationed working terrier, whose marvelous head is topped by a grand silky knot, and whose soft, wise expression echoes from his large round eyes, the Dandie Dinmont has a curved outline and a crisp double coat of mustard or pepper. Mustard refers to coat colors ranging from reddish brown to pale fawn; and pepper, from dark bluish black to light silvery gray. The Dandie stands from 8 to 11 inches at the shoulders, his length measures 2 inches less than twice his height (a dog 10-inches tall measures 18 inches long); weight in

A pepper-colored Dandie Dinmont Terrier, one of England's most unique terrier breeds, was originally fashioned to hunt badgers, weasels and other undesirables in the landscape.
OWNER, NANCY HERMAN.

working condition is 18 to 24 pounds. The skull is well domed and broad between the ears, which are low and 3 to 4 inches long; muzzle is deep and strong; cheeks tapering. Neck is muscular and set well into shoulders; body is long and flexible; tail is 8 to 10 inches long and shaped like a scimitar. Forelegs are short with good development; hind legs, like fore, are set wide apart, but not unnaturally so as to interfere with his free and easy stride. The Dandie coat is distinctive for its pily or penciled appearance, the intermingling of hardish and soft hair (3 to 1). Topknot plus ear feathering and muzzle furnishings give the Dandie a look all his own.

OWNER SUITABILITY

Dandie Dinmonts are a less popular terrier breed, though they make excellent family pets and show dogs—plus they are unique enough in appearance to turn the heads of your neighbors. They can be stubborn, but they are terriers and this comes with the territory. They were developed from competent hunting stock so they have strong varmint inter-

A Dandie in mustard, enough to spice up any dog person's life.
OWNERS, MARVIN AND SHARON GELB.

est and may dart after a squirrel while being primped for the show ring. Training should start early as they can be yappy, making them annoying to neighbors and intruders alike. Never harshly treat a Dandie; be considerate and consistent in your training.

146

Growth

Dandies weigh 8 to 10 ounces at birth; by the age of three to four weeks they should weigh about 3 pounds. Dandie breeders say that growth rates vary greatly from litter to litter, from puppy to puppy. Dandies are born with dark smooth coats: peppers appear black and tan, and the mustards will have black ticking on the body, ears, tail and muzzle mostly black and golden on the top of the head. The puppy coat, which is softish at birth, is stripped at around 12 to 15 weeks of age to encourage growth of the double rough coat. The harder coat takes two to three months to come in, and may need to be stripped again before the correct adult coat comes in. The correct crisp-to-the-touch coat will be a mixture of one-third soft, linty hair and two-thirds hard hair. The puppy coat needs to be combed daily through the first year to avoid matting and to give it a "rolling" appearance. By nine months, most Dandies will have their full size, though the chest drops by 18 months; some males may take up to two-and-a-half years for the chest to

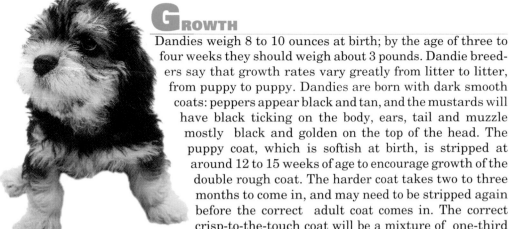

Most Dandies are born very dark with their actual pepper or mustard coloration coming in by five to seven months.
OWNERS, JAMES AND BARBARA MONROE.

develop completely. Dentition is not usually a problem, though shorter-muzzled dogs are prone to lacking molars and premolars. The topknot will grow out and turn creamy white or silvery white by one year of age. Adolescents require more activity than adults, and all Dandies like being walked.

The puppy coat is softer than the adult coat. After the first stripping or two the coat develops into the desirable mixture of hard and soft hair.
OWNERS, JAMES AND BARBARA MONROE.

Health

The long-backed, short-legged Dandie is subject to back (intervertebral disc) problems, as are other long, low dogs. Prevention includes choosing from quality stock and limiting stair climbing, jumping, and other high-impact activities, while keeping off excess weight. Hip dysplasia, kneecap luxation, and excessive ossification of the long bones occur. Among the most common injuries incurred by Dandies is torn ligaments, especially the anterior cruciate (a ligament supporting the hind leg). Arthritis commonly affects older dogs. Ear infections and ear mites are common, making regular ear inspection vital. Although the Dandie doesn't shed, grooming needs are considerable, and a professional is needed. Dandies average a good 13 years of life.

Mustard puppies have a considerable amount of dark hairs on the body: at birth only the top of the head reveals the golden coloration.
OWNERS, JAMES AND BARBARA MONROE.

Dandie Dinmont Terrier

Doberman Pinscher

Bred as a guard dog for a tax collector by the name Dobermann, this stout-hearted, able-bodied working dog is the picture of strength and ability. OWNERS, ANN E. NELSON, GIANNA CROUCH, DVM, AND JOE REID.

DESCRIPTION

Cutting an imposing figure of fearlessness and musculature, the Doberman Pinscher should appear as a medium-sized dog with a square body. He is essentially compactly built for both endurance and speed and ideally stands $27\frac{1}{2}$ inches for males, 2 inches less for females. The head is described as long and dry, like a blunt wedge. The eyes are moderately deep set and almond shaped; ears are set on high and small, cropped and carried erect or naturally drop; top skull flat; stop slight; well filled in under eyes. Neck is well arched and carried proudly; chest broad with well-defined forechest; ribs well sprung; belly tucked well up; hips broad; back short and firm in a straight line. Tail is traditionally docked at second joint. Fore and hindquarter angulation are alike, legs straight and parallel to one another. The coat is smooth, hard and close lying. Colors include black, red (brown), blue and fawn (Isabella), with or without clearly defined tan markings. Other colors are disqualified from the show ring. White markings are undesirable.

Doberman puppies thrive on pleasing their masters. Your puppy should be alert and inquisitive. Show puppies should have dark pigment at a young age as these tan-pointed puppies show. OWNER, BETTY CUZZOLINO.

OWNER SUITABILITY

The Doberman Pinscher excels as a family dog and guardian of home and property. Dobermans bond closely to their family and need to be indoors with them. They do well with children if introduced correctly. Keenly intelligent with a strong desire to please his master, the Doberman can be trained to be a formidable guard dog of intense strength and ability. They do well in obedience and police work. In the hands of the right people and from a quality breeder, the Doberman is sweet and biddable, never mean or aggressive. Dobies are very short-coated and don't do well in colder climates.

Choose a Dobie pup from proven lines. Be aware of possible compulsive disorders in the breed such as flank sucking and dancing disease, which can be problematic though not life-threatening.

GROWTH

Dobermans generally throw large litters, and puppies develop rapidly, making proper nutrition a strong concern to the breeder. Tail docking and dewclaw removal generally performed at about three days. Ears usually cropped, where practiced, around seven weeks. By eight weeks, most Dobies weigh between 15 and 20 pounds, and by nine to ten weeks present a good indication of what they will look like when mature, at around two years of age. Owners should select for temperament, strongly considering the

By nine to ten weeks the puppy should show its adult balanced proportions, including eye shape and ear placement.
OWNER, JANE SILVER.

temperament of the parents and the extent of temperament testing performed by the breeder. New owners must ensure a highly nutritious diet throughout the first two years of life to ensure that this rapidly developing breed is of sound body. Do not supplement calcium. Owners need to be firm but gentle and always consistent in their training. Plenty of quality socialization and training is particularly imperative throughout adolescence.

HEALTH

Protective mothers of guardian breeds like the Doberman provide excellent care and abundant affection to their puppies.
OWNER, BETTY CUZZOLINO.

Doberman puppies need continual socialization and lots of praise to develop into adoring and loving companions.

The Dobie should be a house dog, not a kennel or outdoor dog. Grooming needs are very minimal, though exercise and training requirements are high. A disease known as cardiomyopathy badly affects the breed, in the forms of congestive heart failure and sudden death. Breeders strive to rid lines of this fatal problem. The Dobie is known to have several skeletal problems. In addition to hip dysplasia, a condition commonly referred to as wobbler syndrome (actually cervical vertebral instability) affects dogs four to ten years of age, ranging in effect from minor lameness to near paralysis of the hind legs. Osteosarcoma is also reported. A skin disease referred to as color mutant alopecia occurs, especially in blue Dobies, and results in a lackluster coat, scaly skin, papules, and alopecia—it is treatable. Von Willebrand's disease is documented, presenting the common signs of prolonged bleeding and the formation of subcutaneous hematomas and protracted diarrhea, often bloody. Hereditary immune system disorders are also reported, as is congenital renal hypoplasia (a condition similar to kidney failure) and inherited metabolic liver defect. Hypothyroidism occurs and can be treated most effectively.

Dobies in good health, without cardiomyopathy, live to ten years. Generally, black Dobies have excellent coats and blues have the best dentition though are more prone to skin and coat problems.

Doberman Pinscher

English Foxhound

DESCRIPTION

The stouter Foxhound, the English Foxhound stands 23 to 24 inches at the shoulder on the straightest legs possible. The head is of full size, but should not appear heavy. Ears are set on long and lying close to the cheeks, often rounded. The bite must meet squarely, never overshot (pigmouthed) or undershot. Neck is long and clean, never throaty, tapering nicely to shoulders which are long, muscular and well sloping. Chest girth over 31 inches and back ribs very deep; back and loin muscular; tail well set on and carried gaily, not over back. Elbows must be straight and well let down by a long true arm. The standard states, "Every Master of Foxhounds insists on legs as straight as a post, and as strong." Knuckling over is not acceptable. Bones cannot be too large in the feet, which are round and catlike. Coat is short, dense, hard and glossy and the Foxhound colors can be any good hound color (tricolors, bicolors or pieds, which is white with hare, badger, yellow or tan).

A classic hunting hound in classic hound colors, the English Foxhound is a courageous pack hound with a cheerful yet determined disposition. OWNERS, EMILY LATIMER AND SUZY REINGOLD.

OWNER SUITABILITY

Foxhounds are not popular choices as pets, even though they offer owners an even-tempered, mild companion dog. They are dog oriented, as they were developed as pack dogs, and therefore do well with another Foxhound or other dog. Although they enjoy people and children and bond closely to their family, Foxhounds are generally outdoor dogs and should be kenneled. Their hunting instincts are strong and the need for exercise is more than for your average Beagle!

Foxhound puppies gain about a pound a week until six weeks. Although their care is similar to Beagles, they do not thrive on an indoor existence as a Beagle does. AGENT, GISELLE SASKOR.

GROWTH

Foxhounds generally weigh about one pound at birth and develop evenly and with good pace. A very natural breed, few developmental problems are encountered. However, it is also a very specialized breed, developed for a specific purpose. Uninitiated owners are strongly advised to thoroughly research the breed and to work closely with a breeder/experienced owner in raising and training their dog. Foxhounds require special care, special training, and a specialized diet to truly excel as the hunting dogs they are.

As one of the least popular of all breeds in the U.S., there are less than five litters of English Foxhounds registered annually. This little puppy and proud mom should feel pretty special!
AGENT, GISELLE SASKOR.

HEALTH

A very natural and unexaggerated canine, the English Foxhound enjoys relative freedom from hereditary problems and is highly tolerant of disease. Perhaps of greatest danger to these dogs is injuries sustained on the hunt and in overexuberant play. Some back (spinal) problems have been reported, including osteochondrosis. Thrombocytopathy, a blood disorder, is unique to Foxhounds. Grooming is minimal, but the ears and eyes must be checked at least weekly for signs of infection and foreign objects. Deafness occurs in some lines.

Virtually free of hereditary problems, a hardy, long-lived easycare purebred, the Foxhound will make a handful of dog owners very happy this year.
AGENT, GISELLE SASKOR.

By six months of age the Foxhound has gained at least 80 percent of his height, though it will take up to a year or more to mature fully.
OWNER, SILLA E. TURNER.

English Foxhound

151

English Setter

DESCRIPTION

The glamorous and elegant English Setter is both symmetrical and substantial of build, a sonnet interpolating strength, grace and stamina. The breed is never coarse or extreme in appearance. His flat coat is well feathered and silky and its ground white color is flecked with black, liver, or lemon. The fancy employs the term belton to describe the English Setter's coat coloration. The head is long and lean, stop well defined, and harmonious in size and proportion to body. The skull appears oval from above; head planes being parallel; occipital protuberance somewhat defined. Muzzle long and square; flews fairly pendant; cheeks smooth; eyes dark and nearly round and fairly large; ears well set back and low. Neck is long and graceful; topline level; chest sufficiently deep; tail tapering and feathered with straight and silky hair. Shoulders close together; legs straight and parallel to each other; elbows and hocks with no tendency to turn in or out. The coat is flat without curl or wool; feathering on ears, chest, abdomen, under thighs, back of legs, tail, never overdone to hide dog's true lines. Height: 25 inches for dogs; an inch less for bitches. The belton color pattern is characterized by light or dark ticking or roaning. Color possibilities: orange belton, liver belton, lemon belton, blue belton and tricolor (blue belton with tan markings).

As elegant as any sporting dog can be, the English Setter has hunted by man's side for centuries and today prospers as a loyal and stylish companion.
OWNER, A.L. POLLEY.

OWNER SUITABILITY

A perfectly English breed, the English Setter has the manners of the Royal Family, though is more adept at avoiding scandal and conflict. He is a peaceful, regal soul who is as laid back and easygoing as a dog can be. He regards children with much favor and is infinitely patient with them, no matter how much they tug on his ear feathers! In avoiding conflict, he

If ever an Englishman fit into an American family, it's the English Setter—adaptable, easygoing and always ready for activity.
OWNERS, ARDYS McELWEE AND JANICE BURGESSON.

can be quite stubborn, creatively so, for he is a thinking dog. He is an excellent family and apartment dog who can still perform as a hunting dog if trained, though his field drive is quite sedated. Basic obedience training must be pursued from the very beginning.

GROWTH

English Setters at birth show a white coloration, or white with black hairs on the ears and black pigmentation to the nose. The coat begins to show its color as early as three days after birth. By three weeks, coat color and pigmentation are apparent, though it is not until full maturity (around two years of age) that the coat reaches its full potential. Breeders encourage plenty of grooming, especially during adolescent coat change. Even twice daily during a heavy shedding period is not too much, and particular attention must be paid to the heavy fringing and feathering. Sexual maturity has shown to be very varied in the breed, from as early as six months to as late as 18 months for males.

By three weeks of age the breeder can determine the color a puppy will be. Pigmentation is darkest on the ears and the belton or roaning begins to emerge during the first week of life.
OWNER, MARIANNE CAMERON.

Owners should select for physical soundness and temperaments that are even and sweet, never shy or hyperactive.

HEALTH

Progressive retinal atrophy (PRA) and hip dysplasia both occur and should be checked in all breeding stock. Congenital deafness also concerns breeders, and all pups should be examined for signs of deafness—which can progressively worsen with age. A rare and unusual condition known as juvenile amaurotic familial idiocy, believably caused by a metabolic defect, is marked by increased nervousness, muscle spasms, and decreased learning ability and awareness of surroundings. The onset is usually around one year, with death usually occurring during the ensuing year. The English Setter has demonstrated susceptibility to skin problems, including dermatitis, pyoderma, and demodectic mange. Subaortic stenosis and primary ciliary dyskinesia are reported by vets. The hallmark tail requires special care, as it is subject to wounds which often prove difficult to heal. The English Setter often lives to 14 years, with cancer being among the most common causes of death.

A litter of "Llewelyn Setters," an attempt to recapture the original type thought to be lost for generations. All English Setters are born solid white.
OWNER, KEVIN R. LAGER.

Select for active, happy puppies that display the English Setter's sweet, even temperament.
OWNER, MARIANNE CAMERON.

English Setter

English Springer Spaniel

DESCRIPTION

The sweet English Springer Spaniel is a neat, compact member of the spaniel family, medium in size with long pendulous ears and a moderately long, glossy coat. The body is deep and the legs are suitably strong, able to carry him with ease. His carriage is proud and free. Above all he is without exaggeration, beautifully balanced and well knit with good bone. The back is level and short, with well developed thighs, good feet and a docked tail. Topline is never longer than his height and ideally nearly equal. Shoulder height for dogs is 20 inches; 19 inches for bitches. Weight: 49 to 55 pounds. The head's beauty relies on its refinement and should be impressive and balanced. Adults must never appear leggy, short-necked, heavy or oval-skulled, steep-shouldered, hare- or splay-footed. The coat is flat or wavy on the body, medium in length; the ears, chest, legs, tail and belly are nicely fringed; coat is never rough or curly. In color the Springer can be black or liver with white markings, white with black or liver markings; tricolor; blue or liver roan; never lemon, red or orange.

Of all British land spaniels, the English Springer Spaniel is the highest on leg and raciest in body; he is symmetrical, athletic and beautiful to behold.
OWNERS, DR. JOHN R. AND DIANE C. OSTENBERG.

OWNER SUITABILITY

A biddable companion and prime family dog who is sufficiently merry and easily controlled, not high strung, aggressive or shy. The Springer must be included with the family and does not do well in a kennel environment. As the breed standard

When deciding upon a Springer, you are selecting an indoor family dog. If not permitted to be with the family, the Springer is denied the opportunity to become the responsive, all-around companion he is born to be.
OWNER, DEBORAH MALTBY.

English Springer puppies are confident about their curiosities: choose a spunky puppy who is eager to be handled.
OWNER, DEBORAH KIRK.

describes, he must be friendly and eager to please, quick to learn and willing to obey. Less-well-bred dogs may tend to be stubborn or overly timid; some may be bold in a bad-dog way—nipping and growling. An even temperament and the obvious spaniel style are key to selection.

GROWTH

Springers weigh from 10 to 15 ounces at birth. They are born with incomplete pigmentation and coloration which may not be completely developed until as late as one year. Springers are known to continue developing and maturing till as late as two years. Tails should be docked to about one-third and all dewclaws removed as early as possible. By eight weeks, pups should weigh 8 to 10 pounds. Owners should select for an adaptable dog who is active yet responsive to human commands. Aggression and dominance are not common but can be a problem if not properly handled from a young age. Young Springers are notoriously good eaters and prone to obesity during the formative months. Owners must control this while ensuring proper nutrition with high-quality diet. As the puppy coat is dropped during adolescence, extra weekly/daily grooming time is required, with professional assistance recommended about every six weeks.

Springers grow at a good rate with appetite rarely being a problem. Don't overindulge the puppy during the 12-to-24-week stage as many breeders report weight problems during this time. OWNER, LIBBY O'DONNELL.

Young puppies profit from regular socialization so that their transition to a human family is a natural, less traumatic one.

HEALTH

Springers commonly enjoy life into the mid-teen years. Aside from the other older-dog problems, Springers are prone to obesity. Owners should maintain a regular exercise program throughout the dog's life and feed sensibly. The ears and eyes of the Springer need to be checked carefully. Eye problems include retinal dysplasia, central PRA, ectropion and entropion, and glaucoma—responsible screening

Springers are generally long-lived dogs: it pays to select from a line that is virtually free of any of the genetic problems to which the breed is prone. OWNER, KATHYRN KIRK.

is a must. The ear problems are much simpler, mostly including infection (otitis externa) and mites, and can be largely prevented by regular cleaning and grooming. Hip dysplasia also occurs. Some skin problems are reported by owners, and the rare unusual condition called Ehlers-Danlos syndrome is marked by serious lacerations to the skin from apparently minor accidents. Veterinarians report Springer cases of red-blood-cell disorders, cardiomyopathy and myasthenia gravis (associated with muscle weakness).Springers are normally healthy and vigorous canines who enjoy and require plenty of play and training exercises.

English Springer Spaniel

English Toy Spaniel

DESCRIPTION

A queer little fellow, the English Toy Spaniel is endowed with an oversized head, dome shaped, looking chubby though not coarse. He is short-nosed with a very short muzzle, a broad square jaw, and a slightly undershot bite. The ears are very long and set low and the expression reveals his intelligence and charm. He has a compact body, square and deep, with a broad back. The neck is moderate in length and tail is docked to a length of 2 to 4 inches. The coat is profuse with good fringe on the ears, body, chest, and legs. Four color possibilities include red and white (Blenheim); tricolor (Prince Charles); ruby red; and black and tan (King Charles). The ruby-colored dog is permitted to have a small white patch on the chest, but not elsewhere. The dog should be able to move with good reach and drive due to his straight-boned front and nicely angulated rear assembly. Ideal weight for an adult is 8 to 14 pounds.

The red and white English Toy Spaniel is called Blenheim, celebrating one of the original breeds used to create today's breed. This is Champion Cheri-A's Lord Andrew, the number one English Toy Spaniel of all time.
OWNERS, JOHN WOOD JR., MARY DULLINGER-CUNHA AND JEROME ELLIOT.

OWNER SUITABILITY

Comical and sweet, the English Toy Spaniel, or King Charles Spaniel as he is sometimes called, is a delicate but sturdy breed who needs a smart owner and handler. Despite what some may call an unusual appearance, he is a perfectly normal, trainable dog. Young children are not ideal to handle young puppies due to their fragility and large domed skull. He enjoys being with his people and bonds very strongly with his caregivers.

The head piece makes the breed distinctive. The prominently set and very large eyes must be carefully attended.
OWNER, MARY DULLINGER-CUNHA.

GROWTH

The small English Toy begins life at a hearty 5 to 10 ounces, and by eight weeks should weigh 4 to 5 pounds. Puppies are born with incomplete pigmentation that soon comes in. Breeders report no unusual developmental or growth problems. English Toys mature at a good rate, attaining full height and sexual maturity generally around one year of age. Coat and body development are generally not complete until around two years of age. Poor eating habits are rare, as is overeating. No specialized diet is required, though owners must ensure that proper bone development, both of the limbs and of the skull, is achieved.

HEALTH

The ETS requires little special care, and on average lives from nine to 15 years. Like other toy dogs, the English Toy is predisposed to luxated kneecaps and other joint problems. Frailty of bone

English Toy Spaniel puppies are pleasantly plump, growing at a steady rate with little difficulty.
OWNER, PATRICIA A. ZBOCK.

should be avoided. Eye problems are noted by breeders, owing in part to the prominent setting of the eyes. Breathing difficulty (attributable in part to the brachycephalic head structure), diabetes mellitus, congestive heart defects, umbilical hernias and incomplete fontanel closure (a soft spot on the skull that remains after maturity) affect members of this breed. English Toys are not difficult to groom but do require consistency, especially the coat on the legs and ears. The long, well-furnished ear leather may invite ear infections, especially in hot weather, and the undershot bite makes regular dental care even more important.

A red (ruby) puppy with a small white chest marking that should fade with maturity and a tricolor (Prince Charles) puppy exemplifying two of the four allowable colors.
OWNER, PATRICIA A. ZBOCK.

English Toy Spaniel

Field Spaniel

DESCRIPTION

A medium-sized hunting dog who is not without his beauty and nobility, the Field Spaniel is a symmetrical, sound and free-moving dog of great activity and endurance. Adult dogs stand 18 inches, bitches 1 inch less; he should appear somewhat longer than tall. The head is well proportioned; the ears are moderately long and wide; muzzle long and lean and in no way snipy or squarely cut; lips are close fitting. The neck is long and slightly arched, muscular and clean; back is level and firm; chest is deep; tail set on low and docked to balance the dog. The coat is single and moderately long, always dense and glossy, flat or slightly wavy. Overdone coats interfere with the dog's working capacity and are therefore incorrect. In color the Field Spaniel is black, liver, golden liver, or roan (all possibly with tan points).

Heavier than the Cocker but equally merry, the Field Spaniel was designed with stamina, docility and soundness in mind. OWNERS, JAMES AND LUCY GALLAGHER.

OWNER SUITABILITY

Active but not high strung, the Field Spaniel is an even-tempered spaniel breed with a natural intelligence about him. Many Fields are used by hunters in England and the States, though the numbers in both countries are small but steady. The dogs are completely comfortable with children and enjoy being indoors as much as outdoors. He may become boisterous with his voice so careful correction is required.

Few people ever see Field Spaniels in the fur and even fewer ever see a roan-colored one! It is said that crosses to Springers brought about roan Field Spaniels.
OWNERS, E.B. ALEXANDER AND SARAH W. EVANS.

GROWTH

Newborns weigh around 6 ounces. However they do grow at a good rate and will weigh 4 to 6 pounds by eight weeks of age. Tails docked (to one-third) and dewclaws removed at three to five days. The Field Spaniel usually reaches its full weight by nine months of age, with full maturity at 11 to 13 months for bitches and 12 to 16 months for dogs. Puppies should be outgoing and not show any signs of fear. Feeding should be twice a day until seven months of age, and once a day thereafter, depending on the dog and his unique qualities (activity level, metabolism, etc.).

One of the least popular of all recognized breeds, the Field Spaniel is bred by a handful of individuals in the States. Overall this is a reliable breed base and most puppies are healthy and problem-free. ONWER, LYNN G. FINNEY.

HEALTH

Because of the breed's few numbers, little veterinary research has been conducted. Hip dysplasia is reported, as well as pyometra. The extent of both these conditions is not well known. Breeders also note that a hypothyroid condition sometimes develops in females after whelping. Field Spaniels have shown a sensitivity to anesthetics, and your veterinarian should be aware of this. Due to the Field Spaniel's limited breed base, some lines may be affected by problems which have cropped up due to interbreeding with Springers.

Field Spaniels develop at a steady rate, reaching maturity between 11 and 16 months, depending on dog and sex. OWNERS, GEORGE AND DOROTHY O'NEIL.

Puppies may be reserved upon first meeting though the breed typically shows great affinity for human company. Socialization at any early age will nurture these valuable traits. OWNER, LYNN G. FINNEY.

Field Spaniel

Finnish Spitz

DESCRIPTION

The foxlike Finnish Spitz glories in his brilliant red color, pointed muzzle, small upright ears, dense northern coat and curled plumed tail. Of utmost importance is his symmetrical, square body and natural unexaggerated features. Ideally the male at the withers is $17\frac{1}{2}$ to 20 inches; females 2 inches less. The head is refined and clean cut; eyes are almond shaped with black rims; ears set on high; skull flat between ears; pronounced stop; lips black. The neck is well set; chest deep; ribs well sprung. Quarters are balanced and moderately spaced to afford brisk, light movement. The coat is double, with outer coat long and harsh with straight guard hairs, pants or skirt on thighs; longer hair on neck and back; undercoat is soft and dense. Color is bright and clear and varying in shades from pale honey to deep auburn.

The face of a fox——pointed muzzle, upright ears and a bright red color——the Finnish Spitz is known for this resemblance as well as his characteristic yodel-like bark. OWNERS, TOM T. AND MARG G. WALKER.

OWNER SUITABILITY

Alert and always vocal, the Finsky has much to tell his owner, who is often quite amused by this little dog's perception of the world around him. Typical of the spitz breeds, the Finnish Spitz is very smart and knows much more than his trainer (or so he thinks). He can be difficult to train as he is naturally resistant to advice, no less correction. If training is fun and on his terms, he learns with the speed of a fifth grader. Keep the Finsky's yodeling to a minimum, or the neighbors will soon complain. Owners should be patient and understanding of the breed's quick mind and bouncy temperament. He should be a happy homebody who loves to run and play. The Finnish Spitz is very adaptable and makes an excellent choice for a family wishing to adopt an adult dog.

The Finnish Spitz has the gloriously dense coat of his Nordic dog cousins and a curled plume tail. In Finland he is still a talented hunting dog sometimes called the Barking Bird Dog. OWNERS, TOM T. AND MARG G. WALKER.

160

GROWTH

At eight weeks, the Finnish Spitz should weigh 7 to 9 pounds. Full height is achieved at approximately one year; however, they will continue to mature and fill out until two to three years. At birth, puppies are quite dark; by eight weeks, they are a "paper-sack brown"; and at approximately one year they will become red. Ears should be erect from a young age. Finnish Spitz puppies require abundant socialization and human contact. Prospective owner should select for the friendly, happy puppy. Properly reared adolescents will display an outgoing temperament; however, breeders note that there is a breed tendency toward aloofness.

The epitome of alertness—by law puppies are eager and friendly.
OWNERS, HEATHER STORE AND CHRISTINE ROESLER.

HEALTH

Because of the limited breed base (and relative newness of the breed) in English-speaking countries, veterinary research is lacking. However, one breeder reports that his veterinary friends in Finland tell him "that if there were no dogs other than Finnish Spitz in Finland, the vets would starve to death because Finnish Spitz are very healthy and almost never have to see the vet." However, prospective owners should seek a health guarantee from the breeder, and look for screening of eyes, hips, thyroid, etc. Breeders report no special dietary needs, though owners should follow a breeder-prescribed diet, especially for the first year.

Puppies will appear somewhat leggy as they can reach their full height one to two years before full maturity. Always select for temperament over physical balance in the puppy.
OWNERS, HEATHER STORE AND CHRISTINE

Finnish Spitz shed only twice a year, when grooming is imperative. They do not shed at other times. Dry dogs well after baths to avoid possible hot spots.

Finskis are "paper-sack brown" until they are one year old; consider the brilliance of the dam's coat to see just how fox red your puppy will become.
OWNERS, HEATHER STORE AND CHRISTINE ROESLER.

Finnish Spitz

Flat-Coated Retriever

DESCRIPTION

Powerful and racy, the Flat-Coated Retriever is a dog of moderate substance, well proportioned and never cobby, with his hallmark straight and *flat*-lying coat. The Flat-Coat's head is long and clean, a fairly flat skull with flat cheeks and a deep muzzle, well filled in between and beneath the eyes, which are set wide apart. Ears are smallish, close to the head and not low-set like a hound's or setter's. The neck is long and smoothly flows into the shoulders, which are well laid back. Topline is level; ribs deep; moderate tuckup; forechest prominent. Quarters assembled for good, clean drive. Coat is of moderate length and density; high luster but never woolly, curly, short, silky or fluffy; feathering creates impression of a full coat, never bushy or stringy. Color is always solid black or liver. The dog stands 23 to 24$\frac{1}{2}$ inches, bitches 1 inch less.

Developed by British game hunters, the Flat-Coated Retriever enjoys working close to the hunter and is a capable and professional retriever on land and in the water. OWNERS, PHILIP AND SANDRA PARK, LIBBY BAARSTAD AND LANA GRIFFIN.

OWNER SUITABILITY

Everyone's best friend, the Flat-Coat shimmers with personality like his glistening coat. He loves all people and has never met a stranger. A hunting dog by nature, he thrives on activity and can be trained to perform a bagful of chores. Even-tempered and friendly to a fault, the breed is rather unpopular as a choice for a pet though he has what it takes to be that perfect family dog.

In either coat color—solid black or liver—the breed makes a multi-talented, sensible and tractable companion dog. OWNER, KURT D. ANDERSON.

GROWTH

At eight weeks, Flat-Coats weigh 12 to 14 pounds. In general they are slow to mature (two to three years), though individual rates vary. Full height is achieved by eight or nine months, possibly adding an inch or so after that. Prospective owners should look for an unreserved, outgoing pup. Flat-Coats do not look like Labs with long fur. They are lean and should have a long lean head, a coat that is either fuzzy or flat and silky. Typically, the fuzzier the puppy the more

Flat-Coat puppies should have longer, leaner heads than Labradors, though not as pronounced a difference as adults show.
OWNERS, STEVE AND NANCY WICKMARK.

coated the adult. Pups are born in their adult color, either black or liver. Liver dogs have liver pigmentation on the eye rims, nose, and lips. Eyes may be hazel through black, darker preferred. Pups have little to no feathering at this age. It may take three years for full adult coat to emerge. Adolescent dogs experience very little color change, though any white markings usually disappear at this time. Adolescents may do things their own way but learn quickly. They are not necessarily dominant but need structure and consistency. Growth may be uneven at this time, and dogs especially may appear gangly between six and ten months.

Generally, fuzzy puppies will have more adult coat than pups with little hair. Young pups do not have feathering, which emerges with the young adult's coat.
OWNERS, STEVE AND NANCY WICKMARK.

HEALTH

The Flat-Coated Retriever as a breed enjoys its limited numbers, which have allowed breeders to keep a tighter rein on possible breed-specific health problems. As it stands, HD has a low incidence in the breed, and all breeders must offer proof of HD screening. Other major breeder concerns are cancer and patellar luxation. At this time it is not clear, particularly with cancer, if there is a breed-specific link to this problem or if it is more environmental/individually generated. Always look for breeders who show awareness and concern for these and any other possible problems, such as bloat and hypothyroidism. The breed is typically a good eater and requires no specialized diet. Owners should keep off the excess weight, however, as these dogs were never meant to have the bulk of a Labrador Retriever. Grooming needs are not demanding or specialized though regular maintenance is required. Flat-Coats live to around nine or ten years, some to 14.

Flat-Coated Retriever

French Bulldog

DESCRIPTION

The solid little French Bulldog is compactly built and heavy boned. His hallmark feature is his bat ears, which are broad at the base, rounded at the top, high set and not too close together, erect with the orifice to the front. He weighs in no more than 28 pounds (over 28 pounds disqualifies the dog). The head is large with a flat skull and rounded forehead; the muzzle is deep and broad with well-developed cheeks. Neck is thick and well arched with loose skin about the throat; chest is full and deep; body short and well rounded; tail straight or screwed, never curly, but tapering from thick root to fine tip. Forelegs are short and straight and set wide apart; dewclaws may be removed; hind legs are longer than forelegs. Coat is short and moderately fine. Colors vary and include all brindles, fawn, white, brindle and white; unacceptable colors include solid black (with no trace of brindle), mouse, liver, black and tan, black and white. Nose must be black (except on lighter colored dogs).

A symbol of the English "perfected" by the French, the *Bouledogue Francais* cuts a gentlemanly figure with both politeness and charm, despite his sordid origins. (Imagine how scandalized the British were to see their national dog "shrunk" by the Frogs. True drama!) OWNER, SARAH SWEATT.

OWNER SUITABILITY

A good-sized dog in a small-dog frame, the Frenchie comes equipped with a giant bag of personality and comic bits. He is a clever little dog with a giant heart which he will share with everyone. Very tolerant of children and thriving on family life, Frenchies are adaptable and always keen on pleasing you. They love the family and are most protective, making competent watchdogs. This is a sensitive breed who does not like extremes in temperature. Some Frenchies snore.

Frenchies are muscular little dogs with heavy bone and smooth coats: they come in colorful combinations and have colorful, playful personalities to match.
OWNERS, MARK A. AND BETH A. CARR.

164

Growth

The average birth weight is 6 ounces. By eight weeks, most dogs weigh about 5 pounds. From this point onward, dogs will tend to grow more rapidly than bitches of the same litter, maturing at a larger size as well. Breeders strongly caution owners to apply utmost discretion in choosing their Frenchie. Ill-bred dogs are chock full of problems, both in health and temperament. Well-bred dogs are worth the wait and effort. French Bulldog adolescents are full of life, spunky, and delightful to the owner who has an enjoyment of playtime. Young Frenchies are inquisitive and love to clown around. Owners are advised to initiate early training to avoid stubbornness. Full maturity is attained around two years of age, though full height and sexual maturity occurs some time earlier. As the dog matures, the coat will change texture, and color in the brindles (more brindling will appear).

Breeders have achieved balance in both physical type as well as temperament. Frenchies are sufficiently reserved, not unduly boisterous but happy and good-natured. (Puppies may be embarrassingly silly for a month or two longer than expected.)

Puppies never quite grow into their ears.

Health

The most serious problem affecting the breed today is its apparent susceptibility to cancer. Owners must query breeders about the cancer history in their lines. The most common problems, however, are associated with oversized and overweight dogs. Breathing difficulties, heart complications, and back/vertebral problems are all fostered by a too-big Frenchie. Owners should select their dogs with a discerning eye and properly feed and exercise them thereafter. Von Willebrand's disease, which affects many other breeds as well, is an inherited blood disorder affecting both coagulation and platelet function. Skin allergies are not uncommon, and short tails and skulls are noted birth defects. Intervertebral disc disease occurs but is fortunately not common. Aside from proper diet and plenty of moderate exercise, the Frenchie demands little in the way of special care. Frenchies live ten to 12 years or more.

A bat-eared dreamfest: puppies showing off their eagerness, handsome girth and imaginative coloration.

French Bulldog

German Pinscher

DESCRIPTION

Well balanced and smooth coated, the German Pinscher is a medium-sized dog of solid conformation and a flowing outline. His head resembles a blunt wedge, strong but not heavy; eyes dark and oval; ears set high and V-shaped, cropped or flop; neck is strong, not short or stout, not throaty. Chest is moderately wide; compact and short coupled, with short back, slightly sloping. The tail is set high, docked to three joints. The coat is short and dense and colored in fawn to stag red; or black and blue with tan points. He stands 17 to 19 inches tall.

A farmer's terrier gone purebred—the German Pinscher (in England simply called Pinscher) handily fills in the gap between two well-known breeds, the Miniature and the Doberman Pinscher. The Pinscher, more ancient than both these breeds, has a small but dedicated following.
OWNER, SOCORRO ARMSTRONG.

OWNER SUITABILITY

An easycare, handsome breed that demands very little and returns abundantly. This is an affectionate, versatile breed. He is not a miniaturized Doberman but actually more natural and ancient than that breed. Breeders emphasize that these are not apartment or condo dogs, and that they require daily romps and training, a fenced yard, and plenty of human interaction. (A bored, underexercised Pinscher can become a destructive Pinscher.) He is obedient and easily managed in the home. There are a number of quality sources in the States and England, though his numbers are limited at present.

The black and tan pattern in the Pinscher flashes appeal and pedigree purity. The breed deserves recognition for its good sense: a sensible, obedient disposition and an unexaggerated, natural body type.

German Pinschers at eight weeks weigh 9 to 10 pounds on average. They reach full height between 10 and 12 months, but do not attain full maturity until 18 to 24 months, with bitches typically slower to mature. Owners should select for a square pup with strong rear angulation and a nice topline. Coloration should be a deep red, which will generally darken with age. Bites are rarely a problem but should be checked. Dewclaws always removed; ear cropping, which is optional, is generally performed between eight and ten weeks. Puppy canine teeth may be retained and therefore require removal by your veterinarian. Breeders set four months to one year as the adolescent period. During this time growth may be uneven and growth spurts are common. The adolescent Pinscher is known to be headstrong, highly intelligent and sensitive to its surroundings. These dogs require obedience training from a young age, and consistency is imperative. German Pinschers are known for their excellent memory, and once a command is mastered it should never be forgotten—unless intentionally so! Properly reared and socialized dogs make great companions and protectors. Two adult males should not be kept together, however.

A Pinscher litter is a rare and wonderful thing! Few Pinschers are bred even in Germany these days, though some litters can be located both in England and the States. Contact the breed club to locate a breeder in your region of the country.
OWNERS, DANIEL H. AND RHONDA L. PARKS.

HEALTH

While training and socialization are vital, the German Pinscher is otherwise an easycare companion, having very little grooming requirements and no specialized dietary needs. Most important to the good health and healthy attitude of this breed is daily exercise. Breeders report no serious health problems facing the breed today, and cite a life expectancy of 12 to 15 years on average.

Unlike selecting a puppy from a more popular breed, finding a healthy, problem-free Pinscher puppy should be as easy as finding a breeder.
OWNERS, DANIEL H. AND RHONDA L. PARKS.

German Pinscher

German Shepherd Dog

DESCRIPTION

The German Shepherd Dog is an agile, balanced dog who is longer than tall, with a notably deep body and smooth curves. The impression of the animal must be one of strength, muscular fitness and substance, never spindly or clumsy. Height for males should be 24 to 26 inches; 2 inches less for females. The head befits the breed's nobility and quality, it is cleanly chiseled and without coarseness or fineness. Ears are moderately pointed and in proportion to the skull, always carried erect (never cropped or dropped). The neck is relatively long, strong and clean cut, without loose skin. The withers are higher than the back and slope into the relatively short back, which must be straight without sag or roach. Chest is deep and carried well down between the legs; ribs well sprung and long, not barrel shaped or too flat. Tail is bushy with a slight saberlike curve, extending to hocks. The thigh is broad and nearly forms a right angle; the hock joint and foot (metatarsus) is short and tightly articulated. The GSD has a medium-length double coat, with straight, harsh hair, close lying or slightly wavy; neck and legs furnished with slightly longer hair. Coat must never be soft, silky, too long, woolly, curly or open. The breed should have strong rich coloration commonly seen in sables, black and black/tan, not favoring pale blues or livers, and *never* solid white.

The "mystique" of the German Shepherd is characterized by strength, muscular fitness and substance. This is Champion Altana's Mystique, the number one show dog of all time, and we are honored to have her grace our pages! OWNER, JANE A. FIRESTONE. AGENT, JAMES MOSES.

OWNER SUITABILITY

A dog among dogs, the German Shepherd is a popular choice for a companion and protection dog for many good reasons. He is handsome, intelligent, obedient, affectionate and even-tempered. Well-bred Shepherds, given proper socialization and competent training, arguably offer an owner the best of all possible worlds. He is never aggressive nor spooked at a person's approach. Ideally a friendly, adaptable and fun-loving family dog who provides ample protection for family and property.

No breed has a record of service and devotion to mankind to compare to the German Shepherd. He serves daily in countless areas of service, not the least of which is as a home companion and watchdog. OWNER, NATALY JACOB-LAUVIER.

GROWTH

Puppy weight at eight weeks varies considerably, from 6 to 18 pounds, the average being 12 to 14. Owners should select for puppies which are outgoing and friendly. Breeding stock must *never* be submissive or aggressive. Skeletal growth is rapid in the Shepherd, with muscular growth lagging somewhat behind. This often results in an adolescent who is leggy (as one breeder puts it, "geeky") in appearance. Proper diet, often with vitamin and mineral supplements, is vital to correct development. Maturity also varies considerably, with some dogs fully mature at 16 months and others not until three years. Bitches are usually fully mature by two years of age. Sexual maturity is generally around eight to ten months. Ears should be erect between ten and 12 weeks, though late rising ears are possible. Ears may dip during teething. The tan areas of the coat will intensify until 18 months to two years.

With the high incidence of hip dysplasia in the breed, be sure the puppy you choose is derived from screened parents. Don't let your haste interfere with the long and comfortable life of your dog. OWNER, ROBERTA LAUFER.

HEALTH

The German Shepherd has had tremendous popularity the world over. This unfortunately has led to overbreeding and the advancement of many diseases and conditions. It is most important that prospective owners choose their Shepherds with utmost discretion and caution. Owners cite behavioral problems as a major concern, and temperament testing of breeding stock should be a requirement. Hip and elbow dysplasia and other bone/joint problems (panosteitis, hypertrophic osteodystrophy and myasthenia gravis), eye problems (pannus, cataracts, retinal dysplasia, and Collie eye), cancer (osteosarcoma), urinary and intestinal tract problems, hemophilia A, von Willebrand's disease, heart problems, bloat and epilepsy are all documented in the breed. Health certificates and screening, obedience and working titles, and longevity in breeding lines should attract new owners. The well-bred Shepherd averages 12 robust years of life, with little special care. While shedding can be quite abundant, little more than brushing and combing is required.

In a breed as popular as the Shepherd, choose a puppy that is outgoing, not aggressive or oddly shy. The dam should be approachable and appear balanced, strong and calm. OWNER, ROBERTA LAUFER.

Puppies ten to 12 weeks are just beginning to get ears up and to run on all fours. Don't overexercise a puppy whose bone is not fully developed and never overfeed a Shepherd. These two maxims can help to ward off the possibility of orthopedic problems in the future. OWNERS, KAREN HARMS AND TED BROZOWSKI.

German Shepherd Dog

German Shorthaired Pointer

DESCRIPTION

The German Shorthaired Pointer is a keen and enthusiastic hunter with a graceful outline, clean-cut head, powerful short back, deep chest, sloping shoulders, solid bone, and a taut coat, which might be called short. Symmetry and balance must be achieved at first glance. The head must be neither too light nor too heavy; the skull is broadish; line to forehead must rise gradually without definite stop; muzzle is long and never pointed or dish-faced (like the Pointer's). Ears are broad and fairly high set, not too long. Eyes are medium sized; dark brown color preferred (yellow eyes are to be avoided); nose is brown (spotted or flesh-colored nose to be avoided); perfect level bite. Shoulder blades lie flat and well laid back, never loose or straight; long upper arm with good reach. Coat is short and thick and tough to the touch; skin is close and tight. Tail should be firm and set high, never curved over back or toward head, and always well carried. Dogs should weigh

"All-purpose" best describes the German Shorthaired Pointer: companion, watchdog, show dog, obedience dog and the most versatile hunter on the market!
OWNER, SUSAN HARRISON.

55 to 70 pounds, bitches 10 pounds less. Dogs stand 23 to 25 inches; bitches 2 inches less (1-inch variation severely penalized). The coat is colored in solid liver or combination of liver and white, in America never black, red, orange, lemon, or tan any where on coat and never solid white. In England solid black or black and white acceptable, although never tricolored.

OWNER SUITABILITY

The German Shorthaired Pointer is an active, high-energy dog who is most content in a country setting where he can exercise regularly. Perhaps too high strung for apartment life, the GSP does not thrive in a confined environment. He loves kids, with whom he is both outgoing and gentle. He is a hunting dog with a super keen nose. Training is not difficult with a well-adapted dog and complete control is essential for a reliable hunting dog.

Don't let these two laid-back Shorthairs delude you: this is an active, on-the-move outdoor dog that needs plenty of exercise and stimulation (not that he won't enjoy resting by your side at a long day's end).

170

GROWTH

The eight-week-old German Shorthair should weigh 15 pounds. Growth will continue at a fairly rapid rate until four months or so, at which time it will level off. Proper feeding, possibly with supplementation, is vital during these fast-growing four months. With proper nutrition, full height is commonly attained by ten months, with full maturity not attained until two-and-a-half to three years. Good bites are very common in the breed, and a slightly overshot bite may correct itself by physical maturity. Owners should expect very active adolescents with emerging hunting instincts, which are very alive in this breed. Plenty of daily time should be spent channeling this great exuberance to avoid destructiveness.

HEALTH

Essentially a hardy, hard-working sporting dog, the German Shorthair commonly lives to be an active teenager. Hip dysplasia, entropion, von Willebrand's disease (type II is rare but inherited), and thrombocytopathy (another blood disorder) are of limited occurrence in the GSP. Chronic superficial keratitis (a progressive, though treatable, eye disease) and eversion of the transparent third eyelid (nictitating membrane) are common eye problems. While cancer (particularly fibrosarcoma and melanoma) is reported, kidney failure, heart attacks, and severe arthritis are more common serious conditions affecting the older Shorthair. Cases in GSPs of a rare and unusual condition called amaurotic idiocy marked by progressive uncoordination and confusion, culminating in death, have been reported. Meningitis (brain inflammation) has some minor occurrence in the breed. Though grooming is minimal, ear infections can be common. Feeding and exercise must be regulated to avoid the occurrence of bloat.

A substantially built medium-sized dog, the GSP is a lot of puppy by eight weeks of age. The breed is as alert as the newly risen sun, and about as bright!

Choose a puppy that is confident and outgoing. Avoid high-strung or aggressive puppies. A calm, stable temperament makes for ease of trainability as well as livability. Owners must be consistent and firm to keep the GSP attentive and out of trouble.

German Shorthaired Pointer

German Wirehaired Pointer

DESCRIPTION

The famed wire coat affords the German Wirehaired Pointer with a water- and weather-proof coat as well as his distinctive eyebrows, mustache and beard. Males stand 24 to 26 inches; bitches no more than 2 inches less; height deviations are not tolerated as larger or smaller dogs lack in field performance ability. Weight for dogs 55 to 75 pounds; for bitches 45 to 64 pounds. The head is moderately long with rounded ears hanging close to head; medium stop; fairly long muzzle; dark brown nose (spotted and flesh-colored noses are penalized); lips somewhat pendulous. Neck is medium length and slightly arched; back sloping to croup; chest deep; tuck up apparent; tail set high and docked to about two-fifths. Shoulders are well laid back; forelegs straight with close elbows; hindlegs moderately angulated and parallel. The outer coat is wiry, straight and harsh, flat lying about 1 to 2 inches in length. Short, smooth coats are severely penalized. Color is liver and white, spotted, roaned or ticked, or solid liver. In England black and white is acceptable; solid black and tricolors are penalized in both the U.S. and England.

A wire-coated gundog of immeasurable stamina and ability, the German Wirehaired Pointer revels in his multifaceted talents, not unlike his Shorthaired cousin. The breed was engineered to point, track and retrieve, combining the tasks of a whole kennel of Continental hunting dogs. OWNERS, RICHARD AND JUDITH ZALESKI.

OWNER SUITABILITY

An intelligent and amazingly versatile breed of hunting dog, the German Wirehair is a rugged worker and a biddable companion. Above all he is a people dog, and if his people are hunting people, he is happier yet. For a strongly driven hunter, though, he is remarkably calm indoors, if trained from his youth to abide by house rules. A good family pet who accepts other dogs, though not as willingly as some other hunting breeds since these dogs very typically work alone.

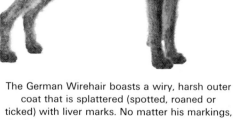

The German Wirehair boasts a wiry, harsh outer coat that is splattered (spotted, roaned or ticked) with liver marks. No matter his markings, he is a tough working dog and an affectionate home companion. OWNERS, JEFFREY AND LISA GEORGE.

172

GROWTH

By eight weeks, the German Wire-hair will weigh 15 pounds, and will continue to grow at rapid rate until four months. Properly balanced feeding, with some supplementation, is very important during these first four months. The full height of the German Wirehair is attained by ten months, and full maturity follows around two to three years. When choosing a puppy, note consistency of coat (problems ranging from shorthair to woolly coat reported) and especially temperament. GWPs should be very affectionate. The German Wirehair is not a kennel dog. Training should be firm and strict yet with gentle commands. The GWP needs reassurance or may become aggressive with other animals.

German Wirehairs grow at a healthy pace, though full maturity isn't reached until two to three years of age. OWNER, BERNEE BRAWN.

HEALTH

Although the German Wirehair stems from similar stock as the Shorthair, Wirehair breeders report few hereditary diseases in common with the GSP. Skin (especially cysts) and dental problems are their major concerns. Hip dysplasia, von Willebrand's disease, and eye problems such as entropion also should be considered. Bloat may possibly affect some Wirehairs. Owners must check regularly for ear infections and foreign matter in the eyes and ears. Grooming the wire coat necessarily involves stripping, which on a dog this size can be time-consuming. Diet and exercise should be regulated.

For a show puppy, the consistency of the coat should be considered, though temperament as always is the most important factor. OWNER, BERNEE BRAWN.

Due to the responsible ethics of Wirehair breeders, few congenital or hereditary problems are reported in this breed. Fortunately acquiring a healthy puppy does not present much difficulty for interested persons. OWNER, REGINA SCHWABE, DVM.

German Wirehaired Pointer

Giant Schnauzer

DESCRIPTION

A true working breed, nearly square in proportion, and the largest and most powerful of the German schnauzers, the Giant Schnauzer is a robust, active animal. He stands $25\frac{1}{2}$ to 27 inches for males; 2 inches less for bitches; medium heights are more desirable than over- or undersize. His head is strong and rectangular; skull moderately broad between the eyes; cheeks flat; muzzle strong and well filled under eyes; bite complete and scissors; ears cropped or uncropped, set high on skull. Neck is moderate in length and well arched; body compact and short coupled; shoulders flat and somewhat sloping, forming right angle for maximum extension; high withers; forelegs straight; brisket fairly deep; elbows set close to body. Chest is medium in width with well-sprung ribs, breastbone noticeable; tail set moderately high, docked to second or third joint. Hindquarters not overbuilt or higher than shoulders; stifles well bent; upper thighs well bent; feet catlike, well arched. Coat is hard, wiry and very dense, double-coated; coarse hair on top of head, with beard and eyebrows essential. Color possibilities are pure black or pepper and salt (black and white hairs, appearing grayish). Markings are highly frowned upon.

The very portrait of a home guardian, the Giant Schnauzer cuts a bold and valiant figure; his robust, strongly built frame and courageous, spirited disposition give him a winning edge as companion and protector. OWNERS, KEVIN E. SCHRUM AND KYLE STEIGERWALD.

OWNER SUITABILITY

A highly qualified guardian breed, the Giant Schnauzer is self-confident and perfectly suited for protection work. As a family animal, he also shines as he admires his human friends, though he is cautious of strangers. This is a playful spirit who can play pretty rough, so children must be closely supervised. Despite his natural dominance and territoriality, he doesn't have a mean bone but functions as a level-headed, thinking working dog.

A matter of taste in America, a matter of law in England, the natural or drop-eared Schnauzer possesses an appealing if less sharp appearance than his crop-eared *Bruder*. OWNER, NEU BERTAM.

174

GROWTH

The average litter size is seven, with larger litters common, resulting in whelps ranging from a mere 6 ounces to over 1 pound. Tails are docked to the second or third vertebra between two and four days. Removal of front dewclaws optional, but rear dewclaws, when they occur, must be removed, also between two and four days. Optional ear cropping is done between six and 12 weeks, depending on litter maturity and breeder practice. Giants undergo a rapid growth period starting around 12 weeks, continuing for several months thereafter. Owners must monitor growth and are advised to follow a prescribed diet, with possible supplementation. Note some reports of vitamin-B_{12} malabsorption. Adolescence is marked by the emergence of dominance and protectiveness, and these highly esteemed qualities must be properly channeled.

The puppy coat will also give way to the distinctive harsh coat, and stripping practices will begin. Giants attain their fully mature stature some time around two years of age.

Feed and exercise your fast-growing puppy with moderation. Too much too fast can only produce negative effects on a Schnauzer pup. OWNERS, KEN AND ROBIN GREENSLADE.

HEALTH

Although the Giant is subject to many diseases and conditions, most of these have been greatly controlled through responsible, limited breedings. Hip dysplasia and bad temperament are perhaps the greatest owner concerns, and HD screening and temperament testings should be requirements. Some Giants suffer from osteochondritis (a cartilage condition that results in lameness). Skin and digestive problems occur but in isolated incidence and not inherent in the breed. Eye problems such as retinal dysplasia have been reported though not common. Giants live on average ten to 12 years. Bloat can be a problem with this large breed, so owners are cautioned to provide plenty of water at all times, feed smaller meals, and limit exercise after all meals. Grooming involves very considerable stripping, and some clipping. Exercise requirements are high, and training from an early age a must.

The show Giant is an elegant and athletic dog. Proper conditioning and training require ample exercise space for a dog as long-limbed as the Schnauzer. OWNER, K. AND R. GREENSLADE.

Adopting a guard-dog breed requires more experience and understanding than a smaller breed with less potential to harm others. First-time owners need not apply. OWNERS, KEVIN E. SCHRUM AND KYLE STEIGERWALD.

Giant Schnauzer

Golden Retriever

DESCRIPTION

A working dog blessed with a rich, lustrous golden coat of a resilient quality and medium length, the Golden Retriever displays an intelligent and friendly expression, a dog of perfect symmetry, powerful, active and sound. The head is broad and gracefully arched with a well-defined, but not abrupt, stop; foreface is deep and wide. Eyes, conveying the breed's true personality, are medium large, well set apart, dark in color. Ears rather short and falling towards the cheeks. Bite must be scissors, full dentition with no obvious gaps. Neck is medium long and merges into well-laid-back shoulders; body short coupled, deep through chest; brisket extends to elbow; loin wide and deep, short, with little tuck-up. The Golden should never appear slabsided, narrow chested, with shallow brisket or excessive tuck-up. The tail is thick with good feathering underneath. The double coat is dense and water-repellent; outer coat is never silky or coarse but close-lying and either straight or wavy; natural ruff with moderate feather on back of forelegs and underbody. Coats must not be excessively long, open, limp or soft. Color varies but should never lack a rich tone (too pale or extremely dark); white markings or black hairs are not acceptable. Height for males 23 to 24 inches; females $21\frac{1}{2}$ to $22\frac{1}{2}$ inches; deviation of more than 1 inch in either direction is a disqualification.

As author Nona Kilgore Bauer calls her beloved breed, the Golden Retriever is truly "A Dog for All Seasons." Versatility and devotion define this breed, making the Golden ideally "A Dog for Life."
OWNERS, WILLIAM AND MARIE WINGARD AND JAMES AND PAMELA COBBLE.

The Golden Retriever's unabashed smile reveals that he has *never* met a stranger.

OWNER SUITABILITY

Ideal Golden owners are active, outdoor-oriented people who like to hike, jog, hunt, swim and who want a dog to share their lives with. Although the Golden spends considerable time outdoors, he loves being inside where he is an integral part of the home life. Goldens shed....and fastidious persons may not cope well with this amount of coat. He is foremost a retriever and therefore very orally fixated: the puppy will attempt to drag, pull and carry anything he can fit into his mouth. He also loves water, but proper introduction is necessary to not "dry up" his water instincts. The Golden is an intelligent breed who thinks probably too much, and may worry about his every move. This affects training, which must be undertaken with care and sensitivity. While the breed is gentle, he is not inactive and needs to be occupied. Essentially the Golden is a loving, all-around wonderful dog for a suitably caring, available owner.

Birth weight among Goldens varies. The seven- to eight-week-old should weigh 7 to 12 pounds. Owners should select for a sturdy pup with straight legs; clean, dense coats; black nose and footpads, and dark pigment around the eyes. Coat will darken with age. Breeders note that a good indicator of adult coloration is the color of the pup's ears. Females generally reach maturity around one year, males around two years. Both males and females typically attain their full-blown beauty and intellect by three years. Adolescent Goldens require great amounts of exercise, and regular outlets for their oral fixations. They also require supervision to keep mischief and danger to a minimum. Owners must guard against excess feeding and strive to keep their dog lean to prevent health problems. Basic training can (and likely should) begin as early as seven weeks.

Since most owners choose the Golden Retriever for its personality and family-dog appeal, temperament is the first criteria for all breeders. OWNER, JULIE. McKINNON.

Health

The Golden's tremendous popularity over the past few decades has led to a greater incidence of some canine diseases and conditions. Puppies should be selected only from HD-screened parents as hip dysplasia occurs too commonly. Eye problems known in the breed include entropion, ectropion, cataracts, retinal dysplasia, PRA, trichiasis, and distichiasis. Hereditary cataracts are also well documented and eye screening is an excellent idea. Von Willebrand's disease, which affects so many other breeds, also occurs in the Golden. Hypothyroidism, diabetes mellitus, subaortic stenosis, and epilepsy are also reported. Cancer claims an increasing number of Goldens' lives, and veterinarians note particularly leukemia, lymphoma, and bone cancer. While grooming is a simple matter, it must be performed regularly—shedding is year 'round. Goldens live to 12 years, though some experience their "golden" years to 16 or 17. Into their teens, their faces become gray or white.

Given the many possible congenital problems in the Golden Retriever, be selective and discriminate with your choice of a puppy. Screening the parents helps to ensure that your Golden live a long and healthy life with less risk of disease. OWNERS, LISA SMITH AND PAULA M. ASHBY.

A puppy's coat may darken with age; a rich, lustrous golden color is more desirable in a show puppy than is a light blonde color. OWNERS, ARTHUR AND CHERYL CARL.

Golden Retriever

Gordon Setter

DESCRIPTION

A clearly marked black and tan setter of substantial muscle and bone, the Gordon Setter is a stylish, active hunting dog of good size. Males stand 24 to 27 inches, females 23 to 26 inches at the shoulder. His characteristic head is rather deep and fairly heavy, chiseled finely to suggest the Gordon's elegance and dignity. Ears are low-set and fairly large, well folded and carried close to the head. The muzzle is fairly long and not pointed. Neck is long and lean without throatiness; topline moderately sloping; body short and chest deep. Tail is short with triangular feather, and placed correctly so that carriage is not too gay and "flags" properly. The quarters assembly provides for long strides and powerful drive. The coat is soft and shining, not curly but straight or slightly wavy; ears, stomach, chest and legs have longer hair. Dogs must be deep coal black with rich chestnut or mahogany markings.

The "black and fallow setting dog" we know today as the Gordon Setter hails from Scotland and is distinctive in appearance and character.
OWNERS, SUZANNE LACH AND MARY ANN ALSTON.

OWNER SUITABILITY

Intelligence naturally accompanies a dog's regal bearing and this well depicts the Gordon Setter. More strong willed than many hunting breeds, the Gordon requires considerable early training. His hunting instincts are strongly intact and he is easily distracted by pigeons and squirrels in the park. A sizable, athletic dog, he is an uncommon choice for apartment dwellers and boredom in a confined area is torture for the Gordon. On the whole, he is a gentle and friendly dog who delights in the company of children.

Intelligent and strong-minded, the Gordon is a thinking dog.
OWNERS, JOANNE VAN ALLER AND MICHELLE OSTERMILLER.

GROWTH

Litter size averages eight to 12. Weight between 10 to 12 ounces. Tan coloration is apparent at birth and deepens by eight weeks. Red puppies occur and can be registered but not shown and should never be bred. Metabolic rates and nutritional requirements vary within the breed. It is best to consult the breeder of the dog for specifics regarding feeding and supplementation, especially for the first year. An amazingly slow-to-mature dog, the Gordon may peak in physical beauty as late as six years, with the coat taking up to four years to reach maturity.

Since Gordons grow more slowly than many breeds, new owners must take care to provide an adequate diet. The puppy's breeder can give you the best idea of the needs of dogs from his line of Gordons.

HEALTH

The Gordon enjoys basic good health; the breed prefers plenty of exercise and training outdoors with its master. Because of its abundant coat, regular grooming is a must; the long drop ears may encourage ear infections. Pads should be checked weekly and kept free from excess hair. Guard against heat stroke. The common problems affecting other breeds affect also the Gordon, namely HD, PRA, and thyroid imbalance. A less common canine disorder known as cerebellar cortical atrophy is marked by failing coordination and an awkward gait—signs usually begin around six months of age. Because it is recessive, both parents must carry the trait, and known carriers should never be bred. Dogs suffering from this degenerative condition are most often euthanized. Veterinarians report cases of inherited retinal dysplasia. Life expectancy is over ten years.

The Gordon has a fair amount of coat for a sporting dog. The young puppy should become accustomed to a regular grooming regimen.
OWNER, SUE DREXEL.

Gordon Setter

Great Dane

DESCRIPTION

The wonder dog known as the Apollo of dogs for his great size, the Great Dane stands 32 inches (preferably) with females 2 inches less; the male must not stand less than 30 inches, the female not less than 28 inches. Provided the dog is well proportioned and maintains the Dane breed type, taller is favored. The Dane's head is rectangular, long and finely chiseled with a strongly pronounced stop. Eyes are medium in size and deep set; ears set high, medium in size, cropped or natural (cropped ears must be carried uniformly erect). The neck is firm and well arched; withers slope into a short, level back; forechest well developed; chest deep and broad; brisket extends to elbow; tail set high and tapering to hock joint (when excited or moving, the tail curves slightly). Quarters facilitate good reach and drive. The coat is short, thick and glossy. The Dane can be brindle, fawn (with black mask), blue, black or harlequin (white with black torn patches).

Who could imagine the elegant Great Dane of today aggressing a wild boar? Fortunately this dreary task is no longer set before the great German Mastiff and he enjoys life as a well-endowed guardian, companion and show dog. OWNER, TERRI LONCRINI.

OWNER SUITABILITY

Danes are big dogs....great big dogs. Although he doesn't know how big he really is, he is surprisingly gentle and nimble. Most owners say that Danes even do well in apartments. Thankfully he is even tempered and not aggressive, though with professional handling can be trained for

Great Dane puppies in blue, just one of the five acceptable colors in the breed. OWNER, DIANA BARTLETT.

protection work. He is also very sweet and truly adores children (who may think he is a pony!). Danes are essentially happy and easygoing: watch their tail wag (and remove the breakables from the endtables). For his good health and balanced psyche, regular exercise is a must.

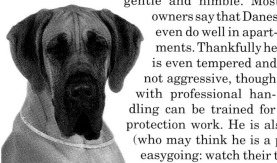

The natural falling ears (or drop ears) give the breed a softer, benign appeal. OWNER, CAROLYN DEAN.

GROWTH

Newborn Danes range between 12 and 24 ounces. Weaning is common by five to six weeks. By eight weeks, a weight of 20 to 25 pounds is to be expected. Danes experience a rapid growth period from four to about ten months of age. A top-quality food of moderate protein content should be fed. Do not supplement to push the already fast growth else you risk more growth and bone problems. Owners are strongly advised to feed a breeder/veterinarian-prescribed diet. Excessive feeding can lead to growth-stress problems. Breeders recommend regular veterinary checkups during this time to help monitor the dog's growth. Teething commences around two months and may affect ear carriage. Avoid calcium supplements. Danes attain physical maturity around two years.

HEALTH

Despite its great size, the healthy Great Dane demands little special care. Grooming and ear care are minimal. The Dane requires a fenced yard and a good diet, but the breed's mellow, gentle disposition lends itself to carefree daily walks and easy trainability. Unfortunately, the Dane suffers from many health problems that involve bones, eyes and skin—from tonsillitis to cancer

Due to the rapid growth periods during puppyhood, breeders strongly recommend a low-protein high-quality diet. Overfeeding and overexercise will badly stress a growing Dane pup.

to heart disease. Bloat is also a common problem. Hypertrophic osteodystrophy (HOD) can affect pups at around four months, through their fast-growing period. Heart problems may affect three or four year olds. Wobbler's syndrome can also affect the Dane's nervous system from three to 18 months of age. Hypothyroidism is another possible occurrence. Harlequin Danes may show a tendency toward deafness. Prospective owners absolutely must research the breed carefully before acquiring a Dane. Talk to breeders and owners; talk also to your veterinarian. Danes have a short, though varied, life expectancy, ranging from five to ten years. Breeders report dogs up to 14 years of age but acknowledge that these are exceptions. Danes over four years will require special diets that will have to be adjusted accordingly as aging continues.

In choosing a Great Dane you must be prepared to accept that the dog may not live as long as most other breeds. Your heart would be better to research and find the very best litter where the breeder's stock has been screened and the life spans of the grandparents are known.
OWNERS, TOM AND DEE MOONEY.

Merle puppies, though not acceptable by the standard, occur in some litters. Merles may suffer from deafness and perhaps other problems related to the potentially lethal merle gene.
OWNER, DOROTHY J. CARLSON.

Great Dane

Great Pyrenees

DESCRIPTION

As majestic as the mountains that give him his name, the Great Pyrenees or Pyrenean Mountain Dog (as he is known in England) surpasses the masses in size, beauty and elegance. His regal bearing, unwavering disposition and glorious white coat qualify his distinctiveness. The male Pyr stands from 27 to 32 inches and bitches from 25 to 29 inches. Weight according to height, 85 to 100 pounds. The wedge-shaped head with slightly rounded crown is perfectly proportionate to the dog and never heavy. Muzzle blends in smoothly with skull; cheeks are flat; no apparent stop; slight furrow between eyes. Eyes are medium sized and ears small to medium, rounded tips and V-shaped. Neck is medium length with minimal dewlap; back level; chest moderately broad. Tail reaches to hock and is well plumed. Shoulders well laid back, close to body; elbows close to body; forelegs straight; hindquarters well angled. The breed is double coated: outer coat coarse and straight, if a little wavy, over a dense woolly undercoat; ruff on neck and shoulders, pantaloons on legs. Coat must never be curly or stand-off. Color is solid white, or white with markings of gray, badger, reddish brown or tan (markings never covering more than one-third body).

Majestic, mountainous and snow white, the Great Pyrenees cuts a romantic European figure. He is as even tempered as he is beautiful, graced with kindness, strength and nobility.
OWNERS, GUY AND KAREN JUSTIN AND VALERIE A. SEELEY.

OWNER SUITABILITY

A strong figure cut on the top of a hillside barking with resonant confidence, the Great Pyrenees is "tops" as a watchdog. Today's Pyr, however, lacks the "I-can-pin-a-wolf" temperament and will more likely itch his nose on an intruder than bite him. He should be calm and must be socialized with people. Roaming is not an unusual complaint, as is shedding. With children whom he knows, he is gentle, though he can step on young ones accidentally. Aggressiveness towards other dogs is likely, though he's perfectly accepting of cats and other pets. Despite his grand size, he adapts well to small homes and doesn't need as much exercise as most mountain-sized dogs.

More commonly seen in European circles, badger and wolf-gray markings on the head (and possible body) are acceptable and characteristic.

GROWTH

Puppies weigh a hefty 1 to $1\frac{1}{4}$ pounds at birth. Pups are born white, except those having the badger markings, which are apparent very early on. Pups are born with pink nose, lips, and eye rims, which should be dark by eight weeks. Pups grow rapidly and at eight weeks females weigh 12 to 14 pounds, males 16 to 18 pounds. Full height is generally achieved by 18 months, though the dog may perhaps gain an inch or more. Despite the rapid growth, the breed is slow to develop, not reaching full maturity until three years or so. Owners should select for a pup bred from HD-cleared parents. Puppies should be self-confident, outgoing and responsive; a degree of independence is a breed characterisitic. Owner should look for a scissors or even bite, straight and par-

Fortunately the Pyr exhibits few temperamental problems. Most dogs are gentle and easygoing, adaptable to most lifestyles. Consider the good disposition of the dam when you select a puppy.
OWNER, LARRY HELMSTETLE.

allel front and rear (avoid cowhocks), and check the movement of the pup. There usually comes a time when the adolescent dog thinks he knows it all. Growth may be uneven at this time and growth spurts are common. Puppies generally will overeat, so owners should avoid overfeeding them—size will come in time. The adult coat change may come any time between six and 12 months and is usually influenced by the climate. The coat change may also be uneven and the dog may temporarily take on a ragged appearance. Typically the badger markings fade with age, except the wolf-gray markings, which remain dark throughout life.

HEALTH

The breed's large size and plentiful coat are certainly considerations. Grooming needs and feeding requirements are considerable. The breed's health, however, is very strong. Pyrs are highly resistant to disease and often live past 15 years of age. The major problems affecting the breed are bone and joint related, including HD, slipped patella (knee), achondroplasia (excess ossification of the long bones), and brittle bones. Blue eyes also occur. Less common are such problems as mono/cryptorchidism, deafness, and cleft palates. Owners are encouraged to examine lines carefully and to follow a breeder-prescribed diet, especially during the formative years. High-impact exercise should be limited.

The puppy's light badger markings on the head will fade with age. The Pyr's coat is extraordinary, as is the shedding. While the breed can thrive outdoors, it greatly admires human company.
OWNER, STEPHANIE A. WOLK.

Great Pyrenees

Greater Swiss Mountain Dog

DESCRIPTION

Large and powerful, the Greater Swiss Mountain Dog must appear sturdy and well balanced. This is a tall dog, standing $25\frac{1}{2}$ to 28 inches; females $23\frac{1}{2}$ to 27 inches. Color must be shiny black with glossy rust-red markings on cheeks, above eyes and on all four legs; white blaze symmetrical on muzzle and chest. The Swiss coloration rule is that red always lies between black and white. His head is flat and broad, with slight stop, and the skull and muzzle are of equal length. The eyes are medium in size and neither deep nor prominent; ears are medium, triangular and set high; lips clean; no dewlap. The neck is moderate and clean. The body length to height is 10 to 9; the back is moderately long and straight; chest deep and broad with slightly protruding breast bone. Tail is

Like his longhaired cousin the Bernese Mountain Dog, the Greater Swiss Mountain Dog waves the classic Swiss flag: black, white and red (the red *always* lies between the black and white).

fairly level and reaching hocks. Shoulders are long, sloping and strong; forelegs straight; withers high and long; croup long and broad. The coat is dense and 1 to $1\frac{3}{4}$ inches in length; undercoat thick.

OWNER SUITABILITY

An active, tall dog who needs considerable exercise time outdoors, the Greater Swiss Mountain Dog is described as an intelligent, friendly dog who makes an excellent companion. The breed is considerably rare though interest grows in the States and England. He is a good obedience worker and is "programed" as a helper. The breed presents few socialization problems, loves people and is even in temperament and never aggressive to people or shy to the approach of strangers.

The Swissy is placid and approachable. By origin and definition not a guard dog, the breed was developed to pull carts, to work in stables, and to herd on the farm. He is a competent watchdog though he lacks the instincts of the true mastiff breeds. OWNER, TERRY MEHLE.

GROWTH

A seven- to eight-week-old Greater Swiss Mountain Dog will weigh 18 to 20 pounds. Owners are encouraged to contact the parent club and research the breed before selecting their dog. Temperament qualities are important, and dogs should never be shy or aggressive. Exercise and training requirements are high from an early age—long walks are especially appreciated. Follow the breeder's prescribed feeding plan, as rapidly developing breeds may require low-protein diets and more frequent, smaller meals. A persevering cart puller, the Greater Swiss does best with early obedience training, puppy kindergarten and other forms of socialization.

HEALTH

This solidly boned dog enjoys relative good health, owing in part to its limited and responsible breeding. However, because its popularity is growing from a small breed base, owners should select carefully to better ensure soundness. The GSMD is prone to bloat—feed smaller meals a couple times a day. Adults eat less food than their size might connote. Check into bone development in the line, as HD, elbow dysplasia, osteoporosis, and joint abnormalities are potential problems. Swissies live eight to ten years, typically longer in healthy lines.

Socialization is the key to a GSMD breeder's program. Fortunately, due to the outstanding ethics of breeders, the GSMD is a confident, healthy canine with limited congenital concerns. OWNERS, JIM AND CHERI BARTON AND TERRY MEHLE.

Don't rush your GSMD through puppyhood. They grow quickly on their own so don't supplement and always limit protein intake during the formative months. OWNER, CATHERINE O. COOPER.

Greater Swiss Mountain Dog

Greyhound

DESCRIPTION

The symmetrically built Greyhound is of generous proportions with a long head and neck, capacious body, powerful quarters, arched loin and well-laid-back shoulders. The head is long and narrow with fair width between the ears; stop is nearly imperceptible. The ears are small and fine in texture, sometimes called rose shaped. The jaws are powerful and well chiseled. The eyes are oval and set obliquely; in color they are preferably dark. Shoulders are muscular with the appearance of being loaded. The forelegs are perfectly straight and chest is deep with well-sprung ribs. Loin is powerful and well cut up in the flanks. The hinds are very muscular with well-bent and let-down stifles. Feet are hard and close, described as more harefooted than catfooted. The tail is long and fine, tapering to a slight upward curve. The coat is short and firm in texture. Colors include black, white, red, blue, fawn, fallow, brindle or any of these broken with white. Weight for dogs is 65 to 70 pounds; bitches 5 pounds less.

Like a thoroughbred race horse, the Greyhound has no rivals as a professional wind hound and "speed merchant." His conformation perfectly enables his task: to run.
OWNERS, TAD W. AND ELLEN C. LOWDERMILK.

OWNER SUITABILITY

Greyhounds are the racehorses of the canine world, incredibly fast and aristocratic in carriage. More so, they are delightful dogs who can make great pets for a family or person willing to accept the responsibilities involved with the breed. He is a gentle dog, not necessarily high strung as has been reported; he is a child of the wind, which is to say when he roams he does so at 40 mph (and therefore must be fenced and supervised). Greyhounds retired from racetracks make wonderful, viable pets for the right dog person. These ex-professionals require much patience as they lack "pet" and socialization skills and are unfamiliar with domestic life (i.e., racetracks don't have doors, windows, steps, balls, or tables).

A gentle soul, the Greyhound is at once an affectionate, quiet house dog as well as an enduring athlete of untrackable stamina.
OWNER, LAURIE RENAUD.

GROWTH

Size at birth varies considerably but is generally one pound or more, with bitches generally smaller than dogs. Pups are born with proportionately long tails which they "grow into." Special care is required during early puppyhood to prevent tail injuries. Coloration is not considered in the standard, and Greyhounds can essentially be any color. Some colors will change with age. Greyhounds grow with good rate and generally reach full height by nine months of age. Development continues until as late as three years, when dogs are considered to be at their physical prime. Sexual maturity is often late in this breed, with some females not experiencing their first heat cycle until after two years of age. Adolescent Greyhounds are high-energy canines who require abundant physical activity and relish opportunities to sprint and run. Greyhounds should be kept lean and fed a proper diet.

Since most persons acquire Greyhounds as adult retired race dogs, few owners have the joy of seeing and raising Greyhound puppies. In fact only a handful of non-race-dog litters are whelped each year, compared to the hundreds of race-dog litters. OWNER, STACY POBER.

HEALTH

Possibly the most athletic of all domestic dogs, the Greyhound demands abundant regular exercise. A high-fenced (these dogs are great jumpers too!) open yard in which the dog can romp and run off lead is requisite. The breed has demonstrated sound health and freedom to such common problems as HD; however, short spines and esophageal malformations are documented. There seems to be a tendency in the breed to develop skin irritations of the tail. Greyhounds are known to be sensitive to drugs, particularly sedatives, in part due to their low body-fat content. Hemophilia A, marked by excessive bleeding, is also known. The most common complications suffered by the Greyhound are the result of injuries owing to the breed's explosive physical abilities. Life expectancy is about ten years; however, some ex-racing Greyhounds live only seven years, owing to the rigors of the track and possible use of steroids. Adopted rac-

The Greyhound boasts being the only full-size breed that is HD-free! Owners must be warned of the breed's sensitivity to drugs, including some heartworm preventatives and sedatives. OWNER, DONNA A. HESS.

When raised with people and other dogs, Greyhound pups mature into fun-loving, biddable companions. They are easily socialized and most adaptable to family life. OWNER, STACY POBER.

ing Greyhounds will need lots of dental care and Nylabones as their teeth are generally badly neglected—professional scaling at the vet can help douse the Greyhound's "dragon breath." Extra teeth are common in some Greyhounds. Young racing Greyhounds have proven susceptible to babesiosis, a tick-borne condition. Owners in the southern U.S. should be specially wary.

Greyhound

Harrier

DESCRIPTION

A large-boned scenthound who works in packs, the Harrier is a notably sturdily built hunting dog who is strong and tireless. The Harrier stands 19 to 21 inches (give or take an inch). Movement and coordination are of utmost importance for the Harrier, so soundness of the fore and hindquarter assemblies must be emphasized. The forequarters are moderately angulated with long sloping shoulders, with elbows set well away from ribs; front legs are straight with plenty of bone. The hindquarters balance the front, musculature well developed, capable of good reach and drive. The head nicely balances the dog; the expression is gentle, sensible yet alert. Eyes are medium in size and can be brown or hazel in color, darker colors preferred. Ears are good sized, set on low and lie flat to cheek.

Hail the Harrier, one the rarest recognized breeds in the world! Despite a long history as a working pack hound of England, today the Harrier works tirelessly for a very small fancy.
OWNERS, KENNETH AND MIRIAM NELL.

The coat is short and dense, glossy; the tail, which is long and set on high, has a bit of a brush on the underside, carried high. Colors vary as with all hounds.

OWNER SUITABILITY

An uncommon choice as a family dog, the Harrier is principally a working pack dog, a true hound dog. Nevertheless, the same attributes that acclaim the Beagle also recommend the Harrier. He is very family-oriented and likes to be counted in family activity. This is an easycare, easygoing dog who is light-hearted and affectionate. Harriers have a high pain tolerance and can take the tugging of toddlers. They have few problems with housebreaking and can make super-tidy housepets, though they are not for apartment dwellers. Active owners are ideal. Harriers do not need a heavy hand for training, and do not need to be corrected twice. They are independent as are other hounds and may exhibit potential hound-dog proclivities: howling and digging. Never banish your Harrier to the backyard—he needs love and attention, especially through adolescence.

Don't believe any other book! The Harrier is a great family dog and *can* live indoors. For some, he offers more than a Beagle, and certainly less problems. He is long-lived and gets an A+ on his bill of health!
OWNERS, KENNETH AND MIRIAM NELL.

GROWTH

At seven to eight weeks of age, Harrier pups are 9 to 10 pounds. By about nine months, a puppy has reached his maximum height, though not fully mature until 18 months. When selecting a Harrier puppy, avoid shyness and find the friendly, frisky one. Be prepared to wait for a litter, as breeders are reluctant to breed since demand for the breed is practically nonexistent. A show puppy should have good bone and substance: avoid tails curving over back, roachy toplines, slight muzzles and light eyes. Tricolored puppies may lose their dark saddles and become bicolored adults.

HEALTH

The Harrier is known (to those few who know it) as a very healthy and vigorous dog. While the incidence of HD in Harriers is limited, it is known to occur; no problems reported with eyes. Epilepsy and seizures have been known in the breed. The close, weather-resistant hound coat requires little grooming, though the ears should be cleaned weekly. Breeders have reported some dental problems, and owners should strictly follow a dental hygiene program. Regular exercise is vital to the healthy-minded Harrier.

Trainable and friendly, the Harrier outshines many rowdy hound types: he is even clean indoors, which you can't say for that "Snoopy" dog!
OWNER, BETTY M. BURNELL.

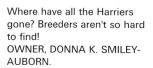

Where have all the Harriers gone? Breeders aren't so hard to find!
OWNER, DONNA K. SMILEY-AUBORN.

Harrier

Havanese

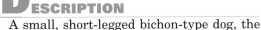

DESCRIPTION

A small, short-legged bichon-type dog, the Havanese is sturdy under his soft profuse coat. Havanese stand $8\frac{1}{2}$ to $11\frac{1}{2}$ inches without variation and move with a characteristic springy gait. The breed should not appear square and should appear longer than tall. Forelegs and hindlegs are short though the dog should not appear close to the ground. The head is of medium length and proportionate to body size. The eyes, large, dark and almond shaped, are the windows to the Havanese's soul, revealing his affectionate, gentle and happy nature. Expression greatly depends on the eye shape and color. Small or round eyes, or insufficient pigment, are incorrect. Topline is straight and rises slightly over the croup. Neck of moderate length; ribs well rounded; feet compact and well arched; tail set high and carried curled over the back with a long silky plume. The Havanese has a soft under and outer coat, which ranges from straight to curly. Curly coats may cord; wavy coats are desirable. The coat is never trimmed, except the feet which need to be neatened. Adult coats can reach 6 to 8 inches in length. Coat color ranges from pure white to shades of cream, champagne, gold, black, silver, chocolate or any combination of these (including particolors and tricolors). Adults weigh 7 to 13 pounds.

Communist contraband smuggled into democracy: meet the Havanese. Formerly Cuba's best kept secret, the Havanese, or Havana Silk Dog, derives from the same family as the Maltese and Bichon Frise, only he is more colorful! OWNER, LINDA COSNER.

Allergic to cigar smoke? The Havanese politely volunteers his services. Non-shedding and perfectly hypoallergenic, the Havanese proves fantastically pleasing—and prefers "non-smoking" too. OWNERS, JAMES A. AND KATHARINE R. RODGERS.

OWNER SUITABILITY

The Havanese epitomizes a happy dog, "puppylike" for all his days. Breeders recommend these perfectly sized house dogs for families with children as well as for the elderly. The breed demands human intervention and thrives on homebodies. The breed is odorless and does not shed: persons with allergies are prime candidates. Havanese are trustworthy off-lead, train readily and excel in obedience competition. When properly socialized and introduced to new people and environments, the Havanese is gentle and accepting. The breed inherently knows every child on the earth, though may be aloof and shy with unfamiliar adults. Although Havanese make easily trained indoor dogs, they have some unexpected outdoor abilities: they are hardy swimmers and love the water; they can herd small animals (or young children); and they make excellent trick dogs.

GROWTH

Havanese puppies require gentle handling and protection. Puppies at eight weeks of age may weigh 2 pounds. Eight weeks is the minimum age that a Havanese should be released to a pet owner. Potential owners must avoid shy puppies as well as litters that are overly inbred. The puppy coat begins to be replaced by the adult coat at around eight months. Although the puppy coat may tend to tangle, typical of most breeds that experience a coat change, the adult coat requires less maintenance. Some woolly coats may tangle even as adults. Color changes should be expected from black puppies (which may turn to silver), and darker colored puppies may become lighter and then darken once again with age. Maturity is reached between 15 and 16 months. Breeders recommend a quality food throughout the dog's life.

Choose a hot-blooded Havanese puppy who likes people. A shy puppy can develop into a fear biter and be a difficult adult to handle.
OWNERS, ELIZABETH VARGO AND LINDA COSNER.

The Havanese puppy's coat is more prone to tangling during its coat change. The young puppy's soft coat should be brushed a few times weekly to accustom the dog to a grooming routine.
OWNER, I. HANIN.

HEALTH

The Havanese is an impressively healthy dog with few health problems. Once the puppy is old enough to go home (eight weeks), he should be fairly hardy. All toy puppies are sensitive and somewhat fragile given their wee size. As with other bichon dogs, breeders screen for juvenile cataracts and PRA though the incidence in the breed is not alarming. Exercise requirements are easily met and the Havanese is lively and active throughout the day, inside and outside the house. Dogs should be groomed three times weekly, and the coat is easy to take care of. Life expectancy is 14 to 16 years.

With puppy faces like these, is there a question why the Havanese is making such a huge splash in the pet world?
OWNER, ELIZABETH VARGO.

Havanese

Ibizan Hound

DESCRIPTION

The deerlike Ibizan Hound possesses the jumping ability and ear carriage of a jack rabbit (his part-time quarry) and yet the true nose of a scenthound, although counted among the sighthounds. This elegant dog stands tall (often on his hind legs); on his fours he is $23\frac{1}{2}$ to $27\frac{1}{2}$ inches at the withers, females stand $22\frac{1}{2}$ to 26 inches. He weighs 50 pounds, 5 pounds less for bitches. His ears, clean cut lines and pale "lion" coloration purchase his uniqueness. His head is long and narrow, shaped like a sharp cone truncated at the base, according to the American standard. His large and pointed ears, never drooping, bending or creasing, are highly mobile. The neck is long and slender; back level and straight; chest deep to elbow; croup only slightly sloping; tail low-set, reaching hock, and carried in a sickle, ring or saber position. Forequarter angulation is moderate and the shoulders are never loose but elastic and well laid back. Hindquarters well under body; hocks straight. Ibizans can be short coated or wirehaired, one to three inches in length. Color must be white or red, solid or in combination; red can be from the lion color (yellowish red) to a deep red. No other colors are allowed.

Although this elegant sighthound breed dates back to the pharaohs of Egypt, Spain claims the Ibizan Hound as a native breed.
OWNERS, LESLIE D. LUCAS AND GLEN E. BRAND.

OWNER SUITABILITY

Ibizans are elegant, intelligent dogs who are mild-mannered and good companions. Exercise for their long legs is required to keep the Ibizan in shape and happy. He is rather independent and doesn't call for much coddling. Like other sighthounds, he is prey-oriented and will chase a passing cat (a couple city blocks away) so a lead is required on walks. He is obedient though training is required from the start, since he is a dog of ideas and strong will. He is a pleasure indoors and has no doggy odors.

Giving the Ibizan a different look is the wirehaired variety. The adult is covered in a length of one to three inches with a possible generous mustache.
OWNER, FERNANDO GONZALVO RAMON.

192

Growth

Most Ibizans begin life weighing about 14 ounces. The red coloration darkens with age. Ibizans grow rapidly, weighing about 15 pounds by eight weeks, and generally reach full height by one year of age. Full development is not complete, however, until as late as three or four years. A coat change does not occur, other than normal shedding. Ears should be erect by six months. Proper nutrition is vital, and supplementation commonly advised. Young Ibizans require a lot of exercise to keep them happy and growing properly. Owners must pay particular attention to socialization to avoid introverted, aloof, and shy or fearful dogs, which can be dangerous. Sexual maturity for females may be as late as two years of age, or even as early as eight months.

Ibizans, like most other sighthounds, require a special owner. Even as puppies, these are sensitive dogs that require a gentle, loving hand, plenty of exercise time and space, and an owner who appreciates the breed's aloof but noble disposition. OWNER, PAMELA LUTHER.

Health

The Ibizan breed is blessed with a natural, thus far unspoiled, conformation, and a small dedicated fancy. Serious hereditary problems are very rare—HD is rarely reported. Nonetheless, puppies should come from certified and clear breeding stock. Owners report skin problems, including juvenile acne and rashes. This breed is best kept in ultra-sanitary quarters and regularly groomed, despite its easycare short coat. As with other sighthounds, caution with anesthetics and flea dips is advised. The breed's great speed and strength, coupled with its slim, low-fat build, can lead to injuries, especially dislocations and torn ligaments. The Ibizan deserves plenty of exercise and human contact, otherwise the breed may become shy and removed, and deteriorate physically. Ibizans commonly reach the 13-year mark.

Ibizans aren't too graceful as puppies. They experience a gangly stage when they appear to be all leg! Full height is achieved by one year, though the rest of the body may take up to four years to mature. OWNER, LAURA CANO VILLASECA.

Count the Ibizan among the "ear" breeds. The ears *erectus* can be expected by the sixth month, in many cases before. Often teething interferes. OWNER, BILL MULLER.

Ibizan Hound

Irish Red and White Setter

DESCRIPTION

An attractive gun dog, the Irish Red and White Setter is a powerful, athletic dog without sign of lumber or raciness. The head is domed without occipital protuberance like the Red Setter, and the stop is noticeable; muzzle fairly clean. The eyes are hazel or dark brown; ears level with eyes close to head; neck is moderately long, not too thick or throaty. Shoulders well laid back; elbows free; deep chest; hindlegs muscular; stifle well bent; hock well let down. The tail is strong at root and tapering. The coat is fine in texture with feathering, wavy but not curly is acceptable. Particolor pattern of pearl white with solid red; mottling and flecking acceptable, not roaning. Dogs stand $25\frac{1}{2}$ to 27 inches; bitches $23\frac{1}{2}$ to 25 inches.

An old Irish tradition is the Setter in Red and White, though never as popular as the Red Irish Setter. Other than coat coloration, the breeds are much the same.

OWNER SUITABILITY

Sweet and good natured, the breed shares all of the good characteristics of its solid-colored brother, the Irish Setter. He is eager to please and must be instructed how to do so. Bad habits can develop from the dog who is not well adjusted to apartment living. Be firm and loving and this dog will hold you in utmost esteem. Although the hunting instincts are less strong than in days gone by, he is still a competent hunter and functions well in the family unit.

Growth

Litter size varies in the breed, as does whelp weight, which ranges from eight to more than 20 ounces. Pups are generally born white with red markings, which may vary in darkness and generally deepen with age. Red and Whites may occur in Irish Setter litters, since the two breeds derive from the same breed base. In general the breed is slow to mature both physically and mentally; sexual maturity may also come later in the bitch's life. Irish Red and White pups are known to be excellent though indiscriminate eaters, and owners must guard against overfeeding. As with other slow-to-mature, rapid-growing breeds, Irish Red and Whites should be fed according to a breeder-prescribed diet and exercised regularly, though not excessively, until maturity.

With the proper socialization and training, the Red and White adjusts well to family life and is a contented, placid companion animal.

Health

Genetically, the Irish Red and White derives essentially from the Irish Setter, though today certain conformational differences can be noted. Therefore, the Red and White is subject to the same problems affecting the Red. Most importantly, the slowly maturing Irish Setters are subject to bone and joint problems. Breeders should be aware of these problems and screen for them—especially HD. Offering an approved diet of the breeder or veterinarian is helpful, as many of the breed's bone problems can be diet related. Prospective owners should also inquire about eye problems, particularly cataracts, and be cautious in the use of chemical preparations. Life expectancy up to 12 years.

The Red and White Setter has not made his way across the Atlantic in any great numbers, though there are a fair number of dogs in Great Britain. OWNER, SUZANNE HUMPHRIES.

Irish Red and White Setter

Irish Setter

DESCRIPTION

Substantial yet elegant, the Irish Setter presents a portrait of aristocracy colored in a rich mahogany. Standing 27 inches at the withers, 2 inches less for bitches, and weighing 70 pounds, 10 pounds less for bitches. The coat is of moderate length, except on head and forelegs where it's short and fine. The head is long and lean and its beauty is heightened by delicate chiseling along muzzle, eyes and cheeks. The skull is oval, appearing very slightly domed in profile. Neck is moderately long, not thick or throaty. Tail is

The Irish Setter endures as a dog of stature and grace. Few can dismiss the beautiful show Irish Setter, larger and more abundantly coated than field dogs.
OWNERS, RANDY KUBACZ AND MRS. JEAN ROCHE.

fringed and set on nearly level and tapering. Body sufficiently long; chest deep; loins of moderate length. Quarters at sufficient angles and balanced to accommodate a big lively trot, with smooth drive and power. Legs are straight and sinewy; feet rather small and firm.

OWNER SUITABILITY

Having endured the wave of popularity, the Irish Setter has returned to its steady four feet and is a good choice for a sweet, affectionate member of the sporting group. He is elegant and beautiful and acts like a gentleman, preferring the country to the city life. Exercise is key to a balanced temperament. Firm training is required to convince this very smart dog what's what and who's who. He is a loving companion for children and likes to spend time indoors after a good afternoon jog or walk.

Training the young Irish Setter for show should begin at an early age. White spots on the chest, less desirable in the adult, usually disappear on the puppy and should not affect a buyer's decision.
OWNERS, ELAINE AND MICHELLE DE CHAMBEAU.

Litter size varies greatly, from one to 12. Thus, whelp weight varies also, from 8 to over 20 ounces. Coloration of the pups also varies, from dark mahogany to light fawn. Color changes are to be expected, and true adult coloration doesn't emerge until the adolescent coat change. In general, the breed is slow to mature both physically and mentally, with three years common. Sexual maturity may come as late, with some bitches not experiencing their first heat until age three. There seems a notable difference between the development of field and non-field dogs, with the former being smaller, growing more slowly, and maturing more quickly. Irish Setters should be fed a breeder-prescribed diet and exercised regularly throughout the growth period. It is important for owners neither to overtax nor to underwork their dogs during the developmental years.

Puppies are sweet natured and carefree, characteristics that last through adulthood. OWNERS, KENN AND JOAN SADLER.

HEALTH

Grooming and ear care are moderate but very important, as ear and skin infections are well known. Breeding stock should be temperament tested, and puppies should experience early socialization and training. The Irish Setter experienced tremendous popularity during the 1970s, during and after which health and temperament problems surfaced. However, in recent years, many of these problems have been eliminated. Hip dysplasia still affects the breed, and screening is a must. Other common problems also affect the skeletal system, including osteodystrophy, osteochondritis and rickets, all of which appear during the growth period. Eye problems, particularly cataracts, including juvenile cataracts, make screening necessary. Short tails and kink tails are the more common birth defects and can be easily observed. Hypothyroidism, re-

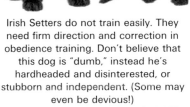

Irish Setters do not train easily. They need firm direction and correction in obedience training. Don't believe that this dog is "dumb," instead he's hardheaded and disinterested, or stubborn and independent. (Some may even be devious!) OWNERS, KENN AND JOAN SADLER.

Temperament is next to godliness, and Irish Setter breeders have been kneeling at the altar of socialization for decades. Most pups will have people-positive, outgoing personalities. OWNERS, ELAINE AND MICHELLE DE CHAMBEAU.

production problems, bloat, and tumors affect the breed. Irish Setters are known to be sensitive to penicillin and chemical preparations, including antibiotics, and your veterinarian must be aware of this. Veterinarians report breed members with vascular ring anomaly and wheat-sensitive enteropathy (affecting the small intestine). Irish Setters live ten to 12 years.

Irish Setter

Irish Terrier

DESCRIPTION

Wiry in movement and wiry of coat, the Irish Terrier is a dog built for action, a dog with great animation, and a dog with a "heedless reckless pluck." The head is long, though in proportion, with a rather narrow, flat skull, not thick. Jaws are strong, sufficiently long, and not cheeky. Bumpy heads are faulted. The coat should be dense and wiry, with a broken appearance, with a sensible beard not overdone like a billy goat's. Neck of fair length; shoulders fine and long; body moderately long; back not short but straight and strong, not dipping; legs moderately long and perfectly straight with good bone; hocks near the ground. Tail should be docked by about one quarter, set high and uncurled. Color should be whole colored in reds or wheaten; white chest mark permissible; adults should be free of black hair. Desir-

He's been called the Daredevil and has more pluck than a chicken farm. He's red, rough and ready and has been badgering the vermin of Ireland for centuries: he may have even helped Saint Pat with the snakes....or was it the Piper? OWNER, STAN WOJEWODSKI, JR.

ably the Irish Terrier is a moderately sized dog weighing 27 pounds for dogs, 25 pounds for bitches; shoulder height is 18 inches.

OWNER SUITABILITY

A fearless daredevil of a terrier, the Irish Terrier is a less common choice as a companion or show dog, though he has much to recommend him. He is still a functional terrier, able to take on vermin with the best of them. Loyal and devoted to family, he is an eager participant in the household business. Digging comes naturally and his healthy portion of pluck can make him boisterous at times.

The standard describes the breed "of good temper, most affectionate, and absolutely loyal to mankind." The breed's terrier instincts are fully intact, and owners must be tuned in to the dog's burning desire to pursue its perceived "adversaries." OWNERS, MARK ESKRIDGE AND REJEAN CHARLEBOIS.

Newborns generally weigh around 8 ounces. Growth is typically even and without complication. Dewclaws should be removed and tails docked by four days. Tails should be docked to two-thirds to three-quarters length. Ear carriage is important in the breed standard, and owners may likely have to tape (or "glue") the ears in proper position until as late as one year of age. A breeder or breed-specialist groomer should be consulted and called to assistance for ear setting.

Young Irish Terrier pups are busy and inventive, giving mom the job of keeping them out of trouble. They are fond of people and socialization is a joy. OWNER, MAUREEN MOSKOWITZ.

HEALTH

The Irish Terrier finds life a breeze. The breed is a relatively problem-free dog with very few documented problems. Breeders report that skin problems are a major concern, and that regular grooming can control these problems, though excessive bathing can aggravate these conditions. Cystine stones, affecting only males, occur in the breed—painful urination is one telltale sign. The terrier family as a whole has shown a predilection to adrenal tumors, though this has not been documented in the Irish Terrier. The breed is a great all-weather companion who thrives on exercise. Firm consistent training is best for the breed, the males of which are naturally aggressive toward other males.

The breed's eyes gain a piercing glance with adulthood. Intelligence and pluck already fill this young pup's eyes. OWNER, MAUREEN MOSKOWITZ.

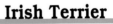

Irish Terrier

Irish Water Spaniel

DESCRIPTION

A loose curly topknot atop a smooth, inquisitive face, the Irish Water Spaniel sports a perfectly balanced frame adorned in crisp liver-colored curls and wags a distinctive rat tail. He is a smart and rugged sporting dog with a cleanly chiseled head, not cheeky, with a large domed skull and gradual stop. The ears are long and abundantly covered with curls. Neck long and arch-

Beneath those crisp liver curls is a robust, strongly built sporting dog. The Irish Water Spaniel thrives on vigorous play and exercise—preferably in the water with a fun-loving owner.
OWNERS, GREGORY M. SINER AND MARCY ROSE.

ing; shoulders sloping; topline strong and level; body of medium length; chest deep; ribs well sprung. The forequarters appear strong and not heavy; forelegs are well boned and medium in length, with sufficient upper arm length for good reach; elbows close in. Rear legs are sound for good swimming power. Coat is necessarily double and abundant all around with dense, tight, crisp ringlets; hair tends toward a natural oiliness. The color is always solid liver, described by the British standard as a "rich dark liver with purplish tint or bloom." Dogs stand 22 to 24 inches, bitches 1 inch less; dogs weigh 55 to 65 pounds, bitches 45 to 58 pounds.

If you wake up to this topknot, you better be ready for an active day.
OWNER, LANDOWSKI.

OWNER SUITABILITY

A fun-loving sporting breed whose distinctive appearance and similarity to the Poodle win him many admirers. He is a natural water athlete and needs an active owner. The Irish Water Spaniel demonstrates great loyalty to his owners, though is less inclined to warm up to unfamiliar people. Children must be instructed to give this quick-thinking, independent dog his space.

GROWTH

Pups are often born with white spots on the chest and toes. These should disappear by six to eight weeks. (White markings are undesirable in the adult.) Eye color may be a pale or light green that should darken to the desirable hazel by maturity. With both of these matters, owners should avoid the extremes when choosing their dog, selecting for the least white and the darker eyes. Development of the Water Spaniel's classic coat begins around four to five months of age. Full adult coat and topknot are usually apparent starting around ten months to one year. Owners should expect to spend plenty of time working and exercising the adolescent, and begin basic obedience training at a young age.

HEALTH

Breeders have long upheld the Irish Water Spaniel, and this good care has contributed to the breed's excellent health and relative freedom from congenital and hereditary conditions. A minor incidence of hip dysplasia, malocclusions of the teeth and a hereditary condition known as patterning (marked by a "patterned" loss of hair) affect the breed. Proper regular grooming is the most vital concern, as the coat tends to mat, resulting in skin irritation. Also, this dense curly coat can easily conceal parasites such as ticks and fleas. Grooming must include trimming the hair in the ears and between the toe pads to prevent infection. The IWS can suffer from a chronic disease that affects their toenails and is often signaled by limping. The Irish Water Spaniel is a high-energy breed with a fearless approach to life. Early channeling of its instincts to training and retrieving greatly contributes to raising the most companionable animal. Lifespan is ten to 12 years.

For show purposes, choose a puppy with good dark pigmentation, a minimum of white spots on the coat, and eyes that are not too light.

A well-trained Irish Water Spaniel contributes to the family's fun and good spirits. Teach the IWS right from wrong early on: he is fearless and inventive—too much freedom can lead to problems.
OWNERS, SUSAN G. ANDERSON AND CAROLYN LANTHROP.

Irish Water Spaniel

Irish Wolfhound

DESCRIPTION

A great-sized, rough-coated Greyhoundlike breed, the Irish Wolfhound stands 32 to 34 inches at the shoulder, with proportionate body length, making him the tallest dog in the world. His sight is keen and his power and swiftness most impressive. The head is long with a not-too-broad skull and a long, moderately pointed muzzle. Overall the head should be neither too heavy nor too light. The ears are small and carried thrown back and folded in repose or semipricked when excited. Neck is rather long, well arched without looseness or dewlap. Chest very deep; back rather longer than short; tail long and slightly curved; belly well drawn up. Forelegs are heavily boned and quite straight; elbows set well under; thighs long and muscular. Coat should be rough and hard, particularly wiry and long over eyes and under jaw. Feet should be moderately large and round. Colors, of little importance, include gray, blue-gray, brindle, red, black, pure white, fawn, and yellow.

The tallest dog in the world sports a rough coat, keen eyesight, and a quiet, docile manner. The male stands no less than 32 inches at the shoulder. OWNERS, RICHARD AND LINDA BELUSCAK.

OWNER SUITABILITY

Lovely, gentle tempered, Irish-happy-go-lucky, protective, and biddable all wrapped up in a tidy 34-inch package! Who can deny that space must be an initial requirement for the Wolfhound: he needs to run and exercise. Nevertheless, he does fine in smaller homes, as he is level-headed and calm indoors; and his food requirements are not as demanding as one might expect from a giant. Children love him and he responds well to them, though he isn't terribly conscious of his bigness, especially during play. They are not naturally aggressive and pay heed to an owner's convincing command.

These toddlers are too young to go to their homes yet. Reputable breeders do not release Wolfhound pups until they are about 12 weeks of age. OWNER, JAMES FOWLOW.

GROWTH

Small litters are common. Average whelp weight is $1\frac{1}{2}$ pounds for dogs, slightly less for bitches. Puppies average 22 pounds at seven to eight weeks. Irish Wolfhounds grow very quickly, making proper feeding and exercise of great importance throughout the developmental years. Puppies should not be crated but allowed freedom of movement at all times (not throughout the house of course), which can complicate housebreaking. Wolfhounds require a lot of nutritious food but may lose interest in food during growth spurts. Owners must ensure that they receive the vital nutrients. Breeders recommend feeding as many as five meals a day for the first year, at which time full height is usually attained. Full maturity is not reached until three to four years. During adolescence, the coat will become coarse and color may change dramatically. The ears, however, should not change. Owners should strive to maintain a Wolfhound that is friendly and outgoing through proper socialization.

The Wolfhound's life expectancy seems but an exponent of his inches: choose your puppy carefully, research the line, maintain contact with your breeder, and find a veterinarian whom you trust.
OWNER, JAMES FOWLOW.

HEALTH

The Irish Wolfhound poses some very serious health concerns. The breed's astronomical growth rate demands a prescribed diet; HD, metabolic bone diseases, and other bone/joint disorders are quite common. Wolfhound puppies should not be crated but allowed roaming ground to help prevent some skeletal problems. Tail injuries and sinus infections are also more common in the Wolfhound than in other breeds. By far the most important owner concern is the Wolfhound's short life expectancy, with males averaging only about five to six years and females six to seven. Bloat, cancer, and heart disease claim the most lives. Proper diet and exercise can reduce the risk of bloat, and careful research and inquiry into breed lines can limit the occurrence of cancer and other diseases. Medicating the Wolfhound requires special knowledge—prescribing by weight alone is dangerous. They are also subject to rhinitis (runny nose).

Given the rapid growth in the breed, Wolfhounds should not be confined in a crate but given room to stretch their ever-growing limbs.
OWNER, LYNN COX.

Litter size in the Wolfhound varies a great deal, from a single puppy to 12 pups. All pups require much of an owner's time and attention, needing to be fed four to five times daily through the first year.
OWNER, JAMES FOWLOW.

Irish Wolfhound

Italian Greyhound

DESCRIPTION

The petite Italian Greyhound is said to look like a Greyhound except smaller and more slender in all proportions. The head is narrow and long, tapering to the nose. Muzzle is long and fine. The eyes are dark and medium in size. Ears are small, fine to the touch, and carried folded at right angles when alert. Ears must not be erect or button shaped. The teeth should meet in a scissors bite (badly under or overshot is faulted); full dentition desirable. The neck is long and slender, with a graceful arch. Body is short coupled of medium length, high at withers, with a curved back and a droop at hindquarters. The tuck-up at flanks is created by the highest point of curve beginning at loin. The shoulders are long and sloping; chest deep and narrow. Forelegs are long and straight, well under shoulders; hinds are long and parallel. His gait is high stepping and both front and hind legs move forward in a straight line. Tail is slender and tapering; feet are hare with well-arched toes. Coat is short with a glossy, soft touch. Colors include black, blue, cream, fawn, red or any of these with white; solid white. Black or blue with tan markings (suggestive of another breed) and brindle are not acceptable. Average weight is 8 pounds, though dogs can vary from 5 to 15 pounds; height ideally is 13 to 15 inches.

Lovingly underfoot, this true toy dog comes from a long pampered history in Italy where it was known as the *Piccoli Levriere Italiani* (meaning Small Italian Greyhound).
OWNERS, JAMES R. BRAY, MD AND SCOTT R. THOMPSON.

OWNER SUITABILITY

The pint-size IG is ideal for small apartments and a great family dog who will interact with household members, though maintain a special loyalty to his chosen member. IGs are great with kids, though supervision is necessary simply because IGs are so small and easily injured. Young pups should never be handled by children. For their size, IGs are quite durable and agile, able to run, climb and leap exceptionally. They are also not overly shy and display excellent friendly dispositions and showmanship in the ring.

Cave canem: beware the dog! Some believe that this famous Latin motto originally wasn't intended for guard dogs, but instead warned people to beware not to *step* on the fragile Italian Greyhound.

GROWTH

For their size, IGs produce rather large litters, with four or five 3 to 7 ounce whelps the average. By eight weeks pups should weigh about 3 pounds and at least begin to show proper ear carriage. Owners should select for sturdy and robust dogs who are responsive, outgoing, and affectionate. IGs develop quickly and may attain full height as early as six months or as late as one year, though they will continue to add substance for another six to 12 months. Skull and jaw development may also continue until about two years. Adolescent IGs are notoriously good eaters for their size and require small feedings throughout the day for proper development and to avoid a hyperglycemic state. Breeders note that Italian Greyhounds generally are more demanding to housebreak than other breeds. Proper and consistent socialization is important to prevent shyness and general reluctance towards strangers.

HEALTH

The Italian Greyhound is among the healthier of the toy breeds, with few congenital and breeding problems. Breeders are greatly concerned with thyroid problems in the breed. Both underactive (with accompanied hair loss) and overactive thyroids occur. The problem is usually not evident until after one year of age and is usually treatable with medication. All breeding stock should be screened for thyroid. Improper dentition (overshot, undershot, crooked and missing teeth) is common, as is receding gums. Prospective owners should carefully check the IG's teeth. Daily gum massage and dental prophylaxis are strongly recommended. Breeders warn of leg fractures, especially common during the formative years. Grooming is minimal, and skin and ear infections are not common problems. Some IGs are susceptible to anesthetics, flea dips and other insecticides. Long-lived, IGs often reach 15 years or more; the average is 12.

Learning to walk for an IG just isn't as easy as "one foot in front of the other." Mom spends much of her day moving puppies about and setting them up on all teetery fours.
OWNER, SUSAN PINKUS.

Don't spoil your baby IG once he gets home. No matter the size of your chosen breed, housebreaking and training are equally important. IGs aren't as easy to housebreak as some other breeds.
OWNER, SUSAN PINKUS.

Italian Greyhound

Jack Russell Terrier

DESCRIPTION

Active and alert, the Jack Russell Terrier is a working terrier of medium size and apparent strength and endurance. The dog stands 12 to 14 inches. The head should be well balanced and of moderate width, narrowing to the eyes, not cheeky. Eyes are almond shaped and small, not protruding, and dark in color. The ears are small and V-shaped, of moderate thickness, button; nose must be completely black (and not brown, white or liver). Neck is clean and sufficiently long to balance the dog; shoulders long and sloping; chest narrow and moderate in depth; back strong and straight; tail set high, strong and carried gaily, not over back, curled, or like a squirrel. Forelegs are strong and straight; hinds smoothly molded with good angulation and bend of stifle. Coat is either smooth or rough: smooth coats have flat but hard hair; roughs are double coated with dense undercoat and coarse wirelike top coat. The color should be predominantly white with black or/and tan markings.

This manly little terrier named for his creator, Parson Jack Russell of Devon, England, derived in the early 19th century to hunt foxes on horseback with his master. The workmanlike JRTs have also been popular show dogs, having participated in England's first dog show in 1862.
OWNER, MICHELE REILLY.

The wire-coated Jack Russells have a coarse top coat and a dense undercoat. Like the smooth coats, they are rugged, individualistic dogs with brains to match their gumption.

OWNER SUITABILITY

Hardy and adaptable, the Jack Russell is an outgoing family dog who is excellent with children and adults alike. They are not snappy or hyper, though they need a firm hand to absorb the house rules. Quick as spitfire, JRTs are high-energy, unspoiled working dogs, who love people, horses and other dogs (though some may be aggressive towards other dominant dogs). Naturally they are diggers and quite inquisitive, many tending to roam. City owners should be wary of traffic as these little dogs can bolt in a wink, and never look up while on a scent.

Growth

Jack Russell Terriers should weigh approximately 3 pounds at seven to eight weeks. Full height is usually attained by one year, though physical and mental maturity take 18 months or more to develop. Prospective owners should select for a healthy-looking, happy and well-adjusted puppy that displays good conformation to the breed standard. Owners should avoid those who are either too bold or too shy. Untypy characteristics to avoid include prick ears, bent legs, bad bites, and heavy coats. Adolescence is marked by the emergence of the dog's true character. Overall temperament should not change but proper breeding and socialization should become apparent in the young dog's development. Smooth coats often develop whiskers at this time and coat color may lighten, especially the black in tricolors.

The Jack Russell puppy should be happy-go-lucky and vigorous. Avoid heavy coats, bad bites, bent legs and prick ears if you are intending on exhibiting your puppy in shows.
OWNER, STRICKLAND.

Health

The JRT in general is a very hardy, healthy and well-bred dog. Feeding requirements are not demanding, but owners are encouraged to acquire a recommended feeding plan from the breeder. Exercise and training requirements are high to keep these hunters happy and healthy. Thanks to breeders' continuing to concentrate on the breed's utilitarian purpose and strong terrier instincts, the JRT has remained quite natural and exhibits no major hereditary conditions. Breeders report lens luxation and hereditary cataracts as two problems that occur and claim that these are primarily in unregistered lines. Owners are encouraged to attain eye-screening certification from the breeder. Patellar luxation (slipped knee caps) and myasthenia gravis (affects muscles) have also been reported in some lines. JRTs live 12 to 14 years and more.

Entertaining the JRT puppy is a full-time commitment. The only thing a JRT does faster than run is think! You have to wake up pretty early in the morning to stay ahead of the JRT.
OWNER, JANET FREDERICKS.

Puppyhood like life is too short.....take time to feel the flowers.
OWNER, JANET FREDERICKS.

Jack Russell Terrier

Japanese Chin

DESCRIPTION

Dainty and smart, the Japanese Chin is a distinct particolored toy breed with a broad, rounded skull and large, lustrous eyes. Petiteness in the Chin is next to godliness and the ideal size is 4 to 7 pounds. Dogs over 7 pounds are shown in a separate class. His coat is profuse, long and silky; it should not appear wavy, silky or flat. More commonly in black and white, the Chin can also be red and white; never tricolor or any other color. Red in the breed includes all shades of sable, brindle, lemon and orange. Markings on all coats must be evenly distributed. The body is described as cobby, of compact, square build, with a wide chest. The Chin's tail is characteristically well twisted and carried up over the back and profusely coated. The little Chin's head is grand and sits on a short, moderately thick neck. The muzzle is very short with a wide nose. Black and white dogs must have a black nose. The ears are small, V-shaped with good feathers. Eyes are dark and prominent, set wide apart. The dog tends to stand up on his toes; feet are somewhat long, small and profusely coated.

Representing the omnipotence of the Divine One in a single sleeve, the Japanese Chin conceals its ancient history and the wisdom of the Buddha.
OWNERS, HAROLD J. AND MARIE A. LANGSETH.

OWNER SUITABILITY

Ideal for a single owner or a family, Japanese Chin are a joy of a toy. The temperament is sweet and charming. Owners relay that this breed is sensitive, eager to please and, for such a peanut, has the memory of an elephant. Chin are taught, not trained, and always have an opinion, though they are not as easily spoiled as many other toy dogs. Socializing is ever important so that the breed's people-adoring personality comes out.

Despite the prudence of Chinese emperors, giving Chin as gifts would be frowned upon in today's politically correct society. What a shame: who could think of a more delightful, peaceable offering?!
OWNER, KIP KOPATCH.

GROWTH

Newborn Japanese Chin average 6 to 8 ounces at birth. Weight at seven to eight weeks should be $1\frac{1}{2}$ to 2 pounds, depending on the variety (under or over 7 pounds). Owners should select for good conformation and avoid frail pups and pups with overly prominent eyes. Breeders warn of the high potential for eye injuries to pups and encourage owners to question any scarring or teary eyes. Proper eyes should be clear and dark. Chin develop with good rate and few complications, reaching adult size by ten months, though the coat will continue to mature. Adolescence is marked by an extreme coat change in which the "fluffies" disappear and the dog can even appear quite naked for a period. Extra grooming will be required during this time. Chin are by nature sweet and charming companions, and owners should strive to maintain and develop these qualities through proper socialization and caretaking.

Chin puppies should be sturdy and not frail. Due to the high potential of eye injuries in the breed, avoid pups with overly prominent eyes.
OWNER, KIP KOPATCH.

HEALTH

The Chin enjoys a long life, commonly 13 or more years. Chin are excellent indoor companions and have reportedly few serious medical concerns. Some sources report a tendency toward spinal disc problems in middle-aged dogs. The Japanese Chin requires plenty of daily grooming to keep its coat healthy and clean, thus preventing skin irritations. Pads, eyes and ears require special attention. The hair between the toe pads must be kept trimmed to avoid irritation. The breed's large prominent eyes must be checked for scratches and foreign body intrusion, and the ears kept dry and free of excess hair and wax. The brachycephalic muzzle may present breeding difficulty if of faulty construction. Overheating must be guarded against. Fractured limbs are a common injury, owing to their fine construction—owners must ensure proper nutrition as a preventative measure. Dentition must also be checked for excessively undershot bites. Cramped teeth require special daily cleaning.

Choosing a Chin isn't always black and white: the breed comes in other appealing colors too, including reds, brindles, lemon and orange.
OWNER, KIP KOPATCH.

Japanese Chin

Japanese Spitz

DESCRIPTION

A handsome Nordic breed in a profuse pure white standoff coat, the Japanese Spitz bears an undeniable resemblance to the American Eskimo and Samoyed and for good reason, as all these breeds derive from similar stock. The Japanese Spitz stands 12 to 14 inches tall and has an alert and intelligent expression. The head is medium in size without coarseness, moderately broad and slightly rounded. The muzzle is pointed but not too long or thick. The nose and eye rims should be black. The eyes are dark, oval shaped and set obliquely. The ears are small and angular, standing erect. The chest broad and deep; hindquarters well proportioned and moderately angulated. The tail is a full plume, moderate length and curled over back. The outer coat should be straight and standoff with a soft, dense undercoat: the whole body is covered with along coat and there is a visible mane on the neck and shoulders.

Looking for a snow beauty that everyone else in the park doesn't have? The Japanese Spitz may be just right to ski his way into your heart and home. He's half the size of the Samoyed and calmer than your average Eskie, the perfect apartment or igloo partner.

OWNER SUITABILITY

Although the Japanese Spitz has been known in England since the early 1950s, the breed has never truly caught on. He may be half the size of the more popular Samoyed but is every bit as sprightful and friendly as his snow cousin. His size makes him desirable as an indoor dog, though he thrives on the brisk outdoors. Why not be the first on your block to have this priceless spitz breed? He makes a marvelous choice for a home with children and his alert nature and big-dog bark serve him well as a watchdog. He is protective and fairly affectionate for a spitz dog. Good examples can be located in the States too.

GROWTH

The eight-week-old Japanese Sptiz weighs 5 to 6 pounds. These dogs mature quickly, reaching height and possibly full size by eight months. Owners should select for an outgoing puppy with clear, bright eyes having no signs of tearing or potential tear stains. Complete black pigmentation should be apparent at an early age. During the adolescent stage, generally six to eight months, a little dominance may emerge, and owners must ensure that the dog learns its proper place in the family. The fluffy puppy coat will drop out and be replaced by a stronger, whiter coat. Combing out the dead hairs greatly facilitates this changeover. The Japanese Spitz is really quite an undemanding breed and owners can expect few complications during the growth period. Breeders note that these dogs become barkers only if permitted; therefore, owners

The expression of the Japanese Spitz plainly reveals his alert and affectionate nature.

should take the prescribed precautions recommended by breeders and experienced owners.

HEALTH

Veterinary research on this lesser known breed is genuinely lacking. However, breeders

Keeping your white darling as pure as the driven snow requires considerable care. Be sure you are ready to commit to brushing the Spitz daily to keep his coat looking its snow-white best.

report that the breed is very free from debilitating hereditary conditions. One major breeder concern is patellar luxation. Other aspects of good health such as feeding and grooming are undemanding for the breed. Breeders report no specialized dietary needs. Shedding can be an owner's concern, greatly reduced by regular combing; however, bathing is needed infrequently. In such cases, dry dogs well to avoid possible hot spots. Breeders report that the coat is virtually self-cleaning. The breed's exercise requirement is moderate only.

Japanese Spitz

Keeshond

DESCRIPTION

The Keeshond is a medium-sized spitz in a wolf-gray coat, distinctive for the "spectacles" around his eyes, his ruff and his trousers. He stands 17 to 18 inches and is a well-balanced, short-coupled dog. Notable too are his foxlike expression and his small pricked ears, and his full-plumed tail curled over his back. The head is wedge shaped and should have a definite stop; the eyes are almond shaped and brown in color; ears are triangular and high on the head. Eyes should not be round or protruding, nor light in color; spectacles are an absolute must in a well-bred Keeshond; ears may not drop; apple heads are faulty as are misaligned teeth. The body is compact and the back is straight; forelegs are straight, with hinds complementing this angulation.

Naturally handsome and well dressed in his culottes and trousers, the Keeshond smiles with charm and bespectacled eyes.
OWNER, JOANNE REED.

The coat is abundant with long, straight, off-standing hair, complete with mane on neck, trousers on hind legs. Coat must not be silky, wavy or curly, with no visible part.

OWNER SUITABILITY

A perky, accommodating Dutch boy who is never as content as when he's near his people, the Keeshond fits into many living situations, country, city, on land or at sea. He is a rugged, sea-faring dog fully adaptable to a variety of climes, despite his full coat. Keeshonden love to play and children and other dogs are at the top of his list. He is bright and learns quickly, though his strong-willed nature makes a firm, loving hand necessary.

Unlike some other coated breeds, the Keeshond can never be clipped. If you're not into brushing your dog (and vacuuming your home), you may not want to take this nautical Dutch boy on barge.
OWNER, JANICE A. WANAMAKER.

GROWTH

Keeshonden begin life at 8 to 12 ounces. They possess short coats which are almost entirely black, with possibly white markings on the feet and chest. (Dewclaw removal optional but encouraged.) Shoulder markings should be apparent at birth or within a few days, and any white on the feet should disappear by eight or nine weeks. Also by eight weeks, a more abundant coat should be visible, with a light-colored undercoat and black-tipped outer coat. Lighter markings on the legs and feet, shoulders, tail and mane should also be apparent. Keeshonden will experience several coat changes by maturity, and grooming needs are very high throughout the developmental period. By ten months, most Keeshonden reach their full height and continue to add substance and coat until two or even three years. Temperament is rarely a problem and owners should capitalize on proper socialization and training.

By eight weeks of age, the puppy already possesses a typical Keeshond coat, though of course not in full bloom. The developing coat goes through many changes and requires considerable upkeep. OWNER, LINDA MOSS.

Puppies inherit their outgoing, friendly temperaments from their dams. The breed is prized for its affectionate and vital disposition. OWNERS, ERNEST AND DONNA WILLIAMS.

HEALTH

The Keeshond is quite a healthy breed. Many diseases and other problems occur, though most are rare in the breed. The more serious problems include HD, epilepsy, and irregular thyroid. Hip dysplasia is not common, though all breeding stock should still be certified. Epilepsy, more common in dogs than bitches, must be a breeder concern; it usually becomes apparent around three years of age. Underactive thyroid results in dull coats and possibly hair loss but is usually treatable with medication. Kidney disease, evidenced by weakness, vomiting, and convulsions, is reported. Perhaps the most serious concern is tumors, especially skin tumors. Owners must inspect the dog's skin, especially as old age sets in. Shedding is a concern, and more importantly, skin irritations and parasites can be prevented by careful regular inspection (flea allergies are reported). Veterinarians report cases of dwarfism, Tetralogy of Fallot (heart defect), vWD, ventricular septal defect as well as diabetes mellitus in some lines.

While the Keeshond has a number of potential health problems, dedicated breeders have minimized their occurrence. OWNER, SHARON A. ELPHICK.

Keeshond

Kerry Blue Terrier

DESCRIPTION

The Kerry Blue Terrier derives his name from his Irish home county and his distinctive blue-gray color, which is fairly uniform throughout the dog and in the mature dog is any shade of blue-gray from deep slate to light blue-gray (blacker coloration on muzzle, head, ears, tail and feet). This is a well-put-together terrier with a short straight back, with good depth of chest, not round. The head is long yet in proportion to the body; skull is flat with a very slight stop; apparent length of foreface is equivalent to length of skull. Cheeks are clean; ears V-shaped and small, never houndlike or dead. Eyes are dark and small, not prominent. Neck is moderately long and clean. Unlike most other terriers, the Kerry's coat is soft and dense and wavy; harsh and wiry coats are severely penalized. He stands 18 to 19 1/2 inches, bitch one-half inch less; weight for mature male should be 33 to 40 pounds, bitches proportionately less.

Kerry is his county and blue is his color but he is more than "terrier." The Kerry Blue Terrier excels as a working dog, capable not only of ratting but of herding, retrieving, farm work and watchdog duty. Plus he's an exquisite show dog. OWNERS, DR. AND MRS. R. A. REILLY.

OWNER SUITABILITY

An all-around elegant terrier, the Kerry Blue is a marvelous children's dog, a good watchdog and a show-dog emblem of purity. His Irish descent has made him a rugged workman, who is aggressive towards other dogs and who is capable of a day's ground chores. He has a mind all his own and knows how to push your buttons to get what he wants. This is a perfect-sized apartment dog who adapts nicely to many styles of living.

An entertaining, clever terrier, the Kerry Blue can outdo his owners if not properly directed. Devious if fun-loving, this terrier needs an owner on his toes. OWNERS, MR. AND MRS. K. NEILL.

Growth

Newborn Kerries weigh between 8 and 12 ounces. They are born black, possibly with small white markings on the chest or feet, and possibly a few white hairs on the belly. Very rarely a pup is born brown with a pink nose, and some believe that all such dogs should be euthanized for medical reasons. Tails are docked and dewclaws removed at a few days old. The point of the extended tail at maturity should touch the imaginary horizontal line drawn from the top of the skull. Ear carriage is important to the Kerry's appearance and most ears will require setting (or pasting).

The Kerry Blue puppy's ear carriage usually needs assistance; the puppy's black coat will lighten to a deep shade of blue. Puppies that begin to lighten too early may become too light.
OWNER, AILEEN SANTO.

New owners are strongly advised to seek professional or experienced help with setting the ears. The coat will change color from black to blue during adolescence. Most white markings, provided they are not large, should disappear with maturity. Kerries require special and careful socialization for the first year to avoid pugnacity and other anti-social behaviors.

Health

A hardy, versatile terrier, the Kerry possesses a very strong body and sound mind. Aside from stripping (and he is a large terrier), grooming demands are little, though more so to achieve the show coat. Whereas, prior to the last decade, Kerries were notably long lived (over 15 years), in recent times there has been a marked increase in malignant tumors in older Kerries, reducing the life expectancy to under 13. Owners are encouraged to check breeding lines carefully to help reduce the cancer risk. Some eye problems, including entropion and distichiasis, are known. And while hip dysplasia is not considered a problem in the breed, elbow dysplasia is a concern. There is reported a neurological disease that affects the young Kerry, with limb stiffness being an early sign, progressing in just a few months to the inability to walk, called extrophyamido nuclear abiotrophy.

For the one-dog home, a Kerry Blue fits the bill. The breed greatly prefers the company of humans to dogs.
OWNER, AILEEN SANTO.

Kerry Blue Terrier

Komondor

DESCRIPTION

A strong, heavy dog whose imposing muscularity is well veiled under a coat of felty tassel-like cords in solid white. The head appears wider than tall and the eyes are almond shaped and must be dark in color, not too deeply set; blue-colored eyes are not acceptable. The ears hang and are V-shaped. The nose is black in color and wide; nose

Komondors are naturally territorial and wary of strangers. Unlike most other breeds, this dog can live confidently and happily in the great outdoors.
OWNERS, PATRICIA TURNER AND ANNA QUIGLEY.

cannot be flesh-colored. Muzzle is wide compared to skull and coarse, not pointed. The chest is powerful and deep and proportionately wide; rump is wide and muscular and sloping towards the tail, which slightly curves upward at the end and is raised to height of back in excitement; never short, curled or docked. The coat is weather-resistant by definition, dense and double: coarser outer coat hairs trap the woolly undercoat fur to form cords that are strong and permanent. Coat must not be curly or short, straight or silky are undesirable. Color must be white; skin ideally is gray, though pink is deemed acceptable.

OWNER SUITABILITY

A lot of dog and a lot of coat, which looks and feels like rope, the Komondor is a real eye-catcher and a protection dog by definition. Koms need a good owner, with a fenced-in yard for them to protect, and a good trainer. These dogs are large and are naturally aggressive and stubborn, unless correctly channeled. On the hills of Hungary, the Komondor worked alone and has developed into a most independent dog. Socialization to other dogs and people is absolutely essential.

How imposing is this dog! Up to 150 pounds of fearless courage and cords, the Komondor once defended herds in Hungary from predators and today excels as a guard dog and protector.
OWNERS, PATRICIA TURNER AND ANNA QUIGLEY.

#

Newborn Komondorok generally weigh a pound or more and develop with varied rates. Most dogs develop evenly and mature later while others experience rapid growth spurts and mature earlier. Owners should discuss development with the breeder of their dog. Owners should select for dark noses, eyes and paw pads and less pink skin, especially on the ears. Light noses and blue eyes should be avoided. Owners should also avoid dogs showing shyness, which can lead to temperament problems. The adolescent Kom will begin to develop its corded coat, which will not be mature until three years or later. Adolescents may also prove finicky eaters, and this can especially be a problem for dogs who experience rapid growth spurts—a prescribed diet may be required.

Although Koms grow at variable rates, encourage variety in your puppy's diet to avoid his becoming finicky.

HEALTH

The Komondor has proven a hardy breed, resilient to disease. Hip dysplasia, however, has taken its toll but has been largely controlled by responsible breeders. Far more prevalent are skin irritations and infections, especially with the less well-groomed Kom. (Grooming requires special knowledge and skill, and owners must make this commitment.) The Kom seems particularly susceptible to staph infections and dermatitis. Allergic dermatitis (commonly called hot spots) also affects the breed. While treatable, these conditions can be complicated by the breed's coat. Long-time

The puppy's coat is relatively soft but by three to six months shows a cording tendency. Believe it or not, upkeep of the cords is not as difficult or time-consuming as might be expected. A knowledgeable breeder-groomer can provide the specifics of cord care.

breeders have commented that some bitches have lost coat, especially at the shoulders/forequarters region, for no apparent reason. Koms are sensitive to anesthetics and some flea dips. Feeding habits are basic, and plenty of good-quality exercise coupled with regular training is vital to the dog's well-being. The well-kept, well-bred Kom can easily live ten or more years.

It will take approximately one year for the cords to form; by two years the cords are readily apparent. An adult coat can take up to five years to reach the floor.
OWNER, JANET CUPOLO.

Komondor

Kuvasz

DESCRIPTION

A white working dog of exceptional balance, sturdy build and large size, the Kuvasz is well muscled and medium-boned, standing 28 to 30 inches for dogs, 26 to 28 inches for bitches. He is the picture of strength framed by activity and lightfootedness. Of great importance is the properly proportioned head, which is longer than wide. Eyes are almond shaped and set well apart; ears are thick and V-shaped with slightly rounded tips, set well back. Muzzle is in proportion to head length with straight top not pointed. Neck is muscular and of medium length, no dewlap; back is medium in length; loin short and muscular; chest deep with long, well-sprung ribs. Tail is carried low and reaches to hocks. Withers are higher than the back; legs medium in bone; femur is long, creating good bend to stifle. The Kuvasz's full luxuriant coat is double with a fine undercoat and straight to wavy guard hairs; neck and chest are covered by mane; legs well feathered. Coat must be solid white; skin pigment is desirably dark. Weight 100 to 115 pounds for males; 70 to 90 pounds for females. Type and quality more important than size but dogs smaller than 26 inches and bitches smaller than 24 inches are disqualified from the show ring.

One of the dog world's greatest secrets stands before you in the Kuvasz: a graceful, powerful, highly discriminate working dog completely unspoiled by popularity and careless breeding. OWNERS, LYNN BRADY AND C.D. TOWNSEND.

OWNER SUITABILITY

Striking in appearance, the Kuvasz attracts more and more people who want an attractive protection animal that doesn't look like a monster. He is elegant and strong, and, with proper socialization and channeling of his natural territorial instincts, makes an ideal guard dog. With children the Kuvasz is reliable, though is not the tolerant victim like a Golden Retriever. Time must be invested in his exercise and training since this is a large and intelligent animal.

The picture of good health and uncanny intelligence, the Kuvasz was born to protect children. He does not accept strangers readily, always remaining politely suspicious. His devotion and patience are second nature, as is his ability to act on his own. OWNERS, LYNN BRADY AND C.D. TOWNSEND.

218

GROWTH

Kuvasz generally produce large litters, and supplemental feeding may be required. By eight weeks, a Kuvasz should weigh a solid 13 to 18 pounds, with dogs generally the larger. Physical maturity is attained by 18 months, though substance may continue to be added, particularly in males. In addition to good conformation, owners should select for mental soundness of the parents and natural suspiciousness (not to be confused with shyness) in pups. Adolescence is marked by a changeover from puppy to adult coat, which should be short, straight and dense. Plenty of additional grooming will be required at this time to remove the shedded coat and prevent matting. This extra care will be repeated during subsequent seasonal shedding periods. Dominance and guarding instincts will also emerge during adolescence, and Kuvasz are known to challenge their owners during this time—firm consistency of the owner is vital. Proper training and socialization will result in a reliable and loyal companion and guardian.

An upbeat, spirited dog with dominant traits and great size requires an experienced owner to train and socialize. Owners must be consistent or else the ever-challenging Kuvasz will quickly be ruling the family flock.

HEALTH

As is the case with other centuries-old working breeds that have never been overbred, resistance to disease is high and hereditary and congenital problems are few. By far the greatest concern is HD, to which this large breed has been predisposed. Only puppies coming from certified stock should be considered. Skin problems, which commonly affect the plushly coated breeds (especially those with white coats), are known. Proper daily grooming, especially brushing of the dense undercoat, can limit their occurrence. The average life expectancy is under ten years.

A suspicious puppy exhibits the Kuvasz's discerning disposition. Do not confuse this desirable trait with shyness in a puppy.

Kuvasz

Labrador Retriever

Of the three colors in the breed, yellow is the most popular for pet dogs. Black Labradors dominate field trials, and chocolates, the most recent color, are the least commonly seen.
OWNERS, PIERRE AND SUZANNE SAEY.

DESCRIPTION

A sporting dog of undeniable activity and substance, the Labrador Retriever is strongly built and short coupled with chest of good depth and width. The coat, tail and feet well equip this water dog for his work. The coat is close and dense with a water-resistant undercoat and no feather. His "otter" tail is peculiarly rounded in appearance and covered in thick dense coat, gradually tapering. The feet are compact with well-arched toes. The Labrador's skull should be wide with a slight stop; head, clean cut, free from cheekiness; nose wide and eyes medium in size, vary in color as coat. Coat can be solid black, yellow from fox red to light cream, or chocolate from light sedge to chocolate; white chest marks permissible. Nose color should be dark, though fading to pink is allowable; dudley (or pigmentless) noses are disqualified. Dogs stand $22\frac{1}{2}$ to $24\frac{1}{2}$ inches, bitches one inch less; dogs weigh 60 to 75 pounds, bitches five pounds less. Forelegs are straight and true, elbows not in or out, allowing for free and effortless movement. As with all sporting/working breeds, cow and bow hocks are to be avoided.

OWNER SUITABILITY

A dog overflowing with energy, ability and love for his family, the Labrador Retriever is the number one choice for a family dog. Foremost he is adaptable and obedient, does well with regular exercise and is a naturally social animal. Due to the breed's tremendous popularity, acquiring a well-bred, genetically clear puppy is most essential. As a versatile working dog and a field, hunt, and obedience competitor, he has no peer. Exercise and training demands are exceptionally high for the Lab, with some specialists recom-

Locating a Labrador puppy can be as easy as ordering a pizza; finding a healthy puppy from guaranteed stock requires more effort than most eager, hungry owners are willing to put forth. Usually the well-bred puppy is actually cheaper (and *always* so in the long run).
OWNER, SHARON CELENTANO.

mending up to seven miles of daily walking to meet the breed's high-energy output. Children and Labs bond very closely and quickly become inseparable, sharing beds, balls, and breakfast. Adult Labradors make fine options for adoption.

Growth

At seven to eight weeks, Labs should weigh between 9 and 12 pounds, with 10 pounds a good average. Prospective owners should be strongly familiar with the breed standard and select accordingly. Look for well-balanced, strongly built dogs with good bone and a broad head. (It is said that Lab puppies should appear as mature Labradors in miniature.) Avoid thin, long-legged, snipy headed dogs, and also excessively large dogs—a 105-pound mature Lab is *not* a typey specimen. Temperament too should be checked, with shyness and aggression avoided. The tremendous popularity of the breed has given way to many less responsible breeders, and owners are

Don't be discouraged by a breeder's "20 questions." He's not selling a used car—he's seeking a suitable home for a life he's created. If the breeder is pushy and evades your questions, find another breeder.
OWNER, DIANE AMMERMAN.

encouraged to select carefully—a waiting list to be expected for quality dogs. Adolescence is marked by high energy and a strong need for proper social and obedience training. Labs change very little as they mature, developing smoothly and evenly to full adulthood, at about two to two-and-a-half years. The soft puppy coat develops into the true double, waterproof coat by maturity. Labs become more "settled" with maturity.

A couple hundred thousand Labrador Retriever puppies are whelped each year and find new homes—a sign of our active, on-the-move times.
OWNER, SANDRA MacLEON.

Health

The tremendously popular Lab, with its natural vigor and delightful temperament, has some problems that have surfaced due to overbreeding. Owners must select their dog carefully. Major breeder concerns are HD and elbow dysplasia, PRA, and epilepsy. Any breeder not screening for these hereditary problems must be dismissed. Cataracts and retinal dysplasia are other eye disorders that have plagued the Lab, and such conditions as hemophilia B, epilepsy, osteodystrophy, hypoglycemia, hypothyroidism, missing teeth, dwarfism, metabolic liver defect, osteosarcoma, and diabetes are well documented. Cancer claims its share of Labradors as well. Healthy Labs are essentially easycare canines. Grooming needs are minimal, and daily brushing helps to prevent hot spots and other skin irritations. Flea allergies are reported,

Without question, Labrador pups are active and outgoing, thriving on human attention and contact.
OWNER, DIANE AMMERMAN.

and ear infections can easily take root owing to the breed's drop ears and true love of getting wet. A well-bred healthy Labrador can live 11 to 15 years.

Labrador Retriever

Lakeland Terrier

DESCRIPTION

A square and sturdy workman, the Lakeland Terrier is designed for hunting vermin. His rather narrow and deep body permits him to maneuver in rocky dens; his legs are straight and sufficiently long for efficient action to cover ground; his head is rectangular (not wedge shaped), flat on top and moderately broad, cheeks flat and smooth; his working jacket is wiry, two-ply for warmth and protection, hard to the touch. His face and foreleg furnishings are plentiful but tidy. He is a small dog, standing $14\frac{1}{2}$ inches, bitches an inch less; he weighs approximately 17 pounds in hard condition. His eyes are moderately small and somewhat oval, set squarely and fairly wide apart; muzzle is strong, well filled in under the eyes; ears are small and V-shaped; foreface is neither too long or too short; nose is black, not pink or spotted. Neck is long and strong, yet

The farmer's terrier was needed to protect sheep and poultry from foxes that would destroy them. The Lakeland Terrier dedicated himself to this task with a fervor that was neither glamorous or merciful. Unlike other fox terriers, the Lakeland always killed its prey. OWNERS, WILLIAM H. COSBY AND JEAN L. HEATH.

refined; body strong and supple; topline short and level; shoulders and hindlegs well angulated. Colors vary and include solid blue, black, liver, red and wheaten; saddled patterns blue, black, liver and grizzle (combination of the three colors).

OWNER SUITABILITY

Not the most recognizable terrier in the crowd, the Lakeland is a self-confident and fun-loving breed who makes a great knock-about clown for the children. His size is ideal, not so small that he gets stepped on, nor so large that he requires more than an apartment or small home. As terriers go, he is full of himself and feisty, therefore needing a steady hand for training.

Feisty and quick-thinking, the Lakeland makes a reliable, entertaining companion for children. He requires an experienced trainer. OWNER, SUSAN FISHER.

GROWTH

Lakelands generally produce small litters, and whelp size varies considerably. By three months, weight should be between 6 and 8 pounds, with males the heavier. Dewclaws are removed and tails docked at an early age. Some pups are born with short tails that require very little docking. Except for reds, which are born self-colored, Lakeland pups are born black with tan points. Markings will first become apparent as early as two weeks and may not be fully intact until two years. White markings occur, and an excessive amount of such should be avoided. Markings on the belly and feet usually disappear com-

Puppy color changes a great deal over the first few months. This Lakey already displays his saddle markings which usually emerge around three weeks or more.
OWNER, SUSAN FISHER.

pletely. Adolescence is marked by a harshening of the coat—the transition from puppy coat to adult terrier coat. Grooming is important to ease this transition. The Lakeland's terrier temperament may need some tempering, and owners should strive to maintain a dog who is lively, obedient and sociable.

These young pups, with the proper care and attention, can live to over 15 years of age—that's a considerable commitment even though Lakeys require little of their owners.
OWNER, SUSAN FISHER.

HEALTH

Like other dogs long bred for utility and not necessarily for beauty, the Lakeland enjoys good health, with a high resistance to disease and few hereditary problems. Cryptorchidism and undershot bites are the most prevalent breeder concerns, though Legg-Perthes disease and von Willebrand's disease are the most serious. While the Lakeland has never really been overbred, its limited breed base has wisely led breeders to exercise caution against excessive linebreeding. A testament to their health, Lakelands often surpass 15 years of age. Grooming involves a considerable amount of stripping, less so for pet dogs. The ears should be cleaned regularly, and the teeth, especially in dogs with incorrect bites, should receive regular prophylactic care.

Lakeland Terrier

Large Münsterländer

DESCRIPTION

A strong hunting dog noted for his black (or blue roan) and white coloration. This is a well-proportioned dog who moves smoothly and carries himself like a professional. The skull is sufficiently broad, slightly rounded; eyes are medium size and dark in color; ears are broad and set high, lying flat and close to head; teeth scissors and complete dentition required; neck strong, slightly arched; chest wide; shoulders well laid back; back short, coupled, slightly higher at shoulders; hindquarters well muscled. The tail is well set on and carried slightly upward, or level; tip docking optional.

The coat is long and dense with feathering on front and hindlegs and tail. He stands 24 inches, bitches an inch less; and weighs 55 to 65 pounds, bitches 55 pounds. The head should be solid black (with blaze permissible); body is flecked with blue roan and black patches.

Smile and say Münsterländer!
OWNER, KEITH GROOM.

OWNER SUITABILITY

Not a large dog by definition, this is a medium-sized breed who adapts finely to family life, consistently affectionate and loyal. This is a multi-purpose gun dog perfect for the serious sportsman; he is a keen worker and a quick learner. He requires plenty of walks and doesn't mind inclement weather. He also needs an owner who can devote time and affection to him. With proper training he is an easily controlled companion capable of being a handy guard dog.

Although your local deli may stock a cheese by the same name, likely no one in your neighborhood has heard of the Large Münsterländer. Despite its rareness, this handsome German gun dog has exquisite skill and charm few Americans have yet to sample.
OWNER, KEITH GROOM.

GROWTH

Large Münsterländers weigh 12 to 15 pounds at eight weeks. As with all of the rarer breeds, owners must research and understand the breed before making a selection. Despite the breed name, the Large Münsterländer is not that large, and owners should avoid oversize dogs. Owners should select for a healthy, nicely balanced pup, ideally with an all-black head and dark eyes (light eyes rarely darken correctly). With age, the Münsterländer coat color darkens, and flecks appear on the white ground, even filling in once-white areas. (Breeder's tip: brushing back the coat will reveal gray areas of skin on the young dog which will give an indication of adult coloration.) The adolescent generally abounds with energy and must be exercised both physically and mentally. Generally two feedings a day are prescribed.

The Large Münsterländer in black and white stands 23 to 25 ½ inches. For hunters specializing in birds who desire a healthy, easycare companion, this may be your dog.
OWNERS, KEITH GROOM AND LINDA FLINT.

HEALTH

Breeders report very few problems with the breed, and its having been maintained at the hands of only serious and knowledgeable fanciers supports this report. The breed club's testing for hereditary cataracts suggests that this problem is very limited in the breed. The club insists on breeders' screening for this trait. HD scores are also promising, though there is an incidence in the breed.

A close relation is the Small Münsterländer who stands only 19 to 22 inches and is colored in brown (liver) and white. This breed is even more uncommon than the Large though equally appealing.

Large Münsterländer

Lhasa Apso

DESCRIPTION

The full-coated Lhasa Apso is a small dog standing 10 or 11 inches high, bitches slightly smaller. The coat is heavy, straight and hard, appearing long with longest feathers on head, ears, feet and tail. In color the breed varies greatly, described as golden, sandy, honey, dark grizzle, slate, smoke, particolored, black, white and brown; ears and beard are often tipped with black. The muzzle is of medium length and not square; skull narrow, neither flat nor domed; foreface is straight and of fair length; nose black; eyes medium in size and prominence; ears pendant. Neck strong and well arched; forelegs are straight; hind of good angulation, parallel; body balanced and compact, its length from shoulders to buttocks greater than height at withers. Tail is carried well over back in a screw (not like a pot hook) often with a kink at the end.

Looking for an ornamental darling to adorn your monastery: go no further. Cheering up a monk is no easy chore: The Lhasa Apso in its thousand years of existence has brightened up a million lives.
OWNERS, MICHAEL A. SANTORA AND ALAN J. LOSO.

OWNER SUITABILITY

Not to be confused with a toy dog or lap dog, the Lhasa Apso is a small-sized, hardy dog who shines for his beauty and intelligence. His elegance has earned him many favors and he is trusting and independent. Spoiling this dog and taking advantage of his portable size are common links to behavior problems. Begin training at a young age and he will soon become a perfect home companion who fully enjoys the company of children at playtime.

Preparing for the big day, Lhasas are show dogs par excellence. Due to the length of the hair, "rollers" keep the hair protected and give the dogs more freedom to move about in the home.
OWNER, NANCY SEHNERT.

In full coat, the adult Lhasa's coat reaches the floor (even when standing!).
OWNERS, ROBERT AND JANIE BREWER AND CINDY BUTSIC.

GROWTH

Most newborn Lhasas weigh about 6 ounces. Dewclaws should be removed by a few days to facilitate grooming at a later age. By eight weeks, Lhasas should weigh about $3\frac{1}{2}$ pounds. This breed in general develops evenly and smoothly, reaching full maturity around three years of age, though full height is achieved usually by one year. Owners should select for a healthy-looking, friendly and outgoing pup, who is neither frail nor oversize. Temperament is of prime importance, as Lhasas are first and foremost companions. The Lhasa's dramatic coat transformation occurs by eight months, though it will

Lhasa puppies scarcely resemble their parents. Their coats are soft and fluffy and their colors darker. OWNER, NANCY SEHNERT.

take considerably more time for the fully mature coat to peak. Lots of extra daily grooming is essential during the coat transition. Lhasas are known to be stubborn at times, and consistent socialization and training can greatly limit any such tendency.

HEALTH

The Lhasa puppy should appear longer than tall and the tail should be carried over the back in a screw. Consider the puppy's ability to breathe freely. OWNER, NANCY SEHNERT.

The Lhasa is an endearing companion that requires abundant time of its owner, both in terms of grooming and companionship. There seems to be a positive correlation between time spent with owners and longevity. Despite the Lhasa's pillow-dog appearance, the breed actually is quite active and enjoys regular walks and other exercise. Keeping excess weight off is important, as back problems can result from obesity. Grooming needs are

Gain your Lhasa's trust early on. Characteristically chary of strangers, the Lhasa treats his own with respect and obedience; his love is thinly veiled, betrayed by his attendant tongue and wagging plume.

very considerable, with several hours of brushing weekly to keep the coat from matting and developing the subsequent skin irritations. Eye problems, including kerato conjunctivitis sicca and corneal ulcers, can result from hairs on the Lhasa's brachycephalic muzzle scraping the eye. Pet Lhasas can be clipped to somewhat reduce this grooming need. Breeders today are concerned with HD, which has become more prevalent in recent years, and eye problems, for which all breeding stock should be screened—distichiasis and PRA are common. Kidney problems, including kidney failure, are known, though seem to be more line-specific than generalized in the breed.

Lhasa Apso

Löwchen

DESCRIPTION

The Little Lion Dog is thusly called for his fabulous leonine clip, leaving his neck maned, head, feet, and tail with furnishings. This is a tiny dog standing 10 to 13 inches high and colored in any number of patterns or shades of solids. His head is short and proportionately wide; eyes are round and dark; ears pendant, well fringed and long; nose black or brown, according to coat; neck good length and proudly arched. Forelegs straight and fine; body short and well proportioned with a level topline. Hindlegs well muscled. The tail is medium length, with tuft to resemble a plume. The fine, silky coat is fairly long and wavy but never curly.

Convincingly quaffed as the King of the Jungle, the Löwchen reigns as one of Europe's original lion dogs.
OWNER, KAJA DENAAN.

OWNER SUITABILITY

Despite his diminutive size, the Löwchen does not act like your typical lap dog, taking himself and his convincing leonine cut quite seriously. Making a fine indoor companion, he also loves to play outdoors and proves surprisingly resistant to cold weather—many enjoying the snow. When in the home, he is not unhappy to sit with his owner and enjoy quiet time.

Young pups may experience identity crises—growing up a little dog dressed up as a big cat.
OWNER, VIRGINIA DENNINGER.

GROWTH

The Löwchen is a smaller sized dog who should weigh 4 to 6 pounds around eight weeks. Breeders set physical maturity at about 18 months, though full height is usually attained some time earlier. Because Löwchens often change color dramatically as they mature, it is difficult for breeders, let alone prospective owners, to predict with any accuracy what the adult color will be. Owners should select for a healthy-looking, well-balanced dog with a friendly and outgoing personality. Because of the relative rareness of the breed, owners are encouraged to research the breed carefully and talk to breeders before selecting their dog, and be sure to get a lot of information regarding feeding, coat care, and physical development.

Color is a matter of taste and it's difficult to predict the adult color of a puppy. Temperament and good health should be the principal concerns.

HEALTH

The Löwchen has fared well at the hands of its dedicated fanciers, who have developed the breed from a very small breeding base (the Löwchen was labeled "rarest dog" in 1960). This is notable because such problems as irregular thyroid, epilepsy, von Willebrand's disease, and Legg-Perthes disease commonly affect small breed bases. These conditions seem not to be problems in the breed, though prospective owners are cautioned to select dogs carefully with full health inquiries of the breeder. At present, breeders are somewhat concerned with PRA and loose patellas, two common hereditary conditions in the domestic canine. To achieve the breed's hallmark little-lion look, professional grooming is required, unless of course the owner is determined to master the art of clipping. A less difficult to achieve "pet clip" is common for non-show dogs. This breed demands plenty of play time and loves romps in the great backyard.

Puppies showing off their first haircut! Löwchens will need to visit the grooming salon to be clipped in an appropriate leonine style.

The Little Lion Dog thrives on play and enjoys the company of children. They make hardy apartment dogs and can live happily singly, in pairs or in a pride.
OWNER, VIRGINIA DENNINGER.

Löwchen

Maltese

DESCRIPTION

A mantle of white silk covering a gentle-mannered toy dog from the tip of his head to pad of his toe, the Maltese ideally weighs 4 to 6 pounds and is a purebred of unstinting quality and vigor. His head is medium in length and proportion, slightly rounded on top with a moderate stop. The ears are set rather low and drop naturally, covered in heavy feather. Eyes are not set too far apart, dark and round with black rims necessary for proper expression. Nose is black. Muzzle is fine and tapered, not snipy, of medium length. The neck is of sufficient length to carry the head high. Body is compact; back is level, ribs well sprung; chest is fairly deep. Legs are fine

Perfection in pure white, the Maltese sparkles through his snowy mantle with gentle manners, a lively personality and unlimited affection for his devoted keeper(s). OWNERS, J. JOLY III, D. AND S. NEWCOMB AND V. ABBOTT.

boned and straight; hinds are moderately angulated and feet are small and round. The tail is a long plume that is carried gracefully over back. The coat is single; there is no undercoat. Long and flat, it drapes over the sides of the body nearly to the ground. The head may be topped with a knot. Coat is never kinky, curly, or woolly in texture. Color must be solid white, though lemon or light tan on ears is permissible.

The Maltese's pedigree goes back 28 centuries to ancient Malta. As a companion, he has always been prized for his aristocratic bearing and pleasing temperament.

OWNER SUITABILITY

As delicate as porcelain figurines, the Maltese shines as an intelligent and intuitive toy dog of fine regal bearing. Ideally this is the perfect toy dog, sweet and responsive, strongly bonding to his owner. As with all the toy breeds, owners are warned against spoiling these dogs, thereby avoiding a tendency towards yappy insecurity and pouty underfoot poofs! Maltese are very tiny and quick around the house, so be careful not to step on them. He is among the most beautiful of all dogs, and is quite sturdy and hardy under all his silken fluff.

GROWTH

Birth weight is variable, as is mature weight, with 5 ounces being an accurate average at birth. Puppies are born with very light coloration. Eye rim and nose pigment begins filling in soon after birth, and should be complete by three or four weeks. Owners should select for dogs with darkest pigment—and, of course, a sweet, friendly, outgoing personality. Maltese grow rapidly, attaining full size as early as eight months, which also marks the changeover to adult coat. This coat change is generally without complication, but extra grooming attention should be paid. Because of the Maltese's small and narrow muzzle, dental problems are more common in the breed. Owners should monitor the changeover

Breeders may not release Maltese puppies until 10 to 14 weeks. Although quite small, puppies are hardy. They grow quickly attaining full size by about eight months of age. OWNER, ANNETTE FELDBLUM.

from puppy to adult teeth and provide regular dental checkups, particularly through the first year. Retained puppy teeth and misaligned adult teeth are two possible complications.

Lemon spots on the coat are not desirable. In puppies, pinkish areas on the face will gradually whiten. OWNER, CLAUDIA GRUNSTRA.

HEALTH

The Maltese, for all its coat, is a relatively easycare companion. Grooming about 15 minutes a day is required. Because of its single coat (no undercoat), shedding is less than would be expected and the tendency towards skin irritations and infections seems lessened. Lack of pigmentation is a problem, however. By far the most prevalent problems involve dentition, with undershot bites, cramped teeth, and tooth loss in old age common. Temporary (baby) teeth are commonly retained and should be removed by a veterinarian. Cavities are common, and affected teeth should be removed to prevent spreading infection. Patellar (knee joint) luxation is the most common skeletal disorder. Deafness, blindness, monorchidism, and hypoglycemia are all reported in the breed. Tear stains are a common owner complaint, sometimes with corrective surgery necessary. Veterinarians report cases of patent duct arteriosus which affects the lungs. These problems, while numerous, are under control, especially at the hands of good breeders, making for a fairly long life expectancy of about 13 years.

Don't be too severe in your judgment of the dam's coat. Frequently Maltese bitches lose their coat after whelping. OWNER, CLAUDIA GRUNSTRA.

Maltese

Manchester Terrier

DESCRIPTION

The Standard Manchester weighs over 12 pounds and not over 22 pounds; overall he is slightly longer than tall (standing 15 to 16 inches) and he is of sufficient bone and muscle to ensure agility and endurance. Without variation, however, the Manchester is a short-coated black and tan dog with a keen alert expression. The eyes are small and almond shaped; ears are small and V-shaped, hanging close to head or naturally erect, cropped, or button; head is long and narrow, without show-

The Standard Manchester Terrier offers a middle-of-the-road alternative. As handsomely marked in black and tan as any German competitor, he is a medium- sized, sharp-looking terrier that does not spar with other dogs.
OWNER, PAT DRESSER.

ing cheek muscles, and resembling blunt wedge. The muzzle and skull are equal in length. The neck is slightly arched, slim and graceful; chest is narrow but deep in brisket; ribs well sprung; abdomen tucked up; tail tapering. Forelegs straight, elbows lie close to brisket; feet compact and well arched; stifle well turned; hocks well let down; hindlegs carried well back. Well marked black and tan are equipped with rosettes, tan spots on each side of chest above forelegs; white is highly undesirable anywhere on the coat, particularly when measuring more than one-half inch.

In the U.S., the Manchester Terrier's ears are cropped long. In England, the country of origin, they are left natural.
OWNER, PAT DRESSER.

OWNER SUITABILITY

For all the Manchester's virtues, it is mysterious how this British terrier has not impacted upon the pet world more strongly. Some might suggest that he looks like a Doberman shrunk down to a more convenient size! Nonetheless, he is his own breed (and more ancient than the Doberman!). For active people, apartment dwellers, travellers, and many others, this is a perfect-sized dog with an accommodating, unassuming personality. They are confident and good candidates for watchdogs.

232

GROWTH

Manchesters are born nearly all black and weigh about 6 to 8 ounces. The basic tan coloration develops by one month of age, though thumb prints and pencil markings usually take longer. Mismarkings (prospective owners should be familiar with the standard) are usually visible by eight weeks. Dewclaws should be removed by one week. Ear cropping is customarily performed in the U.S. Cropping the Manchester ear is a delicate procedure requiring considerable post-operation care. Owners must be knowledgeable of what is involved. Some Manchesters reportedly suffer from upsets in growth, which may be related to a sensitivity to immunizations. Talk to the breeder and your veterinarian about this possibility.

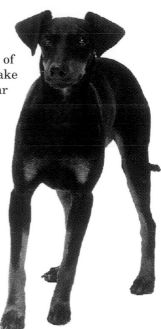

HEALTH

A true terrier without the characteristic terrier coat, the Manchester requires very simple grooming, little more than brushing and combing every other day, plus the regular eye, ear, and paw pad checks. Skin irritations and infections, however, are known in the breed, and they are often treatable with medicated baths and skin ointments. A very unusual skin disorder, called cutaneous asthenia, has been reported, with signs including soft, delicate, moist skin of pale coloration. Hip dysplasia is rare, though epilepsy and vWD occur in some lines. Dentition problems are also rare in the breed. True to their athletic appearance, the Manchesters need abundant physical activity to keep them fit.

An unassuming, friendly chap, the Manchester Terrier lacks popularity but little else.

Breeders have done an outstanding job keeping the Manchester a basically problem-free, natural breed

Manchester Terrier

Maremma Sheepdog

DESCRIPTION

Majestic and grand in size and stature, the Maremma Sheepdog is a solid white, solidly built dog with a beautifully fitting, long coat, which is rather harsh and slightly wavy. The head is conical in shape and large; skull wide between ears and narrowing to foreface; muzzle not snipy. Eyes are bold and not large or small, not sunken or prominent; ears are small and V-shaped, set high on head. Neck is strong and of medium length, no dewlap. Shoulders are long and sloping; forelegs well boned, not heavy, appearing straight. Body is well developed with a broad and straight back, loins slightly arched. Hinds are wide and powerful; hocks well down and moderate bend of stifle. The tail is set on low and reaching below hock. The coat affords the dog a thick collar, a close undercoat and well-covered tail. Coloration should be pure white, though shading of ivory to pale fawn is permissible. He stands $25\frac{1}{2}$ to $28\frac{1}{2}$ inches; bitches two inches less.

Italy's guardian of the flocks is the Maremma Sheepdog, in Italian *Cane da Pastore Maremmano-Abruzzese*. His Italian name pays tribute to the two extinct mountain dogs that were combined to create the modern breed.
OWNERS, GORDON AND ANNE LATIMER.

OWNER SUITABILITY

This is not a well-known breed in England or the States, though he has a strong following in Italy. He is available in both countries, however, and good breeders can be located in most corners of the countries. The breed shares many attributes with the Kuvasz and Great Pyrenees, for whom he could be mistaken. His is a lively, courageous dog who appears aloof, though is quite friendly and approachable (not necessarily by strangers). Maremmas need attention and lots of exercise availability. They are likely too large and outdoorsy for indoor living, though he is notably adaptable. He makes an excellent guard dog.

GROWTH

Born white without exception, the Maremma usually weighs about a full pound. Nose, eye rims and lips are pink and darken by eight weeks of age. By eight weeks he weighs 12 to 18 pounds, males the heavier. By 18 months he will reach his full height and continue adding substance through his second year. Some Maremmas aren't fully mature until three years of age. An outgoing puppy who is not shy makes the best choice; the breed does not have an aloof air. Eyes darken by four weeks. Not difficult to mistake for a young lamb, the puppy coat is soft and woolly, not long but thick. The harder, non-curly coat comes in between six and 12 months. Growth spurts are common—avoid overfeeding the puppy. By 18 months, the Maremma becomes an adult temperamentally.

HEALTH

As with most large breeds, skeletal problems concern breeders most: hip dysplasia, achondroplasia and slipped patellas. Given the small breeding base for the Maremma, these problems are likely line-related and not reported with great consistency. Overall, the breed is a hardy one and easy to care for. Maremmas can easily overdose on anesthesia and great care is advised when administering the drug. Make your vet aware of this. Brush the Maremma regularly to avoid potential skin and coat problems, like hot spots or eczema.

Maremma pups, similar to Kuvasz and Pyrenees pups, are more aloof than pups of other breeds.

Few Maremmas have found their way to American shores, though the breed is recognized in England. In Italy the dogs can still be found working at high altitudes protecting their charges.
OWNERS, GORDON AND ANNE LATIMER.

Maremma Sheepdog

Mastiff

DESCRIPTION

The grandeur and dignity of the Mastiff are relayed by his massive size and overall symmetrical and powerful structure. Dogs stand a minimum of 30 inches at the shoulders, bitches $27\frac{1}{2}$. He is of rectangular construction, his length being somewhat longer than his height at the withers. Musculature and heavy bone create the depth and breadth desirable. His head is massive with eyes set wide apart and dark, medium in size, no visible haw; ears are small and V-shaped; skull broad and rather flat with well-marked stop; muzzle short and broad, blunt. The neck is powerful and slightly arched without much loose skin. Topline is level and firm; chest wide, deep and rounded; slight tuck-up; back straight; tail set on moderately high; shoulders not loose; elbows parallel to body; legs straight; hindquarters well developed; stifle moderately angulated, not straight. The coat is double with the outercoat coarse

Descending from ancient lines of giant dogs, the Mastiff outdoes and outweighs most all his molosser compatriots. He can weigh as much as 200 pounds for his mere 30 inches! OWNER, NANCY HEMPEL.

and medium short; undercoat is short and close lying; no fringe on underbody, nor is the coat long and wavy. Colors are fawn, apricot, and brindle with muzzle, ears and nose ideally black; minimal white on chest permitted.

OWNER SUITABILITY

So you want a BIG dog? The Mastiff is a true giant with a proportionately sized heart. For the family who has the room and lifestyle to accommodate such a big dog, the Mastiff makes a great choice, as he loves people and adapts to a variety of living situations. He does not thrive on a totally outdoor living situation. Some Mastiffs actually survive in apartments and condominiums. Mastiffs have large appetites and require a strong, gentle handler and trainer. He is not stubborn and is a slow thinker—give him time to learn and he will.

The only thing Mastiff puppies do fast is grow. In their first year they can attain 140 to 185 pounds. At eight weeks of age, the puppy will weigh from 28 to 36 pounds. The following ten months of life are dramatic.

GROWTH

Newborn Mastiffs weigh from 1 to $1\frac{1}{2}$ pounds. The breed grows rapidly, and supplemental feeding is generally required from an early age. By eight weeks, males commonly weigh around 35 pounds, with bitches several pounds less. Mastiffs are naturally big dogs, making it absolutely senseless to select for *extra* big-boned animals, which is a common advertising claim. Excessive mass, whether bred for or brought on by overfeeding, is a Mastiff killer. Owners should select for well-constructed, healthy and vibrant pups having friendly, outgoing personalities. The parents should possess solid heavy bone, outgoing temperament, short tight coat, broad square head, and deep massive

Yes, your Mastiff puppy will become super large. Don't be impatient and overfeed him. Breeders advise adding excellent sources of protein to the diet and *not* using vitamin and mineral supplements.
OWNER, ROBERT S. JONES.

body. Adolescent Mastiffs are known to develop self-confidence problems, which require a sensitive, patient owner to overcome. Skin problems should also be watched for during the pubescent time. Mastiffs generally reach full height by 16 months, though will continue to add substance until three years of age.

HEALTH

The Mastiff is a low-keyed, easygoing dog of great size. While not the most active, Mastiffs require a good-sized yard to wander about, ideally for hours a day. The Mastiff requires less food than one might imagine judging from its sheer size, so feed according to a breeder/veterinarian-prescribed meal plan to best prevent bloat, improper bone development, and excessive strain on the joints and vital organs.

The brindle coloration is not seen as commonly as the fawn or apricot.
OWNER, ZOE A. TICE.

Other problems noted in the breed include ectropion, persistent pupillary membranes, retinal dysplasia, cystine uroliths (kidneys stones), and vaginal hyperplasia. Grooming needs are essentially minimal. Owners should take special note of the many skin folds on the breed, especially around the head area, as skin infections are most likely to originate here. Also check the eyes and ears regularly, cleaning them as necessary. Breeders warn that medical costs will be double those of the average dog simply because of the Mastiff's large size. The life expectancy of the larger Mastiffs is seven to ten years; the smaller ones may make it into their early teens.

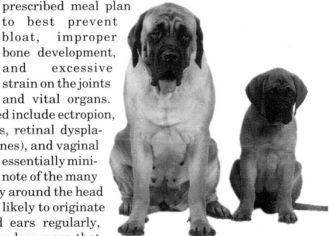

Don't select a puppy for sheer size and bulk. Statistically, smaller Mastiffs live a few years longer than the grander larger dogs.
OWNER, NANCY A. PITAS.

Mastiff

Miniature Bull Terrier

DESCRIPTION

Standing 10 to 14 inches tall, the Miniature Bull Terrier is a strongly constructed, proportionate dog with a long, deep head and a full oval face. Head should be filled up completely without any indentations and forehead is flat from ear to ear. Ears are small, thin and close together; eyes are small, well sunken, and triangular, with a piercing glint. The teeth are perfectly regular. Neck is very powerful and long; back is short and strong; body well rounded with good spring of rib; chest broad from withers to brisket; underside with a graceful upward curve. Tail is short and set on low, tapering to a point. Shoulders strong without heaviness; legs are heavy boned, not coarse; forelegs of moderate length; hinds are parallel and well developed with well-bent stifle. Feet are compact and catlike. Coat is short and flat and colored in pure white or predominated by any other color with white.

Like the Miniature Bull Terrier's spirit itself, this breed is catching on like fire! The enviable little brother of the Bull Terrier, the Miniature courageously asserts himself with the most competent guardian breeds, in spite of his fewer inches.
OWNERS, LORA J. LERCH AND PATRICIA W. EDWARDS.

OWNER SUITABILITY

This relatively new breed is perhaps many people's dream come true: an attractive Bull Terrier breed without the exaggerations that make the standard BT so unusual. The Miniature BT gets a "ten" for perfection of size, though he is a little too small to have the guard-dog power of his bigger brother. He still makes a fabulous watchdog, fits into all lifestyles, is active and alert, and very funny to live with. Kids adore this breed, and females particularly have proven good family dogs.

Don't let the word "miniature" fool you: this is an active, high-energy breed that needs a like-minded owner. Ideally suited as a family dog, the Mini Bull may do well in an apartment if given ample walking/exercise time. Females are said to be more suited to urban life.
OWNER, ANNE MARIE BERGEMANN.

GROWTH

The well-bred Mini Bull has proven a healthy animal with few developmental problems. Mini Bulls develop smoothly to maturity, at which time they should not exceed 14 inches at the shoulder. Because of the relative rarity of this breed and the genuine lack of information available to the public, owners should spend extra time talking to breeders and contacting breed clubs before making an educated selection. The Mini Bull is a high-energy companion with considerable exercise and training requirements. Feeding should be in accordance with a breeder-prescribed diet to meet the breed's high-energy demands and to help ensure smooth and easy development.

Robust, bold and cocky, the Mini Bull possesses great confidence and determination from early puppyhood. As with most other bull breeds, training is demanding and requires an owner patient and clever enough to undo the breed's stubborn nature.
OWNER, JAMES GAIGNAT.

HEALTH

Little can be found regarding hereditary and congenital defects of the Miniature Bull Terrier, but the information the authors have suggests few problems. This is remarkable, for the Mini Bull is both a bantamized breed and a breed which has developed from a relatively small breed base. However, it is true that its parent breed, the Bull Terrier, also has very few hereditary problems. Deafness in lines should be carefully checked, and the incidence of stud tail, inguinal and umbilical hernias considered. Otherwise, it seems the most significant owner concern is protecting this high-energy mite from its own lack of fear and ofttimes overzealous nature—injuries, especially lacerations and broken bones, are the most common health problems confronting owners of this breed. Grooming needs are minimal, though exercise and training requirements are high.

Who could ask for more in such a pint-sized package? Despite the breed's small size, the Mini Bull has proven free of health and genetic problems that trouble other bantamized breeds.
OWNER, ANNE MARIE BERGEMANN.

Miniature Bull Terrier

Miniature Pinscher

DESCRIPTION

The compact Miniature Pinscher is a short-coupled little dog with a smooth coat and a fiery big spirit. He stands 10 to $12\frac{1}{2}$ inches tall and is generally square, though females tend to be a little longer. The head is well proportioned to the body and tapers, but is never coarse. The eyes are full and bright, slightly oval; ears small, set high and drop or erect; skull flat, tapers toward muzzle, which is strong and proportionate to skull, not fine. Neck curves gracefully and is muscular, not throaty. Back level; body compact and slightly wedge shaped; forechest well developed; loin short; croup level with topline; tail set high, docked. Shoulders clean; legs strong and straight; feet closely knit; hindquarters set wide apart. Coat must be smooth and hard, with a lustrous finish richly colored in stag red or black or chocolate with rust red markings. Thumb marks (patches of black or chocolate hair) between front foot and wrist will disqualify a dog, as will a white mark larger than one half-inch in dimension. Uniquely, the MinPin moves in a hackney-like gait, with high-stepping action, with forelegs and hind legs moving parallel; good drive from rear.

The first title your MinPin will acquire is the mortgage to your home: Self-possessed and proud, this toy dog prefers to own the home in which he dwells.
OWNER, ROBERTA McCARTNEY.

A born show man, the Miniature Pinscher easily gains his second title too: Champion. Although the show ring is dominated by red MinPins, there are many excellent black and tan show dogs to contend with.
OWNER, ANN NELSEN.

OWNER SUITABILITY

MinPins are praiseworthy, smart dogs with a lot of energy. Necessarily these dogs need attention, understanding and outlets to channel their abounding inertia. Begin housetraining immediately. Some dogs tend to be yappy; properly directed they make great watchdogs. Children must be instructed that the MinPin has his limits and cannot tolerate too much poking and yanking. MinPins can be set in their ways and do not adapt to new environments or children too readily. They are affectionate and responsive to their owners.

No one has ever explained to the MinPin that he's in the toy group. Therefore, having no conception of his size, he struts, prances and picks fights like the proud Doberman he thinks he is!
OWNER, ROSE J. RADEL.

GROWTH

The MinPin is an exceptionally healthy toy breed that rarely suffers developmental complications. One possible problem is cleft palates, and all puppies should be checked for evidence of such. Also, large litters commonly require supplemental feeding to sustain good health. Tails are docked and dewclaws removed by five days. Ear clipping is generally performed around three months. It must be done by a professional. Owners should look for solid-bodied pups which exude good health and outgoing personality. Coat color changes are the norm. A light red tends to darken with age, while mahogany adults were born almost entirely black. This makes selecting for color difficult with young pups. Mismarkings, including white spots and thumbprints, are serious faults that owners should check for. (Small marking may disappear as the coat color matures.)

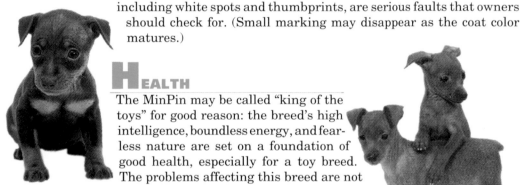

The good nature and responsiveness of the dam can only help ensure the temperament of your chosen puppy. Owners should treat the MinPin with fairness and consistency, never spoiling, teasing or ignoring the dog.

HEALTH

The MinPin may be called "king of the toys" for good reason: the breed's high intelligence, boundless energy, and fearless nature are set on a foundation of good health, especially for a toy breed. The problems affecting this breed are not common but include Legg-Perthes disease (the deterioration of the femoral head in the absence of bacteria), PRA, deafness, kidney stones, and lack of pigmentation. Skin diseases are more commonly reported, and prospective owners should check into this occurrence of the breeder's lines and also ask breeder and veterinarian for preventive measures to be taken. Lack of pigmentation most commonly affects the nose, toe nails, and eye rims and can lead to skin problems later in life. Injuries are not uncommon, owing to the breed's zest and small size. Dislocations, broken limbs, and skin wounds are all highly possible, as are hernias. Owners *must* provide their MinPins with plenty of mental stimulation and physical activity throughout the breed's average 12-year life span.

A chocolate and rust MinPin puppy at a few weeks of age.

If you're looking for a sedate lap dog, turn the page! MinPins outsmart, outrun and outyap most of its toy-dog peers—actually he has no *peers*, he is the King of Toys. OWNER, MARLENE DUNBURY.

Miniature Pinscher

Miniature Poodle

DESCRIPTION

The Miniature Poodle stands between 10 and 15 inches; he is therefore larger than the Toy Poodle but smaller than the Standard. The eyes are very dark and oval, not round, protruding or too large; the ears are close to the head with long leather but not too excessive fringe; skull is moderately rounded with a slight but definite stop; cheeks flat; muzzle long, straight and fine, with slight chiseling under eyes, and should not appear snipy. The shoulders are well laid back and not steep; forelegs straight and parallel; feet are oval and rather small, not paper (lacking padding) or splay. Hindlegs are straight; stifles well bent. The coat should be curly, naturally harsh in texture and always dense; although seen uncommonly, the coat may be corded with tight even cords. The Poodle can be clipped in any of the four acceptable fashions: Puppy, English Saddle, Continental, and Sporting. Poodle colors should be even and solid (varying in shades is allowable): colors are blue, gray, silver, brown, cafe-au-lait, apricot and cream. Particolored dogs are disqualified from competition. Noses, eye rims, lips, toe nails and eye color should adhere to the dog's color.

When perfection is reached in the Poodle, it is breathtaking. Prancing about the show ring in pompons and fringe, the Miniature Poodle has few competitors.
OWNER, ROBERT A. KOPPEL.

Who are the Poodle people? They are regular dog people with heavy duty scissors and clippers; they never sneeze since Poodles never shed; they are proud, smart trainers with the brightest dogs in the world.
OWNER, JUDITH BRAY.

OWNER SUITABILITY

The most popular of the Poodles, the Miniature Poodle fits into more lifestyles, the perfect blend of good tastes—not too "standard" and not too "toy." The Miniature Poodle is frisky and oh-so smart. All Poodles are keen on training and revel in pleasing their owners. Some Poodles get spoiled by their primp-happy owners. This is unfortunate as these dogs have naturally wonderful temperaments; they like people and other dogs, and listen more intently than any other breed.

GROWTH

Litter size averages six to ten, with whelp size 6 or 7 ounces. Tails are docked during the first week, leaving just under two-thirds of the original length. Poodles come in a wide variety of solid colors and color changes from puppyhood to maturity should be expected. The Poodle's hallmark coat grows rapidly but will not attain full-blown maturity until some time after the first year. Sexual maturity too is often not until after the first year. Owners are encouraged to select their puppy carefully, inquiring about health and temperament, and ensuring proper breeding. Grooming should be initiated at an early age to accustom the dog to this routine and to assist the adult coat in its development.

HEALTH

The breed's handy size, high intelligence, and delight of human company are all outstanding characteristics. Grooming needs are great, for regardless of the chosen coat style, professional clipping will likely be required. The importance of careful selection must be emphasized here, for many problems occur in the breed, though their incidence is quite varied. Ear, eye, and skin problems are common, including ear infections; distichiasis, tear duct abnormalities, cataracts, rod-cone degeneration (at three to five years) and PRA; atopic dermatitis, inherited sebaceous adenitis and seborrhea. Serious diseases and conditions such as von Willebrand's, Legg-Perthes, kidney stones, achondroplasia, epilepsy, and amaurotic idiocy all occur but are not common. Prospective owners must also watch for cryptorchidism, missing teeth, and improper bites. Poodles may have a sensitivity to rabies vaccinations.

Most of all, true Poodle people are selective. As the most popular of the Poodles, there are oodles to choose from. A poorly bred Mini promises years of yappy, snappy disappointment. Likewise, don't spoil your Mini or else you'll ruin a potentially marvelous, attentive companion. OWNER, MARYANN K. HOWARTH.

Miniature Poodle

Miniature Schnauzer

DESCRIPTION

While handsome and stylish, the Miniature Schnauzer is first a sturdily built, muscular dog and a robust and active terrier. His coat is harsh and wiry, short enough for smartness, and he is colored in pepper and salt, black and silver or solid black. He stands 12 to 14 inches and is nearly square in proportion. The head is strong, rectangular and of good length with small, deep-set oval eyes, with V-shaped ears set on high, dropping forward to temple or cropped with pointed tips. Head is never coarse or cheeky. Teeth must meet in scissors bite; level or under or overshot is undesirable. Neck is well arched and blends into shoulders; body short and deep; chest moderately broad; forelegs straight and smoothly muscled; elbows close in; hinds slanting and strong, well bent at stifles. The tail is set on high and docked, carried erect. The coat has a dense undercoat and is clean on neck, shoulders, ears and skull; the hair on the legs and facial furnishings are harsh and thick, never silky. The color white is highly undesirable, whether a patch or the whole coat.

The only popular terrier to not derive from the British Isles, the Miniature Schnauzer in salt and pepper can sprinkle any owner's life with a little feistiness and good spirits. OWNERS, LARRY AND GEORGIA DRIVON.

As showy and sophisticated as the Schnauzer may be, he is a people dog through and through and chooses to be treated with intelligence and kindness. Train a Schnauzer early on to avoid leash stubbornness, dog-aggressiveness, and dominance problems. OWNER, CAROL P. BEILES.

OWNER SUITABILITY

Prime companion dogs, the Miniature Schnauzer, of all terriers, has civilized notions about life. It is not too common to find a Best in Show Miniature Schnauzer burrowing after a gopher. This is not to say that he doesn't dig...most breed members have moved on to professional gardening and landscaping. He is a pleasant house dog who enjoys people's company, though he may be suspicious of strangers. He likes his food and takes eating seriously. Always guard against overeating. Children and Minis are compatible if properly introduced and if the children avoid teasing the dog.

Growth

Miniature Schnauzers are generally of smaller litters, with three to five puppies the average. Whelp size ranges from 4 to 9 ounces. Dewclaws are removed and tails docked by the first week. Ears are cropped between nine and 11 weeks and performed by an experienced professional. Growth should be notable and consistent. By eight weeks, pups should stand 8 inches at the shoulder; by four months, about 11 inches. Owners should select for proper conformation, particularly noting height and tail length. Coat color has a broad range of possibilities. Owners should expect color changes as the adult coat emerges and matures, with markings becoming more distinct.

Health

A Miniature Schnauzer in good health is one fine, robust canine. However, several serious conditions are known in the breed. Urinary tract problems and kidney disease are well documented. Avoid vitamin-C

Choose from a healthy line of Schnauzers from a breeder who has screened his stock for a few generations for possible health concerns. Anyone can find a Schnauzer: it takes knowledge and commitment to find the right one.
OWNER, GERALDINE KELLY.

Miniature Schnauzer breeders dedicate themselves to the potential eye problems in the breed. A recent problem known as "hot eye" can affect a dog within two to three days and cause total blindness by the fifth day if not treated immediately by a specialist. Talk to your vet about this condition.
OWNER, GERALDINE KELLY.

supplements. A specific type of follicular dermatitis occurs commonly enough to have as a common name "Schnauzer comedo syndrome." Achalasia, a defect in the esophagus which makes feeding difficult, is noted in puppies, and juvenile cataracts affect some dogs. Other eye problems include retinal degeneration, kerato conjunctivitis sicca, and PRA. Some problems of the reproductive system include pseudohermaphroditism and cryptorchidism. Legg-Perthes disease, metabolic liver defect, and von Willebrand's disease are also reported in the Miniature Schnauzer. All this makes proper selection of your Miniature Schnauzer of the utmost importance, and the extra time spent should pay off handsomely with a hardy, healthy dog. Schnauzers enjoy and require lots of activity to keep their busy minds and bodies healthy and contented. Grooming demands are considerable, especially for the show-type coat. Owners should expect to pluck their dog every two to three months, and professional assistance, especially for clipping, is a good idea.

Miniature Schnauzer

Neapolitan Mastiff

The most shocking dog in the world, the Neapolitan Mastiff conjures images of a living, breathing, drooling gargoyle. As if resurrected from ancient times, nothing compares to the Neo and his primitive approach to life as a domesticated canine.

DESCRIPTION

A large-boned, massive animal of impressive appearance, the Neapolitan Mastiff possesses a large, broad head, a well-pronounced stop; large nose, deep muzzle and flews. The eyes are set forward and rather rounded; ears are small and the neck is stocky and very muscular—dewlap reaching point of neck. Shoulders are long and slightly sloping; elbows not too close to body. Body is longer than tall; broad chest; topline straight; loin broad; thighs long and broad; moderate stifle; powerful hocks; front feet turn out slightly. Tail is thick at root, tapering to tip, customarily docked by one-third. The coat is short and dense, hard in texture without fringe. Colors include black, blue, gray, and brown; brindles possible in all colors; white chest star or toe markings permissible. The Neo stands 26 to 29 inches and weighs no less than 110 to 154 pounds.

OWNER SUITABILITY

The Neapolitan Mastiff is a strong dog, a large strong dog who is not your typical family dog. Ideally, Neos are devoted one-person dogs. They are bigger and stronger than you—only dominant, experienced owners need apply. Neos are too big to play with kids, and smart children instantly retreat when a bounding 175-pounder comes barreling down the hill. Neos are messy: messy eaters, messy players, messy dogs; they are best kept outdoors and if kept indoors, consider adjusting your home owners' insurance or selling everything of value destructible. Neos cannot handle stairs, but they do enjoy eating banisters. Realize that Neos were bred for protection work and are naturally inclined to bring down an opponent. For his one owner, the Neo is immensely loyal, and a childlike and unpredictable joy to own. Make no mistake, the well-trained Neo adores people and yet remains instinctively protective.

"Cute," you say? Perhaps. This little darling will grow up to eat you out of house and home, and then may eat your home. Keep your Neo outdoors to avoid him remodeling the house. OWNER, DANIEL PELLEGRINO.

GROWTH

Neos, of course, are very large dogs. By eight weeks, a weight of 20 to 30 pounds is average. Neos are also dense in composition, making every pound seem like a pound and a half. Growth rate is rapid: don't overfeed the puppy as too much weight too fast will lead to bone and joint problems. Full maturity takes a good two years to occur. Owners must take time to study and meet the breed before choosing it. Be wary for the Neo's popularity has given rise to many unknowledgeable breeders. Prospective owners should see the parents: cute puppies grow to be humongous ugly adults. Socialization of puppies is needed to convert the introverted Neo. No Neo moves gracefully, no matter the age. Puppies will limp at four to six months due to loose ligaments—give him aspirin—he'll grow through this stage. Adolescence is marked by the emergence of the strong dominance inherent in the breed. Until four months of age, puppies pee indiscreetly and need a lot of water to avoid dehydration.

HEALTH

The mighty Neo demands much of its caring owner, not the least of which is hygiene. Neos are notoriously sloppy eaters and excessive droolers. Owners must wipe their Neo after every meal, as would a mother her one-year-old child. The breed's abundant, loose skin requires cleaning and frequent baths–don't worry about drying out the skin. By far the greatest breeder concerns are orthopedic, especially hip and elbow dysplasia, osteochondrosis and arthritis. Foodwise, the Neo needs high carbohydrates and fat, less protein, plus vitamins and minerals. Dry dog foods are not recommended for proper growth. Puppies need only moderate exercise and must avoid high-impact activities, as young Neos are only "loosely" put together. Keep the ears dry and clean to prevent infections. Many Neos are near-sighted:

Thinking about a Neo? Think again. Consider consulting your veterinarian, your insurance company, your analyst and someone who is surviving life with one of these fabulous, challenging monsters! And then re-read this article.
OWNERS, JANET HACHBARTH AND SUSAN CHURCH.

never abruptly awake a sleeping Neo. These dogs are commonly sensitive to anesthetics and tranquilizers. Nephritis is known to affect young and old dogs subjected to excessive cold. Neos *die* in the heat and humidity—shade and water are absolute essentials to survival. Hose them regularly in the summer weather. According to breeder-veterinarian Sherilyn Allen, the Neapolitan Mastiff has a low thyroid hormone level, which can lead to muscle weakness, stiffness, cardiomyopathy, incongruent bone growth, recurrent skin problems, and gastric and intestinal motility that may predispose to bloat. The low thyroid is a breed characteristic and responsible for the Neo's unusual appearance: thyroid replacement therapy can correct these problems but will make the dog look less and less like the majestic living relic of a gargoyle he is meant to be. Who needs Frankenstein when you can live with a Neo!

Neapolitan Mastiff

Newfoundland

DESCRIPTION

Heavy in body, bone and coat, the Newfoundland is well balanced and strong with a proud and dignified head carriage. This is a large and heavy animal, standing 28 inches tall for males, 26 inches for females, and weighing 130 to 150 pounds, females 30 pounds less. The coat is flat and water resistant, ultimately important for this swimmer's work. The outer coat is coarse, full and moderately long with a soft, dense undercoat. The Newfoundland's head is massive with a broad skull and well-developed occiput and cheeks. Eyes are relatively small, deep set and well spaced. Ears triangular with rounded tips and also rather small. Head is essentially free of wrinkles with

From the coasts of Newfoundland swims in this web-footed wonderdog, overflowing with personality, gentleness and Canadian pride.
OWNERS, CAROL BERNARD BERGMANN AND PEGGY HELMING.

a clean-cut, broad muzzle. Neck is strong and long to accommodate head carriage; back is strong and level; chest full and deep; tail is broad at base and strong without kinks. Quarters assemblies facilitate good reach and drive. Solid colors include black, brown, and gray and each may be marked with white. The particolor Newfoundland is known as Landseer and is white with black markings.

OWNER SUITABILITY

It is hard to find fault with the Newfoundland. Newfs are among the most loving and gentle of all dogs, wondrously athletic (especially for water sports), and silly for kids. He is also large enough to deter an intruder (unless the intruder realizes that a Newf is no fighter). He is too large for city life but adapts well to indoor life since your Newf will enjoy his nap as much as the next 150-pound canine. He should be outgoing with an unmistakable love-life attitude. Be soft on him because he is sensitive and can lose heart or become jumpy if treated harshly.

Although bronze in color, the Newfoundland is a gold-medal swimmer and companion, a great sports dog for the family that's ready for fun and fur.
OWNER, LINDA MOWINS.

GROWTH

Most Newfoundland whelps weigh over 1 pound, and some as much as 2 pounds. Rear dewclaws when present should be removed. Rate of growth varies in lines and with individuals. However, the average weight for an eight-week-old is 15 pounds. That same dog should weigh between 70 and 80 pounds by six months. Full height is attained by 18 months, but full maturity can come as late as three years. In general, temperaments are excellent. Pups should be friendly and sweet and present few behaviorial problems during adolescence. Owners need to select for physical soundness, noting the bone structure and coat qualities of the parents. Young dogs should be fed a prescribed diet and exercised with caution.

Newfoundlands can grow quickly, putting on half their size by six months of age. Less commonly seen are the Landseer, a work of art in black and white.

HEALTH

The Newfoundland is one of the longer lived giant breeds, provided that daily exercise and quality attention are never lacking. We say this because most of the problems suffered by the breed are the simple result of inadequate care, including skin infections, eye irritations, obesity-related lameness, kidney stones, and heart failure, and heat stroke. Owners must always be on guard against bloat. Owners must feed their Newfs properly, guarding against excess. Grooming need be performed daily, preventing mats, moist dermatitis (hot spots), and helping to keep the breed cool. Hip dysplasia and similar orthopedic problems are known. All breeding stock should be carefully screened and documented. There are cases of hypothyroidism in the breed. Swimming is ideal exercise for these dogs, both because of their natural affinity to it and because of the low-impact steady-resistance quality. Newfs enjoy swimming into their late years. Newfoundlands love the companionship of man and healthy, well-maintained ones often live to 10 or more years. Veterinarians note that Newfs are very sensitive to anesthetics.

Newfs listen as slowly as they move and think. Praise them repeatedly with convincing tones and they'll respond in their own time. Impatience and punishment can only ruin a Newf.
OWNER, HARFILD SÜLZEN.

Newfoundland

Norfolk Terrier

DESCRIPTION

A working terrier of small proportions, the Norfolk Terrier has ears that are neatly dropped to his head, V-shaped and velvety, carried close to his cheek. He stands 9 to 10 inches and weighs 11 to 12 pounds. For his compact size, he has good substance and bone and is a free-moving and hardy workman. His coat is hard and wiry for protection, measuring $1\frac{1}{2}$ to 2 inches in length, with a good undercoat. He has furnishings on his head, ears and neck, and some on his legs, but overall is kept neat in appearance. His head is slightly rounded and wide with a wedge-shaped muzzle and a well-defined stop. The neck is of medium length and strong; chest moderately deep; tail docked for balanced outline; forequarters well laid back and hind broad and strong; hocks well let down and straight. The Norfolk comes in all shades of red, wheaten, black and tan, and grizzle; dark points not a fault; white marks are not desirable.

A natural, hardy and friendly terrier in a crisp wire coat, the Norfolk Terrier provokes his British countryfolk to call him a "perfect demon" in the field, versatile enough to go to ground after vermin and always agreeable with his fellow Norfolk folk.
OWNERS, JOHN F. AND PAMELA G. BEALE.

OWNER SUITABILITY

Norfolks are confident, scrappy small terriers who thrive on family life and the attention of children. He can play for hours and yet is able to adapt his schedule to yours. Ideal for apartment living due to his small size. Digging and barking are the usual complaints. He is a fast learner and enjoys training sessions. Early training is recommended to keep his yap and digging in check. Norfolk puppies are extremely jaunty and playful; they may even try the patience of their owners. Obedience training and plenty of exercise time are requisite.

The Norfolk's ears fold forward and are described as expressive dropped ears.
OWNERS, LINDA HARING AND HOWARD AND BRIDGET HOLZHAUSER.

GROWTH

Norfolks in general come from small litters of four or fewer. Average birth weight is 5 ounces. Tails are docked (by about one-half) and dewclaws removed during the first week. Norfolks grow and develop quickly. By eight weeks, average weight is 3 pounds; at six months, 10 pounds. Ideal weight at maturity is 12 pounds. Full height is achieved before one year of age. Adolescence is marked by the emergence of the hard adult coat. Stripping and extra grooming time are required. Norfolks become more serious and even-tempered with maturity.

HEALTH

The Norfolk, like its Norwich cousin, enjoys excellent health and relative freedom from serious hereditary diseases. Of the two breeds, the Norfolk is the more natural and therefore less prone to health problems. These little terriers are packed with spunk and vigor. They truly enjoy the outdoors and will romp and dig for hours. Their fearless nature and strong hunting instincts can easily get them into their share of trouble. Breeders cite skin problems as the most prevalent health concern. Allergic reactions (including to flea dips) have been noted, and owners must ensure proper diet (with essential fatty acids) and grooming for their dogs. Proper grooming becomes a relatively simple matter once the practice of stripping (plucking) is mastered, as only a small amount of clipping is required. The Norfolk may be more susceptible to ear infections than its erect-eared cousin, and owners must regularly inspect the eyes for signs of injury and irritation. Most important is early introduction to grooming, as these independent-minded terriers can strongly resist. These dogs commonly live to become hardy teenagers.

If you are seeking a small terrier breed, bolt after a Norfolk! There are many reasons to choose this assertive but ever amenable British tot. Norfolk people tend to congregate at dog shows. Find an all-breed show and you're likely to find a Norfolk litter.
OWNER, KAREN ANDERSON.

Norfolk babies are spirited and inquisitive. Generally the breed enjoys excellent health, and finding a healthy puppy rarely presents a problem.
OWNER, KAREN ANDERSON.

Norfolk Terrier

251

Norwegian Buhund

DESCRIPTION

The lightly built Norwegian Buhund is medium in size with a keen, alert appearance. The head is lean and rather broad between the ears; wedge shaped with medium-length muzzle. Ears are placed high, erect, and sharply pointed; neck is medium length without loose skin. The eyes are dark brown in color. Forelegs are lean and straight; body strong and short, but light; chest deep and back straight with firm loins, slightly drawn up. The hind legs are strong and a little angulated. Tail is set on high, short and tightly curled over back. Coat is close and harsh, but smooth with soft undercoat. Colors include wheaten, black, lighter reds, and wolf-sable. Small white markings not objectionable. Buhunds stand 18 inches tall, bitches somewhat less.

If you need a "hund" for your "bu," this is your dog! The Buhund (farm dog) derives from Nordic sheepdogs and celebrates his diversity as a herder, hunter and general farm hand. OWNERS, MR. AND MRS. A. A. MOLE.

The Buhund's temperament lends itself to work as a guard dog and a guide dog. His natural sweet disposition and high intelligence make him a pleasure to train as well as live with. OWNER, VAN ETTERUK-KROOS.

OWNER SUITABILITY

A clean, natural breed more commonly seen in Europe but accepted in Great Britain at dog shows, the Norwegian Buhund is one of the most adaptable little dogs. His versatility and even temperament have led him to much assistance work with the deaf and blind; he is ideally suited to children. He is exceptionally obedient but is a thinker, and therefore can become bored with repetition. The Buhund is a real people dog, more so than the Husky and many other spitz breeds, and most adaptable to an owner's mood.

A lightly built, husky-type dog with personality and good looks, the Norwegian Buhund comes in many attractive colors and patterns. What could be a more exotic addition to your home than a Buhund in wolf-sable! OWNER, NORAH D. GANDER.

GROWTH

The eight-week-old Buhund weighs 8 to 10 pounds. Birth color may be many different shades of gray, clearing towards its adult coloration by eight to 12 weeks. After this time, little color change can be expected; rather the coat will become richer and gain in its clarity. Buhunds mature at various ages. Generally, full height is reached by 8 to 12 months; weight by 12 to 14 months. Full maturity may come as late as two years. Adolescence marks the puppy-to-adult coat change. The Buhund's plush double coat will require plenty of brushing during this time, as well as during the twice-annual shedding periods. Adolescent males may express dominance at this time, particularly towards other dogs—proper training and socialization are required.

HEALTH

The Norwegian Buhund derives from true working ancestry and has been developed to this day for soundness and function. The Buhund requires plenty of exercise with its human family and consistent training (one breeder notes the importance of teaching the recall and down commands at a young age); the breed delights in herding when given the chance. Grooming needs are not excessive, but regular maintenance of the

Hunting for a Buhund in America will require some doing. In addition to Norway and its neighboring Continental countries, England and Australia have a fair share of Buhund breeders.

coat, particularly during seasonal shedding periods, is requisite. Feeding requirements are undemanding, though new owners are encouraged to follow a breeder-prescribed diet. The breed enjoys general freedom from most hereditary and congenital problems. The British fancy reports a concern with hereditary cataracts and acknowledges the work of a team of geneticists and eye specialists, which working with the fancy have reduced this problem tenfold. Owners should insist on eye certification from all breeding stock.

Norwegian Buhund

Norwegian Elkhound

DESCRIPTION

The hardy gray hunter, the Norwegian Elkhound is classically Nordic with his prick ears, wedge-shaped head, tightly curled tail, dense winter coat and keen expression. The Elkhound stands $20\frac{1}{2}$ inches, bitches 1 inch less; and weighs 55 pounds, bitches 7 pounds less. He is square in profile and close coupled with good bone. The head is broad, the ears without loose skin; eyes are very dark brown and medium sized; his ears are set high and firm, very expressive; stop clearly perceptible; muzzle tapers without pointiness. Neck is medium length and not throaty; back is straight; chest deep and moderately broad; tail set on high, tightly curled and carried over back. Front and rear quarters are balanced in angulation and development, enabling the dog to move with agility and endurance. The coat is thick and weather resistant, lying smooth to the body with a soft woolly undercoat. The preferred Elkhound color is medium gray; black tipped hair determines the darkness of gray; muzzle, ears and tail tip are black. Sooty or patchy coloration is undesirable, and any dog colored in another color (such as red, brown, solid black, or white) is disqualified. In Europe the Elkhound is accepted in solid black.

Bring home a relic of the ancient Vikings, the Norwegian Elkhound is a stout and hardy hunter with Stone Age fossils in his pedigree.
OWNERS, PATRICIA CRAIGE AND JEFFREY AND NAN-EISLEY BENNETT.

OWNER SUITABILITY

Elkhound people are among the most committed of all breed fanciers. Much about the breed is mystical as Elkhounds seem to be well-rounded and personable, biddable and playful. Since they are a high-energy breed, they are not recommended for the elderly or lazy. He is sharp in mind and appearance and makes a keen watchdog, making use of his hearty bark. Elkhounds learn quickly and offer few challenges to his partner: praise him much and he will continue to respond positively.

GROWTH

Litter size and birth weight varies greatly in the breed, generally with a direct correlation between the two. Average whelp size is 12 ounces, though may be as little as 5. Dewclaws should be removed during the first week. Most pups are born black, some dark gray. White markings commonly occur on the feet and chest; provided they are small, they should disappear as the coat takes on its distinctive gray color, starting by a few weeks. Elkhounds become sexually mature some time between six months and one year, though full maturity is reached between 18 to 24 months for females, and as late as 30 months for males. The plushly coated Elkhound will require extra grooming during adolescence when the mature coat emerges, as well as during his seasonal shedding periods.

HEALTH

Grooming can make or break the Elkhound. The breed is a naturally

A happy, socialized Elkhound puppy makes the best choice. Breeders spend many hours socializing puppies as well as screening stock for potential eye problems before breeding. OWNERS, FRED AND MARGARET SHARIS.

healthy one, with few hereditary problems and a high resistance to disease. However, proper diet and grooming are essential to nurture this healthful state. Grooming is a very simple though potentially time-consuming matter, with plenty of daily brushing and combing needed. Skin problems are common in the Elkhound, and many of these can be reduced by proper grooming. Moist dermatitis (hot spots) is common. Seborrhea occurs, but it is more dietary than grooming-related. Subcutaneous cysts also occur. With regard to diet, the Elkhound has a somewhat unique metabolism with a highly efficient digestive system. This results in increased absorption and utilization of foodstuffs. Diet must be adjusted accordingly and vitamin and mineral supplements are often recommended. Owners should follow the advice of the breeder/veterinarian on this matter to avoid potential complications. Of a more serious, though less common, nature are PRA and kidney disease. Glaucoma and rod/cone degeneration can affect the Elkhound's eyes; rod dysplasia results in the puppy being nightblind by six weeks but preserving day vision until two to three years. Your prospective breeder should screen for these problems.

Elkhounds are adaptable and playful, though they prefer active owners in country settings. An apartment dweller with a 9-to-5 work routine will not be the Elkhound's ideal keeper. OWNERS, FRED AND MARGARET SHARIS.

Norwegian Elkhound

Norwich Terrier

A small, vigorous terrier with a sporting, fearless big-dog attitude, the Norwich Terrier will burrow his way into your heart as he is loyal, gay and affectionate. OWNERS, RUTH L. COOPER AND PATRICIA P. LUSSIER.

DESCRIPTION

With sensitive prick ears and a resultant fox-like expression, the Norwich Terrier is a small working terrier, like sized to his Norfolk brother. Ideally he does not stand more than 10 inches at the withers and weighs about 12 pounds. The coat is weatherproof, wiry and hard, lying close to the body with a definite undercoat. There are whiskers and eyebrows, otherwise the coat is short on the head, ears and muzzle. Key to the Norwich's coat is its natural appearance—only minimal tidying is necessary. He comes in all shades of red, wheaten, black and tan and grizzle; white marks not desirable. The eyes are small and oval shaped, dark with black rims; his expression keen and fox-like. Ears have pointed tips and are erect, medium in size. Skull is broad and slightly rounded; muzzle wedge-shaped; definite stop; a scissors bite. Neck is medium in length and strong; body moderately short, compact and deep; tail medium docked of sufficient length to grasp. Shoulders well laid back; elbows close to ribs; legs straight for digging; feet round with thick pads; hinds broad.

Some Norwich Terriers have standing ovations to their fame, as does 1994 Westminster Best in Show Champion Willum the Conqueror. OWNERS, RUTH L. COOPER AND PATRICIA P. LUSSIER.

OWNER SUITABILITY

The Norwich is a clever little terrier, a great child's companion and an untiring watchdog. He adapts well to city life, though his heart of hearts links him to the country, where he can play in the fields and chase mice, etc. Raised with a cat, he does well; otherwise he may want to chase it, too. These little terriers enjoy the outdoors and will romp and dig for hours. Their fearless nature and strong hunting instincts can easily get them into their share of trouble. The elderly find the Norwich and his brother Norfolk delightful companions capable of brightening the bluest of days.

GROWTH

Litter size for the Norwich is generally small, containing four or fewer pups. Birth weight averages about 5 ounces. Tails are docked (by about one-half) and dewclaws removed during the first week. Norwich grow and develop quickly. By eight weeks, average weight is 3 pounds; at six months, 10 pounds. Ideal weight at maturity is between 12 and 14 pounds. The characteristic erect ears of the Norwich should be upright by ten to 12 weeks. The ears

Since the Norwich and Norfolk Terriers were considered the same breed until 1979, litters may yield either breed. These Norwich puppies show great promise as crowd pleasers and homemakers.
OWNER, KAREN ANDERSON.

may rise and fall during the teething period. Full height is achieved before one year of age. Norwich puppies are extremely jaunty and playful; they may even try the patience of their owners. Early obedience training and plenty of exercise time are requisite. Adolescence is marked by the emergence of the hard adult coat. Stripping and extra grooming time are required. Norwich become more serious and even calm with maturity.

HEALTH

The Norwich and Norfolk Terriers are closely related breeds. In fact, it was only recently that the two were considered separate. Health information is similar for both dogs. Excellent health and relative freedom from serious hereditary disease are breed qualities. Norwich are prone to Caesarean sections unlike the Norfolk. The greatest owner's concern most commonly is guarding against injury. Breeders cite skin problems as the most prevalent health concern. Allergic reactions (including to flea dips) have been noted, and owners must ensure proper diet (with essential fatty acids) and grooming for their dogs. Proper grooming becomes a relatively simple matter once the practice of stripping (plucking) is mastered, as only a small amount of clipping is required. Owners must regularly inspect the eyes for signs of injury and irritation. Most important is early introduction to grooming, as these independent-minded terriers can strongly resist. These dogs commonly live to become hardy teenagers.

Norwich grow rather quickly. Toddlers are surprisingly hardy and outgoing. Puppies weigh around three pounds by eight weeks.
OWNER, KAREN ANDERSON.

Norwich Terrier

Old English Sheepdog

DESCRIPTION

The bobtailed shaggy Old English Sheepdog is a medium-sized dog with a profuse coat over a muscular, thickset body, capable of agile movement and an elastic trot. The OES coat is not the proverbial mop—instead it is profuse without being excessive and the eyes are covered by shag, though vision is never impeded. Soundness is most important in this compact, square dog who stands 22 inches or more, an inch less expected for bitches. The eyes are brown or blue, sometimes one of each; ears are medium and flat to the head, moderately covered with fur; skull is rather square with a well-defined stop; the nose is big and black. Neck is fairly long and the dog is taller at the loin than the withers, thereby giving the breed a unique topline. The tail is docked close when not naturally bobbed—the breed is sometimes called Bobtail for this feature. Forelegs straight; hind round with well-let-down hocks. The coat is of a hard texture, not curly or straight but desirably shaggy—the dog's coat must not distort his natural outline. The hams (rear thighs) are the most densely coated. The color is gray, grizzle, blue or blue merle, with or without white. Browns and fawns are objectionable.

Ye olde Bobtail, the Old English Sheepdog or OES lacks the possession of a tail but little else. In England this tailless wonder assisted the herdsmen with sheep and drove other livestock. His tail was removed so that his charges didn't grab him by the rear. OWNER, JERE MARDER.

An excellent family dog ideally sized for the kids, the OES delights in rolling with little people. Puppies should be supervised and trained early. OWNER, ARLENE PIETROCOLA.

OWNER SUITABILITY

Fluffy but strong, the Old English Sheepdog is a self-sufficient, nicely tempered canine. He can be excitable and strong-minded. The OES also loves children and plays rough, so the youngest of the family need to be supervised when rolling with the OES. He is fearless and makes an excellent guard dog, though he is by nature a herder, not a fighter. Firm handling and specific corrections are necessary to keep your OES obedient.

258

Growth

Newborn Sheepdogs weigh from 10 to 16 ounces. They are born black and white with an unpigmented nose. The nose should begin to gain pigmentation by a few days and be complete by eight to 12 weeks, though some take much longer. Tails are docked a few days after birth; they should be taken back as close to the body as possible. Owners should select for a solid, healthy-looking pup who exhibits the desired square construction and the jovial outgoing personality. Prospective owners should check that the nose is black and well pigmented, front legs are straight, and movement is sound. Blue eyes and even odd-eyes occur; though not faulted, the darker eyes and eye rims are preferred in the show ring. For the pet owner, eye color, as well as coat color, is a matter of preference. Grooming needs are great from a young age, and are even greater during the adolescent coat change and seasonal shedding periods.

The Bobtail mom should be approachable and people-oriented, never suspicious, shy or nervous. Her pups happily inherit her disposition. OWNER, ARLENE PIETROCOLA.

Health

The OES has its fair share of health problems, which is not to say that the breed is an unhealthy one. On the contrary, the breed's average life span is from 10 to 15 years. Most importantly, HD is a real problem, and screening a must. Wobbler syndrome (cervical vertebral deformity), a condition characterized by malformation at the lower spine, is documented; it usually begins as partial lameness of the rear quarters and can progress to total quadriplegia, with the first signs usually in evidence between three and 12 months of age. The most common problems affecting the breed involve the skin and coat. Veterinarians also report on eye problems including cataracts. Deafness occurs in some lines. Grooming is very demanding—and vitally important. Owners should commit at least four hours weekly to coat care. Particular attention must be given to the areas of the ears, neck, chest, legs, and paw pads. The ears and pads must be kept free of excess hair to help prevent irritation and infection. Other less common problems reported in the breed are juvenile cataracts and prepubertal vaginitis; the latter usually clears with the first estrous cycle.

Don't choose the moppiest or mopiest puppy! Look for an outgoing puppy with medium coat length, big bone, a square outline and straight legs. OWNER, ARLENE PIETROCOLA.

Old English Sheepdog

Otterhound

DESCRIPTION

Lean and large, the rough-coated Otterhound stands 24 to 27 inches tall with an imposing head that is large and fairly narrow; bitches stand about an inch shorter. Males weigh 75 to 115 pounds; bitches 65 to 100 pounds. In addition to his shaggy, crisp coat, which has a water-resistant woolly undercoat, and an essential oily feel for his bred-for work, the breed is known for his keen nose, which is extremely sensitive. The dog is slightly rectangular and ideally in good musculature and fit. The square muzzle and very slightly domed skull are nearly equal in length; eyes are dark and deeply set, with a little haw; ears are long and pendulous and low set; jaws powerful. Chest is deeper than wide; ribs well sprung; tail long and tapering with good fringe and carried like a saber. The coat must not be shaped for the show ring, but natural. Dogs come in all colors including whole colored, grizzle, sandy, red, wheaten blue, black and tan, blue and tan, black and cream, liver, tan and liver, tan and white. The Kennel Club does not permit liver and white dogs, nor white dogs with separate black and tan patches.

Be the first one in your swamp to have an Otterhound! To the dismay of the otters in your neighborhood, this waterproof wading hound dog stands 27 inches tall and abounds in many abilities besides otter hunting.
OWNERS, GAEL LEWIS AND JACK AND ANDREA McILWAINE.

OWNER SUITABILITY

An athletic burly hound dog, a natural water worker and hunter, the Otterhound is such an unusual choice for a pet...so why not! His rough coat is appealing; he stands tall and proud; he loves children and an on-the-move family. His bark is enough to frighten your neighbor's intruder as well as your own. On the field and in the water he is enduring and an easycare hardy sportsman. Many people believe that the Otterhound's first love is water—this is not true—his first love is *mud!* Exercise is important to keep him happy and fit. Being a hound he is gregarious, friendly, sweet and devoted. Owners must be aware that this is a scent hound: "when the nose goes down, the hearing goes off!"; and a pack hound—the owner must be leader of the pack and the dog loves a home environment. Fences are a must.

Teach the puppy when he is young, impressionable and manageable. Otterhounds are smart and instinctual; unless otherwise instructed, they are more likely to follow their noses than your commands.
OWNER, ROBIN ANDERSON.

GROWTH

Otterhounds weigh one pound at birth, about 6 pounds at four weeks. By the age of seven to eight weeks, an Otterhound puppy should weigh 20 to 25 pounds. By six months of age, he has reached three-quarters of his adult height. Otterhounds come in many colors, and coat color changes are considerable, both during the growth period and after. At six to eight months, the adolescent will begin to develop its adult coat and color. Most pups appear nearly black at birth (except livers and other light colors) but begin to show hints of their adult coloration by two weeks; this is especially true of black and tans but also for grizzles and reds. Tricolor puppies may become grizzle adults. In general, the Otterhound's color lightens with age, and this is true throughout the dog's life. Owners should select for health, insisting on proper screening certificates, and outgoing personalities. Undershot and overshot bites are somewhat common and should be checked for. Adoles-

Motherhood...smotherhood...ain't ever an easy job. Teaching a litter of Otterhounds the ropes can give the best of dams a bad hair day.
OWNER, ROBIN ANDERSON.

cence may be marked by the gangly uglies, especially during the coat change. Appetites may suffer. Never choose a puppy who shies away from people. The adolescent's activity level settles down, and feeding amounts level off at six months.

HEALTH

The breed faces two serious problems, namely hip dysplasia and thrombocytopathy. The importance of proper breeding cannot be overstated here, for at one time these two conditions were widespread in the breed. Interestingly, while so many Otterhounds possessed HD, few actually showed symptoms of it—making testing all the more important. Canine thrombocytopathy is a blood platelet defect, and while responsible breeding has greatly reduced the incidence of this defect, all puppies should be tested for it when seven to eight weeks old. Skin cysts and tumors have been commonly reported in the breed. Proper grooming is vital to prevent other skin problems, as the breed's long, rough, woolly coat can mat, causing irritations and also easily masking parasites. One good brushing weekly will do the job. These dogs should be exercised cautiously during their first year of life so as not to encourage orthopedic problems, with swimming an excellent choice. Dogs typically live to ten or more years.

Adolescence is a challenging time for the Otterhound: all this hair; these legs are too long; these ears, that tail; hormones raging and not an eligible Otterhound in this whole darn swamp.
OWNERS, JACK AND ANDREA McILWAINE.

Otterhound

Papillon

DESCRIPTION

The Papillon is a dainty fine-boned little dog named for his wonderful butterfly-like ears (in his native France, *papillon* means butterfly). He stands an elegant 8 to 11 inches, and not taller. His eyes are dark and round and must not be bulging; ears should be erect and carried obliquely, able to "move like the wings of a butterfly," or they may be drop and completely down (labelled Phalene–in French, moth). The head is small with a medium, slightly rounded skull and a fine muzzle, much thinner than the skull. The topline is straight and level with a medium-deep chest and tucked-up belly. The tail is long and set high and covered with a flowing plume. To allow free movement, the Papillon should have well-laid-back shoulders and straight forelegs; his hips should not be stiff when moving. The coat is abundant and silky, made up of fine resilient hair which is flat on body but frilly

From the pillows and ottomans of French and English nobility, the Papillon sits among the most gentle and elegant of the toy breeds, a perfect dwarf of the spaniels from which he derives.
OWNER, PAT JONES.

on chest. The breed is always particolored with a clear white foreface blaze (or streak) and noseband preferred; color other than white should cover both ears and eyes. The face should be symmetrically marked. Colors can be red or black and tan, but not liver.

OWNER SUITABILITY

Who likes to be a typical toy dog these days? The Papillon is a tough mini-canine, sublime for his grace and elegance. Temperamentally he is friendly and outgoing and prefers to be a doer. Laps are fine but not for too long. Paps, for all their big-dog attitudes, are still dainty dogs who are not recommended for households with young children (under ten years of age). Paps are intellectual tots who prefer an owner who appreciates their subtleties, beauty and pleasant ways. Paps train easily but can be yappers if not corrected consistently early on.

The butterfly lends its name to the Papillon for its beautiful, animated ears.
OWNERS, LOU ANN KING AND JOHN OULTON.

GROWTH

Litter size is generally four or five, and whelp weight averages 4 to 5 ounces. The color of the young puppy often changes by maturity (e.g., bicolors can become tricolors). In general, blazes tend to narrow. Owners should select carefully, and insist at least on information about the sire and dam. Papillon bitches should never be bred before their second or third season. Small bitches (4 pounds or less) should never be bred. Don't be alarmed if the new mother has a very poor coat, as Paps commonly blow their coat after whelping. Ask to see a picture of the bitch before breeding. Papillons mature quickly, reaching

Select a friendly Papillon pup who is neither nervous or unresponsive. The dam often blows her coat upon whelping, so don't misjudge her by her appearance. Nevertheless, she should be happy, alert and friendly. OWNER, CYNTHIA SILVERS.

full height by eight months. Full maturity is usually attained by ten to 15 months. Retained puppy teeth can be a problem, and any puppy teeth still in the mouth at seven months should be extracted by a veterinarian.

HEALTH

The Papillon enjoys good health for a toy dog, free from many of the diseases affecting its diminutive relatives (e.g., congenital heart disease, hydrocephalus, and hypoglycemia). It is also relatively free from HD and PRA. However, luxated patella (knee) and epilepsy must be screened for by breeders. Entropion rarely occurs. The Papillon is susceptible to broken bones and other such injuries simply because of its small size and fine bones. Grooming demands are not great, but regular brushing and a small amount of trimming are required. Importantly, the areas around the ears, anus and paw pads must be neatly kept to prevent infections. While the Pap is a lively breed, his exercise requirements can be easily met in the confines of the home, though walks and outdoor play are greatly appreciated. Papillons live 12 to 15 years, often more.

Although moths may be less romantic than butterflies, the Phalene is as elegant and graceful as his erect-eared brother.
OWNER, MICHELE KUNSLI.

Papillon

Pekingese

DESCRIPTION

The imperial Pekingese is quaint and highly individualistic, undeniably Chinese with resemblance to the lion in boldness and impression. The skull is massive and broad, never domed, with a broad black nose that is characteristically short and flat, with a deep stop; and large prominent eyes, dark and round; the ears are described as heart shaped and rather long, not set too high. The body is heavy in front, with ribs well sprung and broad chest; level back; forelegs short with firm, well-shaped hinds; feet must be flat with toes turning out, not round. The Peke is medium sized and should never weigh more than 14 pounds. His coat is straight and flat but mostly long, with a thick undercoat, and a profuse mane around the neck and shoulders. Colors include red, fawn, black, black and tan, sable, brindle, white and particolor, all with black masks and spectacles. The particolor should have a broken color pattern on the body and a white saddle. The tail is a long straight feather, set high and lying over the back.

As proud and independent as the big cat, the Pekingese celebrates an ancient Chinese ancestry and is unmistakably Oriental in expression, philosophy, and quaintness. OWNER, NANCY H. SHAPLAND.

OWNER SUITABILITY

Without a moment's doubt, the Peke is full of himself, possessed of self-esteem and boldness. No animal with this level of attitude cannot be all brains and, even if he is not an *original* thinker, the Peke is aware of his superiority, treating his castlemates with generic cordiality. He can be stubborn for all his independence and is not the ideal family dog. To his own, he is devoted and attentive.

Tell your Peke he's pretty, dainty and delicate and he's liable to prepare for battle: the lion in your Peke makes him courageous, bold, and combative, though he trains easier than your average lion. OWNER, LINDA NOLKER.

GROWTH

Newborn Pekes weigh 4 to 6 ounces on average. Weight at eight weeks is 1½ to 2 pounds. The Peke develops quickly and smoothly, with few complications. Breeders need be concerned with inguinal and umbilical hernias, eye problems and injuries, as well as cleft lips and palates, and prospective owners should inquire about these. By ten weeks, the puppy's construction can be evaluated. Prospective owners should note the fore and hind limb construction and be sure the pup moves with soundness. Grooming needs begin at a young age and are particularly important during the emergence of the adult coat and during the annual shedding period, when matting of the

Dramatic and discerning, Pekingese puppies are born with sense and sensibility. With so many colors to choose from, new owners can be overwhelmed: look close to the skin to see the likely adult color of your puppy.
OWNERS, MARY GAY AND GINNY FERGUSON.

undercoat is likely. Coat color may change in reds and fawns, which tend to lighten as the adult coat takes its place. (Breeder tip: usually the hair color closest to the skin is a good indicator of adult coloration.) Pekes need to be fed a balanced diet from a young age, and owners must guard against obesity.

The Pekingese coat goes through many changes before adulthood. Brushing through the first year is essential to assist growth.
OWNERS, SANDI GIBSON AND LINDA NOLKER.

HEALTH

The Peke proves an easycare companion. His plush coat requires on average a couple hours of weekly care, but no special skills or clipping is required. Owners must keep the eyes, skin wrinkles, and anus clean and free of debris. Diet, too, is not demanding, as Pekes do well on most balanced meal plans. Most of the breed's health problems are related to its conformation. As an achondroplastic dog,

the Peke is susceptible to urinary calculi and the degeneration of intervertebral discs. Physical defects such as short skulls, flat chest, and insufficient nasal passages can easily occur in uncareful breeding plans. The most common problems involve the eyes, ranging from diseases such as juvenile cataracts to hair irritations, distichiasis, PRA, and "dry eye" (due to an inadequate opening of the lachrymal duct). Breeders diligently screen for eye problems. The Peke can easily live to 14 years.

Pekes are long-lived companions that bond with a chosen companion for life. Are you ready to acquire the heart of this noble lion?

Pekingese

Pembroke Welsh Corgi

An enchanted little dog with the face of a fox and the body of a dwarf, the Pembroke Welsh Corgi weaves many an age-old yarn about his beginnings a thousand years after Christ. OWNERS, MRS. ALAN R. ROBSON AND RUTH L. COOPER.

DESCRIPTION

The Pembroke Welsh Corgi is a medium-sized, amply boned dog who is moderately long and low—he stands 10 to 12 inches tall and ideally weighs 27 pounds, 2 pounds less for bitches. He is distinguished from the Cardigan Welsh Corgi by his docked tail. His attractive head is foxy, although not sly in expression with slightly chiseled foreface (bone not filled in under the eyes and cheeks slightly round). Eyes are oval, not round or protruding or deep set like a pig's; in color they are dark, not yellow or blue but not true black either. Ears are erect and medium sized with rounded points; neck fairly long, slightly arched and clean. The ribs are slightly egg-shaped and moderately long with a deep chest, not too low to the ground. Forelegs are short with forearms turning inward slightly so that front is not absolutely straight; elbows well fitting; hindquarters moderately angulated. The coat is double and medium in length, with a noticeable ruff; hair straight and maybe wavy but not wiry or marcelled and never fluffy (very long with exaggerated feathering). The Pembroke is self-colored in red, sable, fawn, black and tan, with or without white. White does not predominate to appear as ground color, i.e., whitelies; mismarks and bluies (with smoky cast to portions of coat) are highly undesirable.

OWNER SUITABILITY

A working breed, the Pembroke Welsh Corgi revels in a challenge and excels in obedience training as well as other formal exercises like agility, herding and tracking. His cow-heeling heritage makes him a little nippy when the family herd gets too unruly. Smart owners get a head start on training the Corgi before he trains them. His legs are short but this doesn't curtail his need for exercise. He has much energy and much talent to share with a willing kinsman.

Pembroke puppies are energetic and creative. Begin training early to channel his time and talents. He doesn't force his affections and is sensitive to moods and limitations: an ideal house dog by any definition. OWNER, BETH MAGNUS.

GROWTH

Litter size varies considerably, and whelp size varies accordingly, with the average around 10 ounces. Dewclaws are removed and tails docked (as necessary according to length at birth) at an early age. Most pups are born a grizzled brown or black and tan; some pups have white markings. An eight-week-old male Corgi weighs about 8 pounds, females slightly less. Ears usually erect by four weeks or so, but may be as late as four months. Taping may be required for ears not erect by three months. (The ears may drop temporarily during the teething period.) Corgis mature slowly: while most growth is complete as early as six months, it may take three years for the breed to reach full maturity. Growth is often uneven, with the ears and feet seeming to grow first and the rest of the body catching up later.

Choose a sociable, outgoing puppy before he chooses you! Pembroke puppies epitomize alertness and individuality. If you go home with two, make sure they're opposite sexed.
OWNER, JULIA S. CLOUGH.

HEALTH

The Pembroke has proven a hardy, easycare companion, enjoying life into the double-digit years. Grooming needs are minimal, but owners must ensure a proper diet and guard against excess—overweight Corgis are prone to back problems. Stair climbing and high-impact exercises can also lead to back and joint problems. As with the Cardigan, eye problems are the more common complications, with PRA, lens luxation, and secondary glaucoma all found in the breed. Hip dysplasia is also known, and though its effects seem less debilitating in the Corgi, it is of course still highly undesirable. Cervical disc (neck) and back problems are known, as is epilepsy. All breeders must screen for hips and eyes (including retinal dysplasia). A rare and unusual problem known as cutaneous asthenia (Ehlers-Danlos syndrome) is reported in the breed; signs include loose skin of a velvety texture, and skin lesions. Otherwise, prospective owners should carefully

You may never see your puppy at this tender age as breeders must be cautious about visitors until the pups are five weeks or more.
OWNER, COOK.

examine the dog's bite, as overshot and undershot are both common, and a more serious defect called "shark mouth" (upper jaw extending far beyond lower jaw) also occurs, though more rarely. Veterinarians report cases of vWD, patent ductus arteriosus (affects lungs), and kidney stones. Pembrokes live 14 years on average.

Pembroke Welsh Corgi

Petit Basset Griffon Vendéen

DESCRIPTION

Tousled and carefree, the Petit Basset Griffon Vendéen is a small, low-to-the-ground, rough-coated scent hound, toughly constructed and bold in character. Both dogs and bitches stand 13 to 15 inches at the withers, not taller. He is essentially 50% longer than he is tall and of good bone. His coat should be harsh to the touch and long, though not exaggerated, woolly or silky; his natural (untrimmed) coat with his beard and moustache and long ears give the breed a wonderful appeal. His head is well proportioned and carried proudly; eyes are large and dark; ears narrow and fine; skull domed and oval, with obvious occiput. Neck is long and strong, not throaty; back is level with slight arch over loin; chest deep; tail medium and set high, carried saberlike. Forelegs are straight with a slight crook acceptable; hinds show good bend of stifle. In color, the breed can be white combined with lemon, orange, black, tricolor or grizzle.

Beneath this unrefined coat and tongue-twisting name is your average cute Frenchman with a penchant for rabbit hunting. The PBGV raises his melodious voice to tell of his happy mood and the scent of fresh bunny in the air. OWNER, JANE E. CHESMEL.

This is not a Dachshund! The feet may turn out slightly but otherwise the PBGV's elbows should be close to the body with straight forelegs (a slight crook is acceptable). OWNER, N. QUADLING.

OWNER SUITABILITY

Called the rustic French hound, the PBGV (his popular acronym) is a charismatic, charming hound with a lot of voice and a surprisingly independent spirit. For all his self-confidence and boldness, he is still willing and happy to please. For a hound (no less a basset) he is not laid back, but full of life and the love of life and his people. He likes hunting and other outdoor sports and enjoys sharing his games with the children.

In France the Petit Basset Griffon Vendéen is a popular pack dog for hunting as well as a companion. For show purposes, the breed must have a white ground color. OWNER, ANDRE FRANCHI.

GROWTH

By eight weeks, the PBGV should weigh 8 to 9 pounds. Age of physical maturity varies but is approximately 18 months. Prospective owners should select for the active puppy, the happy extrovert. The temperament of the parents should also be critiqued; ideally the breeding stock exhibits a good and loving nature. A degree of stubbornness and/or bravado is to be expected. Owners should avoid any dog with crooked legs or who exhibits shyness. Color changes are common in the breed, with dark colors tending to fade and pale colors darkening. Adolescent dogs require consistent training and socialization and require plenty of exercise and time outdoors. The breed, true to its ancestry, delights in hunting

Petit Basset Griffon Vendéen puppies are gregarious and playful. Consider the good temperament of the dam. She may be a little stubborn and cautious though always approachable and friendly.
OWNER, MARILYN CROWNSBERRY.

(or just aimless wanderings through the woods) when given the opportunity.

HEALTH

The PBGV is a very old breed, long maintained by French hunters as well as serious dog fanciers. The apparent result is a hardy, healthy dog, reportedly free of hereditary and congenital problems. One breeder concern is epilepsy, and responsible breeding has greatly reduced its incidence. Of course, screening and certification are always good ideas. Neither feeding nor grooming is demanding. Owners are encouraged, however, to feed a breeder-prescribed diet, at least for the first year of growth. Grooming is a simple matter but must be performed weekly. Special attention should be paid to the ears, keeping them clean and free from infection. Also, the areas around the mouth and anus should be kept clean and checked for infection. Some light trimming

As a relatively new breed in the U.S., the PBGV enjoys good health untainted by reckless popularity and overbreeding. Fortunately he's not for everyone: boisterous, stubborn, and less than biddable, he's cute enough to get away with it.
OWNER, CAROL A. STRONG.

of these three areas may be required. Be sure your veterinarian is familiar with this lesser known breed.

Petit Basset Griffon Vendéen

Pharaoh Hound

DESCRIPTION

The amber-eyed, chestnut-colored Pharaoh Hound is a graceful sight hound with clean-cut lines and a distinct nobility and litheness. The breed stands 23 to 25 inches as a male; 21 to 24 as a female. He has fine, large ears that are very mobile and carried erect, a long and chiseled skull and a flesh-colored nose that, like his eyes, must blend with his coat. The head is carried high on a long, lean and muscular neck. The topline is almost straight and the tail tapers like a whip. Shoulders are strong, not loaded, and sloping; forelegs straight; hinds with moderate sweep of stifle. Coat is short and glossy. The coat can be tan or chestnut with desirable white markings on the tail tip and chest (called the star). White, however, must not spot on back of neck, shoulders, back or sides of dog.

Were the Phoenicians still marauding in the 20th century, they'd surely leave the Pharaoh Hound in the Maltese Islands! No fault of his own, the Pharaoh Hound is only progenerated by a few proud fanciers that still see the timeless value of this 6000-year old purebred gaze hound. OWNERS, G. VON ZECH, LIZ HANLEY, AND N. AND B. SOWERBUTTS.

Adolescent Pharaoh Hounds are all limbs and lack the breed's characteristic grace and balance.

OWNER SUITABILITY

Pharaohs are unassuming and extremely sensitive, more suited to the well-adjusted adult household than the unruly married-with-children arrangement. Except for humans, the Pharaoh is the only other mammal capable of blushing. He is active, but not so much so that elderly folk can't keep up with his exercise needs. Pharaohs also adapt well to apartment life and are behaved in the house. They do not do well in kennels. Be conscious of socializing the pup to different experiences and lots of people, otherwise he may tend towards the overly shy. His hearing, like his eyesight, is stupendous, so he is easily distracted during training.

GROWTH

Pharaohs are born in their adult colors and experience a very normal growth pattern. Puppies are highly independent, and this quality is desirable when choosing your puppy. Grooming needs are minimal, though keeping the ears clean is essential from puppyhood. Older dogs should have their anal glands checked regularly.

HEALTH

The Pharaoh Hound's sensitivity extends somewhat to his health as well. He has a known sensitivity to veterinarian-prescribed drugs, so be sure your vet is particularly aware. This also includes flea collars,

Not many people have the joy of meeting a Pharaoh Hound puppy. Only a few litters are born each year and breeders are highly selective about the animals they choose to mate.
OWNER, DEBORAH KIDWELL.

powders and dips, to which many Pharaohs are allergic, as well as anesthetics. Never be casual about medicating a Pharaoh Hound. Because of the fragile nature of the tail, it can be broken; should this occur keep the area well lubricated until completely healed to avoid complications developing from a dry skin condition. Elbow calluses can occur—choose a gentle skin cream. Due to the limited number of Pharaoh Hounds, few hereditary problems have resulted from indiscriminate breedings. Pharaohs live 15 to 17 years.

The Pharaoh Hound defies the definition of a sight hound—his hearing and scenting abilities are superior, and his temperament is neither aloof nor standoffish.
OWNER, MARLENE HINES.

Pharaoh Hound

Pointer

DESCRIPTION

First and foremost, the Pointer is an alert, hard-driving hunter; his power is compact and his agility graceful. The head piece of this hunting dog is noble and carried proudly; the skull is medium width, approximately equal to muzzle length, with a slight furrow between the eyes and cleanly chiseled cheeks. The muzzle is deep without pendulous flews. Ears hang naturally and reach below lower jaw with little or no folding; they are not round but rather somewhat pointed. Eyes are intense and round. Neck is long and dry with a slight arch; shoulders long and thin, sloping; elbows well let down; chest deep rather than wide; back solid with only a slight rise from croup to shoulders; tuck-up not exaggerated; tail tapering, never too long or docked; hindquarters powerful for good drive. The Pointer stands 25 to 28 inches for dogs, 2 inches less for bitches; he weighs 55 to 75 pounds, 10 pounds less for bitches.

The prototypical hunting dog, the Pointer sports a lithe, athletic frame. He can be mistaken for none other, though he makes a companionable family dog and proves a fine show dog as well. OWNER, PHYLLIS B. KROLL.

The Pointer's head is the stamp of the oldest of all sporting breeds. OWNERS, RON AND CAROLYN TWYMAN.

OWNER SUITABILITY

A popular choice among hunting enthusiasts, the Pointer is less popular as a pet though he is ideally suited towards home life. He is a talented field dog, for which reason he has so many followers in this arena. Pointers are also exceptional with children and even prove tolerant of toddlers. Exercise and a fenced-in yard are essentials for this active working dog.

Show Pointers tend to be larger and heavier boned than field Pointers. For pet considerations, the show line puppies are more congenial and calmer in the home. OWNERS, DEN AND ELSA LAWLER.

GROWTH

Pointers produce moderate to large litters, with whelp size ranging from 10 ounces to more than 1 pound. In general, purely hunting dogs (those bred from field lines) are smaller and mature to a smaller size than Pointers bred for show. All Pointers should demonstrate good steady growth, weighing in around 4 pounds by three weeks. Supplemental feeding may be required for slow-growing pups. Coloration at birth is highly varied, with lemon-colored dogs typically born solid white and other colors born

Pointer puppies raised in the home are sweet and people-oriented. Look for the puppy that is friendly, well put together, and attentive. OWNER, MARY ANN GRACE.

with large patches or markings that may change with maturity. Ticking becomes evident around three weeks of age. Owners should select for outgoing, vibrant pups of obedient, well-constructed parents. Those desiring a hunting dog should select from field lines. Show owners should look for dark eyes, solid-colored non-houndy ears, and of course good conformation.

The Pointer's ideal family has well-adjusted children, an active but not chaotic schedule, a home with a fence, and time to devote to an athletic, even-tempered dog. OWNER, MARY ANN GRACE.

HEALTH

The Pointer has proven an easycare canine, having few inherited problems. Most important is early socialization and training. These are high-energy, hard-working dogs originally developed for long days in the field. Grooming needs are minimal, though some skin problems (including demodectic mange) occur, making regular brushing and coat inspection necessary. Hip dysplasia is the most serious breeder concern, and an unusual and rare disease known as neurotropic osteopathy has been documented in the Pointer; signs such as self-inflicted injuries usually appear between three to nine months of age, with degeneration of the spinal cord the root cause. Entropion, PRA, gout, and umbilical hernias occur relatively infrequently.

Pointer

Polish Lowland Sheepdog

DESCRIPTION

A muscular dog in a fairly long, thick coat, the Polish Lowland Sheepdog is a medium-sized, cobby dog whose appearance is alert and lively. His head is medium sized and not too heavy, carried moderately low. Stop is well defined, nose blunt and skull moderately broad and slightly domed. The eyes are medium in size, hazel to brown in color. The ears are called heart shaped, large at base and set moderately high. Neck is medium in length without dewlap. Shoulders are well placed, legs straight; body is rectangular rather than square, with deep brisket and distinctly marked withers; back level; broad loin. Hindquarters are well angulated with broad thighs. The coat is long, dense and shaggy, of a harsh texture with a soft undercoat. All colors are acceptable. He stands 17 to 20 inches tall; bitches 16 to 18 $\frac{1}{2}$ inches.

PON...that's short for Polski Owczarek Nizinny, the original name of this traditional Polish working dog. The PON's list of credentials is as long as his pedigree: a huggable, shaggy, no-shed dog that's medium sized with a giant heart.
OWNER, SUE AINSLEY.

OWNER SUITABILITY

A furry dog who doesn't shed, the Polish Lowland Sheepdog comes to order! PONs, as they are called (acronym for their Polish name Polski Owczarek Nizinny), are magnificent family pets with great affection for children. As an independent worker, the PON naturally makes decisions for himself and therefore tests his owner regularly. PONs have incredible memories and remain very loyal to all family members. He exhibits self-control and is generally equable in his dealings with people and in his decision-making.

You can tell the PON is thinking, but he needs a smart, on-his-toes owner to keep up with him. Adults sustain a suspicious air which the puppy has yet to adopt. Your puppy will be pure puppy: friendly, happy and playful.
OWNER, DORENE W. ZALIS.

274

Once upon a PON, God created a perfect teddy bear to watch over the flock. Today the Polish Lowland Sheepdog has inherited new flocks of Americans to shepherd and adore. OWNERS, THOMAS M. WASON AND LOANA J. SHIELDS.

Growth

A PON at eight weeks should weigh about 8 pounds. The young PON is a shaggy-coated, tailless "teddy bear." Of course, prospective owners must take the time to learn about this breed, its conformation and heritage, before making a final selection. In addition to good health and conformation, owners should select for temperament, avoiding pups who are nervous or awkward. Adult PONs should be naturally suspicious, aloof with strangers but never cowardly. PONs grow at a good rate. Breeders set physical maturity at about 18 months of age. Adolescence is marked by the development of an undercoat and coat color changes. A temperament change from friendly puppy to suspicious adult is to be expected.

Health

Because of the genuine rarity of the breed and its relative newness in the English-speaking world, little veterinary research is available on the breed. According to breeders and veterinarians in Poland, there is insufficient evidence to conclude on hereditary conditions. It seems that the PON is subject to the common problems that affect all dogs, and that conditions affecting this breed is more individual than breed-specific. Naturally, breeders and owners should take the reasonable precautions of screenings for PRA and HD. Breeders in the U.S. note that some skin inflammation and allergic reactions have

Although temperaments vary from puppy to puppy, even a timid PON will become a delightful companion dog. OWNER, LOANA J. SHIELDS.

been noted, making proper year 'round grooming very important. PONs live ten to 12 years or more.

Polish Lowland Sheepdog

Pomeranian

DESCRIPTION

The tiny Pomeranian weighs from 3 to 7 pounds; show dogs ideally weigh 4 to 5 pounds. He is a cobby short-coupled dog, appearing alert and intelligent. Foxlike in expression, his head is wedge shaped and well proportioned. The eyes are bright and almond shaped; ears are small, carried erect; the skull is not domed; muzzle rather fine but not snipy; with a scissors bite. The neck is rather short; topline level; ribs well up and rounded; chest is fairly deep but not too wide. The tail should be turned over the back and carried flat, profusely coated. The Pom should be sufficiently laid back in shoulders; forelegs straight and of medium length. He stands well up on his toes. The coat consists of a thick undercoat with a longer, glistening outercoat of standoff guard hairs, harsh to the touch. Limited trimming permitted for tidiness. In color the breed can be red, cream, sable, brown, blue, white, black, orange, beaver, and particolor (with even patches).

The tiny Pomeranian sparkles with character and friendliness. Today he is a toy dog of choice and does his best work on your lap (or in the show ring, if you're inclined to see him strut his Pom stuff). OWNER, JOSE A CABRERA.

OWNER SUITABILITY

Naturally mischievous and inventive, the Pomeranian makes a delightful house dog and a hardy outdoor dog as well. His thick coat makes outdoor living more a possibility than his size intimates. Poms live to be carried about and pampered, but owners are advised against too much cuddling and cooing lest your Pom become unsociable and even nippy. As a companion he is gentle, affectionate and consistent, able to take the handling of children.

Because Poms come in a variety of colors, they're fun to collect. A pack of Poms is as common as a flock of sheep, which incidentally their larger ancestors used to herd in Germany. OWNERS, MR. AND MRS. WILLIAM A. KERR.

GROWTH

The Pomeranian, being such a small dog, naturally produces small litters. Whelps range from 3 to 5 ounces, though smaller whelps are not uncommon. Newborn Poms, particularly the smaller ones, require extra breeder attention for the first few weeks to ensure proper development. Rate of growth varies considerably in

Never pick a Pom for color alone. Consider the temperament of the dam and the litter. If you are not impressed by their friendly nature, move on.
OWNER, BENEDETTO.

the breed. In general Poms mature at an early age, with full height attained around seven months. Coloration at birth also varies considerably and is subject to change as the adult coat comes in. The coat takes three or four years to mature, but by one year the adult coat is present. The two-month-old is long and fluffy; at three months, the coat sheds and looks ragged; by five months, the pup will look nearly short-coated from the shedding; by ten months, the first double coat will be present. Owners should select for outward signs of good health, and an intelligent, outgoing personality. Extra grooming time is essential during adolescence to assist the coat change.

A Pomeranian adult *never* weighs more than 7 pounds. An eight-week-old puppy may weigh 1 1/2 to 2 pounds. Don't accept an oversized puppy—not even for a discount! You'll more than pay for it later.
OWNER, BENEDETTO.

HEALTH

The good-natured and lively Pom places few demands on his owner. He is considered by many to be the most intelligent, obedient, and hardy of the toy breeds. Grooming needs are not excessive, though several weekly sessions are necessary, with some trimming required. Like other toy dogs, the Pom is prone to tooth loss as it ages, and regular dental care, including brushing, is strongly encouraged. Feeding demands are normal. The Pom is affected by the common problems affecting the toys. Patellar luxations (loose knees), open skulls, low blood sugar, and cryptorchidism all occur in the breed, though their incidence is limited. Dwarfism, hydrocephalus, hypothyroidism and patent ductus arteriosus (affecting lungs) have been reported by vets. Known eye problems include PRA and tear duct abnormalities. Due to the breed's small size, injuries such as dislocations and broken bones must be guarded against. Poms often live into their teens, with heart and kidney problems the more common causes of death.

Pomeranian

Portuguese Water Dog

DESCRIPTION

Built for the water, the Portuguese Water Dog is a swimming, curly-or wavy-coated and ruggedly built dog. He is medium sized, standing ideally about 22 inches for a male, and 19 inches for a female. The Portie's head is distinctively large but well proportioned, with exceptional breadth of topskull. The eyes are medium in size and well apart, dark in color. The stop is well defined and the muzzle substantial. The nose is broad. The neck is straight, short, and round with strong muscles and no dewlap. The chest is broad and deep. Tail is not docked and thick at base and tapering, a fifth extremity for swimming. The front and hind assemblies are powerful and balanced. The feet are round and rather flat with webbing of soft skin between the toes. The coat can either be curly with compact cylindrical curls or wavy, waves instead of curls with more sheen to it. Dogs are clipped in the lion or retriever clip. In color the Portie can be white, black, and shades of brown; with or without white.

If you'd rather be fishing, why be there alone? Here's the original fisherman's dog. The Portie's ancestors retrieved broken nets or an overboard tuna, herded schools of fish, and carried messages from boat to boat to shore. OWNERS, DR. LOU GUTHRIE AND STEVEN BEAN.

OWNER SUITABILITY

An athletic, outdoors dog who is outgoing and industrious, the Portuguese Water Dog outshines most other water dogs for both brains and beauty. The Portie enjoys moderate popularity as a companion animal though his versatility and mild ways should recommend him to many. He is a competent retriever, an excellent water worker, a worthy watchdog and a great friend for the kids. His winning ways and kind disposition will continue to gain him new swimming and fishing partners.

In the lion clip, the Portie defies expectations: a cat that swims willingly. The breed is a loyal and affectionate companion, an admirable watchdog, and the spirited, athletic pet your active family is dying to take on board. OWNERS, CHRISTINE NOYES AND STEVEN DOSTIE.

278

GROWTH

The eight-week-old Portie weighs from 8 to 10 pounds. The breed is slow to develop, reaching full height some time around 18 months and not attaining full maturity until four or five years. Owners should look for friendly, happy puppies, never shy or timid, with good activity level both in individuals and the litter. Coloration remains essentially the same, except that white markings typically diminish. Pigmentation should be dark. Two coat types are apparent at this age: curly, with curls apparent (curling at the edges); and wavy, having straight hair with a wave but no curl at the edges. The coat type visible here will determine adult coat type. Adolescence is marked by high activity, which coupled with the breed's high intelligence can pose a real challenge. Breeders call the adolescent Portie a *real* teenager, very demanding, and in need of obedience from an early age. Growth is steady, and eating habits should remain constant, always guarding against obesity.

Select a vibrant puppy with dark pigmentation and some enthusiasm about meeting you. The breed does not have the vivacious outgoing personality of a Golden Retriever but instead is more reserved, though never shy or timid.

The adolescent Portie is far from "perfect in every way," a true teenager that will challenge his master's commands and demands. Establish a rapport with the young dog early on—don't wait to start training.
OWNER, KRISTIN COFIELD.

HEALTH

Perhaps the most important aspect of Portie health is exercise and training. These are high-activity, very smart dogs who can easily self-destruct if *not* stimulated on a daily basis. While this aspect may take much of the owner's time, the breed's grooming needs do not. He does not shed. The coat is hair, not fur, and grooming needs, while simple, should be discussed with a breeder/professional. There are three main hereditary concerns of breeders today, namely HD, PRA, and an unusual condition called storage disease, characterized by an enzyme deficiency. Storage disease can be checked by a blood test as early as at six weeks of age. Prospective owners should inquire about (and insist on a guarantee against) a history of patterned hair loss, which can be genetically passed.

Posing for a family Portie portrait.

Portuguese Water Dog

Pug

DESCRIPTION

Square and cobby, the Pug is compact of form with well-knit proportions and hard muscles. He weighs 14 to 18 pounds. The head is decidedly large, massive and round, but not apple-headed. The eyes are large and dark, globular in shape with a soft expression. The ears can either be rose or button, but always thin, small, and soft. The wrinkles are large and deep and the muzzle is characteristically short, blunt and square, but not upfaced. The bite is very slightly undershot. The neck is strong and thick, slightly arched. Back is level and chest wide. The tail is set high and curled tightly, preferably double. The forelegs are very strong and straight with moderately laid back shoulders and elbows under the withers. The hinds are strong with moderate bend of stifle and short hocks. The coat is fine and smooth, glossy, but not hard or woolly. Pugs come in silver, apricot-fawn, or black, with clearly marked black on muzzle, ears, cheek moles, forehead thumbmark and back trace.

Once napping beside the monks of Tibet, the seat of William, Prince of Orange, and the cell of Napoleon's wife, Josephine, the Pug has found colorful bedfellows through the years.
OWNER, HAZEL M. MARTENS.

OWNER SUITABILITY

Adventurous and adaptive, the Pug is an easygoing small dog whose flexibility and talents make him a likely option for any contemporary dog owner. Pugs must be counted among the most functional of the toy-sized dogs, though he is not called upon to perform the tasks of his mastiff ancestors—who is? Nevertheless, he is a useful yard helper and home assistant, easily trained and happy to be helpful. Due to their short faces, they tend to snore and wheeze, though this is not serious. He likes children and other dogs.

Here's a lot of dog in a small package. That could be the Pug's motto and is: *Multum in parvo*. The Pug's tidy package of charm, dignity and serenity makes him attractive to a variety of owners with good taste.
OWNERS, RONALD AND ELIZABETH PIZZANO AND DORIS ALDRICH.

Growth

The Pug's weight at birth ranges from 4 to 9 ounces. True to its mastiff heritage, full maturity may not be reached until three years, though full height is reached by 10 to 12 months. Adult coloration is visible at a young age, though color will modify and clarify with maturity. Owners should select for a dog of good substance and outward signs of good health. The puppy's legs should be checked for straightness, the nose for proper breathing and freedom of sinus passages, and the eyes for clarity and freedom of protrusion and scratches. Sexual maturity for bitches is complete between nine and 12 months. Undershot bites are somewhat common in the breed and result in an up-faced look. Incorrect bites usually do not correct with maturity.

Be selective about your Pug puppy. Check for clear eyes (not cloudy or overly prominent), straight legs, bites that are only slightly over, and apparently normal breathing. Your pup's mom should have these same conformational features.
OWNERS, ALEXANDER AND AMY WHITE.

Health

The Pug, both a dwarfed dog and a brachycephalic breed, is prone to hereditary defects. Cleft lips and palates, elongated soft palates, and inadequate nasal passages are all possible congenital defects. The Pug's breathing commonly has a snoring-like quality; only if extreme can this signal sinus and/or nostril problems. While HD is rare, slipped stifles are rather common, and breeders should screen for this defect. Though not common, veterinarian data indicate cases of calculi (kidney stones), kerato conjunctivitis sicca, and subaortic stenosis. Among the most common health concerns are injuries, particularly of the eye. Checking the eyes for scratches and irritations should be part of the daily grooming regimen. Also, skin irritations starting in the wrinkles of the Pug's skin are common, and owners must keep these wrinkles clean and dry; the same applies to the ears. Otherwise, grooming is a simple matter.

The Pug can easily develop Tasmanian Devil characteristics if spoiled properly: he can be notoriously devious, greedy, and nasty tempered. Treat him kindly and consistently and that same Pug will be clever, affectionate, and endearing.

Healthy Pugs are typically good eaters, and owners must guard against obesity, causing such problems as heart attacks and spinal complications. Excess weight also lessens the breed's tolerance to heat, which is characteristically low. Entropion and Legg-Perthes disease also are documented. Pugs live 12 to 14 years.

Pug

Puli

DESCRIPTION

The light-footed, heavily corded Puli is a miracle of a little canine capable of strenuous work. Most distinctive for his dense weather-resistant coat made up of woolly cords, round or flat. He stands 17 inches, 16 inches for females and is tightly knit, medium boned and square in proportion. The head is medium in size with rather large, almond-shaped eyes, and high-set, hanging ears. The skull is slightly domed and broadish with a defined, not abrupt

Yes, this is a dog! And a smart one at that. The Puli's history is entwined with the sheep industry of his native Hungary. He is agile, light-footed, and surprisingly muscular under his thick moppage.
OWNER, CONSTANCE PETERSON.

stop. The muzzle is strong and straight. The neck is medium length, strong and not throaty. The chest is moderately broad and deep and the loin is short and moderately tucked. The tail is carried well over the back. Well-laid-back shoulders and straight forelegs with round and compact feet with well-arched toes. The hindquarters are well developed and balanced with the front. In color, the Puli is rusty black or black, shades of gray, and white; the skin has a bluish or gray cast. Solid colors are preferred with only small white marks on chest tolerated by show judges.

Only a fraction of the size of his Komondor cousin, the Puli makes a more functional house dog. His corded coat requires regular though not excessive attention. The puppy slowly grows into his cords and may not have a mature coat until a couple years of age.
OWNER, JANE SABLE.

OWNER SUITABILITY

Pulik love to play. They prefer an active owner who has time to spend; children are ideal untiring playmates for the Puli. Well-bred Pulik are not aggressive, though naturally protective of family. For all his camouflaging cords, the breed has been unable to disguise his stubborn streak. Training must be gentle but firm. Pulik with the upper hand can be unpleasant animals, though in general they are super-disposed to training and enjoy time with their owner. Pulik are also notorious vermin exterminators by nature, and extra training will be required should this trait be undesirable by the owner.

GROWTH

Birth weight is highly varied in the breed. Puli puppies have a short smooth coat that develops with maturity. Most pups are born a solid black, and with maturity attain their adult black or shade of gray coloration. Pulik can also be white, and such dogs are born white, making color selection rather easy. Ears and tails are left natural, though dewclaws are removed during the first week. The Puli is a hardy, high-energy breed, and these qualities are no better witnessed than in the adolescent Puli. Plenty of exercise and obedience training is required. Additional grooming time too must be spent on the adolescent as his thick adult coat assumes its proper place. The coat can be brushed out if the owner prefers to not have a corded dog. The traditional corded coat emerges by four to six months. Pulik are intelligent and ofttimes free-spirited animals, and young dogs can certainly test their owners.

Well-socialized Puli puppies will be curious and direct about their curiosities, friendly to people, and generally pleasant. The dam may be sensibly suspicious but not too headstrong, nervous or high-strung.
OWNER, GEORGINA DIOSLAKI.

HEALTH

The Puli's rarity largely accounts for the limited veterinary information available on the breed. However, its exceptionally long life expectancy (over 15 years) is a testament to the breed's fine health. Its working origin coupled with its limited and responsible breeding suggest a hardy, disease-resistant canine. The primary breeder concern is HD, and all breeding stock must be screened. Skin problems are likely in dogs with neglected coats. While little to no trimming is involved (and the Puli's look is often described as unkempt), owners should plan to spend at least one hour weekly keeping their Puli tangle- and mat-free, removing dead hair from the plentiful undercoat. Also excess hair should be removed from the ear and anal regions to prevent infection. While eye injuries are not common, they can easily be concealed beneath the abundant facial furnishings and should be checked for. Pulik are lively, energetic, and notoriously intelligent. They require daily exercise and mental stimulation to keep healthy.

Don't buy a Puli on a whim. This novelty act can live to 15 or 18 years! That's a long commitment to a living creature. If you're committed, the Puli will not disappoint.
OWNER, MARY WAKEMAN, DVM.

Puli

Rhodesian Ridgeback

DESCRIPTION

A handsome and strong houndlike hunting dog named for his peculiar *ridge* along his *back,* essential to the breed as its characteristic feature. It is clearly defined, tapering and symmetrical, beginning behind the shoulders and running along the back to a point between the prominence of the hips, and containing two identical crowns. This is a short and dense-coated dog, whose coat appears glossy; he is colored from light to red wheaten, possibly with small white marks on chest and toes. He stands 25 to 27 inches tall, bitches an inch smaller. The head is of fair length with a flat and rather broad skull and long, deep muzzle; jaws level and powerful; lips clean and close fitting. The ears are rather high and wide at base, medium in size. Neck is fairly strong and not throaty. The chest is not too wide, but notably deep with well sprung (not barrel-like) ribs. Forelegs are perfectly strong and heavy in bone, compact feet; hinds muscular with well-let-down hocks. The tail is tapering and strong, with a slight curve upwards, not curled. Dogs weigh about 75 pounds; bitches 65 pounds.

The Ridgeback comes by his name honestly. The ridge is formed by hair along the spine growing in the opposite direction to the rest of the coat.
OWNER, LINDA G. HOTHAN.

OWNER SUITABILITY

Owners considering the Rhodesian should know that this robust hound of a dog was bred to hunt lion. He is therefore strong and aggressive, not to suggest vicious. His exercise requirement is very high—the breed prefers a country life to the cities. Today's Ridgeback, well removed from the African jungles, has developed into a fine companion who enjoys playing with children. Assume that he plays with great vigor and may be too rough for many children. Training should be firm to nurture a well-balanced, responsive companion dog and superior watchdog.

A tough, no-nonsense hunter bred to kill wild game in the African jungle can surely make a lovely dinner companion. The Ridgeback today makes a worthy, capable pet for an experienced dog person and family.
OWNER, JUDITH LICHTMAN.

Growth

Litter size is generally large in the breed, and whelp size varies considerably. Rhodesians can be essentially of two different color types: reddish brown with a dark nose or liver with a self-colored nose. Color at birth is not a good indication of adult coloration, but, as early as two weeks, when pigment starts to develop, basic adult coloration can be determined. In general, red dogs darken with age, while liver-colored ones lighten. With the exception of the ridge, the Rhodesian presents a very natural appearance, and owners should select for a happy temperament and healthy appearance. The breed requires proper training and socialization throughout its formative years to develop into the desired outgoing family-oriented dog. Behavior problems such as shyness and aggression are documented—never choose an overly bold or timid pup.

Finding the right Ridgeback litter is your battle cry. Of all breeds, the Ridgeback must be socialized at a young age so that puppies are not aggressive, stubborn, and unmanageable.
OWNER, ULLA-BRITT EKENGREN.

Health

The Ridgeback's ridge poses a unique problem to the breed. Because it is believed to be caused by a gene complex and not a simple recessive factor, a condition called dermoid sinus can theoretically appear in any Rhodesian line. Dermoid sinus is characterized by the appearance of a sinus ("canal" or "funnel") either above (towards the head) and/or below (towards the tail) the line of the ridge. These sinuses grow down toward the spine, making corrective surgery dangerous. Euthanasia is usually the humane option. Hip dysplasia, hypothyroidism, vertebral deformities, deafness, and other common canine conditions may also affect the breed, though responsible breeding has largely limited occurrence. Grooming is a cinch, and the ridge presents no special grooming concerns. Care with anesthesia is advised.

Ridgebacks aren't ordinary hounds. They tend to be aggressive toward other dogs, suspicious of strangers, and more protective and territorial. Of all hounds, this breed is the best candidate for guard-dog duty.
OWNER, LINDA G. HOTHAN.

Rhodesian Ridgeback

Rottweiler

DESCRIPTION

Not a huge dog, the Rottweiler is a medium-large, compact dog noted for his solid black flat-lying coat with clearly defined rust marks. He is known for his strength and agility and stands 24 to 27 inches, bitches 2 inches less. Length of body is slightly longer than tall (9:10). His head is broad between the ears and of medium length; in profile, forehead moderately arched with well-developed stop and good bony ridges to eyes. The eyes are medium and almond shaped, colored darkly (never yellow or odd eyed); eye rims must not be hairless. Ears are pendant and triangular, well set apart. Muzzle is broad at base and tapering with well-developed chin and broad black nose. Correct scissors bite and full 42-tooth dentition important. Overshot and undershot, wry mouth and two or more missing teeth disqualifies a dog from showing. The back is firm and level; chest broad and deep (approximately 50% of the dog's height); croup only slightly sloping. Tail is docked short and close to body. Legs are strongly developed and straight with heavy bone, not close together; hinds balance forequarters; stifle joint is well turned. Built for trotting, the Rottie should move with sureness and balance; bowhocked and cowhocked dogs must be disregarded. The coat must be straight and dense, not wavy, curly or long; the undercoat exists but is not visible through the coat.

The butcher's dog of Rottweil has gone on to fame beyond all Germany's dreams. The most popular dog of the decade is a powerful, mastiff-drover dog colored in black and tan. OWNERS, MARTIN AND FLORENCE THOMSON.

OWNER SUITABILITY

The well-bred Rottie is a gentle, family-loving animal and a natural guard dog. Temperaments vary: some are independent, aloof and less friendly while others are outgoing and gregarious with everyone. He is a medium-large dog of incredible strength who must be properly trained and socialized to love people. Rotties are active dogs and very agile for a dog of their size, capable of jumping and running with ease. They are well mannered enough to live indoors and are happiest when with their people. Attack training of any kind is highly discouraged else his already protective nature be overstimulated and therefore uncontrollable. To a degree, all Rotties are aggressive and are unsuitable for timid or unconfident owners.

Never select a Rottie for bigness alone. He is a big dog, no doubt, but his greater virtues are his sound temperament, good hips, and desire to please his master. OWNERS, SCOTT AND LISA COTE.

286

GROWTH

Birth weight ranges from 12 to 18 ounces, though pups from very large litters may weigh less. Growth is relatively slow at first, but then should quicken. Weight at eight weeks should be about 14 or 15 pounds. Prospective owners must avoid the overly large Rottweilers so commonly advertised, as these dogs are much more prone to skeletal problems, including HD, as well as bloat and other complications. The Rottie is naturally a big dog, making it senseless and harmful to select for even larger ones. Prospective owners need to select carefully, insisting on health certificates and proper screening of breeding stock. Check the movement (gait) of both puppies and parents, and of course insist on good even temperaments in both. Avoid the shy Rottie and any pup coming from aggressive parents. The importance of socialization and training cannot be overstated. Maturity is reached between two and three years.

The Rottweiler puppy is outgoing and friendly, not suspicious or shy. The dam should be likewise, neither too protective, aggressive or nervous. OWNER, ROBERT C. SARRO.

HEALTH

Temperament and HD are Rottie breeders' two main concerns. Prospective owners should insist on temperament-tested parentage and early socialization of the pups. Owners should continue socialization and enroll in puppy kindergarten to help ensure a sound Rottie temperament. Only pups from HD-clear parentage should be considered. Rottweilers have proven unusually susceptible to parvovirus, and this has become an important concern of breeders. Other known problems affecting the breed include entropion, retinal dysplasia, osteochondrosis, and pancreatic disorders; these are limited in occurrence. Some breeders have also reported dietary complications, and owners are advised to inquire about this and follow a breeder-recommended feeding plan. Grooming needs are minimal, though abundant training and plenty of exercise are required. Guard against heat stroke. The Rottie can live to ten-plus years, with heart disease, cancer and bloat the common causes of death.

Everyone and his Fraüline is breeding Rottweilers these days. You can't afford not to be selective. Make sure the parents and grandparents have been screened for hips. Screening is not a show-dog thing: who wants a Rottie that limps at age two and must be euthanized at age five? OWNER, ROBERT C. SARRO.

Rottweiler

Saint Bernard

DESCRIPTION

The Saint Bernard is a balanced, tall and muscular dog with a very powerful and imposing head. The skull is massive and wide, with noticeable wrinkles (not exaggerated); muzzle is short and does not taper; nose is very substantial and black; ears set high with strongly developed burr; eyes medium size, set more to front than sides, set moderately deep, dark brown. Neck is set high and very strong with pronounced dewlap (not overly developed). Chest is moderately deep and very well arched, not reaching below elbows; back very broad and perfectly straight (sway backs and overly long backs are very incorrect); legs well developed and muscular with moderately angulated hocks (not cowhocked or bent too much); hindquarters not straight with strong pasterns; forelegs straight, not

The Saint Bernard bears the saintliness and name of the Archdeacon Bernard de Menthon, founder of the Hospice in the Swiss Alps, where he has saved well over 2,000 lives over the past centuries.
OWNERS, DR. CLYDE E. AND CATHERINE E. DUNPHY.

out at elbow. Tail broad and long, very heavy, hanging straight down or slightly bending (never erect or rolled over back). The coat can either be very dense and shorthaired, lying smooth, or longhaired or medium length, plain to slightly wavy (not curly or shaggy). The dog should stand at minimum $27\frac{1}{2}$ inches at shoulder; bitches stand 25 inches. In color the dog is solid white with red markings or solid red with white markings; brindle patches with white.

Bernard puppies should not be canonized until they have been properly schooled. The breed does well in the home though can thrive on a mostly outdoor life.

OWNER SUITABILITY

A giant saint, the Saint Bernard is a blessing for the right owners. He loves family life and revels in the company of children. Cold weather doesn't bother him, nor does a mostly outdoor existence, though he is biddable and reliable in the home. Although he is a clean animal, he tends to slobber, so owners should be forewarned. Generally he is not the most extroverted soul, but is rather the deep, slow thinker. A very deliberate animal capable of competent guard work and of a beautiful even disposition.

288

GROWTH

Litter size is generally large, though smaller litters occur. Whelp size is typically just under a pound. Saint Bernards grow at a remarkable rate, particularly during the first year when 25 or more pounds may be gained in a month. Growth may be uneven, resulting in a temporarily disproportionate-looking dog. Owners must be knowledgeable of the breed and are encouraged to work closely with their veterinarian through the first year. Feeding a high-quality food in restricted, prescribed

This three-pound toddler will gain about 25 pounds per month for the next few months.

amounts has proven best. Allowing these pups to eat to their full or feed on lesser quality food has often resulted in growth complications, as has oversupplementation. The best start to proper growth, of course, is good breeding, and owners are encouraged to shop carefully and insist on screening for hereditary conditions. Temperament is rarely a problem, but suffice it to say that an unruly Saint Bernard is a 200-pound problem. With proper upbringing, the Saint Bernard should mature to a courageous, devoted, gentle canine.

Giant breeds grow rapidly and often problematically. Owners must never overfeed or supplement the puppy. Diet greatly affects a puppy's orthopedic well being.

HEALTH

The Saint Bernard is a rapid-growth giant breed, making it susceptible to a variety of skeletal and bone-related problems. Hip dysplasia is a very serious problem—owners must select only from HD-clear lines. Pituitary abnormalities are common, owing in part to the breed's acromegalic nature; these most commonly result in bone-growth problems, excess skin, and diabetes mellitus. Bloat and cancer (especially bone cancer, osteosarcoma) are not infrequent. Entropion, ectropion, and distichiasis are less serious problems. Hemophilia B and epilepsy are infrequent but are reported.

Despite the only moderate popularity of the Saint Bernard, new owners must still be cautious about the selection of a puppy. Be sure the parents and grandparents have been screened for the many problems reported in the breed. Your hours of research can add years to your new puppy's life.

Saint Bernard

Saluki

DESCRIPTION

The dignified Saluki is an elegant and graceful sighthound with characteristic deep far-seeing eyes, a lovely long and narrow head, and long legs. The adult Saluki stands on the average 23 to 28 inches tall. The skull is not domed, nor is the stop pronounced. The ears are long and covered with long, silky hair. The eyes are dark to hazel and bright, not prominent. The neck is supple and long, and the chest deep and moderately narrow. The shoulders are sloping and set well back; forelegs are straight; hip bones are set well apart and stifle is moderately bent, low-to-ground hocks and well-arched long toes. The Saluki's construction lends itself to its light, effortless gait in which the body is lifted off the ground, not flung forward. The coat is smooth throughout except on ears, legs, back of thighs which are graced with long, silky feathers; in the smooth

As ancient as civilization itself—some say—the Saluki predates all other domesticated breeds and has bred pure since the time of Alexander the Great (329 B.C.). Today he remains a regal purebred of keen sight and intelligence.
OWNERS, CHRISTINE McINTYRE AND CHARLIE COPE.

variety, all feathers are absent. Salukis can be white, cream, fawn, golden red, grizzle, silver grizzle, deer grizzle, tricolor; but never brindle.

OWNER SUITABILITY

Only a special person should be owned by a Saluki, an ancient regal breed whose elegance and exotic charm cannot be exceeded. Salukis move with the grace of a cat; they also sleep in a ball like a cat and clean themselves similarly. They can live in congenial harmony with other breed members or other dogs. Intelligent and aloof, these animals are not overly demonstrative yet are friendly, playful and enjoy entertaining the family. Some breed members can be nervous and high strung if improperly reared and socialized.

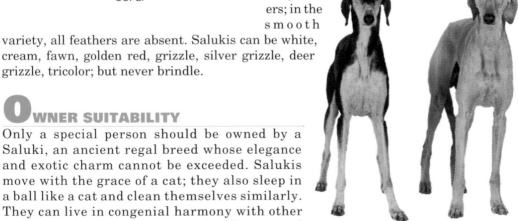

Dignity mixes with gentleness to create the Saluki expression. The Saluki is a sensitive companion animal who must be regarded and trained with both virtues that engender his expression.
OWNER, P. REYNOLDS.

Birth weight and growth rates vary in the breed, though most pups grow rapidly during the first months. Size at maturity also varies, with some lines typically larger than others. Owners should select for sound construction and balance and pay special attention to temperament. It is important to visit the parents, or at least the dam, and consider her temperament. Note that Salukis usually drop their coat after whelping a litter. The breed matures slowly, taking as long as four years to complete. Salukis need room to grow and should not be kenneled or crated for extended periods.

Although Salukis prefer the royal treatment, spoiling them can do as much harm as good. Provide the Saluki with soft bedding to avoid the possibility of calluses.
OWNER, EILEEN BARBIERI.

Adolescence usually lasts a couple years. Proper socialization is imperative. Young Salukis are known to be sly, to test their owners, and to wander if given the chance. A pleasant home environment is essential to developing a happy, well-balanced dog.

HEALTH

The Saluki's freedom from most hereditary problems affecting the domestic dog is partially attributed to centuries of highly selective breeding in its native Arabia. Even HD and cryptorchidism are rare. However, as every rose has its thorns, the Saluki is among few breeds to demonstrate a tendency to develop psychosomatic illnesses. These illnesses usually affect the skin and/or digestive system and are believed to be stress-related. Socialization and companionship are vital to this dog's health. The Saluki does not fare well alone or confined nor does it do well in the company of overbearing or intimidating breeds. Other special concerns include bedding, as the Saluki may develop serious calluses, including on its breast, if not provided with soft bedding. Fussy eating can also be a problem, and provided a good-quality diet is most important. Sensitivity to anesthetics due to their lack of body fat must be considered, as well as susceptibility to flea dips and barbiturates. A limited occurrence of heart disease, PRA, and cancer is reported. Salukis commonly live 13 to 16 years when properly maintained.

Purebred dogs pass on their physical features as well as their behavioral traits. Salukis often assume this characteristic cross-legged position.
OWNER, MELINDA CAMARDELLA.

Saluki

Samoyed

DESCRIPTION

The beautiful Samoyed, with his lush coat of glistening white, is constructed as a legitimate working dog. Beyond his dignity and "Snow White" grace, he must be agile and strong, though his full-bodied ruff doesn't make him look so rough. The dog is close-coupled, and therefore not long in back; ideally dogs should be strong in back and muscular, with deep chest and well-sprung ribs, a strong neck, straight front, moderately long legs, particularly strong loins, well-bent stifles. The Samoyed is a dog of substance and his bone is heavier than one might expect from a medium-sized dog who stands 21 to $23\frac{1}{2}$ inches (females 19 to 21 inches). Nevertheless, he is not so massive as to interfere with speed and agility, nor is he heavy and clumsy; neither is he light or racy. The outer coat should stand straight out from the body and the undercoat should cover the whole body and be soft, thick like close wool. An abundant coat is desirable, though quality must be considered first—it must be weatherproof! The Samoyed's lovely head and smiling expression are of paramount importance. The skull is wedge shaped and broad, not round or apple headed, with a medium muzzle. The ears are strong and thick, erect and triangular with slightly rounded tips. The eyes must be dark, not blue; nose should be dark, though dudley noses are not penalized. The tail is moderately long, profusely coated and carried forward over the back or side. The dog can be pure white, biscuit, or cream; no other colors are acceptable as Samoyeds.

A working dog by definition, the Samoyed's ancestors herded reindeer and pulled sleds while the Arctic sun bleached their coats snow white.
OWNER, CHERYL A. WAGNER.

Only a fool would try to put the Samoyed smile into words.
OWNERS, MRS. REYNOLDS-PARNHAM.

OWNER SUITABILITY

Despite their snow-white coat and love of the snow, Samoyeds are indoor dogs as their love of their people is not exceeded by anything. More often placid than not, Sams can be willful and somewhat stubborn too, thereby requiring a good loving disciplinarian as an owner. Shedding occurs three times per year (depending on climate) and is extensive. Barking is not a problem in the breed, if properly trained, but no doubt they are vocal (some owners claim they talk). If you work all day and must leave your dog, spare the Samoyed the agony. These dogs demand attention and can become destructive if ignored. Their sweet dispositions and absolute devotion to man make them appear even more beautiful than their lovely exteriors.

Growth

The Samoyed is a natural and hardy breed having few breeding complications. Puppies develop rapidly and are soon inquiring about their environment. Ears are usually erect by six weeks, though they may drop during the teething period. Weight at eight weeks varies from 9 to 13 pounds. Owners should select for an outgoing, friendly puppy who is square in outline, with all four feet firmly on the ground, toes pointing forward. The coat should be thick and woolly, eyes dark, head broad, and muzzle short. It is important that nose, eye rim, and paw pad pigmentation be dark. Adolescents are known for their destructiveness and big appetites. Between six months and one year, the coat change occurs, and plenty of grooming is required, as during the shedding periods.

Health

The well-maintained Samoyed of proper breeding enjoys excellent health and can be expected to live into its teen years. Hip dysplasia, deafness, dwarfism, PRA and other eye problems are known but have been largely limited by re-

If a Samoyed's personality and smile do not sparkle like an icicle, it simply isn't a Samoyed. Temperament is all in the Samoyed. These dogs have interacted closely with man for time immemorial and understand the human species better than anyone.

sponsible breeding. Blue eyes occur (often accompanied by albino characteristics) and are a disqualifying fault. This certainly can lead to health-related complications. A few known Samoyeds have suffered from myasthenia gravis (muscle weakness), pulmonic stenosis (lungs), and some reports indicate a genetically linked zinc deficiency. Samoyeds must be protected against the sun and obesity. A northern breed, Sammies can fall victim to heat stroke and exhaustion. The white coat can suffer sunburn, leaving brown patches. Obesity both lessens the dog's tolerance to the sun and can lead to other health problems. Older Samoyeds are known to develop kidney disease and cancer. Some lines are known to be very sensitive to anesthesia.

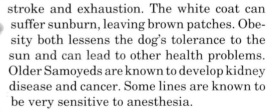

Keeping the Samoyed pure white requires less time and care than might be imagined. A quality coat provides near self-cleaning insulation for the dog. OWNERS, C.E. KIGHT AND CHARLOTT J. CONNIFF.

Samoyed

Schipperke

DESCRIPTION

The impudent sailor, the Schipperke is always well dressed in his black cape, jabot, culottes and ruff. His face is foxlike, although his tail is not, as he is decidedly tailless. This mischievous little mariner stands a mere 11 to 13 inches, lady sailors an inch less. He is square in profile and thickset, casting a unique silhouette, with a slope from shoulders to croup. The skull is of medium width, appearing round, with oval rather than round eyes that are small and dark brown. The ears are small, placed high and erect, never drop. The neck is of moderate length and proportionate; topline is level; chest is broad and deep, reaching elbows; ribs are modified oval and croup is broad and well rounded. Shoulders well back; forelegs straight; hind appearing lighter than forequarters; hocks well let down and stifles well bent,

How easy is it to bring home a faithful sailor!? The Schipperke glows like a black diamond in the "ruff" and is a true find for the proper nautical family. He's small, foxy and Flemish!
OWNERS, DOM AND CLAUDIA ORLANDI AND BRENDA S. BIBLE.

not overly angulated. The coat is distinctive for its ruff and cape around the neck, culottes on rear of thighs and jabot across the chest. It must be abundant, straight and slightly harsh with a dense undercoat. In color the Schipperke is black; in England and Europe other self-colors are permissible, such as creams and fawns, though these are not showable in the U.S. and Canada.

OWNER SUITABILITY

"The best little house dogs," Schipperkes are fond of children and do exceptionally well in the family situation. They become ready protectors for their families and place trust in each member of the family. They are independent and intelligent and need a devoted family to spend time with. Overall they are quite friendly, though reserved around strangers (who never remain strangers for long).

Schipperkes can become very people-oriented but should be exposed to different adults and children at a young age.
OWNERS, VIKKI INGRAM AND ANN WALTHALL.

294

Growth

Though smaller litters are the norm, litters of as many as eight do occur. Average birth weight is 5 ounces. Tails and dewclaws are removed during the first week. By eight weeks, Schipperkes weigh around 5 pounds. Growth rate is varied, but in general full height is achieved between six months and one year. Full maturity, however, may be as late as three or even five years. Bite is subject to change and should be monitored for the first year. Puppies should be colored in a deep black and have triangular ears that sit high atop the head. The soft puppy coat will change to the more coarse adult coat around five months. The abundant coat with distinctive ruff may not be completely developed until after one year.

Health

By far one of the healthier and longer lived of all canines, the Schip has been known to attain 20 years of age. Hereditary abnormalities are very rare, as are any other breed-specific problems. The most common problems faced by Schipperke owners are allergy-related, ranging from asthma to dermatitis. Proper grooming of the easycare coat can help limit some of these problems and certainly helps in early detection. The Schipperke requires more dental attention than most other breeds. This includes regular professional-type cleaning. Entropion occurs, though not to any great degree. Two serious conditions that are occasionally encountered are epilepsy and Legg-Perthes disease. These are possibly more line-specific and should be inquired about. The Schip is an active and highly trainable breed, and owners should capitalize to the fullest on these qualities.

Ever alert and distractible, Schips need structured feeding and training times. Young ones sail through puppyhood always looking for an enticing port or new dock to explore. OWNER, CAROLYN KROSINSKY.

Schipperkes make excellent house dogs and train with little difficulty. Although only 1/24 fathom high, the Schipperke measures up as a watchdog, proving very protective of his family.
OWNERS, DR. CHARLES MORGAN AND PATRICIA NIGEY.

Schipperke

Scottish Deerhound

DESCRIPTION

The Deerhound resembles a rough-coated large-sized Greyhound—he stands not less than 30 to 32 inches as a male, for bitches 28 inches and upward; males weigh 85 to 110 pounds, bitches, 75 to 95 pounds. He must not appear coarse due to excessive size, but always symmetrical and of good bone, capable of easy and true action. The head is long, carried high, and well balanced. The body itself is long, very deep in brisket, with well-sprung ribs and great breadth across hips. The forelegs are strong and quite straight, with elbows neither in nor out. Thighs should be long and muscular, with good second thighs and well-bent stifles, well-arched loins and a goodly tucked-up belly. The coat should be harsh and wiry, shaggy and thick, about 3 to 4 inches in length, not woolly, though a mixture of silky and hard hair is generally acceptable in the U.S. Feet are close and compact with well-knuckled toes. Ears are set on high and eyes are dark and moderately full with a soft look in repose. The tail is long and slightly curved. In color the dark blue-gray is commonly preferred over the others, though he comes in lighter grays or brindles and yellows, sandy red, red fawn with black points. A white blaze on head or collar is unacceptable.

Deer Season! Here's a proud 32 inches of dog once used to remove antlers off the Scotch plains. Today, although athletic and trainable, this mythical beauty is more likely to be chasing the family cat or a unicorn than any wild quarry.
OWNER, JOHN D. HOGAN.

OWNER SUITABILITY

Gentle dignity in a mudless coat, the Scottish Deerhound is a reticent gentleman and most obedient. Deerhounds are intuitive and responsive to mild correction. They are very tall and seemingly aware of their size, as they are easygoing with children. Of course, exercise is essential for the harmony and balance of this athletic running hound. He does not wander and enjoys being close to his family.

GROWTH

Litters are generally large, both in number and size. Eight pups weighing 1 to 2 pounds is the norm. Pups are born black, usually with white spots on the chest and toes. The coat will lighten and grizzle with age. Removal of dewclaws optional. Growth rate varies between lines and even in individual dogs. It is often sporadic and can be influenced by genetic and environmental fac-

Puppies have abundant energy and need supervision and rest during their growth spurts. Crate training is not advised for Deerhounds.

tors. Typically Deerhounds grow rapidly for the first year and must be ensured a nutritious diet. While obesity is rarely a problem, over-nutrition can lead to growth problems. Full height is attained by 18 months, though full maturity usually takes about three years. Deerhounds generally do not mature sexually until after one year of age. Adolescent Deerhounds need to be protected from their own energy, especially during any awkward periods when growth is uneven and balance and coordination suffer.

Bloat claims many Deerhounds' lives. Breeders advise owners to feed smaller meals and to limit exercise.
OWNER, BETINA ADAMS.

HEALTH

Deerhounds in general live long, healthy lives. Getting them smoothly through the growth period is critical, as complications in growth and development are certain risks. Knowing your dog's line is important, and feeding a breeder/veterinarian-prescribed diet and offering plenty of exercise are necessities. The Deerhound's exercise requirements remain high throughout its life, diminished of course during the senior years. Because of this high-activity level, coupled with the breed's deep-chested conformation, owners must especially guard against bloat, which claims a fair number of the breed every year—the usual precautions of smaller meals and limiting exercise before and after feeding are givens. Care with anesthetics is advised. Grooming is not excessive, but owners should expect to spend about an hour a week brushing and lightly trimming the coat. Fortunately, HD is rare in the breed, but should nonetheless be checked. Heart problems are known to affect older dogs. Cystine uroliths also affect the breed. Life expectancy is between ten to 13 years.

Scottish Deerhound

Scottish Terrier

The Scottie is the tops for many an admirer: he's been at the foot of Scottish kings, American presidents, and many a Best in Show judge. This flawless lady is Champion Gaelforce Post Script, the 1995 Westminster Best in Show winner.
OWNERS, DR. VANDRA L. HUBER AND DR. JOE KINNARNEY.

DESCRIPTION

Very compact and very muscular, the Scottish Terrier is an intensely wirehaired terrier weighing 19 to 22 pounds (bitches a pound less), who appears solidly powerful for his diminutive size. The skull is long and of medium width with a good-sized black nose, square and level jaws, and evenly placed teeth in a scissors or level bite. The ears most definitely are small and prick, set well up on skull, pointy with short velvety fur on them. Eyes are set wide apart and almond in shape, not round or light colored. The neck is moderately short, not clumsy, and thick and the shoulders are sloping. Chest is broad and deep, well let down between the forelegs. The body is moderately short and well ribbed up with strong loin, deep flanks and very muscular hindquarters. Of great importance are the legs, which must be short and heavy in bone; the forelegs are straight or slightly bent, never out at elbows; stifles well bent and legs straight from hock to heel. Feet must be round and thick. The shortness of the legs and deep chest give the Scottie a peculiar gait where the forelegs incline slightly inward. The tail is about 7 inches long, never cut, and carried with a slight curve (not over back). The coat is rather short (about 2 inches). In color, the Scottie is steel or iron gray, brindle or grizzle, black, sandy or wheaten. Slight white marks on chest permissible.

A joyful find for an intelligent, level-minded owner, the Scottish Terrier puts on no airs, doesn't make merry without reason, and doesn't give away his heart without a long-term commitment.
OWNER, DONNA M. CONE.

OWNER SUITABILITY

Those who love the Scottie tell us that you don't fall in love with him at first sight, though living with him will convince anyone to his side. Scotties think they are large dogs, with the boldness and courage to match. He is independent and therefore difficult to obedience train and often slow to housebreak. The Scottie tends to be a rather dour, sober fellow who knows that life is serious and that it is to be met with dignity. They are adaptable and enthusiastic at work; sensitive to praise and blame; enjoy well-behaved children; and prefer attention in their own prescribed doses.

GROWTH

Weight at birth is 6 to 8 ounces. Pups may be born black, brindle or wheaten. Color will begin to clear in a few weeks, when a better determination of color is possible. White spots on the chin and chest occur, and provided they are not large, usually recede by maturity. Owners should select for large-headed (in proportion to body of course), long-backed pups with a solid stance and good movement. Eyes should be clear and dark, never round, and the tail free from kinks. Growth is typically without complication, though conformation is subject to change. Front legs may lose their straightness and eyes may lighten as late as six months, for example. Full height is achieved some time around one year, with full maturity coming later. Grooming the terrier coat must begin at a young age and stepped up during the changeover to adult coat. Plucking is usually performed every two to three months, depending on the growth of coat.

If you're heading for the show ring with your Scottie puppy, look for a large head, long back, smooth movement, and character befitting this assertive little terrier.
OWNERS, LOIS MILLER AND JANE ROBINSON.

HEALTH

The Scottie is a hardy little dog with a strong resistance to disease and high tolerance to pain. Scotties enjoy life and generally exhibit zest and fortitude. Owners must guard against overfeeding, as excess weight can lead to back problems. Stair climbing and similar activities should be limited during the first year and the older years. Several hereditary diseases are known to affect the breed, including von Willebrand's disease (a blood platelet disorder) and craniomandibular osteopathy (an unusual and little understood disorder affecting the jaw bones). These both are rare. A breed-specific hyperkinetic disorder known as "Scottie cramp" is believed to be a recessive trait found in the breed. It is characterized by intermittent spasms in which the limbs, back and tail muscles become rigid. Treatment is available. Symptoms may appear as early as six weeks. Thyroid problems, hematomas of the ear, and allergies are more commonly reported and can often be treated. Achondroplasia, deafness, and lens luxation are also rarely reported. Kidney disease and various carcinomas are the ailments of older dogs. Life expectancy is about 12 years, although some reach their late teens. Grooming needs include professional stripping and usually involve an hour or two each week.

Scottie cramp is no joke and can interfere with playtime and standing ovations.
OWNERS, JACK AND MARGARET BANKER.

Scottish Terrier

Sealyham Terrier

Named for the estate of his creator in the late-19th century, the Sealyham Terrier possesses a unique coat comprised of hard and soft hair: there is nothing else soft about this terrier, a game slayer of badgers, foxes and otters.
OWNERS, FRANEL BROWN, CHRISTINE STEPHENS AND P. STUCKEY.

DESCRIPTION

Above all the Sealyham should appear perfectly balanced, a terrier of great determination and purpose with extraordinary substance. He stands about $10\frac{1}{2}$ inches at the withers and weighs 23 to 24 pounds (height more important than weight). The head is long, broad and powerful, not coarse and perfectly balanced. The skull is very slightly domed with a shallow indentation between brows and a moderate stop. Cheeks are smooth and flat without heavy jowls; nose black (not white, cherry or butterfly). Eyes are very dark, set deep and fairly wide apart. Ears are folded level with top of head, well rounded at tip, thin, and not leathery. Prick, tulip, and hound ears are bad. Neck is of good length and reach, refined at throat; shoulder well laid back, not too muscular; forelegs strong with good bone; chest well let down (not down on pasterns, knuckled over, bowed, or out at elbow). Hindlegs are not as long as forelegs, and less heavily boned; hindquarters powerful, stifles well bent, hocks well let down (not cowhocked). The body is strong and short coupled; topline level. The coat is weather resistant with a dense undercoat and a hard wiry top coat, neither curly nor silky. In color, the Sealyham is all white with lemon, tan or badger markings on the head and ears. Markings on body and excessive ticking not favored.

OWNER SUITABILITY

Energetic and loyal, Sealyhams make ideal children's playmates, perceptive watchdogs and competent workers. Bred for the hard work of catching badgers, foxes and other vermin, the Sealy has a strong digging and chasing instinct that needs channeling. Today's dog is more elegant and more likely to be seen sweeping around the show ring than burrowing after badgers. Their high-energy level may be more than an elderly person can readily handle.

ROWTH

At eight weeks, Sealyhams weigh 5 to 7 pounds. Tails are docked to one-third to one-half during the first week. Full height is reached around eight months; full maturity comes around 12 to 18 months. Owners should select for a pup having a solid white body, free of markings (some markings acceptable for the pet dog), with dark eye rims, dark brown oval eyes, and medium-length back. The head should appear large for the body; the legs be straight; the tail carried high. The eight-week-old coat is smooth, not fluffy. The Sealy experiences a gradual coat change around four to five months, which usually coincides with the teething period. Stripping facilitates this process. Color may lighten during this change, especially if the coat is clipped. Adolescent dogs may prove "piggy" eaters and do require exercise. Aggression toward other dogs may be experienced around 18 months, but is outgrown if dealt with properly.

The Sealyham may not upset the badgers in your neighborhood, though his big-dog bark is quite a deterrent for would-be intruders. OWNER, FRANCE BERGERON.

HEALTH

The major breeder concerns involve the eyes, skin and coat. Retinal dysplasia, evident from birth, and lens luxation are both known in the breed. Congenital retinal dysplasia, often accompanied with cataracts, results in early blindness. Glaucoma occurs and is reportedly the result of lens luxation. Most skin and coat conditions are allergy-related. Early detection of allergens is most important, and prevention includes checking into the breeding lines, and subsequently ensuring proper diet and grooming. Epilepsy and deafness are also breeder concerns. Grooming needs are considerable, as professional grooming is often required. Owners should expect to spend at least an hour a week maintaining the Sealy's plentiful double coat. He is in no way a show piece for the home but is definitely an active dog that requires plenty of exercise and playtime. Owners must guard against back injuries, for while the breed is not prone to them, its long-backed, low-to-the-ground construction makes such injuries real possibilities. Sealys usually live 12 or more years.

Sealyham Terrier

Shetland Sheepdog

DESCRIPTION

"A show Collie in miniature" aptly describes the Shetland Sheepdog: this is a small, longhaired, rough-coated working dog whose outline is distinctly symmetrical and whose refinement is not shy of perfection. Without variation, the Sheltie stands 13 to 16 inches. The refined and expressive head is shaped as a long, blunt wedge that tapers slightly from ears to nose; correct expression is achieved through the perfection of the balanced parts. The ears are small and flexible, placed high and carried three-fourths erect, with tips falling forward. Correct ears are essential—they must never be hound, prick, bat or twisted. The eyes are medium in size, almond shaped and dark brown or blue (in merles). The stop is slight but definite, neither prominent or undefined. The skull is flat, not domed; cheekbones flat, not prominent; muzzle well rounded, not snipy. Neck is arched and chest is deep with brisket reaching point of elbow, not narrow or shallow; back is level and not too long or short, neither swayed nor roach; ribs must be well sprung and not slab-sided or barrel. The tail is sufficiently long, not too short or twisted. The forequarters must be sufficiently angulated with good length of upper arm. The coat is double with a long, straight, harsh outer coat and a short, furry, dense undercoat, with mane and frill abundant. Short and flat coats, softness or silkiness, smooth coats and lack of undercoat are faults. Colors include black, blue merle and sable with white and/or tan. Faded colors, white body spots and brindles are not desirable.

The Shetland Sheepdog, affectionately called the Sheltie, derives from Border Collies bantamized on the Shetland Islands. Indeed he appears to be a perfect miniature of today's Rough Collie. OWNERS, KATHLEEN SCHMUTZ AND LINDA S. GRIFFITH.

When selecting a puppy, temperament not color should be your first concern. Puppies, like their dam, should be friendly and responsive.

OWNER SUITABILITY

A well-socialized, calm puppy makes the most ideal Sheltie to adopt as a pet. The breed makes excellent family dogs who are gentle with children. Shelties tend to be busy dogs and therefore need employment (or a lot of play). Be aware that the Sheltie is a vocal dog and his bark is very high—save your fillings, teach him not to bark at a young age. Very easy to train, Shelties are adaptive and will tolerate children introduced later into the family, and yet protect them, recognizing they belong to his flock, too. Sensitive and happy, Shelties have a lot of love to share and sense an owner's mood instinctively.

GROWTH

Birth weight ranges from 4 to 10 ounces. In general, coloration at birth is a good indication of adult color, except some gold and mahogany appear very dark and lighten with age, and tricolors and blue merles often have very little to no sable at birth, which should appear by two to three weeks. Blue merles are typically grayish blue with black marbling. White markings change little, except that the blaze usually lessens. Coloration is largely a matter of personal preference, though more than two-thirds white and sables with blue eyes should be avoided. Owners should select for well-socialized, lively and friendly pups. Adolescent Shelties can be somewhat coatless, leggy, gangly, and less attractive than the mature adult. Prior to the coat change, the color may turn a drab grayish hue. It may take two or even three sheddings of this coat to attain the full adult coat. During teething, the ears may prick or drop and may require assistance, either weights or braces as necessary. The testicles may be as late as 12 months in descending.

If reared with love and gentle discipline, the Sheltie puppy will never lose his natural sparkle and will grow to become a treasured, perfectly behaved companion dog. The breed is intelligent and keenly perceptive of its owner's moods and feelings.
OWNER, SHERRY LEE.

HEALTH

The well-bred Sheltie proves a hardy, highly intelligent dog that can live well into its teen years—Shelties have been known to exceed 16 years of age. Skin problems seem to be on the rise, and the breed's plush coat requires lots of brushing, especially during the shedding season. Specialized care such as trimming is minimal. Grooming should be done daily to prevent mats and subsequent skin problems. Exercise requirements are average. The breed's good disposition makes training a pleasure, and owners should capitalize on this. Eye problems are a major concern. Breeders feel that the eye conditions are being bred out, but potential owners should be aware that such conditions as PRA, cataracts, ectasia syndrome (a retinal vessel problem), and trichiasis are reported in the breed. Insist on eye-screened breeding stock, and have your pup tested as well to head off any possible problems. Other problems, all limited in occurrence, include HD, thyroid deficiency, epilepsy, nasal solar dermatitis ("Collie nose") cryptorchidism, deafness, pemphigus, vWD, and dwarfism.

Not for the child who is whining for a Shetland Pony, the Sheltie does not take kindly to the zealous mauling of toddlers. Older children who respect a dog, however, are the Sheltie's best friends.
OWNER, SHERRY LEE.

Be sure to check the blue-merle puppy's hearing by calling it or clapping your hands. This color pattern is more prone to deafness than the others.

Shetland Sheepdog

Shiba Inu

DESCRIPTION

A perfect dog in miniature: the Japanese Shiba does not have a small dog appearance, but rather a large, muscular dog scaled down to perfection. He is, however, a small dog (judging by the yard-stick not the attitude-stick) standing only $14\frac{1}{2}$ to $16\frac{1}{2}$ inches, bitches, 1 inch less. The head is a blunt wedge with well-developed cheeks and defined stop; muzzle moderately thick; nose black; lips close fitting, black in color; eyes deep set and almond shaped sloping slightly upward—not round or unoriental in appearance; ears are small, triangular, and pricked, ideally with furnishings; neck is of medium length; back straight and level; loins broad and muscular; chest deep; tail set on high, thick and carried curled or sickled over back. Proportions are slightly longer than tall. Forelegs are straight; hindlegs are well muscled with medium bend of stifle. The coat is double, harsh and straight on the outside, soft and dense on the inside. Colors include red, red sesame, and black and tan; other colors such as white, cream, pinto, brindle occur but they are not true Shiba colors, belonging instead to the other native breeds of Japan.

More miles per gallon than any of its small Japanese competitors, the Shiba Inu corners the market on personality, attitude, and ingenuity. All grown up, this is the author's first Shiba, Jacquet's Tengu, bred by Rick Tomita. Tengu is smarter than any Shinto god, doesn't share his secrets, and refused to edit his caption.
OWNER, ANDREW De PRISCO.

"The most beautiful girl in the world" is Maikohime of Akatani, known in the author's home as "Kabuki," a theatrical whirlwind of mischief and kisses. Kabuki never has a bad day, always waking up to the greatest morning of all!
OWNER, ANDREW De PRISCO.

OWNER SUITABILITY

His appearance is eye-catching and enchanting, yet the Shiba is not for everyone. These are quick and high-strung little dogs with big ideas and as much energy and industry as Japan itself. They are clean and catlike in their habits, even attempting to climb onto tables and windowsills. They love to be outdoors but are very comfortable inside as well, though they tend to tear about the house if you let them. No doubt the Shiba knows he's special and his owner must know he's special too. Training is challenging because the Shiba thinks he's smarter than you are and doesn't see much gain in silly repetition. All in all, Shibas have a problem being told to do things that they don't think they want to. Show dog puppies should have mouths inspected daily, since many Shibas are real idiots about having their mouths touched. Shibas have strong fleeing instincts and are very prey-oriented—quick-footed and quick-minded (likely they'll only hunt for themselves). If you like one Shiba, you'll love a second—of the *opposite* sex.

GROWTH

Shiba puppies are very dark, nearly black, with the adult color developing by five or six weeks. The ears will stand naturally by the age of eight to ten weeks. The Shiba is such a natural breed that few dramatic changes occur. Puppies are individualistic from the moment they can waddle. Obedience training is essential early on. Shibas will resist lead training unless introduced from young puppyhood. *Never* attempt walking a Shiba off lead. Shibas may make a honking noise when excited—don't be alarmed.

HEALTH

Grooming needs are not excessive, though a weekly brushing keeps the coat clean and mat-free. During bi-annual shedding season, combing with a medium steel-tooth comb helps to move the undercoat along, as will a hot bath. Some Shibas despise water and no amount of getting used to will help. Be firm and good-spirited, the Shiba will challenge you constantly. The Shiba is a most hardy dog, though some dogs are more sensitive than others. Keep ears and anal glands clean; be aware of flea infestation and hot spots. Hip dysplasia and PRA are not major problems but screening is still advisable. Some lines have proven predisposed to heart murmur and thyroid deficiency. Some dogs suffer from slipped knee caps. Shibas live 12 to 16 years.

Shibas dance and celebrate their Japanese heritage on their toes, as Kabuki effortlessly demonstrates. True to her name, Kabuki uses her dramatic soprano voice freely whenever her freedom is challenged. OWNER, ANDREW De PRISCO.

Shiba mothers are very serious about their roles. The Shiba is a natural breed and experiences few health problems. Puppies will be unique from a very early age but should always be people-oriented. OWNERS, RICHARD TOMITA AND KAREN STEITZ.

Let not the author's bias or these fuzzy urchins sway you, the Shiba grows into a strong-willed, often needlessly creative canine who requires an experienced, ready-to-go owner with a sense of humor. Like *cats,* they're clean, cunningly intelligent and highly trainable! OWNERS, RICHARD TOMITA AND KAREN STEITZ.

Shiba Inu

Shih Tzu

DESCRIPTION

The Shih Tzu is a proud toy dog of noble bearing and arrogant carriage whose long, flowing coat, distinctive facial furnishings, top knot and tail plume over his back assure his unmistakably pure Chinese lineage. Despite the acknowledged variation in size, the Shih Tzu must be compact and solid, of good substance and weight (10 to 16 pounds). Ideally he is 10 to 10½ inches, never less than 8 inches nor more than 11 inches. The head is round and broad, in balance with the dog. The eyes are large and round, not prominent or close-set, looking straight ahead. The ears are large and heavily coated. The skull is domed and the stop is definite; muzzle is short and square, not downturned. The neck is well

Just what the eunuch ordered: the Shih Tzu, the perfect little person dressed in lion fur, a tribute to the Buddhist deity and centuries of meticulous breeding. The "chrysanthemum-faced dog" still adds color to many homes and palaces today.
OWNERS, GREGORY AND TAMMARIE LARSON AND SUSAN BLETZINGER.

set on and of sufficient length to allow for high natural head carriage. The body is short coupled and sturdy, slightly longer than tall, not leggy. Chest is broad and deep, not barrel. Tail is set on high and heavily plumed over the back. Shoulders fit smoothly into body; legs straight with well-bent stifles; hocks well let down. Coat is luxurious and double, possibly with a wave. Hair on head is tied up. All colors occur and on particolored dogs, the white blaze on forehead and tail tip are desirable.

Shih Tzu owners profess that these are not dogs.....and perhaps they are pocket-sized deities...but they still require grooming, training, and care like any less divine house dog. Best of all, Shih Tzu are affectionate and trusting to all.
OWNER, GINGER J. RABER.

OWNER SUITABILITY

Few dogs are as unconditionally loving as the Shih Tzu. These are truly little people cocooned in silky fur who intuitively understand your every word and respond accordingly to your feelings. They are the epitome of toy dogs, love to be spoiled and carried around, yet they do not become rotten and obnoxious like some other toys. They bond very closely with the lady of the house and are playful and accepting of other dogs and children.

GROWTH

Shih Tzus weigh 6 ounces at birth. All puppies should be checked for cleft palate and cleft lip, which are passed recessively in the breed. Pups are born smooth coated and their puppy fuzz grows quickly—by seven weeks they look like long-coated dogs, and by three months the chrysanthemums are in bloom! The first puppy clip will be due by six months. Coloration is largely a matter of preference, and coloration varies considerably in the young pup. Not until the adult coat change can true color be determined exactly. Owners should select for dogs having dark, well-pigmented noses, except liver-marked dogs, which may have liver noses. Also check for clear eyes and avoid lethargic dogs or dogs with overdeveloped rears. Owners should be strongly familiar with the standard regarding the tail, legs,

Select a puppy that is not experiencing breathing difficulty, with clear, non-protruding eyes, and that is neither lethargic nor overly excitable. Show dogs should exhibit dark pigmentation without overdeveloped rears.
OWNER, POLLIOT.

and head and select accordingly. Temperament should also be considered, avoiding shy or surly dogs. Introduce grooming early on since the Shih Tzu has a high-maintenance coat unless clipped down.

HEALTH

Shih Tzu are susceptible to slipped stifles, which can be corrected through surgery. Most important is proper grooming, including care of the eyes; their protruding eyes are susceptible to lacerations, and their lids and lashes can sometimes be irregular. The eyes should be checked for excessive/insuffi-

The puppy clip ideally suits the young Shih Tzu with play on his mind.
OWNER, GAY PAYNE.

cient tearing and treated accordingly. Pinched nostrils (stenotic nares) may occur around six to eight weeks due to their short muzzles. Affected dogs may snort and sniffle with a watery discharge from the nose. These dogs must be guarded against heat stroke and respiratory difficulties in general. Owners should expect to spend at least two hours weekly keeping the coat lustrous and mat- and tangle-free. The teeth require regular cleaning and scaling. (If the teeth are crooked or the bite incorrect, more care will naturally be required.) The most serious hereditary conditions include renal cortical hypoplasia (a kidney disease) and cleft palates and lips. Umbilical hernias are also hereditary and can be seen from six to eight months. Thyroid malfunction, von Willebrands, cherry eye, and eye ulcers also concern breeders. With proper care, well-bred Shih Tzus commonly live into their teen years. Clean up after your Shih Tzu *promptly* to avoid any "messy snacking."

Shih Tzu bond closely with their owners and therefore need a completely committed and available keeper. If you're not at home all day, the Shih Tzu politely asks you to turn the page....or to get him a nanny.
OWNER, GAY PAYNE.

Shih Tzu

Siberian Husky

DESCRIPTION

The Siberian Husky is an enduring, well-furred working breed of typical northern characteristics, including his brush tail, pricked ears, and alert, friendly expression. His pleasing head is medium sized, slightly rounded on top with a medium-length muzzle, not snipy or coarse, tapering gradually to the nose, not pointed or square. The eyes are almond shaped, brown or blue or one of each color; ears are medium size and triangular. The neck is medium in length and arched. Chest is deep and not too broad; back is straight and strong, not weak, slack, or roached, with level topline. The tail is well furred and shaped like a foxbrush, gracefully carried over the back. The shoulders are well laid back, not straight or loose, and the forelegs are straight and parallel, with close elbows. The hind-legs are moderately spaced and well muscled with well-bent stifles and well-defined hocks. The feet are oval and not long. The double coat is medium in length and the outer coat hairs are straight and smooth lying, not harsh to the touch and off-standing. Siberians can be colored most variously, from black to pure white, in some eye-catching patterns not found in other breeds, usually with a typical Nordic mask on the face. The coat must not be so long as to obscure the outline of the body. The Siberian stands 21 to $23\frac{1}{2}$ inches at withers, bitches 20 to 22 inches. Dogs weigh 45 to 60 pounds; bitches 10 pounds less.

Engineered for endurance hauling over the frozen tundra, the Siberian Husky takes the command "mush" with great seriousness. Sledding his way to Best in Show is Champion Kontoki's E-I-E-I-O looking F-A-B-U-L-O-U-S at four and a half years old. OWNERS, N. WISNIEWSKI, B. MOYE, M. DePALMA, AND T. OELSCHLAGER.

OWNER SUITABILITY

Among the most beautiful of all dogs, the Siberian Husky enthralls his owners with his unaffected, friendly air and love of children and play. These are high-energy, high-emotion dogs who thrive on people and relate exceedingly well to their owners. He is easily bored and thrives on the companionship of another dog (or even a cat). His need for exercise is great, nearly always bursting with get-up-and-go, and he loves being outdoors. Due to his incurable need to make friends, he is a lousy guard dog.

Siberians are robust, working dogs that require much daily exercise. They do not adapt to life indoors as well as most other dogs. Any northern breed designed for running cannot be trusted without a fence and must be walked on lead. OWNER, KATHLEEN KANZLER.

GROWTH

Birth weight ranges from 12 to 16 ounces. Coloration varies greatly, and many different colors and color patterns are possible in the same litter. Eye color too varies, with brown, hazel, and blue eyes (including odd eyes) possible. Cryptorchids are not uncommon. More important than color is pigmentation. Growth rate varies in the breed, and familiarity with specific lines is helpful. Dogs which experience rapid growth spurts will likely experience a gangly, awkward stage, usually around four to six months. Prescribed feeding adjustments may be helpful. Maturity may come as late as three years. Siberians may prove picky eaters. In general, the breed does best on smaller meals having a relatively high-protein content. Young dogs may develop loose stools, which may signal that a higher protein ratio is required.

For such a popular breed, the Siberian Husky doesn't present many problems for selection. Be sensible and evaluate the puppy's good temperament, consider the dam's friendly, calm manner, and ask about the breeder's conscientious screening of his stock.
OWNER, MARGARET COOK.

HEALTH

The Siberian enjoys good general health with few breed-specific problems. Fortunate for the breed, Siberian breeders began early testing for HD, making the breed today one of the least affected by the condition. Eye problems are more common and a major breeder concern. Huskies are affected by PRA, corneal dystrophy, cataracts, and others. These are all of limited occurrence, and only dogs coming from eye-screened parentage should be considered. As with other plushly coated northern breeds, daily brushing is a must to prevent skin problems, including zinc-deficiency skin disorders, dermatitis, hot spots, patchy coat, etc. The breed's tolerance to heat is naturally less than other breeds, making such precautions as not allowing excessive exposure to direct summer sun, reduced exercise in the heat, and allowing plenty of water in warmer weather necessary. The Husky's endurance is phenomenal and his daily exercise requirement is fairly high. Puppies from racing-dog lines may be too hyper as home pets.

Training should begin early to convince the Siberian of the benefits of learning.
OWNER, MARGARET COOK.

When the eight-week-old is ready to go home, he should be gentle, eager and friendly.
OWNER, C. RAND.

Siberian Husky

Silky Terrier

DESCRIPTION

The blue and tan Silky Terrier is a true toy terrier with a coat *silky* in texture, otherwise straight, single and glossy—not so long as to reach the floor nor to obscure body outline, well groomed but not sculpted in appearance. The profuse hair on the head forms a topknot, colored in silver or fawn. The Silky stands 9 to 10 inches at the shoulder, no more or less. The head is wedge shaped and strong, moderately long. The ears are small and V-shaped, carried erect and set high on the head. The skull is flat and the stop shallow. The neck is medium-long and fine; topline level, without a dip; chest is medium-wide and deep to the elbows; body moderately low-set and tail is docked, set high, well furred without plume. The shoulders are well back; forelegs straight and rather fine boned and feet are catlike and small. The thighs are strong but not heavy, with well-angulated stifles and low hocks. The blue coloration varies from silver blue, pigeon blue or slate blue and the tan is always deep and rich.

A 20th century spin-off of two popular toy terriers, the Silky Terrier combines the virtues of the Yorkshire and Australian Terriers. The Silky has the best of both worlds: the charm of a toy dog and the bravery of a terrier. OWNERS, WILLIAM A. AND STEPHANY S. MONTELEONE.

OWNER SUITABILITY

The lively Silky Terrier is an ideal, easycare miniature terrier. His coat, comprised of near-human hair, does not shed and he loves being indoors with his mom and family. Yet, he is not *just* a lap dog; he is hardy enough for outside and reportedly has been used for hunting in Australia. They tolerate children but do not enjoy being constrained by toddlers. He is easy to train, and despite all his silk has remained "a dog" and an instinctive one at that! He is not high-strung so treat him like a terrier, not a toy.

All rise for a terrific little dog that doesn't leave his toys or hair all over the house. When trained properly, Silkys are responsive and obedient. A problem Silky is a spoiled Silky. OWNERS, GINNY CURTIS AND NORMA BAUGH.

Silkys at eight weeks weigh $2\frac{1}{2}$ to $3\frac{1}{2}$ pounds. Dewclaws should be removed and tails docked to one-third during the first week. Color changes on the body to a silver-blue to slate-blue with tan face and feet and fawn-colored topknot. Physical maturity is attained usually by 18 months, when full size and adult coat and color are completely developed. Ears prick by four months. Silky puppies should be outgoing and friendly. Shy puppies may become fear biters. Silkys need plenty of socialization and time spent with their human family. They have a strong need for discipline and consistency. Well-raised Silkys become protective of their family and home territory and make great watchdogs.

Silky puppies aren't too silky from the beginning. The coat takes nearly 18 months to reach maturity.
OWNERS, M. L. AND S. STEGEMANN.

HEALTH

The average life expectancy of the Silky is about 12 to 13 years, though individuals have been known to reach near 20. The breed is a hardy, actually rugged dog adorned with a luxuriant coat. Grooming needs are not excessive, with frequent 15-minute sessions generally prescribed. Only a little trimming is required. Regular exercise and consistent disciplinary training are musts. As a breed the Silky Terrier is relatively free from health problems, although the common conditions affecting the "toy" breeds, including hypoglycemia, cryptorchidism, patella (knee cap) luxation, kidney stones, and diabetes mellitus, may occur. Legg-Perthes disease is documented. Additionally, though rare, a condition known as storage disease has been found in the breed. Affected individuals are often normal at birth but fail to grow properly, and later succumb to the disease.

By four months or before, the Silky puppy's ear will stand up naturally.
OWNERS, M. L. AND S. STEGEMANN.

Silky Terrier

Skye Terrier

DESCRIPTION

Despite his name, the Skye is twice as long as he is high. An elegant terrier with a profuse coat falling straight down the sides of the body. The coat is hard and straight and forms a characteristic veil over the forehead and eyes, and the ears are fringed with long feathering. Ideally the Skye reaches only about 10 inches, bitches $9\frac{1}{2}$ inches. The dog should be long, lean and level. The head is long and strong with medium, close-set eyes, dark in colors and symmetrical ears, carried prick or drop. The drop ears tend to be larger. Muzzle is just moderately full, not snipy. The nose must be black (dudley, flesh or brown-colored noses disqualify). The neck is long and gracefully arched and backline level. Tail is long and well feathered. Shoulders well back, not loose or tied; forearms straight and sound; chest deep with oval-shaped ribs. Large harelike feet pointing forward for preference. Hinds short and straight. Skyes are self-colored in black, dark or light gray, silver platinum, fawn, cream, all with black points, but no distinctive markings.

Only experienced, discriminating dog owners dare sign up for a lifelong excursion to the Isle of Skye. The Skye Terrier has no limits on style, elegance and dignity, plus he's a manly terrier, fearless, territorial, and a tad clannish.
OWNERS, ROXANA L. ROHRICH AND GLEANNTAN KNIS REG.

OWNER SUITABILITY

As his fanciers will acclaim, as terriers go, the Skye's the limit! This is a sensitive and spirited terrier breed who knows his people and needs his people to know him. Like any other good terrier, he is somewhat stubborn and needs a firm hand in training. Although stubborn and seemingly fearless, remember the Skye is sensitive and does not respond well to harsh scolding. He's a great indoor dog but enjoys moderate exercise. He's not the best friend of many children and is more likely the choice of experienced dog folk.

The drop-ear Skye Terrier is commonly seen and can occur in the same litters as the prick-ear variety.
OWNER, CATHERINE McLEOD.

GROWTH

When buying a Skye, what you see is *not* what you get! Young Skyes are small and adorable with little coat and an undeniable resemblance to Mickey Mouse. Skyes grow to be bigger than a mouse or a Yorkie, for that matter, and should be considered a big dog (with little-dog legs!). The coat invariably comes in soft and by five months is replaced by good-textured hard hair. Puppy coats that remain cottony will not improve; good-textured hair at this age only gets better. Dogs with narrower heads have little problem with their ears rising. Dogs with good fore-face need assistance in getting their ears up. Getting *both* ears up takes some doing—including clippering the hair on the ears to lighten them up. Teething doesn't help either. Puppy colors do change, though not dramatically. Often a band of color may indicate the adult color. The Skye has a demanding

Trust your breeder about what your Skye puppy will grow up to look like. In time the puppy's coat, ears and color will evolve to look more like that of a Skye Terrier.
OWNER, JOAN FINGAR.

coat and from puppyhood it must be attended. The coat is not mature until 18 months of age or more. Both drop ears and prick can come in the same litter. Prick-eared Skyes should only be bred to the same. Keep an eye out for the puppy's teeth as the correct bite is most important in the breed and missing molars and premolars are a common problem.

HEALTH

All in all, the Skye is a hardy, long-lived dog. Owners must realize that the adult dog has a high-maintenance coat. Daily brushing guarantees a mat-

"I'm going to Disneyland!" Mouse ears are more predictable than Skye ears.
OWNER, DIAN TEBO.

Before these two darlings fly away from their dam, notice that two prick-ear pups came from a drop-ear mama. Training the Skye requires a steady, experienced hand and a pint of patience.
OWNERS, SUSAN PARSONS AND ROBIN STILES.

free coat. A tangled Skye coat is a true horror. Kinked tails, usually detectable at birth, occur frequently and are undesirable, although they are not described as faults in the breed standard. Juvenile limp affects the forelimbs of many Skyes around three to eight months of age. Limiting exercise is helpful at this time, though the condition is most always self-correcting. A more serious forelimb condition known as premature closure occurs in Skyes. It can only be positively identified through X-ray and many breeders are screening for it. A rare nervous system disorder marked by an enlarged foramen magnum is characterized by unusual compulsive behaviors such as ear scratching. This is not well documented in the breed. Veterinarians report a genetically linked copper toxicity as well as an inherited metabolic liver defect.

Skye Terrier

Smooth Fox Terrier

DESCRIPTION

Swift, enduring and powerful aptly describes the Fox Terrier, who should embody the symmetry of the Foxhound. The Smooth Fox must have a smooth, flat, but hard, dense and abundant coat. He is by no means leggy, nor is he short on leg, able to cover a lot of ground, and he possesses a desirably short back. He does not stand taller than $15\frac{1}{2}$ inches at the withers, and the length of back should not exceed 12 inches. Ideally he weighs about 18 pounds, though weight is no fair assessment of a terrier's fitness. The head is flat and moderately narrow, not much stop, gradually tapering from eyes to nose. Cheeks are not full. The nose is black, not white, cherry or spotted. The eyes are dark and moderately small, rather deep set and full of fire; ears are V-shaped and small, dropping forward to cheek, never rose, prick or tulip. Neck is clean and not throaty; chest deep, not broad; ribs deep and well sprung; shoulders long and sloping, elbows close; forelegs straight; feet round and compact, not large. The hindlegs are responsible for power in movement and they must be strong and muscular, with good reach of second thigh and well-curved stifles. White must always predominate on the coat: he can be solid white, or white with tan, black and tan, or black. Brindle, red and liver are highly undesirable.

The cleverly made hunter stands solidly on his four legs, the perfect picture of fitness, endurance, and strength: the Smooth Fox Terrier embodies the active terrier with eyes full of fire.
OWNERS, MICHAEL AND SUZANNE SOSNE.

OWNER SUITABILITY

Perhaps of all breeds, Fox Terriers are for everyone...almost. These are sturdy, clean little dogs with a lot of spirit and personality, able to fit into any lifestyle if given a fair chance. They are easily trained, easily groomed and easily loved. The Fox Terrier needs to be properly socialized to mellow his terrier heart. He loves to bark, and digging is a talent which needs to be expressed. Firm reprimand is all the Fox Terrier needs to understand your wishes.

He is at once obedient and attentive: life with the Fox Terrier is *smooth* and easy.
OWNER, LINDA HILL.

Fox Terriers weigh 3 to 4 pounds at eight weeks. Physical maturity is attained by 18 to 24 months. Tails docked and dewclaws removed by the end of the first week of life. Tail docking is important and should only be performed by an experienced breed-knowledgeable person. Essentially one-third of the tail should be removed. Owners should select for a pup with a good, long, lean skull, without any bulky bone, especially behind the eyes (known as cheeky). The legs should be parallel, feet small, very tight, with well-arched toes. Avoid pups with toes turning either in or out, as well as pups with rear legs that are very close together. The ears usually become erect around teething time. Proper ears and bite cannot be guaranteed until seven months. Typical of the terriers, adolescent dogs often test their owners' authority. Consistency and firmness are the keys.

A feisty addition to your family's den: the Smooth Fox Terrier puppy should be friendly and busy, adding happy commotion to anyone's life.
OWNER, DEBRA DEHNE.

HEALTH

The Fox Terrier is a hardy and exceedingly well-constructed canine with a life expectancy of over a dozen years. While not a problem breed, the Fox Terrier is affected by disorders of the eyes and bones. Lens luxation, distichiasis, and cataracts are all reported in the breed. The few bone problems (hip dysplasia is rare) include shoulder dislocation and Legg-Perthes, which affects other terriers as well and involves deterioration of the femoral head, resulting in progressive lameness. Deafness, goiter, subaortic stenosis, pulmonic stenosis, recessive ataxia (usually occurring at two to four months of age, the result of a spinal cord defect that causes uncoordination which may progress to paralysis) are uncommon. Myasthenia gravis is a musculature disorder that appears to be associated with an enlarged esophagus in the Smooth Fox. Grooming is minimal, little more than a couple once-overs a week.

An ideal first dog for the inexperienced, the Smooth Fox is a user-friendly choice.

Smooth Fox Terrier

Soft Coated Wheaten Terrier

DESCRIPTION

A well-balanced, steady sporting terrier whose battle cry is moderation: the Soft Coated Wheaten Terrier shuns all exaggeration—in structure and presentation both, he is a middle-of-the-road terrier. As his name denotes, his coat is soft and silky and his color is wheaten, preferably warm in tone. He stands 18 to 19 inches at withers, bitches, 1 inch less; and he weighs 35 to 40 pounds, bitches, 5 pounds less. The head is well proportioned yet moderately long and rectangular in appearance; eyes are medium in size and slightly almond shaped; ears small to medium in size and dropping slightly forward; skull is flat and clean; not cheeky; defined stop; muzzle strong; nose black and large. Neck is medium in length, not throaty; back is strong and level; chest deep; ribs not round but well sprung; tail docked; feet round and compact. Forelegs straight; hinds are well developed; stifles well bent. The adult coat is an abundant single coat and must not be woolly or hard, crisp or cottony, curly and standaway, or straight. The wheaten color varies in shade and may have stray red, white or black guard hairs, though the overall color must appear wheaten.

As Irish, smooth, and strong as a keg of ale, the Soft Coated Wheaten Terrier reigned in the Old Country as an all-around hunter, terrier, guard dog and companion. His soft coat exposes his big heart, less aggressive and scrappy than most other terrier breeds.
OWNERS, HELEN WILSON AND ELENA LANDA.

OWNER SUITABILITY

A pliable personality and a good heart, the Wheaten is an excellent family dog and a competent watchdog. Alert and responsive, he delights his family members with his fun-loving approach to life. As a puppy he looks much like a stuffed toy, but under all his soft wheat he is very much a terrier. They love to be doing something: occupy your Wheaten before he gets into too much mischief. He can be stubborn—no surprise for a terrier—so be firm and kind and he will respond.

On the large side for a terrier, the Soft Coat excels as a watchdog. He is fairly territorial and ever so protective of his family.
OWNERS, NEIL AND DIANA EDWARDS.

318

GROWTH

Birth weight is 5 to 8 ounces. Tails are docked and dewclaws removed soon after birth. Potential coloration at birth varies greatly, ranging from a light gray to almost completely black. Brown or reddish brown birth color is most common. Nose and paw pads should be black by three weeks. The birth color will change dramatically as the pup matures. During the younger months, a black mask and black stripe down the back are common and will fade with maturity, culminating in the Soft Coated's hallmark wheaten color. By their senior years, Wheatens whiten and lose their warm tone. Extra daily grooming is required throughout the coat change as matting is a definite problem. Owners should avoid puppies born blonde, lacking pigmentation, and those with yellow or green eyes, as these are genetic faults. Soft Coats are generally not big eaters. They typically require high-protein diets, possibly with vitamin-mineral supplementation.

The Soft Coated puppy wears his heart on his sleeve...who could ask for a more eager puppy?! OWNER, HILTON.

HEALTH

The Wheaten's heritage of guardian and hunter has demanded that it be a hardy, disease-tolerant animal, which it has proven to be. While veterinary research is not conclusive, it seems that Wheatens suffer from few hereditary diseases; HD and PRA are of very limited occurrence. The major breeder concern focuses on heart problems, as evidence suggests that it may be a breed defect. Older dogs commonly succumb to a heart condition. Veterinarians report cases of lymphangiectasia in the Wheaten. Otherwise, allergies and skin conditions are the most common concerns, as Wheatens have been affected by both. Grooming is rather considerable, with several weekly 30-minute sessions the norm which are helpful to prevent skin irritations and detect any problems in an early stage. Some trimming is also involved and the areas around the eyes, ears, and anus should be kept free of excess hair to prevent infection.

Wheatens are easy to occupy. This little guy thinks he's at the circus.

Soft Coated Wheaten Terrier

Spinone Italiano

DESCRIPTION

A squarely built and sturdy gun dog with a rough and tough coat, the Spinone Italiano stands $23\frac{1}{2}$ to $27\frac{1}{2}$ inches, bitches 2 inches less. Dogs weigh 70 to 82 pounds; bitches 62 to 71 pounds. The head is long and flat, with gently sloping sides; eyes large and fairly round, color deep yellow to ochre; ears are long and pendulous, triangular in shape. Neck is strong and fairly short; shoulders strong and well laid back; forelegs straight; pasterns slightly sloping; chest broad, well let down; topline, slightly sloping from raised withers to loins. Thighs long and strong; hocks well let down; feet compact and round. Coat is thick and slightly wiry, furnished with eyebrows, moustache and beard. Colors include white, white with orange, white with brown; patterns are speckled (roan) with or without patches.

The great Italian hunter, the Spinone Italiano represents one of the Continent's most versatile and ancient pointing dogs. The name derives from the Italian word for thorn ("spino"), which describes his wiry coat. OWNER, F. RILEY.

OWNER SUITABILITY

An adaptable hunting dog of superb trainability, the Spinone Italiano is not familiar to most of us. This is a gentle gentlemanly hunting dog who does well with a family. He is steady and self-confident and largely independent. He is well suited for the company of other dogs and will cohabit with other animals without complaint or issue. His grandfatherly appearance gives him a distinct appeal and he is a natural guardian for children. Spinones should be exposed to the hunt as their instincts are very keen and they respond quickly to training.

The polite pointer, the Spinone expects no less from his master. OWNER, VINOLA VALENTINO.

GROWTH

The Spinone weighs 9 to 11 pounds by eight weeks. Breeders allow two-and-a-half years for physical maturity to complete. Owners are strongly advised to follow the breeder's prescribed feeding and exercise program, especially until maturity. Owners should particularly monitor the bone development of the legs and back. Most Spinones are good eaters, so avoid overfeeding. Adolescence is marked by the changeover to the hard adult coat and some darkening of the coat color. Training and socialization should strive to produce a steady, self-confident canine.

HEALTH

While the Spinone has long graced his native Italy, the breed is relatively new to the English-speaking world, where veterinary data is lacking. It seems apparent that the Spinone is in general a healthy and hardy dog, true to his hard-working hunter ancestry. As with any other deep-chested breed, bloat can occur, and necessary feeding and exercise precautions must be followed. There is also an incidence of HD, and while specific percentages are unknown, owners should insist on screening. Skin allergies have been reported by breeders, as are limited cases of thyroid problems. Grooming is not particularly difficult but is important both for good health and for proper coat development. Ears should be checked and cleaned regularly to prevent infection.

For all his virtues, the Spinone remains a rarely seen purebred who still awaits his day in the sun.
OWNER, F. RILEY.

Although his exterior is one of a docile hunting dog, the Spinone is brave and highly protective of his family. He does nicely indoors but prefers lively exercise and a bird to find.
OWNER, F. RILEY.

Spinone Italiano

Staffordshire Bull Terrier

DESCRIPTION

For his inches and pounds, the Staffordshire Bull Terrier is of great strength—likely for anyone's inches and pounds, he is a wonder of strength. This is a muscular smooth-coated dog, the epitome of activity and agility. His inches are 14 to 16; his pounds 28 to 38, bitches 4 pounds less. The head is short and deep; foreface short, distinct stop; the skull broad; cheek muscles very pronounced; nose black (not pink). The eyes are dark and round, of medium size; ears are rose and half-pricked, not large in size, full drop nor prick. The neck is muscular and rather short, not throaty; body close-coupled with a level topline; deep brisket; tail is natural and undocked, tapering to a point and carried low. The forelegs are well boned and straight, set rather far apart; hinds are well muscled and parallel. The coat is close to the skin and short, in red, fawn, white, black or blue, and any shade of brindle, with or without white. Black and tan and liver-colored dogs are most undesirable.

Bred for the purpose of dog fighting, the Staffordshire Bull Terrier maintains his gameness and spirit despite his change in occupation. A paradigm of loyalty and steadfast honor, Staffordshires make excellent family pets and guard dogs. When acquired from reputable sources, they are infinitely trustworthy. OWNER, MICHAEL GOLDFARB.

OWNER SUITABILITY

Staffordshires require a family or person who have time to invest in them and their education and socialization. These are easily trained dogs: they are eager to please and enjoy being occupied. He is people-oriented and very intelligent, no doubt a high-energy dog with much talent and athletic ability. He is not the choice for a multi-dog household and same-sex dogs will spar. Owners must be aware that this English breed is *not* the Pit Bull and has been slandered by the press for his similar appearance. Staffs come from different stock and are exceedingly trustworthy with no history to the contrary.

The Staffordshire weighs 8 to 10 pounds by eight weeks. Development should be moderate and steady. Overfeeding and supplementation to be avoided. After attaining full height, the Staff will continue to add substance. The skull typically broadens until full physical maturity, some time between 18 to 24 months, with males generally maturing later than females. Owners should look for a strong, outgoing puppy, compact and cobby with strong head and good overall balance. Coloration is unimportant, but owners should

Staffordshires require a caring owner that understands the breed's heritage and doesn't teach aggressiveness toward people or other dogs. In the wrong hands, the Staffordshire can become a dangerous, harmful dog.
OWNER, HARRY L. RODEHEAVER.

select for dark, solid pigmentation to the nose and pads. Adolescence is marked by abounding energy, and chewing problems are common: owners must offer outlets for both. Plenty of early socialization and training requisite to creating a well-adjusted, reliable home companion and watchdog.

The breed is more docile today than in the heyday of dog fighting, as these three well-bred, well-behaved show dogs exhibit. Don't be misled: you still cannot keep two same-sex dogs in the same home.
OWNER, JOAQUIN TORMO ESTEVE.

HEALTH

Very little is reported about medical problems affecting the Staffordshire Bull Terrier, and breeders report few to no breed/line-specific problems in programs. Bilateral cataracts, passed recessively are known to exist, and cleft palates and harelips are congenital problems that occasionally occur. Some dogs are prone to calculi (kidney stones). Early obedience and socialization are required for this strong and determined canine. Injuries, especially to the limbs and joints, are possible. The dog's high tolerance to pain and stoic nature may make early detection difficult. It is very important to know your dog. While grooming needs are minimal, a daily once-over is required. The ears and eyes should be checked for foreign bodies and early signs of infection. They are reportedly susceptible to tumors so owners should check over their dogs' externals regularly.

Staffordshire Bull Terrier

Standard Poodle

DESCRIPTION

The tallest Poodle breed, the Standard stands over 15 inches at the shoulder. The eyes are very dark and oval, not round, protruding or too large; the ears are close to the head with long leather but not too excessive fringe; skull is moderately rounded with a slight but definite stop; cheeks flat; muzzle long, straight and fine, with slight chiseling under eyes, and should not appear snipy. The shoulders are well laid back and not steep; forelegs straight and parallel; feet are oval and rather small, not paper (lacking padding) or splayed. Hindlegs are straight; stifles well bent. The coat should be naturally harsh in texture and always dense; although seen uncommonly, the coat may be corded with tight even cords. The Poodle can be clipped in any of the four acceptable fashions: Puppy, English Saddle, Continental, and Sporting. Poodle colors should be even and solid (varying in shades is allowable): colors are blue, gray, silver, brown, cafe-au-lait, apricot and cream. Particolored dogs are disqualified from competition. Nose, eye rims, lips, toe nails and eye color should adhere to the dog's color.

Perhaps the most recognizable dog in the world, meet *Canis Familiaris Aquatius, le Caniche, der Pudel, el Perro de Lanas,* the Duck Dog: the Poodle. In his duck-hunter's clip, the Poodle remains a most popular and dignified companion dog, show dog, and performance dog.
OWNER, EDWARD JENNER.

OWNER SUITABILITY

Poodles are egotistical dogs and thrive on praise, applause and attention. The Standard Poodle is regarded as the most intelligent of all breeds of dogs. If you are seeking an obedience worker or an easily trained dog, do not overlook this handsome dog. Socialization is a must since the Poodle, for all his brilliance, can be pretty socially retarded and unfriendly towards strangers. Owners must work on his approachability, though with his family he is most affectionate. Poodles thrive on city life and do very well in that environment. Poodles display selective listening and memory, making them a challenge to conquer. This is complicated by their apparent sense of humor: the Poodle's *joie de vivre* is boundless. Owners should be aware of the time a Poodle's coat requires, particularly the Standard. If the show-clipped Poodle gives you the willies, you should consider that these haircuts were devised by he-man duck hunters for their dogs' maximum functionability.

GROWTH

Normal birth weight varies from 8 to 16 ounces. Tail length varies at birth, and proper docking requires experience. Dewclaw removal is optional. Depending on the color expected at adulthood, the puppy may change color as he matures. For example, gray Poodles are born black and change slowly to gray as they get older; apricots are often born a deep shade and lighten to a soft peach color by adulthood. Good pigmentation to the nose, lips, etc., is important. At eight weeks of age, the puppy weighs 5 to 7 pounds. Physical maturity is reached between 12 to 18 months. Choose a friendly, outgoing puppy as personalities do not typically change.

HEALTH

The Standard Poodle, for all its ornate clipping, remains a stalwart dog with some of its hunting ability still intact. Owners should not expect a showpiece but a high-maintenance dog with considerable exercise requirements. Because of the breed's coat and size, grooming demands are great, with professional assistance necessary for all but the simplest clips. Ear infections are common, and weekly cleaning is necessary. Hip dysplasia, especially with larger Standards, and eye problems are both known in the breed. Reported problems include entropion, distichiasis, iris atrophy, and juvenile cataracts. Tear staining may also be a problem. PRA has become an important concern of breeders, and buyers should discuss this before purchase as it can cause blindness. Epilepsy, vWD, some heart conditions, and improper bone development problems are documented. An inherited skin problem known as sebaceous adenitis has been screened for. Bloat is a threat to the Poodle, and the necessary precautions are strongly advised. Some dogs may have bad reactions to rabies vaccinations. Standard Poodles commonly live 10 to 14 years.

The Poodle's coat is more abundant and plush than any other breed. Although it is not necessary to clip the pet Poodle in one of the traditional patterns, the coat will need to be trimmed down for the animal's comfort. Accustom the puppy to clipping at any early age: his first haircut will be a day to remember.
OWNER, KAREN S. GRACE.

The brain pack: the intelligence of the Standard Poodle is nothing short of superlative. He's obviously the smartest of all since, unlike the Border Collie whose intelligence is well known, the Poodle can never be seen chasing sheep. "How droll!" says the Poodle.
OWNER, KAREN S. GRACE.

Standard Poodle

Standard Schnauzer

Once cast on canvas with the Madonna by the likes of Rembrandt, the Standard Schnauzer today has simply been cast aside by the dog-buying public. The Schnauzer is the oldest of the three recognized breeds and counts herding, ratting, guarding, retrieving, and police work among his diverse talents.
OWNERS, GABRIO DEL TORRE AND RITA HOLLOWAY.

DESCRIPTION

A ruggedly constructed, medium-sized dog with a typically dense, harsh coat, accessorized by arched eyebrows, a bristly moustache and good Schnauzer whiskers, the Standard Schnauzer stands a sturdy, well-boned, well-muscled $18\frac{1}{2}$ to $19\frac{1}{2}$ inches (an inch less for females). Height variations are not tolerated in show circles. He is square in proportion, his body length equaling his height. The head is rectangular and long; eyes medium in size, oval and dark brown; ears set high, erect and cropped or uncropped and V-shaped, carried forward (never prick or hound); skull is flat, not domed or bumpy; muzzle strong; cheeks well developed, but not overly; bite scissors. Neck is strong and of moderate thickness and length, nicely arched; topline horizontal; back strong, straight and short; body compact and short coupled; chest medium width; belly moderately drawn up, not excessively so; tail set moderately high and erect, docked (not squirrel-like). The shoulders are sloping and strongly muscled; forelegs straight; hinds muscled and not higher than shoulders; thighs broad with well-bent stifles. The coat is tight, hard, wiry and very thick: undercoat soft and close; outer coat harsh. Two color possibilities include the pepper and salt (combination of black and white hairs creating a dark gray to silver gray appearance) and solid pure black. Top coat color should never appear rust, brown, red, yellow or tan, look spotted, striped, nor lack peppering.

OWNER SUITABILITY

Extremely loyal to his "own people," the Standard Schnauzer is a strong one-man or one-family dog. He is good with children if raised with them. He is rightly labelled territorial and his family is his family, and their friends rarely make it into his inner circle. Thus he is an excellent watchdog and most discriminating in the use of his deep bark. He has a good memory and is very consistent in his likes and dislikes. The combination of his intelligence, trainability and sheer love of fun makes him a prime choice for a companion. He does not always get on well with other dogs and cannot be trusted with small mammals, such as gerbils or mice. He is, after all, an exterminator by trade.

Growth

Standard Schnauzer newborns weigh 7 to 12 ounces and are generally all black in color. During the first few weeks, traces of lighter coloring will appear and spread as the dog matures. Rate of growth varies. Ears may be left natural or cropped. Tails are docked and dewclaws removed in the first few days. By eight weeks, weight should be 7 to 10 pounds. Some dogs may experience early growth spurts, while others may appear undersize yet grow rapidly later. Full height is reached around one year, though full maturity may come as late as three to even five years. Owners should select for the well-socialized puppy. Puppies require constant socialization through young adulthood. Breeders recommend puppy kindergarten and similar socialization/training involvement. The adolescent dog will likely challenge the rules of the household. The coat change will require special care.

In England and many Continental countries, only the drop-ear variety of the Schnauzer is seen. OWNER, DOROTHEE HENNE.

Health

The Standard Schnauzer is a hardy, active, intelligent, long-lived breed, enjoying its 15 to 17 years of life. Most problems are behavioral. Improperly socialized dogs, dogs which are traumatized by improper keeping, and otherwise neglected dogs do poorly. Grooming needs are considerable and vital. As with the Miniature Schnauzer, the Standard is affected by a specific type of follicular dermatitis commonly called "Schnauzer comedo syndrome. " Regular plucking seems to reduce this incidence. Also conjunctivitis caused by hair irritation of the eye is reported, as is PRA. Fatty tumors and adenomas occur in older Schnauzers. Some heart problems also affect the breed, with heart failure a common cause of death in older dogs. Pulmonic stenosis affects the lungs, and calculi the kidneys in some Schnauzers. Some flea and food allergies are also known.

A Schnauzer is truly a dog for life, potentially living to 17 years of age. OWNER, BARBARA M. DILLE.

A socialized Schnauzer puppy is your only choice. Select an outgoing, people-oriented puppy that has been exposed to people and various situations. Since the most prevalent problems in the breed are behavioral, socialization and training are the keys to the ideal Schnauzer companion. OWNER, KOEHL LIWE.

Standard Schnauzer

Sussex Spaniel

DESCRIPTION

Long and low and rather massive, the Sussex Spaniel is a rich golden liver-colored dog who stands 13 to 15 inches and ranges in weight from 35 to 45 pounds. He is a rectangular dog who is longer in body than tall. This is a muscular hunting dog of free movement with a notably somber, serious expression to him. His head is moderately long, not narrow, with a full stop; brows are fairly heavy, with full occiput, appearing heavy but not dull. Muzzle is broad and square, not weak. The eyes are hazel in color and fairly large, without showing too much haw. The ears are thick, fairly large and lobe-shaped, set moderately low. The back is level and long, very muscular in width and depth; the legs are set well under dog and are very short, strong and heavily boned; the hindquarters are full and well rounded, parallel and set wide apart; the feet are large and round. The color is most distinctive in the Sussex, and the golden liver must not be dark liver or puce; the occurrence of white on the chest is not desirable. The coat is abundant, flat, with no tendency to curl; legs moderately well feathered; ears furnished with soft, wavy hair; tail with moderate feather; longer hairs between the toes cover the nails.
The tail is docked from 5 to 7 inches and set low.

From Sussex County, England where the first kennel of these golden liver dogs were developed, the Sussex Spaniel has been distinct for about 150 years. His low-to-the-ground massive body qualifies his slowness; his nose is faster than his feet, but he's determined and can keep up with a hunter on foot.
OWNERS, NORMAN AND CONSTANCE GRENIER.

OWNER SUITABILITY

This is a low-key, warm and loyal breed of dog and his near-human personality is well conveyed by his beautiful hazel eyes. Sussex are never high-strung or aloof. He is a possessive, close-bonding animal, a true family dog who loves to be indoors. Don't be fooled by his size and temperament: he is an active, lively hunter and enjoys this opportunity. He is sensitive, so train him lovingly and he will respond in turn.

What you see is what you get: the Sussex adores family life and is ever content to snooze by his master's slippers. Don't culture a hearth potato: the Sussex thrives on outdoor activity, so give it to him.
OWNER, ANN S. CUMMINGS.

ROWTH

Though a substantial dog at maturity, newborn weight is only 4 to 6 ounces. Tails are docked slightly less than two-thirds and dewclaws may be removed during the first week. Early growth and development slow. Sussex pups weigh only about 3 pounds at five weeks. Growth accelerates after this point, however, and a weight of 6 to 12 pounds at eight weeks can be expected. Physical maturity may take a good two years. Owners should select for a dog with short legs, heavy bone, large feet, and long body. Temperament should be sweet and laid-back. During adolescence, color will lighten. Sunlight is necessary for proper color. Breeders

Begin your Sussex Spaniel's training from the first day. Even the most pleasant of puppies will want to have his way. Early training encourages social behavior and good potty habits. OWNER, ANN S. CUMMINGS.

comment that adolescent Sussex Spaniels are in general less active than other breeds but still require daily exercise. Eating habits are normal, though adults require generally less food than other breeds of the same weight. Obesity to be avoided.

HEALTH

The Sussex Spaniel suffers from few hereditary health problems and enjoys a long life expectancy of up to 15 years. The Sussex is essentially an easycare dog, with grooming and exercise needs not excessive. The dog's hunting instincts are intact, and owners are well advised to provide regular outlets. The long fringe must be kept tangle free, and trimming excess from the areas of the ears and anus is important. The ears of the Sussex are prone to infection and mite infestation, and owners must keep them clean and free from waxy build-up. The serious conditions affecting the breed are congenital heart problems and carcinomas, affecting older dogs. Hip dysplasia has a low incidence, and breeders report that Sussex Spaniels cope well when affected.

The show puppy should have short legs, large feet, and decidedly heavy bone. OWNER, ANN S. CUMMINGS.

Sussex puppies are convinced that the world is a nice place. If you're fortunate enough to find a litter of Sussex Spaniels, you will be challenged to choose the sweetest doll to take home. OWNER, ANN S. CUMMINGS.

Sussex Spaniel

Swedish Vallhund

DESCRIPTION

A fairly long, small dog who appears like a sturdily built working dog. The head is rather long and cut in a blunt wedge. Muzzle rather square; black nose; medium-size eyes of oval shape and dark brown in color; ears of medium size, pointed and pricked. The neck should be long and strong; shoulder blades are long and well laid back; back level with short, strong loin. Chest is long with good depth; chest oval; croup broad and slightly sloping. The hindquarters are well angulated with well-bent stifles and low hocks. Tails are docked or naturally short (if present, tails do not exceed 4 inches). The coat is medium in length, harsh, tight top coat with a soft woolly undercoat. The color is steel gray, grayish brown or yellow, or reddish yellow or brown; ideally there is a dark and well-defined mask and lighter marks around eyes, muzzle, and throat. Dogs should be 13 to 14 inches; bitches 1 inch less—ratio of height to length is 2:3.

A versatile Vallhund may be just what the herdsman ordered! Although his prowess is nipping at the heel of unruly cattle, this skill can be nicely applied to your herd of children and other pets.
OWNER, KATE DUNCAN.

OWNER SUITABILITY

A European breed that has made small strides in Britain and smaller ones in America, the Swedish Vallhund (or Vasgotaspets, as he is known at home) has been called a Corgi of a different color. While he may appear much like those beloved Welsh dwarfs, he is actually higher on the leg and more active and better tempered than the Corgis with a personality that is distinctly his own. Although he may never outrank the Corgi, in whose constant shadow he basks, he is a devoted companion animal, biddable and likes to be involved in the family activity.

A Corgi of a different color, the forest dog of Sweden compares to those Welsh breeds in every respect except color and popularity.
OWNER, MRS. R. BISS.

GROWTH

The eight-week-old Vallhund weighs 8 to 10 pounds. Prospective owners are encouraged to study the breed, attend shows, and visit the prospective breeder before making their selection. Vallhund puppies should be active, bold, happy and friendly. The ears should be small and neat, and the overall impression should be of a little working dog—as one breeder puts it, "almost all devil!" As the Vallhund matures its color will change to a rich sable (wolf sable), and the thick undercoat will grow in. Training requires firmness, and owners must be careful not create an aloof dog by harsh training techniques. As a spitz breed, the Vallhund can be quite vocal. Full maturity is reached between 18 to 24 months.

"Almost all devil" aptly describes the unique Vallhund, who does not shy from the use of his bark and the pursuit of his devilish ideals. A Vallhund promises more than fun to your presently orderly home.

HEALTH

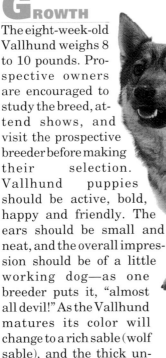

The Swedish Vallhund was long maintained as a working dog in his native Sweden and today's breeders have inherited a dog free from serious hereditary problems. Breeders report no disease problems in the breed, though proper screening for such common conditions as HD, PRA, and others is always a good idea. The Swedish Vallhund is a rather long-lived breed, commonly living 12 to 15 years. The breed's long-backed construction also seems to present no problems, though owners must keep their dogs trim and muscular with healthy feeding. The breed is an active one and requires plenty of exercise. The pleasant and pleasing personality lends itself to easy socialization.

Believe it or not, training the devil ain't as hard as you think. Vallhunds respond admirably to most training and welcome the opportunity to allow you to think for them....once in a while.

Swedish Vallhund

Tibetan Mastiff

DESCRIPTION

Powerful, heavy with good bone, the Tibetan Mastiff has a solemn and impressive appearance. This is a well-coated breed of good quality coat, fairly long, with thick undercoat. The head is fairly broad and heavy; skull massive; muzzle fairly broad; eyes are medium in size and brown; ears also medium and triangular, pendant and carried low. The neck is strong and arched with not too much dewlap; the surrounding mane is upstanding. The back is straight and strong; the shoulders well laid, strongly boned; forelegs straight and strong; chest deep with brisket reaching to elbows. Tail is medium to long, curled over back and well feathered. In color the Tibetan Mastiff can be black, black and tan, gold, or gray; white star is permissible on breast and minimal white on feet. The dog stands 26 inches high; females 2 inches less.

Unless you're on the Dalai Lama's goodwill gift list, you're going to have find this Tibetan treasure on your own. The Tibetan Mastiff is an impressive, formidable guard dog who is naturally territorially and protective.
OWNER, SUSAN ENGLE.

Perhaps the most appealing of color patterns for the TM is the black and tan: could this be a Rottweiler in a plush, long coat?
OWNER, M. PILAT.

OWNER SUITABILITY

A considerably large dog, the Tibetan Mastiff is a protective animal, aloof with strangers but not unfriendly. He is a wonderful companion but not so for everyone, since the teddy bear-like puppy does grow up into a sizable "dog." TMs need a securely fenced-in yard so that he will not wander and so that he knows his territory. Too large for toddlers to roughhandle, he is patient and gentle with children, but more so with *your* children, so do not let strangers or their children approach your dog until they know him. This is an adaptable, independent dog who needs encouragement and proper socialization. He is a nocturnal barker, and his voice is *booming profundis*, like a good guard dog's should be.

Growth

Tibetan Mastiffs are slow to mature and females reach maturity at two to three years; males not until four to six years of age. Size of whelps varies quite dramatically as reports of dogs larger than the desired size have been steady. At 12 to 13 weeks, TMs weigh about 40 pounds. Socialization of young pups is vital to nurture a biddable, amenable adult. The breed can be aggressive and stubborn. The adolescent can become a picky eater.

Your Tibetan Mastiff puppy should only receive moderate exercise and a good protein-based diet that doesn't overstimulate growth with no supplementation. This combination will help to alleviate possible growth problems and poor health conditions to which most large breeds are prone. OWNER, MELISSA WOLFE.

Health

Generally a healthy breed, TMs should be tested for hip dysplasia. Since the Tibetan Mastiff is not a true giant, he may live into his teens. TMs are prone to thyroid deficiencies as well as inherited demyelinative neuropathy, a genetic nerve disorder that affects puppies prior to 12 weeks of age—such puppies are not able to stand. Grooming demands are not great and they shed once annually. The Tibetan is remarkably adaptable to weather conditions, perhaps due to the breed's ancestors surviving the extreme temperatures in native Tibet. They can do well as outdoor dogs weather-wise, though they prefer to be indoors with the family.

The teddy bear appeal goes far with children. However, this trio of teddy bears will grow quickly into sizable dogs who will remain gentle with children they know. OWNER, MELISSA WOLFE.

Tibetan Mastiff

Tibetan Spaniel

DESCRIPTION

An unexaggerated, slightly elongated, well-balanced miniature dog, standing about 10 inches at the shoulder and weighing 9 to 15 pounds, the Tibetan Spaniel carries his head proudly and is a dog of quality, free from suggestion of coarseness. The head is slightly domed, moderate in size, not flat or wide in skull; stop is slight; eyes oval and dark brown, not large and full or light; ears are pendant and medium in size; muzzle is blunt and cushioned; teeth are evenly placed, tongue not visible when mouth is closed. The neck is moderately short with level back and good depth of rib; tail set high; shoulders well placed with slightly bowed forelegs, not loose in front; feet harelike, small and neat. The hindquarters are strong with moderately angulated good stifles, not straight; hocks well let down, not cow. The coat is double and silky in texture. Ears, forelegs, tail and buttocks are longer coated than rest of body; male dogs carry more mane (or shawl) around neck than do bitches. Tibetan Spaniels come in all colors and combinations.

More a miracle of careful breeding practices in Tibet than reincarnation, the Tibetan Spaniel promises dedication through its present life. He is is sensible: sensible in size, attitude, conformation and adaptability. OWNER, ARLENE TANEL.

OWNER SUITABILITY

The Tibetan Spaniel unfortunately falls through the cracks as a choice for a companion: he is not dramatic; he is not vehemently self-centered; he is not pocket-sized or moplike; he is not queer in appearance. Give thanks for such a sensible little dog! The Tibetan Spaniel is just medium-small, with a very large heart and bigger-than-life personality. He is ideal in the home and playful with children. He makes few demands and gives back much in return. The breed is relatively rare but pursuit of this dog will pay back a thousandfold.

Proud despite his lack of numbers, the Tibetan Spaniel is an assertive, big-hearted purebred with class beyond his competitors. OWNER, MRS. K.M. LOWE.

GROWTH

The eight-week-old Tibetan Spaniel weighs about 4 pounds. Despite the small size, the breed is slow to mature, requiring a good three years to develop fully. Owners should select for an outgoing, happy-go-lucky personality; avoid poorly reared, shy dogs showing thin or otherwise poor coat, red (inflamed) ears, and other signs of poor health. The adolescent dog fills out considerably, though gangly periods are expected. Colors may lighten; tricolors are pretty true, except gold will lighten; particolors stay the same, though patches other than black may lighten. The fluffy puppy coat starts to change down the middle of the back at eight to 12 weeks, and by six months the coat is really coming in.

Given the popularity of the Pekingese and other lion-like Orientals, Tibetan Spaniel litters are a dear commodity. Puppies should be outgoing and show every sign of alertness and good health. OWNER, CHERYL A. KELLY.

HEALTH

The Tibetan Spaniel enjoys good health and relative freedom from serious genetic problems. Life expectancy of the breed can be set at 15 years. PRA is a breeder concern but has a low incidence. The breed is also known to be sensitive to fleas and to have a particular dislike of flea collars and other such potential irritants (e.g., owners must ensure that no stool collects on the fur around the anus). Feeding requirements are simple, and breeders recommend avoiding a high-protein diet and not feeding meat scraps— they point to the breed's origin in relatively meatless Tibet. The breed is considered "wash and wear" in that simply combing about three times a week is all that is required, except during the spring and fall shedding periods, when daily combing and pin brushing is required. The breed has easily met exercise requirements. Always guard against heat stroke.

The Tibetan Spaniel's coat requires little care to look its best. OWNER, SANDRA FOURNIER.

With a poster puppy like this, Tibetan Spaniel registrations should skyrocket! OWNER, CHERYL A. KELLY.

Tibetan Spaniel

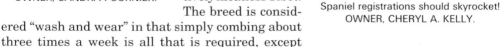

Tibetan Terrier

The perfect skiing partner, the Tibetan Terrier comes with his own snowshoes and an instinctive knack for the slopes. OWNER, JOYCE AYOTTE.

DESCRIPTION

The snowshoed Tibetan Terrier comes to the West from the difficult terrain and harsh climates of his homeland, with his profuse coat and unique feet! The TT is a medium-sized dog with a powerful build, whose square body is well coated with a full and fine outer coat, protected by his soft and woolly undercoat. He stands about 15 to 16 inches and weighs 20 to 24 pounds (though the full range is regarded as 18 to 30 pounds). The head is medium length, not broad or coarse; skull is neither domed nor flat; the stop is marked but not exaggerated; eyes are large and dark brown, neither prominent nor sunken; ears pendant and falling not too close to the head, V-shaped; nose black. Muzzle should not be pointed nor the head long and narrow, as are commonly seen on poor specimens. The body is compact, square and strong; topline level; chest not too wide; loin slightly arched; tail medium length, set on fairly high, curling over back and may have a kink near the tip. The quarters construction provides for a free, easy gait. The coat must be double, with a fall of hair covering eyes and foreface, beard on muzzle, feathering on ears, chest, tail, forelegs, and feet. The feet are large, flat and round, providing traction in a snowshoe fashion. The coat is long, not reaching the ground, and may be wavy or straight, but not silky, woolly or curled. Part over back and neck is natural. Colors include white, golden, cream, gray or smoke, black, particolor and tricolors; chocolate and liver are not permissible in the U.K.

OWNER SUITABILITY

These little people bless their owners with engaging personalities and strong guard-dog abilities, despite their medium size. As with any other surviving breed from Tibet, this is a hardy, enduring animal who is a doer. He is no ornament, though he can stop a crowd and entertain them while he's at it. And yet he's a real homebody, loving his castle and his family (whom he undoubtedly owns). Adaptable to many lifestyles, he is obedient and willing to learn, despite his sometimes taxing stubbornness. Begin housebreaking early and be very consistent.

Treasured for centuries as talismans, the Tibetan Terrier today brings luck to all who welcome him into their home. OWNER, SHERYL RUTLEDGE-SCHULTIS.

GROWTH

Tibetan Terriers begin life at a small 4 to 5 ounces. Dewclaws removed during the first week. Pups average about 5 pounds at eight weeks. Color varies greatly in the breed. Breeders encourage owners not to select based on color, since it is insignificant. Color may lighten or darken with age. Prospective owners should research this lesser known dog and shop for a friendly, playful, inquisitive pup that is healthy, well constructed and typey. Proper coat care is very important, especially during the developmental period. The undercoat should never be removed, and the top coat should never be forced into a part along the back. Avoid frequent bathing, rather brush and comb often.

Due to responsible breeding, Tibetan Terrier litters promise puppies that are as healthy as they are irresistible.
OWNER, SUSAN B. NERDAHL.

HEALTH

Very little medical information is available on the breed. Breeders experience very few problems and there seems to be no serious problems other than general concern for HD and PRA. Exercise demands of the Tibetan Terrier are normal. Dogs do well with moderate daily exercise and greatly enjoy the activity. Grooming demands are not great, but the breed's abundant coat does require regular care. Shedding can be a consideration. The areas around the ears and anus should be kept clean and free of excess hair to prevent infection. The shrouded eyes should be inspected regularly for problem signs. Hernias and lens luxation have been reported in the TT, though responsible breeding has limited their occurrence. Hypothyroidism has been reported.

You can be sure that the adolescent TT will want to become part of your active family. He's personable and good with most people and other animals.
OWNER, SUSAN B. NERDAHL.

Even the most suspicious child will believe this adolescent TT is a Muppet.
OWNER, SUSAN M. CARR.

Tibetan Terrier

Toy Fox Terrier

DESCRIPTION

The Toy Fox Terrier is a mostly white dog with black and/or tan markings. He weighs in at 3 ½ to 7 pounds, and never more. The head is slightly rounded, not apple-headed like a Chihuahua; muzzle is medium long, about same length as skull and somewhat pointed. The eyes are round, dark and prominent, though soft in expression; stop medium; ears point and V-shaped, not too far apart. The neck is moderately long and slightly arched; shoulders sloping; back straight, not sway or round-rumped; tail carried erect and set high (docked to three-fifths); rear legs straight in hocks and strong in thighs; stifles straight; moderate tuck-up; front legs straight with feet pointing forward. The coat is short and satiny (slightly longer at ruff).

One of America's best-kept secrets, the Toy Fox Terrier was recognized by the United Kennel Club in 1936 and since has remained the country's toy of choice. OWNER, ANN MAUERMANN.

OWNER SUITABILITY

Ideally versatile, the tiny Toy Fox Terrier derives from small English hunting dogs and still maintains much instinct. He is affectionate and loves everyone. Protective of his folks, he makes a good watchdog and alarm dog. He is an impressionable little tyke who will pick up your bad habits, so set a good example. Toy Foxes prosper on love and affection. Training poses few difficulties and the breed is a regular winner in obedience competitions. Americans have found the Toy Fox an all-around winner for years!

For such a small dog, the Toy Fox has some big ideas. This brainy tot is arguably the Most trainable of all 4-pound dogs! OWNER, LISA VETTRAINO.

338

GROWTH

Weight at eight weeks ranges from 1 to 2 pounds. Growth rate and age of maturity may vary with lines and individuals. Full size can be attained as early as six months, though up to 12 months is common. Toy Foxes are a unique American breed and owners should purchase puppies that come from recognized lines. Many tiny terrier-like pups are passed off as Toy Fox Terriers—be sure that it's a purebred. Owners should select for strong bones and proper bite, as well as such conformational points as head, eye, and ear shape. Avoid at all costs long backs, weak bones, and any trace of unhealthy skin or irritated eyes.

HEALTH

All in all, the Toy Fox Terrier is a hardy, healthy little dog with no hereditary problems. Breeders strongly emphasize the importance of selecting a healthy pup from healthy lines. Major breeder concerns involve the eyes, bones and skin. Weak insufficient bone can occur in breeding lines, and complications, primarily injuries, are the consequence. Skin problems, primarily allergies, also occur. Exercise requirements are normal. The Toy Fox requires plenty of play and exercise time to be happy and well contented. Toy Fox Terriers are generally good eaters, and adults must be prevented from carrying excess, which can stress the bones and heart.

The original alarm dog, the Toy Fox Terrier can be digitally programmed to do just about anything, from waking you up to reminding you to take your vitamins. These are ideal apartments dogs, perfect for children and the elderly. OWNER, LISA VETTRAINO.

Count the Toy Fox Terrier among the healthiest of all dogs, and the signs of health in the puppy should be as clear as day. Although the puppy may be awkward, he should not be weak or overly excitable. A calm but outgoing puppy is your first choice. OWNER, ANN MAUERMANN.

Toy Fox Terrier

Toy Manchester Terrier

DESCRIPTION

The smaller Manchester breed, the Toy Manchester Terrier weighs less than 12 pounds and is further distinguished from his larger counterpart, the Standard Manchester, by his naturally erect ears, which are wider at the base and tapering to pointed tips. Unlike the Standard, cropped ears disqualifies the Toy from the show ring; additionally the Toy's ears must never be wide, flaring, blunt, or bell-like. Overall he is slightly longer than tall and he is of sufficient bone and muscle to ensure agility and endurance. Without variation, however, the Manchester is a short-coated

A friendly, unassuming toy dog, the Toy Manchester Terrier may be known to some as the English Toy Terrier. By any name, this is a sleek little black and tan dog with a bright disposition.
OWNERS, PETER J. AND PATRICIA LAPINSKI.

black and tan dog with a keen, alert expression. The eyes are small and almond shaped; head is long and narrow, without showing cheek muscles, and resembling a blunt wedge. The muzzle and skull are equal in length. The neck is slightly arched, slim and graceful; chest is narrow but deep in brisket; ribs well sprung; abdomen tucked up; tail tapering. Forelegs straight, elbows lie close to brisket; feet compact and well arched; stifle well turned; hocks well let down; hindlegs carried well back. Well-marked black and tans have rosettes, tan spots on each side of chest above forelegs; white is highly undesirable anywhere on the coat, particularly when measuring more than $\frac{1}{2}$ inch in diameter.

OWNER SUITABILITY

A most uncommon choice among the toy dogs, the Toy Manchester has maintained a steady following in Britain for years and is one of the true English breeds. He is small but not frail, and attractive for his shimmering black and tan coat. Toy Manchesters are affectionate dogs who need a loving partner to train him and share. These dogs can become aggressive and excitable if spoiled or poorly handled. Like most other toys, this dog needs correct handling and socialization to develop his natural sparkling personality.

Even in the puppy, the alertness and intelligence of the Manchester already shimmer.
OWNER, LOUISE H. STRICKLAND.

GROWTH

Size at birth is 5 to 6 ounces. Dewclaws are removed during the first week. Pups are generally born completely black, though minimal tan markings may be visible. The requisite tan markings should be apparent by four weeks. Thumb marks and pencil markings typically take longer to appear. Ear carriage is important, as the candle-flame ears are the breed's hallmark. Never cropped, the ears may become erect as early as one month or as late as six months. Ears which are not erect by six months should be professionally taped. (Early taping is not recommended.) The puppy teeth of the Toy Manchester may require extraction if retained.

HEALTH

The Toy Manchester is an easycare, diminutive companion dog. Grooming demands are very simple, with little more required than brushing and combing every other day, plus the regular inspection of the eyes, ears, and paw pads. He is susceptible to slipped stifle, which can be corrected surgically. His skin is sensitive and he must be guarded against chills in cold and damp weather. Skin infections occur in the breed, and can be limited to some degree by proper grooming. A very unusual skin disorder, namely cutaneous asthenia, has been reported in the larger Manchester Terrier, with signs including soft, delicate, moist skin

The puppy takes some time to get used to being on all fours. Though never frail or weak in appearance, the puppy may appear awkward. The dam should be outgoing and friendly, not high-strung or unpleasant. OWNER, LOUISE H. STRICKLAND.

of pale coloration (because of the close genetic link, this condition is possible in the Toy as well). Epilepsy and vWD have been reported, though infrequently. The Toy Manchester requires more exercise time than most other toy terriers. Toy Manchesters have some history of blood disorders as well as gingivitis and other tooth and gum maladies.

Don't rush through your selection of a puppy from the litter. The Manchester breeder will be able to tell you about the individual personalities in the litter. His advice is more valuable than any impulse or evaluation you could have. OWNER, LOUISE H. STRICKLAND.

Toy Manchester Terrier

Toy Poodle

DESCRIPTION

The Toy Poodle stands 10 inches or under at the shoulder. Diminutiveness is paramount in the Toy Poodle, provided that balance and proportion are achieved. The eyes are very dark and oval, not round, protruding or too large; the ears are close to the head with long leather but not too excessive fringe; skull is moderately rounded with a slight but definite stop; cheeks flat; muzzle long, straight and fine, with slight chiseling under eyes, and should not appear snipy. The shoulders are well laid back and not steep; forelegs straight and parallel; feet are oval and rather small, not paper (lacking padding) or splay. Hindlegs are straight; stifles well bent. The coat should be naturally harsh in texture and always dense; although seen uncommonly, the coat may be corded with tight even cords. The Poodle can be clipped in any of the four acceptable fashions: Puppy, English Saddle, Continental, and Sporting.

The tiniest of the Poodles is too toy to tote a duck like his taller brothers, but he is a most ideal companion and a show dog that rises above the crowd.
OWNER, NORMA STRAIT.

Poodle colors should be even and solid (varying in shades is allowable): colors are blue, gray, silver, brown, cafe-au-lait, apricot and cream. Particolored dogs are disqualified from competition. Noses, eye rims, lips, toe nails and eye color should adhere to the dog's color.

OWNER SUITABILITY

A well-bred Toy Poodle cannot be matched for companionability and affection. This tiniest of dogs glistens with personality and genuineness and adores his mistress (or master) above all others. With proper socialization and diplomatic handling, the Toy Poodle can be an outgoing dog in society. This tot is all brains too, so do not underestimate his ability to perceive his situation.

The Toy Poodle compares to the largest of dogs in intelligence and personality.
OWNER, LYNN DeROSA.

Training can be tricky since owners want to give into the "baby's" tantrums. From the earliest point, let him know that you love him, but you're the boss. Ideally the Toy Poodle is a delight for the toy-dog person.

Growth

At seven to eight weeks, Toys weigh $1\frac{1}{2}$ pounds; full size is reached at six to seven months. Tails are docked during the first week, leaving just under two-thirds of the original length. Poodles come in a wide variety of solid colors, and color changes from puppyhood to maturity should be expected. The Poodle's hallmark coat grows rapidly but will not attain full maturity until some time after the first year. Sexual maturity too is often not until after the first year. Owners are encouraged to select their puppy carefully, inquiring about health and temperament, and ensuring proper breeding. As attractive as they may be, undersize dogs and/or dogs of small bone should be avoided. Health problems and injuries are more common in such animals. Grooming need be initiated at an early age, both to accustom the dog to this regular requirement and to assist the adult coat in its development.

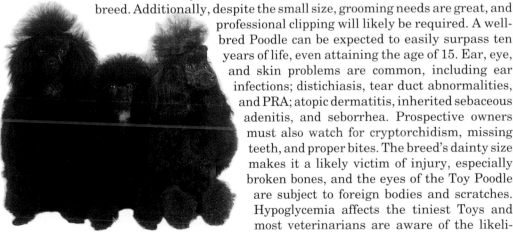

If you're planning to show your Toy Poodle, you're best to scour the dog show catalogues to meet the breeders that are winning. If you're searching for a pet, seek a confident, calm, and friendly puppy with no apparent eye or skin problems. OWNER, PATRICIA A. ZBOCK.

Health

The Toy Poodle enjoys a strong and dedicated following of serious breeders, and the breed's unique look and diminutive size attract a steady flow of new admirers. Prospective owners must select carefully, as there are a number of health problems affecting this breed. Additionally, despite the small size, grooming needs are great, and professional clipping will likely be required. A well-bred Poodle can be expected to easily surpass ten years of life, even attaining the age of 15. Ear, eye, and skin problems are common, including ear infections; distichiasis, tear duct abnormalities, and PRA; atopic dermatitis, inherited sebaceous adenitis, and seborrhea. Prospective owners must also watch for cryptorchidism, missing teeth, and proper bites. The breed's dainty size makes it a likely victim of injury, especially broken bones, and the eyes of the Toy Poodle are subject to foreign bodies and scratches. Hypoglycemia affects the tiniest Toys and most veterinarians are aware of the likelihood of the condition. Poodles may have bad reactions to rabies vaccinations.

Perceptive and sensitive beyond belief, Toy Poodles can learn to do anything you have the patience to teach them. They respond miraculously to kind, gentle training. OWNER, MARION USHER.

Toy Poodle

Vizsla

Description

Worth his weight in solid golden rust, his own color, the Vizsla is a robust and somewhat lightly built hunting dog with a short close-fitting coat. The head is lean and muscular, moderately wide between the ears. The stop is moderate, not deep; muzzle tapers gradually, is square and deep, not dish faced (like the Pointer). The nose is brown, and a totally black nose is very bad. Ears are thin, silky and long; eyes medium in size with color blending with coat, never yellow or "pop" eyed. The neck is strong, smooth and moderately long, without dewlap, and broadening into shoulders; back short; topline slightly rounded to elbows; tail thick at root and docked to two-thirds; forelegs straight; hindlegs moderately angulated to balance front; hocks neither too angulated nor lacking. The unique solid golden rust coat varies in shading; small white spots are permissible; large white chest marks are disqualified, as are noticeable black areas. White marks on feet should not extend above toes. The Vizsla stands 22 to 24 inches for a male, an inch less for females. Over or under $1\frac{1}{2}$ inch disqualifies the dog from show ring.

Developed by the Magyars for hunting, the Hungarian Pointer or the Vizsla has bred pure in his golden rust coat since the 10th century. He is a multi-purpose retrieving gun dog who is light and swift of foot.
OWNERS, RON AND PATRICIA FOLZ.

Owner Suitability

A rewarding and loving breed, the Vizsla closely bonds to all members of his family. While he is an outdoor dog of great athleticism, he should be kept indoors with the family, since he is miserable when separated from his people. Likewise, he does not roam and remains close to home. Even on the hunt, the Vizsla is known to keep their handler in eyeshot. Hunting dogs and family dogs are one and the same and need not be treated differently. His instincts are remarkable and he shows much verve for the chase.

For the show ring, the Vizsla's coat is short, smooth, and close-lying; nonetheless, the breed may have a rough, wiry coat that is bristly and 1 to 1 $^1/_2$ inches in length.
OWNER, M. VOORN.

GROWTH

Vizslas weigh 10 to 14 ounces at birth. Tails are docked by one-third, and all dewclaws are removed. Newborns grow rapidly, reaching nine to 12 pounds by eight weeks. Eye color is often still blue at seven to eight weeks. Eyes will gradually change to blend with coat. When selecting a dog, owners should carefully note temperament. The breed is considered a sensitive one, and pups bred from exclusively hunting stock may not make the best companions if not kept as house dogs. Owners should look for friendly, tail-wagging, face-licking puppies, and always view the parent's temperament and conformation. Owners should avoid pups with yellow eyes or very light colors. The color of the adult nose should be brown, not black. The adult coat change occurs around one year, when the often lighter and softer puppy coat is shed.

HEALTH

Very few problems are reported in the Vizsla breed. Hip dysplasia is not overly common and breeders are continuously working to lessen this incidence further. Other notable problems include entropion and ectropion, incorrect bites, cryptorchidism and monorchidism, as well as allergies. These are the same common problems that occur in most breeds. Some recent studies show occurrences of hypothyroidsm in the Vizsla. Coat care for the Vizsla is minimal, as is shedding. Exercise requirements are high, however, and the breed's hunting instincts are alive and well. Early and continued socialization is important. These dogs do not do well when kenneled and require a consistent, non-aggressive approach to training.

Vizslas are sensitive dogs that thrive on an owner's complete attention. Puppies nevertheless should be glad to meet you and warm up to you in little time. Though sensitive, they should be fearless; though gentle, they are not aloof.
OWNER, LUCILLE JARDIN.

Socialization is vital for the young Vizsla to come out of his shell to become the lively Hungarian hunter he was born to be. The loyal Vizsla hunts better if kept as a member of the family.
OWNER, ANNE DENEHY.

The well-socialized Vizsla puppy is gentle-mannered and demonstrative, adoring the company of humans and dogs alike.
OWNER, JOY LYONS.

Vizsla

Weimaraner

DESCRIPTION

The Weimaraner is unique in many respects: his distinctive mouse gray to silver gray coloration, his light-amber-colored eyes, his webbed feet, and his aristocratic hunting-dog demeanor. He stands 25 to 27 inches, bitches 2 inches less, and is well balanced and the very portrait of grace, speed and endurance—ideally in good working-dog musculature. His head is moderately long, with a moderate stop and rather prominent occiput. Flews moderately deep and straight; nose gray; ears long and lobular. Back is of moderate length, strong; chest deep and shoulders well laid back. The forelegs are straight, elbows neither in nor out; feet firm and compact; and the hindlegs are parallel with well-angulated stifles and straight hocks, capable of effortless, smooth coordination. In America, the coat can only be short, smooth and sleek, its color always solid, with small white mark on chest permitted. The Weimaraner's tail is docked to approximately 6 inches, carried in a confident manner. In the U.K. a long coat variety (coat measuring 1 to 2 inches in length) is acceptable. Long-coated Weimaraners have a feathered tail whose tip may be removed.

Behold the Gray Ghost: the Weimaraner resides in the aristocracy of the sporting dogs, a German creation for big game. His amber-colored eyes, unique gray coat, and sensitive nose have earned him lasting popularity.
OWNERS, ROGER AND JEANNE SHELBY.

OWNER SUITABILITY

Eager to please and perceptive of your needs, the Weimaraner excels as a companion animal, as he does as a hunting dog. This is an all-around dog who loves family life; he will not flourish in a kennel environment. He is a smart and second-to-none obedience and field-trial dog, whose natural retrieving, scenting and trailing abilities acclaim his instinctual superiority. Yet Weimaraners are willful and can be stubborn to train; owners need to channel their industry lest they can be reckless. They often hunt singly and do not do well with strange dogs.

In American show rings, the long-coated Weimaraner is disqualified; in Europe these silky-haired ghosts are frequently seen. Training the Weimaraner requires a patient, experienced handler with ample time to devote to the dog.
OWNERS, MR. AND MRS. P. KELLER.

GROWTH

Newborns weigh a solid 10 to 16 ounces. Dewclaws removed and tails docked the first week, possibly slightly later. Color at birth is an unusual tan to grayish base with dark stripes running the length of the body. Blue pups occur but are disqualified from showing. White markings may also occur and are undesirable. Very limited white marks may well disappear with maturity. The Weimaraner is a soft-coated and soft-skinned breed, and special precautions against injuries are called for. The breed is also known for its awkward walk, which smooths out when gaited. This awkwardness may increase with age.

HEALTH

Weimaraners are hardy dogs who do well in the field and at field trials. They are easycare companions who require little grooming but plenty of exercise. Outlets for their hunting instincts are required. Ear infections are easily acquired owing to the drop-eared conformation. Weimaraners are affected by the common canine ailments,

Some trainers call the Weimaraner a stubborn dog. As such, begin training the puppy early on to discourage chewing, house-soiling, and other bad habits. The puppy is strong-minded but also willing to please.
OWNER, LANCE A. WOLFE.

including HD, entropion, eversion of the third eyelid (nictitating membrane), and cryptorchidism; these occur with no great frequency in the breed. There are two more unusual problems affecting the breed, namely color mutant dermatitis and spinal dysraphism. The first is a skin condition (dermatitis) that affects blue Weimaraners. Breeders note that it is not that severe or common a condition in this breed as it is in others. Spinal dysraphism, while not common, is a severe though non-lethal condition that results in an abnormal (hopping) gait and an unusual stance that resembles a crouching position. It can be diagnosed but is not treatable. Hemophilia A and malignant oral cancers have also been documented in the breed.

Select a puppy that is fearless and friendly. The dam should embody these characteristics as well.
OWNER, ELLEN GREVALL.

If you work all day or live in an apartment, don't torture the Weimaraner, choose another breed.
OWNER, LANCE A. WOLFE.

Weimaraner

Welsh Springer Spaniel

DESCRIPTION

A handy-sized hunting dog colored in rich red and white is assembled for hard work and stamina, who performs in a naturally flat, straight single coat, that is moderately feathered on the extremities and thick to protect him from heavy cover and the elements. The coat is not so long as to interfere with his hunting. He stands 18 to 19 inches, bitches an inch less. The head, well proportioned to the body, is medium in length,

As unspoiled and hard-working as the original red and white spaniels that accompanied hunters centuries ago, the Welsh Springer Spaniel makes the grade as a land spaniel, water dog and companion.
OWNERS, DARLENE K. FERRIS AND A. CANDY CARSWELL.

slightly domed with a defined stop and chiseling below the eyes. Eyes are oval in shape and dark in color (yellow or light eyes are bad); ears are small and shaped like a vine leaf, hanging close to the cheek; muzzle straight, fairly square; nose black or brown (not pink). The neck is long and slightly arched, not throaty; topline level; loin slightly arched; close coupled; chest well developed; tail docked. Forearms of medium length and straight; fore and hinds well boned, not coarse; thighs muscular; moderate bend of stifle; feet round and tight, well arched. The coat is soft to the touch, never wiry or wavy. Color patterns vary, with or without flecking and ticking in the white areas.

An all-around dog, the Welsh Springer doesn't have a bad angle! What little tail there is wags to express this charmer's true feelings.
OWNERS, DARLENE K. FERRIS AND A. CANDY CARSWELL.

OWNER SUITABILITY

What the Welsh Springer lacks in numbers, he compensates in ability and personality. This spaniel offers all the soft-eyed faithfulness of the more popular spaniels in a completely unspoiled package. He learns quickly and remains consistent. He is a reserved animal whose feelings are not worn on his sleeve, though his devotion is no unknown quantity. As a hunting dog, his stamina and ability on difficult terrain recommend him to the serious sportsman. Exercise is a capital must.

GROWTH

Welsh Springers weigh 8 to 12 ounces at birth. Tails are docked and dewclaws removed (optional) at three to five days. Pups are born white with pale tan to red markings. Nose is pink but should darken in just a few days. Coloration and pigmentation will continue to develop as late as six months. Welsh Springers attain full height at about one year, but may require another year to reach full maturity. The breed is a very loving and people-oriented one. Good temperaments are the norm. Adolescence is marked by a peak in the energy level and a strong need for exercise and obedience training. The coat change occurs without complications when assisted by daily brushing. Essentially an easycare dog with little special requirements during the growth period and beyond.

For a devoted family dog with a pleading expression and unabashed loyalty, you've come to the right Welshman. Welsh puppies are friendly to a fault. OWNERS, RICHARD AND SANDRA ROHRBACHER.

HEALTH

For centuries the Welsh Springer has been selectively bred for health and working ability. As a result, coupled with its unexaggerated and natural conformation, the breed is relatively free of hereditary problems. Grooming needs are minimal, though particular care must be given to the ears, keeping them clean and free from excess hair. The dog's considerable fringe requires regular brushing and combing to keep it mat- and tangle-free.

Brittany, smittany....think Welsh! OWNERS, RICHARD AND SANDRA ROHRBACHER.

The Welshie makes an excellent indoor companion but requires time outdoors and thoroughly enjoys exercise, training, and hunting. In addition to the common problems affecting most breeds, such as entropion, cryptorchidism, allergies, etc., epilepsy is reported in the breed. A breeder concern is infertility in the male after three or four years of age. However, for the average owner, this should be of no concern as there seems no link of it to any health problems. Welshies commonly live into their teens.

Welsh Springers have all the charm and less of the problems than their popular sporting dog competitors. OWNER, LINDA S. BRENAN.

Welsh Springer Spaniel

Welsh Terrier

A far cry from his rather scraggly red and black Welsh forebears, today's Welsh Terrier is both a gallant showman and a fun-loving home companion.
OWNERS, KAREN AND R.C. WILLIAMS, JR.

DESCRIPTION

A solid workmanlike terrier with a tight wiry jacket, the Welsh Terrier is a squarely built dog with a solid, good-reaching trot and a fearless, friendly attitude. His head is rectangular, with strong foreface, small V-shaped ears that fold just above the topline of the skull. The eyes are small and dark brown, fairly far apart. The muzzle is one-half the length of the skull. The nose is black. The neck is of moderate length and thickness, slightly arched and clean. The body is well ribbed up and of obvious good substance; the front is straight and shoulders are long; forelegs are straight with upright pasterns; feet small and catlike. Hinds built to give dog free effortless movement, with hocks moderately straight and well-bent stifles. The tail is docked and well set on, completing a square impression of the dog. The color of the jacket is black (or grizzle sometimes) with tan on the legs, quarters and head. Males stand 15 inches at withers, weighing about 20 pounds.

OWNER SUITABILITY

The serious clown, the Welsh Terrier is a somewhat cocky terrier breed with a whole circus tent of amusing antics and sideshows to share. His owners find him engaging and sometimes trying. As a terrier he is strong-willed with definite ideas, albeit many quite original. They need to be taught house manners and respond well to a firm, committed hand. They are athletic and upbeat much of the time and get on well with children, for whom they are super nannies.

At five weeks, the small, boxy Welshie is a bit wobbly. Choose a puppy that is calm and friendly. Excitable puppies can grow into short-tempered, aggressive adults.
OWNER, ERIGN H. SEACORD.

GROWTH

Welshies are keenly aware of their surrounding and don't like to be distracted by training. These spunky, opportunistic terriers are highly intelligent and fairly sensible. *Teach* puppies the house rules and regard them with respect and they will respond accordingly.
OWNER, ERIGN H. SEACORD.

Welshies weigh 6 to 8 ounces at birth, which is remarkably large considering the size of the dam. Litter size is four to six; the record is ten. Puppies are predominantly black in color. The small bits of tan on the feet spread up the legs as they grow, as the tan of the eyebrows spreads up and down to cover the head and ears. Dewclaws removed and tails docked by three to four days. The tan markings or grizzled coat pattern begins to emerge by a few weeks and clarifies with maturity. Full height is achieved by nine months, though full maturity may take 18 months to two years. The ears should be small, V-shaped, and not thin. Adolescence is marked by the coat change, during which the soft puppy coat will be replaced by the hard terrier jacket. Extra grooming is important during this time. The Welshie is a high-energy animal, particularly during its youth. Early obedience training helps create a manageable and more contented adolescent.

HEALTH

Welshies need flea dips since their waterproof coats resist regular sprays. Typically they are not sensitive to such treatment. Grooming needs are considerable, with regular plucking required to prevent possible skin complications. Also, attention must be paid to the areas around the eyes and ears to prevent excess hair from causing irritations. Welshies may develop skin allergies that affect their ears and chest. These allergies are chiefly tied to manmade fibers, so using cotton bedding or furniture throws will help. Medically speaking, the Welsh Terrier is blessed with very few problems. Its limited breeding at the hands of dedicated fanciers can largely be credited for this fact. Entropion and cryptorchidism should be checked, but otherwise no breed-specific problems are reported. Welshies are expected to live ten or more years.

Breeders have done an excellent job with keeping the Welsh virtually problem-free. Welshie puppies like humans almost as much as they like other puppies: notice how the little individualists will look you right in the eye.
OWNER, ERIGN H. SEACORD.

Welsh Terrier

West Highland White Terrier

DESCRIPTION

A varminty pure white terrier, strongly built, and blessed with an old-time showman's self-confidence, the West Highland White Terrier possesses a unique double coat of straight hard *white* hair above a soft, furry, close undercoat. The outer coat must not be soft, fluffy or silky; short coats and single coats are equally objectionable; better yellowed than soft. The skull is slightly domed, gradually tapering from eye to muzzle with a distinct stop; nose is black and fairly large, and furnishings thick, making head appear round. The eyes are slightly sunk and set wide apart, not full but medium in size; ears are small and erect; neck sufficiently long for proper head carriage. The shoulders slope backwards; elbows well in; forelegs short and straight; body compact; back level; chest deep; hinds strong and wide across top; hocks well bent, never straight or weak. Good bone throughout. The front feet are larger than hind; the carrot-shaped tail is 5 to 6 inches in length, straight and carried jauntily, not over back. The dog stands 11 inches; bitches an inch less.

The Westie bests them every time: this solid white angel outshines his varminty competitors in showmanship and companionship.
OWNERS, FREDERICK C. MELVILLE AND MARK AND SALLY GEORGE.

OWNER SUITABILITY

The child's best friend, the little Westie enjoys great popularity for his marvelous ways and steady disposition. He has much energy and enjoys playing outside (or inside) with the kids. Westies make perfect house and apartment dogs and are adaptable to your lifestyle. Additionally, he is among the showiest of the terriers and a smart cookie in the obedience ring. Invest time and love into your Westie and you will have an indispensable family member, who is never too busy to sit and listen to his mom's troubles.

All rise. The Westie is in. "Possessed of no small amount of self-esteem," the standard lands the gavel on this showy defendant: Champion Aberglen Lucky Lindy, winner of many Best in Show awards.
OWNERS, FREDERICK C. MELVILLE AND MARK AND SALLY GEORGE.

GROWTH

Despite the breed's white coloration, it is heavily pigmented. Nose and paw pads should turn black in the first few weeks. The pigmentation may make the skin appear dirty. West Highlands develop with good speed. During teething the ears may drop or fold forward but should stand erect by maturity. If the ears have not begun to stand erect by five months, taping should be done. As the adult coat comes in, the puppy coat should be combed out. The new coat should be plucked early, then about twice a year thereafter. Excessive bathing must be avoided to keep the coat properly hard. Daily brushing and combing with a light

Bring the children to choose your Westie puppy—they're guaranteed a best friend before leaving the breeder's home.
OWNER, MARIAN MOELLER.

wipedown is all that's required. Westies mature mentally often before their first birthday; their bodies catch up by two years.

Playful, assertive, and gay, the Westie is ready when you are, ball in hand. Although he's an excellent apartment dog, don't leave him home too long: he's waiting for you from the moment you leave.
OWNER, MARIAN MOELLER.

HEALTH

The Westie has proven to be an easycare, very hardy and adaptable canine. Grooming demands are typical of the terriers, with stripping and some trimming required on a regular basis. Westies delight in outdoor activities, do well with obedience training, and will not hesitate to combat a varmint if given the chance. The Westie is subject to the common ailments affecting most other dogs, with few breed-specific problems reported. Legg-Calve-Perthes, a bone-related disease; craniomandibular osteopathy (CMO), resulting in extreme swelling of the jaw in pups under one year; and Krabbe's disease (globoid cell leukodystrophy), a degenerative nerve condition, are all rare but have occurred in the breed. Epidermal dysplasia may be inherited in the Westie. Additionally, veterinarians have reported cases of inherited metabolic liver defects, kerato conjunctivitis sicca, hereditary red-blood-cell disorder and a genetically linked copper toxicity. Some dogs have skin ailments. Westies generally survive well to about 13 years, declining rapidly when the end is near. Deafness may affect some lines.

West Highland White Terrier

Whippet

DESCRIPTION

Elegant and fit, the Whippet is a running dog of great speed and power, whose impression must combine both his athletic power and ability with the graceful outline of a purebred sighthound. The Whippet should stand 19 to 22 inches; 18 to 21 inches for bitches. One-half inch in either direction disqualifies. The skull is long and lean, fairly wide between the ears; eyes are large and dark, not light or yellow, never blue or wall eyes (with whitish iris); small, fine rose ears; muzzle long and powerful, not coarse; nose black. The neck is long and clean, not throaty; back broad and firm; brisket very deep; tail long and tapering, carried low in a gentle upward curve, not higher than back. The dog must be able to move smoothly and freely with straight back, straight forelegs, strong pasterns, elbows directly under withers, and well-formed feet. The hinds are long and powerful with well-bent stifles; hocks well let down, never sickle

Faster than a rabbit, mechanical or otherwise, the Whippet was designed for dog racing though today makes a sporting companion dog and an elegant show dog.
OWNERS, MRS. JAMES BUTT, DEBBIE BUTT, E. HANSEN AND A. TRUXAL.

or cow hocks. The coat is short, close and smooth, texture firm. Longhaired Whippets are not acceptable. Colors vary greatly, solids and combinations, including black, white, fawn, blue, gray, brindle, red, and others.

OWNER SUITABILITY

Whippets are extremely clean and quiet, yet vigorous athletes and outdoor jogging companions. The company of children most always delights a Whippet, as they are both patient and tolerant. In colder climes, the Whippet may be better off equipped with a sweater as his tight coat does not give him much resistance to cold. The Whippet is reserved but not rightly called

Although most Whippets would rather be chasing the wind (or the neighbor's cat), they make ideal indoor companions and adapt well to most lifestyles.
OWNER, CEILA DOWNEN.

skittish. He has long thin limbs and is susceptible to injury. Most Whippet people own more than one Whippet, which well bespeaks their appeal and fabulous dispositions.

GROWTH

Whippet newborns weigh 8 to 12 ounces. Growth is rapid, and by eight weeks the puppy should be about 8 pounds. Coloration varies considerably in the breed, and the subject of the Whippet's color inheritance is extensive. Suffice it to say that colors lighten with age, while pigmentation darkens. Eye and nose pigment on very light-colored dogs may take up to a year to develop completely. Any brindling is usually apparent at birth and will clarify with maturity. Full height is attained as early as six months, while full maturity takes 18 months. Whippets are extremely infantile puppies, and owners must avoid fragile or flimsy pups. The young Whippet should be bright, attentive, and fearless. Adolescent dogs grow in rapid spurts and require a high-protein diet and plenty of exercise. The ears may prick during teething. Breeders note that Whippets generally housebreak easily, though are known to be problem chewers.

Whippets can come in most any color. The puppy's pigment may not fill in until he's a year of age. OWNERS, ROBERT E. AND MONA MAYTAG.

HEALTH

The properly bred and maintained Whippet can be expected to be virtually free of health problems. Diet and exercise requirements are considerable, however. The Whippet must be kept lean on a high-protein diet and exercised every day. Owners are strongly advised to follow a breeder/veterinarian-prescribed diet and conditioning program. Diarrhea is common in dogs not receiving the proper diet. Grooming needs are simple, though the breed's thin coat and skin fare best with a gentle touch. Skin lacerations are common, and breeders caution that stitches are likely some time in the dog's life. Demodectic mange is particularly common in pink-skinned whites, and color mutant dermatitis affects blue Whippets. Also, the Whippet has demonstrated a sensitivity to strong flea baths and other medications, including anesthetics and barbiturates. By far the greatest problem in the breed is cryptorchidism/monorchidism, which is common. Life span is 12 to 13 years, sometimes to 16.

The eight-week-old puppy should be neither frail or fearful. Puppies ideally are spry and sprightly, attentive to people, and alert to their surroundings. OWNER, SARAH STEGEMANN.

Whippet puppies are sensitive creatures; too fragile for children, they require gentle handling. Puppies tend to be accident-prone and need close supervision. OWNER, LAUREY WEINER.

Whippet

Wire Fox Terrier

DESCRIPTION

The Wire Fox Terrier possesses eyes full of fire, life and intelligence, neatly folded, small, V-shaped ears, and a gaily carried high-set tail. These three features define the Wire Fox's character. His coat should appear broken, dense and wiry, with hairs having a tendency to twist. He is a working terrier whose bone and strength is substantial for his size. This cleverly made hunter should not appear cloddy, and neither is he leggy or lacking in leg; his short back enables him to cover much ground. He stands $15\frac{1}{2}$ inches at withers, and back measures not more than 12 inches. Weight is approximately 18 pounds, bitches 2 pounds less. The head on the adult measures about 7 inches in length. The eyes are moderately small and dark in color. The skull is almost flat, sloping slightly, the forehead is full and well made up, not too wedgelike. The jaws are strong and the cheeks not prominent. Nose is black and not white, cherry or spotted. The neck is of fair length, not throaty, broadening to the shoulders; back is short and level, not slack. Chest deep and not broad; brisket deep; shoulders sloping steeply; elbows perpendicular to body; feet round, compact and not large. The hinds are responsible for propulsion and therefore must not consist of a short second thigh and a straight stifle; long thighs and well-curved stifles, turning neither in nor out, are correct. White should predominate on the coat; brindle, red, liver or slaty less good, though color is of little importance to the breed.

A dog of dogs, the Wire Fox Terrier excels as a children's companion as well as a show dog. The Wire Fox is many judge's favorite choice for Best in Show; the breed has won the Westminster show more times than any other breed. OWNERS, MR. AND MRS. RICHARD VIDA.

OWNER SUITABILITY

The purebred Wire Fox is an elegant animal who lends a certain sophistication to an owner's home. Yet this is a rough-and-tumble dog of strong terrier instinct. He makes a wonderful choice for children, who love his spunk and incessant desire to play. If socialized and well handled, he is vastly obedient and his stubborn terrier ways are easily overcome. As a show dog, the Wire Fox has few equals. A professional groomer is needed to keep your Fox Terrier looking appropriately thoroughbred—unkempt Wire Foxes can look ratty but loveable.

The Wire Fox is easy in most respects: he is easy to train, easy to live with, and easy to fall for. He is hard only in respect to his coat and his attitude toward vermin. OWNER, ANDREW DiGIORGIO.

GROWTH

Wire puppies at birth are black and white or all white. Black turns to tan on the face, as does some of the black on shoulders, hips, and tail. Nose at birth can be black, black and pink, or pink, but should turn black by eight weeks. Fox Terriers weigh 3 to 4 pounds at eight weeks. Physical maturity is attained by 18 to 24 months. Tails docked and dewclaws removed by the end of the first week of life. Tail docking is important and should only be performed by an experienced breed-knowledgeable person. Essentially one-third of the tail should be removed. Owners should select for a pup with a good, long lean skull, without any bulky bone, especially behind the eyes (known as cheeky). The legs should be parallel, feet small, very tight, with well-arched toes. Avoid pups with toes turning either in or out, as well as pups with rear legs that are very close together. The ears usually become erect around teething time. Proper ears and bite cannot be guaranteed until seven months. Typical of the terriers, adolescent dogs often test their owners' authority. Avoid white, cherry or spotted nose; tail too short; prick, tulip, or rose-shaped ears; bad bite.

If you're planning to show your Wire Fox puppy, look for balance: a long, lean skull, medium bone, parallel legs and small feet. Avoid the puppy whose feet are turning in or out. The dam should be curious and friendly.
OWNER, DEBRA DEHNE.

HEALTH

You can take this puppy anywhere. The Wire Fox Terrier will follow you to the ends of the earth, or at least the forest.
OWNER, DEBRA DEHNE.

The Wire Fox Terrier is commonly considered the classic terrier, both in mind and body. The breed is a spunky, high-spirited canine that requires plenty of training. Grooming demands are considerable, as both stripping and clipping of the terrier coat are required to present that distinctive Fox Terrier look. Proper grooming of the Wire should begin around three months. Problems of the eyes and bones most concern breeders. Lens luxation, distichiasis, and cataracts are all reported in the breed. Hip dysplasia and Legg-Perthes are rare but reported. Shoulder dislocations are far more common. Deafness, goiter, recessive ataxia (usually occurring at two to four months of age, the result of a spinal cord defect that causes uncoordination which may progress to paralysis), pulmonic stenosis and subaortic stenosis are uncommon. Life expectancy is a good 12 years.

Wire Fox Terrier

Wirehaired Pointing Griffon

DESCRIPTION

The gun dog's gun dog, the Wirehaired Pointing Griffon is a medium-sized, harsh-coated pointer and retriever. The head and muzzle are square with only slightly pronounced stop and occiput. The eyes are large and round; ears medium in size, lying flat; nose must be brown; bite scissors. The neck is rather long; back strong and firm; chest not too wide or too narrow; loin strong and well developed; tail docked by one-third to one-half length. The shoulders are long and well laid back; forelegs straight; feet round and firm with close-webbed toes; thighs are long with good angulation, hocks neither in nor out; stifle and hocks strong and well angulated. The coat is double with a medium-length outer coat that is straight and wiry (not curly or woolly) with a less abundant yet water-resistant undercoat of fine thick down. The dog's head furnishings (mustache and eyebrows, ear trims) give the Griffon an untidy appearance. No tail plume. The color of preference is steel gray with brown markings; also chestnut brown or roan, white and brown, white and orange. The coat must not be black.

A "supreme gun-dog" modestly describes the Wirehaired Pointing Griffon. The breed's easy trainability, devotion to family, and general friendly attitude endear him to all who know him. OWNERS, JOE AND MARGE GRYSKIEWICZ.

The Griffon puppy, though never in demand, is happy to meet the demands of most serious owners. OWNER, ELAINE HUNSICKER.

OWNER SUITABILITY

This rare gun-dog breed can be found in both the United States and England—he is of European descent and is a multi-talented hunter, far superior in ability to most other recognized gun-dog breeds. He is athletic and highly trainable and has much more energy for the hunt than even the serious huntsman. In the home he is quiet and affectionate, bonding closely with his whole family. Socialization is a must since some breed members tend to be timid.

GROWTH

Wirehaired Griffon puppies are born white with brown heads. By one week, flecks of brown begin to emerge, and by three weeks the spots and markings begin to emerge. The breed is slow to mature, not reaching maturity until two-and-a-half to three years of age. Selecting owners should avoid oversized puppies—this is a medium-sized dog. The breed is known to be rather sensitive, and owners should certainly avoid the shy puppy, selecting for the outgoing and friendly one. Avoid the soft and/or curly coat—the coat should have a wiry quality, even at a young age. Breeders note that this is an *active* breed but not a hyper-active one. Adolescents should be easy to train, intelligent, and of good temperament.

HEALTH

The Wirehaired Pointing Griffon enjoys relative freedom from serious hereditary conditions. Hip dysplasia does, however, occur, but in low incidence. The breed's wire coat does require weekly attention,

Griffon puppies bond closely with their owners. Choose the outgoing, spirited puppy for the best possible hunting companion.
OWNER, ELAINE HUNSICKER.

namely plucking and light trimming, to be well kept. Matting of the undercoat can lead to skin problems and encourage the harboring of parasites. Particular attention should be paid to the hair around the eyes, mouth, ears, and anus, keeping these areas clean and free from infection. These are hardy working dogs who do best in the hands of sportsmen who provide positive outlets for the dog's strong hunting instincts and work ethic. The Griffon is playful and curious, and should have a fenced yard. Life expectancy is around ten or more years.

So glad to be here!, exclaims the "happy hunter." This puppy is showing off his first point. Most experts agree that the Griffon is only suited for the sporting person or family.
OWNER, ELAINE HUNSICKER.

Wirehaired Pointing Griffon

Xoloitzcuintli

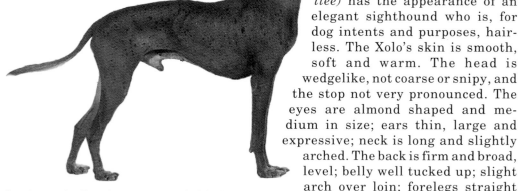

Say that again. Show-low-eats-*queen*-tlee! And it has no hair. The Xolo and its smaller brother, the Mexican Hairless, derive from the Aztec Indians, who regarded them highly for their palliative virtues.
OWNER, BRIAN TERRY.

DESCRIPTION

Clean and graceful in outline, the Xoloitzcuintli (that's *show-low-eats*-queen-*tlee*) has the appearance of an elegant sighthound who is, for dog intents and purposes, hairless. The Xolo's skin is smooth, soft and warm. The head is wedgelike, not coarse or snipy, and the stop not very pronounced. The eyes are almond shaped and medium in size; ears thin, large and expressive; neck is long and slightly arched. The back is firm and broad, level; belly well tucked up; slight arch over loin; forelegs straight and well under body; rear quarters strong with hocks well let down and sufficient angulation for free driving action. The feet are harelike and webbed, with well-arched toes. The tail is set low, long and fine, reaching hock. The breed is divided into three size categories: Standard, 18 to 22½ inches; Miniature, 13 to 18 inches; Toy, under 13 inches. The Toy variety is also called the Mexican Hairless. Dogs can either be completely hairless or coated. Hairless dogs may have some coarse hairs on forehead, toes and tail tip; coated dogs have a short flat and dense coat with no thin or bare batches. The breed comes in many colors: solids, marked and patches.

OWNER SUITABILITY

The Xoloitzcuintli is an unusual dog—if you like unusual, you may like the Xolo. Like other hairless breeds of dog (yes, there are others), he is very much a dog. Essentially the temperaments are consistent across the size ranges, and are dignified, gentle and calm. He is a biddable, hardy breed who is affectionate and devoted. Xolos are often reserved with strangers. The dogs are not easily acquired but there is a reliable pool of breeders in the U.S. from which to choose.

A coated *perrillo* looking for a new home.
OWNERS, ROBERT McRAE AND BERNARD PEARSON.

GROWTH

At eight weeks, the Toy should weigh 2 to 3 pounds, the Mini, 3 to 5 pounds, and the Standard, 5 to 6 pounds. Full size is attained early, between six and eight months. Prospective owners should research carefully before making their selection. In addition to healthy appearing and conformationally sound dogs, owners need to avoid shyness, a common temperament fault. Adolescent dogs may experience behavioral changes, particularly shyness and nervousness. Owners must expect these and be patient and understanding with their dogs. Any such period should pass. Teething youngsters require plenty of chewing outlets. Erect ears may temporarily drop during this time, and potential show pups should have their ears taped.

Nakedness is no cause for shame or fear! The Xolo makes friends freely and fearlessly—he has nothing to hide. OWNERS, LINDA WOODS AND SUSAN CORRONE.

HEALTH

Missing teeth and improper dentition are the most commonly cited concerns. It seems reasonable that the breed may be susceptible to any of the common canine maladies, disorders of the bones and eyes. Skin problems affecting adolescents, particularly males, usually clear up by two years—not unlike acne in humans. Owners need to learn the proper grooming (skin care) techniques from a breeder, and protect their dog at all times from cold and drafts. Xolos generally have a great resistance to parasites, including fleas and ticks. Many exhibit adverse reactions to cortisone, flea preparations and certain heartworm preventatives. Coated Xolos, in their puppy years, may develop mange, but this is treatable by a vet. Other breed defects include sealed ear canals and dropped ears. The Xolo can live 12 to 15 years, and some have reached 20.

Truly a rare breed, the Xolo is the ultimate in hypo-allergenic. Aside from his coat, he's a completely normal dog. OWNER, SUSAN CORRONE.

The Xolo puppy can be treated like any other unclothed puppy: he's susceptible to drafts and cold as well as nicks, cuts and sunburn. OWNER, SUSAN CORRONE.

Xoloitzcuintli

Yorkshire Terrier

DESCRIPTION

The tiny Yorkshire Terrier boasts a floor-length silky garb in blue and tan: his coat is glossy and fine and must be perfectly straight. His head is topped with a topknot, usually with a bow or two fixed in his delicate hair. The head is small and flattish on top; muzzle not too long; good teeth; ears small, V-shaped, carried erect; eyes medium, dark and not prominent with dark eyelids. The body is very compact on this less than 7-pound toy terrier, with a rather short back and level backline. The forelegs are straight with elbows neither in nor out; hindlegs are straight with stifles moderately bent; feet are round. The quality of the coat is of utmost importance and the blue coloration should be dark steel blue, not a silvery blue or blue with fawn, bronze or black hairs. The blue covers the body from neck to tail, while the tan colors the sides of the head, ear roots and muzzle, chest and legs. The tail is docked medium and carried a little higher than back, colored darker than the rest of body.

The Yorkie is all heart and can fit into any loving owner's pocket. These toy terrier's are giant contenders at dog shows, easily conveying their sense of self-importance and high spirits. OWNERS, DR. IVAN AND MARIE KAUFMAN CARDONA.

OWNER SUITABILITY

All five pounds of the Yorkshire Terrier is brimming with attitude and boldness. His miniature terrier heart gives him intense protective instincts and a cavalier bravado one might associate with a dog 20 times his size. Yet, he is a happy lap dog and loves to be toted about by his one-and-only. He is recklessly loyal and a delightful addition to any family. Don't spoil your Yorkie or else he will become as yappy and paranoid as a politician.

Choose the Yorkie if you can commit to having the dog with you through the day. They make excellent traveling companions, love the mall, and can remain quiet as a mouse whenever necessary. OWNER, SHARON L. JONES.

Growth

Yorkies develop slowly and because of their small size are not typically placed in homes until three to four months of age. Puppies are born black with small tan markings at the sides of the head and ear roots, on the muzzle, down the back of the neck, on all four paws and under the tail. All traces of black or sooty puppy hairs must be completely outgrown, lest they spoil the golden tan color. Hair shafts that are too thick will prevent the coat from falling properly. Ears are born drop and will become erect in time, usually interrupted by the teething phase. The puppy coat develops slowly, with the first bow being tied around five months of age. It generally takes eight to ten months for the dog's coat to reach the floor and need protective wrapping.

Puppies are born black with tan markings and eventually grow into their classic blue and tan coats. As with any toy dog, select for temperament above all else.
OWNER, CLAUDIA GRUNSTRA.

Health

The Yorkie lives up to its terrier name with its lively, fearless personality. Grooming needs are very considerable. Abundant daily brushing and combing is required, as well as more specialized care to achieve the ideal coat. The Yorkie faces problems common in most of the other toy breeds, including patellar luxation, slipped stifle, spinal cord problems, and congenital hydrocephalus. Legg-Perthes, a rare disease, has been reported in Yorkies four to 12 months of age. Eye problems such as keratitis sicca, PRA and distichiasis are reported. Digestive difficulties resulting in vomiting and diarrhea are more common in the Yorkie than in some other breeds.

Even the tiniest Yorkie puppy doesn't know his size. This little devil has few cares or fears.
OWNER, CLAUDIA GRUNSTRA.

Hard foods are recommended occasionally for good strong teeth. Both kidney stones and cryptorchidism have been reported by veterinarians. Yorkies commonly live into their teen years.

Despite his propensity for pockets and laps, the Yorkie is a lively, on-his-toes companion, always ready to please.

Yorkshire Terrier

Thanks to All Our Contributors

It ain't as easy as it looks . . .

The authors wish to extend much thanks to the many

Ready when you are...
OWNERS, SANDRA SASSO AND CONNIE M. HARRIS.

breeders who helped in the preparation of the text for this book. Most of the following breeders are acknowleged experts as well as authors in their breed...not to mention friends! We are indebted to the millenium of experience they represent, the thousands of champions they have bred and owned, and the support they have shown us and T.F.H. Publications over the years. Here are some of the most respected and important people in the dog world and our hats are off to all of them:

Stop, you're embarrassing mom. OWNER, WENDY ARCHINAL.

Affenpinscher Mrs. A.J. Teasdale (UK) and Richard and Sharon Strempski of Vroni Kleine Kennels (Danbury, CT); *Afghan Hound* Peter Belmont, Jr. of Elmo, Reg. (Kansas, KS); *Airedale Terrier* Charlotte Schwartz (Fort Myers, FL); *Akita* B.J. Andrews of O'BJ Akitas (Candler, NC) and James Taylor (Hollywood, CA); *Alaskan Malamute* Nancy Brosque of Totempole Kennels (New Ipswich, NH) and Janet Edmonds of Highnoons Kennels (UK); *American Bulldog* John Blackwell (Owasso, OK) and Taylor Brandon (Venice, CA); *American Eskimo* Monica Sellers of Sweetwater Ranch (Lancaster, CA); *American Pit Bull Terrier* Diane Jessup of Bandog Pit Bulldogs (Olympia, WA), Carl Semencic (West Hempstead, NY) and Richard F. Stratton (San Diego, CA); *American Water*

Handstands anyone!
OWNER, LOUISE H. STRICKLAND.

You're in my light.
OWNER, SUSAN M. CARR.

Isabelle at work

Spaniel Lara A. Suesens of Wave Crest Kennels (Sheboygan, WI) and Paul and Lynn Morrison of Little Brownies Kennel (Waterford, MI); *Anatolian Shepherd Dog* M. Kurikir (UK); *Argentine Dogo* Dee Gannon and Linda Smith of Ganymede Kennels (Willingboro, NJ); *Australian Cattle Dog* Narelle G. Robertson of Kombinalong Kennels (NSW, Australia).

Hey. No secrets.
OWNER, SUSAN PINKUS.

Beagle Anna Katherine Nicholas and Marcia Foy (Danbury, CT); *Bearded Collie* Carol Gold (Ontario, Canada) and Chris Walkowicz of Walkoway Beardies (Sherrard, IL); *Bedlington Terrier* Mrs. Shirley Davies of Honeymist Bedlingtons (Scotland); *Belgian Malinois* Kathy Adams for Tri Sorts Belgian Malinois (West Islip, NY) and Sharon Parks Burke and James Burke of Rustyroad Kennels (Wheaton, MD); *Belgian Sheepdog* Peg and Bill Koller of Spectre Belgians (Medford, NY); *Belgian Tervuren* Christine Argento for Doni Zahn-Heule (Northport, NY) and Dr. and Mrs. Newsome of Tacara Tervuren (Edmond, OK); *Bernese Mountain Dog* Lilian Ostermiller (Westtown, NY); *Bichon Frise* Ann D. Hearn of Jalwin Kennels (Atlanta, GA); *Black and Tan Coonhound* Danny May of Harvest Hollow Kennel (Remus, MI); *Border Terrier* Wayne and Joyce Kirn of Towzie Tyke Border Terriers (Bel Air, MD); *Bouvier des Flandres* Debbie Goldstein of Dance on the Wind (Virginia); *Boxer* Richard Tomita of Jacquet Boxers (Oakland, NJ); *Briard* Alice Bixler (Summerfield, FL); *Brittany* Wendy Archinals of Top Shelf

Cheese.
OWNER, DIANE CORDERO.

Brittanys (Amsterdam, NY); *Bull Terrier* Betty Desmond (Claysville, PA); *Bulldog* Linda Teitelbaum Shrink a Bull Kennel (Lawrence, NY) and Mrs. P.M.L. Shore of Foresquare Bulldog Kennels (England); *Bullmastiff* M. Allen of Allen's Bullmastiffs (Warwick, RI).

Cairn Terrier Chris and Ken Carter of Bramblewood Cairn Terriers (Colorado Springs, CO); *Cardigan Welsh Corgi* Eugenia B. Bishop of Cardach Kennels (Cookstown, NJ); *Chesapeake Bay Retriever* Dyane Baldwin of Pond Hollow (Newport, PA); *Chihuahua* Linda M. Glenn of Glindale Kennels (Harrington, NJ); *Chinese Crested* Amy Fernandez of Razzmatazz (Forest Hills, NY) and S.G. and J.A. Gorwill of Alltot Kennels (South Wales, UK); *Chow Chow* Bob and Love Banghart (Santa Anna Heights, CA) and Dr. Samuel Draper and Desmond Murphy of LionTamer Chows (Monroe, NY); *Clumber Spaniel* Eunice Bailey (Eastham, MA) and Edith Donovan (Column, NY); *Cocker Spaniel* Lloyd Alton and Bill Gorodner (Leesburg, VA) and Frank DeVito and Joey Serrano of DeRano's (Long Island City, NY) and Judy Iby (Millford, OH); *Collie* Doris M. Blakeley of Dorwill (Wall, NJ); *Curly-Coated Retriever* Marcy Iler (Boonsboro, MD). *Dachshund* Kaye Ladd of Ladd-Land Kennels (Wexford, PA); *Dalmatian* Sylvia Howison (Howell, MI) and Susan MacMillan of Paisley

Are we done yet?
OWNERS, STEPHEN AND NANCY MACHINTON.

Qu'est ce que c'est?
OWNERS, PAT MENTIPLY AND BARBARA O'CONNOR.

Dalmatians (ST. Paul, MN); *Dandie Dinmont Terrier* France Roozen of Dunsandle (Middlebury, CT) and Barbara Monroe (Chappaqua, NY); *Doberman Pinscher* Colleen Kelso Nicholson of Kelview (Mechaulcsburg, PA). *English Cocker Spaniel* George and Joyce Caddy of Quaine Cockers (Somerset, UK) and Kate D. Romanski (Hales Corner, WI); *English Set-*

I like the one with the camera.
OWNER, DEB REDDER.

ter Kevin R. Lager (Wallkill, NY); *English Springer Spaniel* John and Colleen Nicholson of Soutue (Dillsburg, PA); *English Toy Spaniel* Mary K. Dullinger of Leprechaun (Revere, MA).
Finnish Spitz Dr. Tom T. Walker of Finkkila's Finnish Spitz (Bastrop, TX); *Flat-Coated Retriever* Pat DeBree (Killingworth, CT); *French Bulldog* Beth A. and Mark A. Carr of McBeth's Frenchies

He ain't heavy...he's my brooder.

(Temple, PA).
German Pinscher Roger Brazier (CA); *German Shepherd Dog* Dr. Carmen Battaglia (Lithonia, GA), Charlotte Schwartz (Fort Myers, FL) and Chris Walkowicz of Walkoway Beardies (Sherrard, IL); *German Wirehaired Pointer* Suzette M. Wood (Kissimmee, FL); *Glen of Imaal Terrier* Miss. L.J. Smith of Nicholls Glens (UK); *Golden Retriever* Nona Kilgore Bauer of Chances R Golden (LaBelle, MO); *Great Dane* Victoria L. Robertson (Hawthorne, FL) and Jill Swedlow (Yucaipa, CA); *Great*

Pyrenees Carolyn Hardy; *Greater Swiss Mountain Dog* Dr. Howard J. Summons of Sennenhof Kennels (Sinking Spring, PA).
Harrier Kimberly G. Mitchell of Wesford Harriers (Ukiah, CA); *Havanese* Jerome J. Podell (Silver Spring, MD).
Ibizan Hounds Diana Berry (UK); *Irish Wolfhound* Paula E. Payson of Karadarn Farm (Ashby, MA); Dean Keppler and Kim Tudor (Toms River, NJ); *Italian Greyhound* Donna Bedrick of L'image Italian Greyhounds (Wynnewood, PA).
Jack Russell Terrier Mr. Steve Hutchins of The Ratpack Kennels (Norfolk, England). *Japanese Chin* Steve and Debbie Trout (Rochester, NY); *Japanese Spitz* Mrs. Stephanie Jones of Charney (Oxfordshire, England).
Kuvasz Linda Llyod of Czigany Kuvasz (Dale, PA).
Labrador Retriever Dennis and Patricia Livesey of Amberfield Labrador Retrievers (Ramsey, NJ) and Mrs. B.W. Ziessow of Franklin Labadors (Franklin, MI); *Large Münsterländer* Mr. Keith Groom of Grunjagen (England); *Lhasa Apso* Mary C. Soto of Sunshine Lhasas (Gary, IL); *Löwchen* Herb Williams of Taywil Kennels (Roxbury, CT).
Maltese Kathy DiGiacomo (Fair Lawn, NJ); *Maremma Sheepdog* Mrs. Charlotte Walsh; *Mastiff* Mary Louise Owens of Acorn Hill Mastiffs (Gloversville, NY); *Minia-*

Not now, honey.
OWNER, CINDY SELLITTO.

ture Pinscher Jacqueline Fraser (Kalispell, MT); *Miniature Poodle* Marjorie McCarthy of Cloudspin Poodles (Burke, NY); *Miniature Schnauzer* Narda Riese (Vero Beach, FL).

Neapolitan Mastiff Dr. Sherilyn Allen (Boyertown, PA); *Norwegian Buhund* J. Barringer of Sandyhill (Bethalto, IL), Mr. and Mrs. A. A. Mole (UK) and R.W. and K.A. Frost of Frostisen (England).

Otterhound Elizabeth K. Conway and Donna Emery of Scentasia (Yorktown Heights, NY).

Papilion Charlotte Clem McGowan of Rorralore, Reg. (Newton, MA); *Pekingese* Steve and Debbie Trout (Rochester, NY); *Petit Basset Griffon Vendeen* Mrs. P.J. Aldous of Sweetdean (UK) and Jeffrey G. Pepper (Putham Valley, NY); *Polish Lowland Sheepdog* Kaz and Betty Augustowski of Elzbieta Kennels (Severn, MD); *Poodles* Charlotte Schwartz (Fort Myers, FL); *Portuguese Water Dog* Marianne Murray (Lansdale, PA); *Puli* Mary Wakeman DVM of Szeder Pulik (Ashford, CT).

Rottweiler Joan Klem (Wheaton, IL), Victoria L. Robertson (Hawthorne, FL) and Yvonne Wilson of Kelev Rottweilers (London, England).

Saluki Nan Bodine of Shahtani Salukis (Lakewood, NJ); *Samoyed* Dianne E. Sorrentino of Swo Dawn (Bogota, NJ) and M. Skiandu (UK); *Schipperke* Carolyn Krosinsky (Long Beach, NY); *Scottish Terrier* Muriel P. Lee (Minneapolis, MN); *Sealyham Terrier* Cheryl Jennings (Highland Park, IL); *Shar-Pei* Elly Paulus (New Brunswick, NJ) and Linda Teitelbaum of

Now keep your eye on the.....
OWNER, CAROLYN KROSINSKY.

Ming Yu Kennel (Lawrence, NY) and Peter Belmont, Jr. of Temple Toi, Reg. (Kansas, KS); *Shetland Sheepdog* Charlotte Clem McGowan of Rorralore, Reg. (Newton, MA), Elaine Wishnow of Malashel Kennels (Brooklyn, NY) and Mary Sweeney (Red Bank, NJ); *Shiba Inu* Christine Eicher-Tomita (Rockaway, NJ) and Donald Robinder (Newville, PA); *Shih Tzu* Joe and Joann Regelman; *Siberian Husky* Kathy Kanzler of Innisfree (Chateaugay, NY); *Silky Terrier* Norma Baugh of Amron Silkys (Cypress, TX); *Skye Terrier* Sandra Goose Allen (Madeira Beach, FL); *Smooth Fox Terrier* Lisa Sachs of Fortone (Huntington, NY); *Soft Coated Wheaten Terrier* Linda M. Glenn of Glindale Kennels (Harrington, NJ); *Spinoni Italiano* Ruth E. and Donald L. Adams (Indianapolis, IN); *Staffordshire Bull Terrier* J. Zane Smith of Bullseye (Scarborough, ME); *Standard Schnauzer* Barbara M. Dille of Vortac Standard Schnauzers (White Plains, NY); *Sussex Spaniel* Ann Findlay of Oldholbans (UK) and John Robert Lewis, Jr. of Lexxfield Kennels (Natural Bridge, VA); *Swedish Vallhund* Mr. and Mrs. Peacock of Kinkholure (London, UK).

Tibetan Mastiff Donald and Louise Skilton (Weymouth, MA); *Tibetan Spaniel* Jeanne Holsapple of Tashi (Newcastle, IN); *Tibetan Terrier* Anne Keleman of Ti Song Tibetan Terriers (Novato, CA); *Toy Fox Terrier* Sherry Baker-Scott of Heaven's Sunshine Toy Fox Terriers (Covington, OK).

Vizsla Doris Ratzlaff of Dorratz Vizslas (Oakland, NJ).

Welsh Terrier Bardi McLennan (Newtown CT); *West Highland White Terrier* Dawn Martin (Saylorsburg, PA); *Whippet* Dean Keppler and Kim Tudor (Toms River, NJ); *Wirehaired Pointing Griffon* Vicky Foster

(Hampden, MA).
Xoloitzcuintli Amy Fernandez of Razzmatazz (Forest Hills, NY).
Yorkshire Terrier Betty Dullinger (Kezar Falls, ME).

DOG OWNERS AND BREEDERS

Thank you to all of the following dog owners from around the United States, Europe, and elsewhere for cooperating with our photographer Isabelle Francais and sharing their wonderful, beautiful dogs with our readers. These are the folks to talk to about meeting the breed and finding the right dog. Our apologies to any owners who have been misplaced, lost, or unidentified.

Affenpinscher, Mrs. Patricia Patchen (Chashire, England); Dr. and Mrs. Brian J. Shack (Nesconset, NY); Nancy E. Holmes (New Boston, NH); Highland Kennels.

Afghan Hound, Gregg, Scott and Todd Rechler (Mill Neck, NY); Lucia Brown (Monroe, CT); Renee Wolcott (South Port, NC).

Airedale Terrier, Linda Hobbet (Walnut Creek, CA); Scott and Dottie Boevin; Linda Baake (Chester, CT); Sandra Hamer (Quebec, Canada).

Akita, BJ and Bill Andrews (Columbus, NC); Walter and Victoria Donach (Woodbury, NY); Ruth Zimmerman (Wilmington, DE).

Alaskan Malamute, Mike and Jackie Cosentino (Lebanon, CT); Sandee Reeves and Cheryl Paterson (Blusson, NC).

American Bulldog, Louis Maldarelli (Palisades, NY).

American Eskimo, Margaret A. Cannon (Maryland); Cyndi Richards (Stroudsburg, PA); Marilyn A. Pike (Alden, NY).

American Foxhound, James M. and Judy G. Rea (Clarkesville, GA); Juanita Troyer (Granite City, IL); Lisa Schinker (Waukegan, IL).

American Pit Bull Terrier, Vicki Clensy and Gary Cleary (Sabot, VA); Beth Jones (Clinton, CT); Mary Martin and Mary Happel (Unicopee, MS).

American Staffordshire Terrier, Yunhee and Kihong Kim (New York, NY); Karen Hines (Perkasie, PA); J.D. Waymire (Zoetermeer, Holland); Mary Jean Martin and Ruth Tee-ter (Norton, MA); Judy Haight (Levittown, NY).

American Water Spaniel, Sharon Dougherty (Inver Grove Heights, MN); L.A. Alexander-Suesens (Hilbert, WI); Paul and Lynn Morrison (Waterford, MI); Sandra W. Bracken (Crownsville, MD).

Anatolian Shepherd Dog, Vernon and Di Miles (Sussex, England); Wanda Stutzer and Editha Collins (Stuart, VA); Louise and Elizabeth Emanuel (Clinton, MD); Gayle Bouder (Pleasant Mills, PA).

Argentine Dogo, Joseph Kraer (Effort, PA).

Australian Cattle Dog, Linda Bernard and The Ruben Hortas (St. Petersburg, FL); Bill and Susan Streaker (West Friendship, MD); Rhue Jefferson (Christiana, TN); Jamie Hansen (Elizabethtown, NC).

Australian Kelpie, Philip Delathiere (New Caledonia).

Australian Shepherd, J. Frank Baylis; Kathy Hauer (Fort Collins, CO); Joan Della Rocco (Goshen, NY); Mary-Lou E. Trone (Warwick, NY); Sandra K. Noell (North Carolina).

Australian Terrier, Amy R. Marder, DVM (Cambridge, MA); Debra L. Austin (Ashville, NY); Daniel L. and Pat A. Turner (Norfolk, MA).

Basenji, Dianne T. Bleecker and Gustavo De La Garza (Reddick, FL); Arthur R. Gilbert (Portland, ME); Susan Campeau (Warrentown, NC); Amy Riddle (Shelby, NC).

Basset Hound, Gabrio Del Torre and Pat and Roger Turpen (Lewes, DE); Pamela T. Robbins (Panama City, FL); Laura Bailey (Holliston, MA); Dawn Toune (Weedsport, NY).

Beagle, Mark Lister, Bruce Tague, John and Greta Haag (Alpine, CA); Richard Preston (Brockport, NY); Christine L. Voronovitch (Manchester, CT); Loretta Caterino (New Boston, NH).

Bearded Collie, Penny Hanigan (Rye, NY); Michel Hanigan (Rye, NY); Carol Thurston (Pleasant Valley, NY); June E. Hartzog (Amherst, NH).

Bedlington Terrier, David P. Ramsey (Warwick, RI); Doug Lehr and Desiree Williams (Pennellville, NY); Jean L. Mathieu (Montverde, FL); K. Donovan (Norwalk, CT).

Belgian Sheepdog, Groenendael, William and

Cathy Daugherty (Bethlehem, CT); Julia E. Fiechter (Falls Church, VA); Jan Manuel and Carolyn Kelso (Glen Burnie, MD); Peg Koller (West Islip, NY).

Belgian Sheepdog, Laekenois, Mona B. Moore (Leesburg, VA).

Belgian Sheepdog, Malinois, James and Sharon Burke (Wheaton, MD); Rebecca J. Wasniewski (Cresco, PA); Carol and Frank Knock (Vienna, VA); Kathy Adams (West Islip, NY).

Belgian Tervuren, Joelle G. White (New York, NY); Judy Baumeister and Steve Sorenson (Eau Claire, WI); Robin M. West (Lebanon, CT); Chris Argento (West Islip, NY).

Bernese Mountain Dog, Heather Bremmer (Emmaus, PA).

Bichon Frise, Jerome Podell (Silver Spring, MD); Anita Carolls, Barbara B. Stubbs and Lois K. Morrow (W. Lake Village, CA); Joyan Nolan (Pittsford, NY); Lori Kornfeld (Ridgefield, CT); Estelle and Wendy Kellerman (Floral Park, NY).

Black and Tan Coonhound, Katherine Settle (Sanford, NC); Arilla E. Turner (Sanford, NC); James and Kathleen M. Corbett and Margo Sensenbrenner (Aloha, OR); Linda D. Pincheck (Merritt Island, FL); Jan Brungard (Merritt Island, FL).

Bloodhound, Gretchen Schuecking (Atlanta, GA); Dr John and Susan Hamil and Dr. Marlene Zahner (Laguna Beach, CA); Roberts Sharps (Mount Vernon, NY); Jimmie and Delores Jackson (Eufaula, AL); Mrs. Diana Dixon (Kent, England); Mrs. Doris McCullough (Landenburg, PA).

Border Collie, Sharon Holm (North Tarrytown, NY); Peter and Ann Stacey (Salop, England); Jerri A. Carter (Deltona, FL); Linda Husson (Shohola, PA).

Border Terrier, Wayne and Joyce Kirn (Bel Air, MD); Robin Jones (Blythewood, SC); Betsy Kirkpatrick, Cindy Peebles and W. Henry Odum III (Lynchburg, VA); Teresa Tipton (Trail Hopkins, SC); Hazel Wichman (Morris Plains, NJ).

Borzoi, Debbie Tapley (Westbrook, ME); Lena S. Tamboer (Mahwah, NJ); Amy L. Sorbie (Aurora, CO); Pat Hardy (Scotia, NY).

Boston Terrier, Anna M. Benedetto (Pequabuck, CT); Elisabeth McNeil and Jodi Ghastes (Crownsville, MD).

Bouvier des Flandres, Jeffrey Bennett and Nan Eisley-Bennett (Corona, CA); Debbie Goldstein (Fredricksburg, VA); Debbie Arbucci (Marlborough, CT); Emmy Walters (Raleigh, NC).

Boxer, Richard Tomita (Oakland, NJ).

Briard, Kenneth and Valerie Fox (Clinton, MD).

Brittany, Dr. Dennis and Andrea Jordon and G.K. Nash (Littleton, CO); Theresa Mann (Cornwall, NY); Wendy Archinal (Amsterdam, NY); Sharon Buehler (Schenectady, NY); Betsy Wallace (Rotland, MA); Claire Stidsen. *Brussels Griffon,* Howard Ogden (Cheltenham, England); Cleola Moorhead (Oklahoma City, OK); Cheryl Stevens (Pinellas Park, FL); Terry Page (Raleigh, NC); Doug Matney (Raleigh, NC).

Bull Terrier, W.E. Mackay-Smith (Villanova, PA); Gay Hillman and Jay and Mary Remer (Birdsboro, PA); Karen D. Cook and Marion Dussault (Woronoco, MA)

Bulldog, Robert and Jean Hetherington, Jr. and Margaret K. Curtis (Swannanoa, NC); Connie Gibson (Syracuse, NY).

Bullmastiff, Malinda Raby and Peter Kozel (San Francisco, CA); Steven and Linda Allen (Warwick, RI); Debbie Jones (Churchville, MD); Cindy Sellitto (East Hartford, CT).

Cairn Terrier, Betty Hyslop (Ontario, Canada); Mr. and Mrs. Wallace (Scotland); Jon Lawrence (Commack, NY); Susan W. De Witt (Norwalk, CT).

Canaan Dog, Myrna Shiboleth (Israel); Isabella Zirri (Parma, Italy).

Cardigan Welsh Corgi, Doreen Pargo (Shrewsbury, England); Cindi Bossi (Wilmington, NC); Jacque Schatz (Muskogee, OK).

Cavalier King Charles Spaniel, Cindy Beebe (Wilton, CT); James and Christine Meager (Hatfield, PA); Linda Stebbins (Cresco, PA).

Chesapeake Bay Retriever, Stephen and Margee S. Webb (Parkersburg, PA); Pamela Woodes (North Hampton, NH); Helen T. Siegel (Annandale, NJ); Janice Bykowsky (Garfield, NJ).

Chihuahua, June and Jennifer Ferrante (Hazlet, NJ); Barbara Sporer (North Collins,

NY); Mrs. Keith Thompson (Waukesha, WI); Bonnie Thompson and Katherine Glamona (Fairfield, CA).

Chinese Crested, Arlene Butterklee (Nesconset, NY); Victor Helu (Bethpage, NY); Jackie Wendelkin (Ronkonkoma, NY).

Chow Chow, Robert Banghart and Eileen Baldi (Santa Anna Heights, CA); Frank and Sandra Holloway (Stormville, NY); Linda Albert (Hauppauge, NY).

Clumber Spaniel, Richard and Judith Zaleski (Windermere, FL); Dr. Gerald Nash and Janice Friis (Mattawan, MI); Mrs. G. Bird (United Kingdom); George and Dorothy O'Neill (North Kingston, RI).

Cocker Spaniel (American), Samuel B. and Marion Lawrence (Orlando, FL); Mary Maloney and Lee Bergstrom (Caver, MN); Brigitte Berg (Issaquah, WA); April Stich (West Hartford, CT); Michael Jones (Woonsocket, RI); Judith Beauchamp (South Bridge, MA).

Cocker Spaniel (English), Susan Fiore-McChane and Joan Davis (Clinton, IA); Sue and Annie Kettle (United Kingdom); Helyne Copper (Marstons Mills, MA); Corky Meck (Lancaster, PA); John Poucher (New Market, NH); Tracey Deyette (New Market, NH).

Collie, Nancy McDonald and Joyce Dowling (Manassass, VA); Joe Koehler (New City, NY); Theresa Thomas, (Orange, NJ); Stephen and Nancy Machinton (East Hampton, NY); Duncan C. and Libby Beiler (Milton, PA)

Curly-Coated Retriever, Gary E. and Mary Meeks (Allegan, MI); Mr. and Mrs. Robinson (England).

Dachshund, Kaye Ladd (Wexford, PA); Elisabeth A. Patterson (Allendale, NJ); Diana Bartlett (Pittsfield, MA); Kelli Williams and Duan and Evelyn Pettyjohn (Houston, TX); Dr. Roger and Deborah Brum and Sherry Snyder (Irvine, CA); Mary Jean Martin (Norton, MA); Ruth K. Teeter (Norton, MA); Pat Leone (Califon, NJ); Shirley J. Stummer (Syracuse, NY).

Dalmatian, Stephanie Podejko (Central Square, NY); Ben Riley (Old Hickory, TN); Mrs. Walter A. Smith (Hamilton, MA).

Dandie Dinmont Terrier, Barbara and James Monroe (Chappaqua, NY); Nancy

Herman (Pleasanton, CA); Marvin and Sharon Gelb (Monroe, CT).

Doberman Pinscher, Betty Cuzzolino (Howell, NJ); Ann E. Nelson, Gianna Crouch, DVM, and Joe Reid (Brookshine, TX); Jane Silver (Bar Mills, MA); Elizabeth Kamau (Aurora, CO).

English Foxhound, Silla E. Turner (Walkertown, NC); Emily Latimer and Suzy Reingold (Spartanburg, SC); Giselle Saskor (Ridgefield, CT).

English Setter, Mary Oldham (Fort Collins, CO); Ardys McElwee and Janice Bungesson (CT); Marrianne Cameron (Oakham, MA); A.L. Polley (Ontario, Canada); Kevin R. Lager (Wallkill, NY).

English Springer Spaniel, Deborah Kirk (York, PA); Deborah Maltby (Verona, NJ); Libby O'Donnell (Stratham, NH); Katheryn Kirk (Oxford, CT); Dr. John R. and Diane C. Ostenberg (Boulder, CO).

English Toy Spaniel, Mary K. Dullinger-Cunha and Jerome Elliot (Revere, MA); Susan R. Jackson (Bristol, IN); Patricia A. Zbock (Hamburg, NY).

Field Spaniel, E.B. Alexander (Alexandria, VA); Sarah W. Evans (Potomac, MD); Lynn G. Finney (Lyndell, PA); James and Lucy Gallagher (Upper Saddle River, NJ); Dorothy and George O'Neil (North Kingston, RI).

Finnish Spitz, Heather Store (New London, CT); Christine Roesler (New London, CT); Tom T. and Marg G. Walker (Bastrop, TX).

Flat-Coated Retriever, Kurt D. Anderson (North Haven, CT); Steve and Nancy Wickmark, (Webster, NY); Philip and Sandra Park, Libby Baarstad and Lana Griffin (Fredericksburg, VA).

French Bulldog, Beth A. and Mark A. Carr (Temple, PA); Sarah Sweatt (Minneapolis, MN); Pat Mentiply and Barbara O'Conner (Springfield, MA).

German Pinscher, Socorro Armstrong (Lake Elsinore, CA); Daniel H. and Rhonda L. Parks (Gardeners, PA).

German Shepherd Dog, Roberta Laufer (Liberty, NY); Nataly Jacob-Lauvier (Quebec); Jane A. Firestone; Karen Harms (Rochester, NH); Ted Brozowski (Springfield, MA); James Moses (Roswell, GA).

German Shorthaired Pointer, Susan

Harrison (Fort Lauderdale, FL).

German Wirehaired Pointer, Bernee Brawn (New Hope, PA); Richard and Judith Zaleski (Windermere, FL); Jeffrey and Lisa George (Mount Vernon, OH); Regina Schwabe, DVM (Stony Point, NY).

Giant Schnauzer, Kevin E. Schrum and Kyle Steigerwald (Lake Forest, CA); Neu Bertam (Germany); Ken and Robin Greenslade (Salem, NH).

Golden Retriever, Julie A. McKinnon (Kingston, MA); Lisa Smith and Paula M. Ashby (Bedford, NY); William and Marie Wingard and James C. and Pamela S. Cobble (Spring Lake, NJ); Arthur and Cheryl Carl (Hatfield, PA); Debra Wales (North Anson, ME); Sandra Sasso and Connie Merrick Harris (Hanover, MA).

Gordon Setter, Sue Drexel (Sewell, NJ); Suzanne Lach and Mary Ann Alston (Scottsdale, AZ); Joanne Van Aller and Michelle Ostermiller (Schoharie, NY).

Great Dane, Carolyn Dean (United Kingdom); Diana Bartlett (Pittsfield, MA); Dorothy J. Carlson (North Oxford, MA); Tom and Dee Mooney (Merrimack, NH); Terri Loncrini (Hampden, MA).

Great Pyrenees, Larry Helmstetle (Jamestown, NC); Guy and Karen Justin and Vallerie A. Seeley (Monroe, NY); Stephanie A. Wolk (Windsor, CT).

Greater Swiss Mountain Dog, Mrs. Terry Mehle (Watchung, NJ); Catherine O. Cooper (Martinsville, VA); Jim and Cheri Barton (Forest Hill, MD).

Greyhound, Laurie Renaud (Quebec, Canada); Tad W. and Ellen C. Lowdermilk and Maureen Lucas (Winston-Salem, NC); Stacy Pober (Roslyn, NY); Donna A. Hess (Basking Ridge, NJ).

Harrier, Donna K. Smiley-Auburn (Inyokern, CA); Betty M. Burnell (Scottsdale, AZ); Kenneth and Miriam Nell (Taylors, SC).

Havanese, Linda Cosner (Bedford, PA); I. Hanin (Coublevie France); James A. and Katharine R. Rodgers (Hampstedd, NC); Elizabeth Vargo (Stubenville, OH).

Ibizan Hound, Fernando Gonzalvo Ramon (Valencia, Spain); Pamela Luther (New York); Laura Cano Villaseca (Spain); Bill Muller (Deposit, NY); Leslie D. Lucas and

Glen E. Brand (Livermore, CA).

Irish Red and White Setter, Mrs. Suzanne Humphries (England).

Irish Setter, Elaine and Michelle de Chambeau (Masachusetts); Kenn and Joan Sadler (Belvidere, NJ); Randy Kubacz and Mrs. Jean Roche (Jackson, NJ).

Irish Terrier, Maureen Moskowitz (Selden, NY); Mark Eskridge (Kemptville, Ontario); Rejean Charlebois (Kemptville, Ontario). Stan Wojewodski, Jr. (Guilford, CT).

Irish Water Spaniel, Susan G. Anderson (Altoona, PA); Carolyn Lathrop (Cumberland, MD); Gregory M. Siner and Marcy Rose (Upper Montclair, NJ).

Irish Wolfhound, Lynn Cox (Chapel Hill, NC); Richard and Linda Beluscak (Olmsted Falls, OH); James Fowlow (Elma, NY).

Italian Greyhound, Susan Pinkus (West Orange, NJ); James R. Bray, MD and Scott R. Thompson (Winder, GA).

Jack Russell Terrier, Janet Fredricks (Huntington, NY); Michelle Reilly (Rohrersville, MD).

Japanese Chin, Kip Kopatch (Greene, RI); Harold J. and Marie A. Langseth (Everett, WA).

Keeshond, Linda Moss (Selma, NC); Janice A. Wanamaker (Candia, NH); Donna and Ernest Williams (Jax, FL); Sharon A. Elphick (Wanague, NJ); Joanne Reed (Santa Rosa, CA); Paula Weiman (Rio Rancho, NM).

Kerry Blue Terrier, Mr. and Mrs. K. Neill (North Ireland); Aileen Santo (Multontown, NY); Dr. and Mrs. R. A. Reilly (Lakewood, OH).

Komondor, Patricia Turner and Anna Quigley (Chehhalis, WA); Janet Cupolo (Farmingdale, NY); Ruben Collado (Bosque Farms, NJ).

Kuvasz, Lynn Brady and C.D. Townsend (Whitmore Lake, MI).

Labrador Retriever, Juxi Burr and Sonya Ninneman (Alburquerque, NM); Pierre and Suzanne Saey (Canada); Sharon Celentano (Newburgh, NY); Diane Ammerman (Mahwah, NJ); Sandra MacLeon (Norton, MA).

Lakeland Terrier, Susan Fisher (Oxford, MA); William H. Cosby and Jean L. Heath (Pleasanton, CA).

Large Münsterländer, Keith Groom (United

Kingdom); Linda Flint (United Kingdom).

Lhasa Apso, Nancy Sehnert (Liverpool, NY); Michael A. Santoria and Alan J. Loso (Princeton, FL); Robert and Janie Brew and Cindy Butsic (Greenville, MI).

Löwchen, Virginia Denninger (Macedon, NY); Kaja Denaan (Lambertville, NJ).

Maltese, Annette Feldblum (Charlton, MA); Claudia Grunstra (Maywood, NJ); J. Joly III, D. and S. Newcomb, and Vicky Abbott (McKinney, TX).

Manchester Terrier, Pat Dresser (Medina, OH).

Maremma Sheepdog, Gordon and Anne Latimer (England).

Mastiff, Nancy Hempel (Clearwater, FL); Robert S. Jones (Selden, NY); Zoe A. Tice. (Pleasant Valley, NY); Nancy A. Pitas (Atileboro, MA).

Miniature Bull Terrier, Anne Marie Bergemann (Denmark); James Gaignat (Torrington, CT).

Miniature Pinscher, Marlene Dunbury (Littleton, MA); Ann Nelsen (West Bloomfield, MI); Roberta McCartney (North Ireland); Rose J. Radel (East Hanover, NJ).

Miniature Poodle, Maryann K. Howarth (Jackson, NJ); Judith Bray (Redmond, WA); Robert A. Koppel (New York, NY).

Miniature Schnauzer, Geraldine Kelly (North Falmouth, MA); Larry and Georgia Drivon (Stockton, CA); Carol P. Beiles (Brookville, NY).

Neopolitan Mastiff, Daniel Pellegrino (Kenosha, WI); Janet Hachbarth (Ackley, IA); Susan Church (Philadelphia, PA).

Newfoundland, Linda Mowins (Clay, NY); Harfild Sülzen (Unkel, Germany); Carol Bernard Bergmann and Peggy Helming (Chelsea, MI).

Norfolk Terrier, Linda Haring (Sandusky, OH); Howard and Bridget Holzhauser (Sandusky, OH); Karen Anderson (Monrovia, MD); John F. and Pamela G. Beale (Peterborough, NH).

Norwegian Buhund, Van Etteruk-Kroos (Belgium); Norah D. Gander (South Wales); Mr. and Mrs. A. A. Mole (Turkey).

Norwegian Elkhound. Fred and Margaret Sharis (East Hartland, CT); Patricia Craige and Jeffrey and Nan-Eisley Bennett (Carmel, CA).

Norwich Terrier, Ruth L. Cooper and Patricia P. Lussier (Glenview, IL); Karen Anderson (Monovia, MD); Deb Redder (Weare, NH).

Old English Sheepdog, Arlene Pietrocola (New Milford, NJ); Jere Marder (Chicago, IL); Larry and Angela Stein (Mount Holly, NJ).

Otterhound, Robin Anderson (North Midway, RI); Gael Lewis and Jack and Andrea McIlwaine (Wintersville, OH).

Papillon, Cynthia Silvers (Claremont, NH); Pat Jones (Roswell, GA); Lou Ann King (Solon, IA); John Oulton (Norwalk, CT); Michele Kunsli (Malleloy, France).

Pekingese, Linda Nolker (Mardela, MD); Mary Gay (Gardinek, ME); Ginny Ferguson (Limerick, ME); Nancy H. Shapland (Champaign, IL); Sandi Gibson (Williamson, PA); Linda Nolker (Mardela, MD).

Pembroke Welsh Corgi, Beth Magnus (Cherry Hill, NJ); Mrs. Alan R. Robson and Ruth L. Cooper (Glenview, IL); Julia S. Clough (York, ME);

Petit Basset Griffon Vendéen, Miss N. Quadling (Japan); Jane E. Chesmel (Keyport, NJ); Carol A. Strong (NY); Andre Franchi (Auriol, France); Marilyn Crownsberry (Chicopee, MA).

Pharaoh Hound, Deborah Kidwell (Thornburg, VA); G. Von Zech, Liz Hanley, and N. and B. Sowerbutts (Bensalem, PA); Marlene Hines (Derry, NH).

Pointer, Ron and Carolyn Twyman (Kent, England); Mary Ann Grace (Chatham, NJ); Phillis B. Kroll (Charlotte, VT); Den and Elsa Lawler (Caro, MI).

Polish Lowland Sheepdog, Sue Ainsley (Cleveland, England); Dorene W. Zalis (Rockville, MD); Thomas M. Wason (Naples, NY); Loana J. Shields (Naples, NY).

Pomeranian, Mr. and Mrs. William A. Kerr (Kenmore, NY); Jose A. Cabrera (Miami, FL).

Portuguese Water Dog, Kristen Cofield (Middletown, CT); Dr. Lou Guthrie and Steven Bean (Conroe, TX); Christine Noyes and Steven Dostie (Lewiston, ME);

Pug, Ronald and Elizabeth Pizzano (Northford, CT); Doris Aldrich (Pelham, MA); Hazel M. Martens (San Diego, CA); Alexander and Amy White (Chatham, NY).

Puli, Georgina Dioslaki (Lincoln Park, NJ); Constance Peterson (Los Gatos, CA); Jane Sable (Wilton, CT); Mary Wakeman, DVM (Ashford, CT).

Rhodesian Ridgeback, Linda G. Hothan (Willington, CT); Ulla-Britt Ekengren (Dunstable, MA); Judith Lichtman (Hamden, CT).

Rottweiler, Martin and Florence Thomson (Royal Oak, MI); Scott and Lisa Cote (Fallriver, MA); Robert C. Sarro (MA); Suzanne E. Burris (Tijeras, NM).

Saint Bernard, Michael Parker (Vail, CO); Dr. Clyde and Catherine Dunphy (Carlinville, IL).

Saluki, P. Reynolds (England); Eileen Barbieri (Pine Plains, NY); Christine McIntyre and Charlie Cope (Alto, MI); Melinda Camardella (Elizaville, NY).

Samoyed, Mrs. Reynolds-Parnham (England); Carrie Parma-Dinger (Richland, PA); Cheryl A. Wagner (Roswell, GA); C.E. Kight (Glenwood, MD); Charlott J. Conniff (Balto, MD).

Schipperke, Vikki Ingram (Lancaster, SC); Ann Walthall (Lancaster, SC); Dom and Claudia Orlandi and Brenda S. Bible (Essex Junction, VT); Dr. Charles Morgan and Patricia Nigey (Belford, NY); Carolyn Krosinsky (Long Beach, NY); Chandler Hahn (Winter Haven, FL).

Scottish Deerhound, Betina Adams (Bishampton, England); John D. Hogan (Pauling, NY).

Scottish Terrier, Donna M. Cone (Manchester, MA); Dr. Vandra L. Huber and Dr. Joe Kinnarney (Apex, NC); Lois Miller and Jane Robinson (Greensboro, NC); Jack and Margaret Banker (West Islip, NY).

Sealyham Terrier, France Bergeron (Sherbrooke, Quebec); Franel Brown, Christine Stephens and P. Stuckey (Clouis, CA).

Shar-Pei, Edward Bronson (Wassaic, NY); Dennis Kirby and Deanna Brown (Baccoville, NC); Rose McKinstry (MD); David Melvard (Peoria, AZ); Vicky Teshera (Mulino, OR).

Shetland Sheepdog, Sherry Lee (St. Cloud, FL); Kathleen Schmutz and Linda S. Griffith (Scottsdale, AZ); Linda Zimmerman (Bosque Farms, NM).

Shiba Inu, Andrew De Prisco (Ocean Grove, NJ), Karen Steitz (West Milford, NJ); Richard Tomita (Oakland, NJ).

Shih Tzu, Gay Payne (Middletown, NY); Ginger J. Raber (Fort Myers, FL); Gregory and Tammarie Larson and Susan Bletzinger (Chanhassen, MN); Lynne Bennet (Moore, OK).

Siberian Husky, Kathleen Kanzler (Chateaugay, NY); N. Wisniewski, B. Moye, M. DePalma and T. Oelschlager (Brunswick, OH); Margaret Cook (Easton, MA); C. Rand (Carteret, NY); Maureen Kent (Bow, NH).

Silky Terrier, Ginny Curtis and Norma Baugh (Bristol, ME); William A. and Stephany S. Monteleone (New Orleans, LA); M.L. and Sarah Stegemann (Stephentown, NY).

Skye Terrier, Joan Fingar (Rochester, NY); Dian Tebo (Waltham, MA); Roxanna L. Rohrich and Gleanntan Knis Reg. (Medina, OH); Catherine McLeod (Scottland); Susan Parsons (Grafton, MA); Robin Stiles (Bocawen, NH).

Smooth Fox Terrier, Linda Hill (North Stonington, CT); Michael and Suzanne Sosne (Caro, MI); Debra Dehne (Franklin, TN).

Soft Coated Wheaten Terrier, Neil and Diana Edwards (Howick, Quebec); Helen Wilson and Elena Landa (Belevue, WA).

Spinone Italiano, Vinola Valentino (Italy); F. Riley (Nottingham, England).

Staffordshire Bull Terrier, Harry L. Rodeheaver (New Mexico); Michael Goldfarb (Port Washington, NY); Joaquin Tormo Esteve (Valencia, Spain).

Standard Poodle, Edward Jenner (Burlington, WI); Karen S. Grace (Fishers, NY) .

Standard Schnauzer, Koehl Liwe (Germany); Barbara M. Dille (White Plains, NY); Dorothee Henne (Germany); Gabrio Del Torre and Rita Holloway (Newark, DE).

Sussex Spaniel, Ann S. Cummings (Vineyard Haven, MA); Norman and Constance Grenier (Hope Valley, RI).

Swedish Vallhund, Mrs. R. Biss (United Kingdom); Kate Duncan (Wales).

Tibetan Mastiff, Susan Engle (Dayton, OH); M. Pilat (France); Melissa Wolfe (Herndon, VA).

Tibetan Spaniel, Mrs. K.M. Lowe (North

Ireland); Cheryl A. Kelly (Macedon, NY); Sandra Fournier (Belchertown, MA); Arlene Tanel (Miami, FL).

Tibetan Terrier, Sheryl Rutledge-Schulitis (Catharpin, VA); Joyce Ayotte (Plattsburgh, NY); Susan B. Nerdahl (Wilton, CT); Susan M. Carr (Tolland, CT).

Toy Fox Terrier, Ann Mauermann (Louisville, KY); Lisa Vettraino (Millington, MI).

Toy Manchester Terrier, Louise H. Strickland (Spring Hope, NC); Peter and Patricia Lapinski (Port Orange, FL).

Toy Poodle, Patricia A. Zbock (Hamburg, NY); Lynn DeRosa (Warsaw, VA); Marion Usher (Rhode Island); Norma Strait (Vista, CA).

Vizsla, Ron and Patricia Folz (Woodstock, CT); M. Voorn (Netherlands); Lucille Jardin (Marion, MA); Anne Denehy (Huntington, NY); Joy Lyons (Pompano Beach, FL).

Weimaraner, Mr. and Mrs. P. Keller (Humberside, England); Roger and Jeanne Shelby (Sylmar, CA); Ellen Grevall (Chester, CT); Lance A. Wolfe (Bridgewater, NJ); Audrey R. Soltis (Toms River, NJ); Laurel Lockhart (Liverpool, NY); Diane Cordero (Plattekill, NY).

Welsh Springer Spaniel, Darlene K. Ferris (Milford, CT); Candy Carswell (Milford, CT); Richard and Sandra Rohrbacher (Lafayette, NJ); Linda S. Brenan (Stanhope, NJ).

Welsh Terrier, Erign H. Seacord (Ithaca, NY); Karen and R.C. Williams, Jr. (Shingle Springs, CA).

West Highland White Terrier, Frederick Melville (Sonoma, CA); Mark and Sally George (Sonoma, CA); Marian Moeller (Holcomb, NY); Christine Forbes (Hingham, MA).

Whippet, Sarah Stegemann (Stephentown, NY); Robert E. and Mona Maytag (Dover Plains, NY); Laurey Weiner (Morris, CT); Ceila Downen (Morristown, NJ); Mrs. James Butt, Debbie Butt, E. Hansen and A. Truxal (Paoli, PA); Sharon Sakson (Fairless Hills, PA); Matthew L. Downing (Oakland, FL).

Wire Fox Terrier, Debra Dehne (Franklin, TN); Mr. and Mrs. Richard Vida (Sacramento, CA); Andrew DiGiorgio (Windsor, MA).

Wirehaired Pointing Griffon, Elaine Hunsicker (Havertown, PA); Joe and Marge Gryskiewicz (Nanticoke, PA).

Xoloitzcuintli, Brian Terry (Weston, CT); Linda Woods (Jersey City, NJ); Susan Corrone (Bethany, CT); Robert McRae and Bernard Pearson (MI).

Yorkshire Terrier, Sharon L. Jones (Goshen, CT); Claudia Grunstra (Maywood, NJ); Dr. Ivan and Marie Kaufman Cardona (Guaynabo, Puerto Rico).

Index

Suggested Reading

BY THE AUTHORS

THE MOST COMPLETE DOG BOOK EVER PUBLISHED: CANINE LEXICON

(TS-175) Over 3500 alphabetically arranged entries present over 500 breeds of dog and related topics of breeding, showing, anatomy, health care...includes over 1300 photographs in 896 full-color pages.

WHICH DOG FOR ME?

(KW-227) An overview of the basic breeds of dogs, portraits and basic accommodation needs. 120 pages illustrated by over 100 color photographs.

THE MINI-ATLAS OF DOG BREEDS

(H-1106) Over 400 breeds presented in color with descriptions of each breed's history, portrait, and temperament. A handy sized field guide to the international world of dogs. The most accurate and entertaining guide of its kind. 544 pages illustrated by over 500 color photographs.

THE MINI-ATLAS OF CATS

(TS-152) All the major breeds of cat presented in full color with descriptions of each cat's temperament, needs, physical appearance, as well as likes, dislikes and quirks. A thoroughly amusing browse through the cat world illustrated with fabulous champion kitties. 480 pages with nearly 500 color photographs.

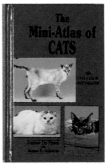

THE RIGHT CAT FOR ME

(KW-238) A current and accurate review of the purebred cat breeds available to the pet owner. Histories of the breeds and the cat's basic needs and personalities are addressed. Photography is stunning—nearly 200 full color photographs in 160 pages.

BY LOWELL ACKERMAN, DVM

OWNER'S GUIDE TO DOG HEALTH

(TS-214) Every owner and potential owner needs this book. It is layperson friendly and includes all of the major diseases of dog. Excellent discussions on all of the terminology used in "Health" sections of *Choosing a Dog for Life,* such as hip dysplasia, entropion, von Willebrand's, etc. Winner of the Dog Writers Association of America's Best Health Book Award 1996. 432 pages with over 300 color illustrations

SKIN AND COAT CARE FOR YOUR DOG

(TS-249) Coat and skin ailments are the number-one reason to bring your dog to the veterinarian. Addressing all the possible problems affecting the dog's skin and coat, this comprehensive volume features the contributions of 14 of the most respected dermatologists, veterinarians and groomers in the dog field. 224 pages with over 200 color illustrations.

DOG BEHAVIOR AND TRAINING: VETERINARY ADVICE FOR OWNERS

(TS-252)

A team of behavior experts join Dr. Lowell Ackerman to discuss the common behavioral problems dog owners face. Behavioral problems are the most common reason for owners to abandon a dog. This book helps to solve many difficult temperament, training and related disciplinary problems. Over 300 pages with full color photographs throughout.

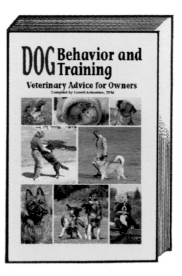

TRAINING BOOKS

EVERYBODY CAN TRAIN THEIR OWN DOG
By Angela White
(TW-113)
256 pages; color photography throughout.

DOG BEHAVIOR
By Ian Dunbar
(H-1016)
224 pages; 135 photographs.

SUCCESSFUL DOG TRAINING
By Michael Kamer
(TS-205)
160 pages, color photographs throughout.

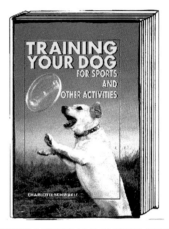

TRAINING YOUR DOG FOR SPORTS AND OTHER ACTIVITIES
By Charlotte Schwartz
(TS-258)
160 pages, color photographs throughout.

JUST SAY, "GOOD DOG"
by Linda Goodman with Marlene Trunnell
(TS-204)
160 pages, over 50 drawings.

OTHER OUTSTANDING DOG BOOKS

PIT BULLS AND TENACIOUS GUARD DOGS
By Carl Semencic
(TS-141)
320 pages, over 300 color photographs.

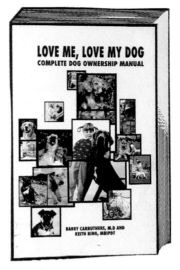

LOVE ME, LOVE MY DOG: COMPLETE DOG OWNERSHIP MANUAL
By Barry Carruthers and Keith Bing
(TS-212)
254 pages, over 140 color photographs.

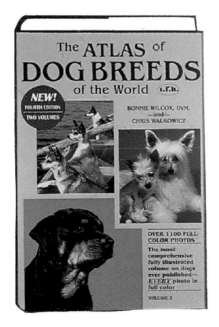

THE ATLAS OF DOG BREEDS OF THE WORLD
By Chris Walkowicz and Bonnie Wilcox, DVM
(H-1091)
912 pages, over 1100 color photographs.